MW01074476

Ingram's Fourth F....

Also by David D. Bruhn

Ready to Answer All Bells

Wooden Ships and Iron Men: The U.S. Navy's Ocean Minesweepers, 1953–1994

Wooden Ships and Iron Men: The U.S. Navy's Coastal and Motor Minesweepers, 1941–1953

Wooden Ships and Iron Men: The U.S. Navy's Coastal and Inshore Minesweepers, and the Minecraft That Served in Vietnam, 1953–1976

MacArthur and Halsey's "Pacific Island Hoppers": The Forgotten Fleet of World War II

Battle Stars for the "Cactus Navy": America's Fishing Vessels and Yachts in World War II

We Are Sinking, Send Help!: The U.S. Navy's Tugs and Salvage Ships in the African, European, and Mediterranean Theaters in World War II

Eyes of the Fleet: The U.S. Navy's Seaplane Tenders and Patrol Aircraft in World War II

Ingram's Fourth Fleet

**U.S. and Royal Navy Operations Against
German Runners, Raiders, and Submarines
in the South Atlantic in World War II**

Cdr. David D. Bruhn, USN (Retired)

HERITAGE BOOKS
2017

HERITAGE BOOKS

AN IMPRINT OF HERITAGE BOOKS, INC.

Books, CDs, and more—Worldwide

For our listing of thousands of titles see our website
at
www.HeritageBooks.com

Published 2017 by
HERITAGE BOOKS, INC.
Publishing Division
5810 Ruatan Street
Berwyn Heights, Md. 20740

Copyright © 2017 Cdr. David D. Bruhn, USN (Retired)

Heritage Books by the author:

Battle Stars for the "Cactus Navy": America's Fishing Vessels and Yachts in World War II

Eyes of the Fleet: The U.S. Navy's Seaplane Tenders and Patrol Aircraft in World War II

Ingram's Fourth Fleet: U.S. and Royal Navy Operations Against German Runners, Raiders, and Submarines in the South Atlantic in World War II

MacArthur and Halsey's "Pacific Island Hoppers": The Forgotten Fleet of World War II

We Are Sinking, Send Help!: The U.S. Navy's Tugs and Salvage Ships in the African, European, and Mediterranean Theaters in World War II

Wooden Ships and Iron Men: The U.S. Navy's Ocean Minesweepers, 1953–1994

Wooden Ships and Iron Men: The U.S. Navy's Coastal and Motor Minesweepers, 1941–1953

Wooden Ships and Iron Men: The U.S. Navy's Coastal and Inshore Minesweepers, and the Minecraft that Served in Vietnam, 1953–1976

All rights reserved. No part of this book may be reproduced or transmitted in any form or by any means, electronic or mechanical, including photocopying, recording or by any information storage and retrieval system without written permission from the author, except for the inclusion of brief quotations in a review.

International Standard Book Numbers
Paperbound: 978-0-7884-5757-9

To the officers and men of the United States, British, French,
Brazilian and other Allied Navies and Merchant Marines
who served in the South Atlantic in World War II

Contents

Photos and Illustrations

Maps and Diagrams

Foreword

This latest book by Commander David D. Bruhn, USN (Ret.), *Ingram's Fourth Fleet*, is a well written, well organized, and extremely interesting history of a little-known aspect of the Second World War: the naval war in the South Atlantic area between South America and Africa. Though not entirely neglected, the South Atlantic theater is usually treated as a small part of the Battle of the Atlantic, leaving historians to write about the smaller theater piecemeal, focusing largely on Germany's surface raiders, the blockade runners, and the Battle of the River Plate in which the *Graf Spee* was scuttled. This work is the first truly comprehensive history of the war in this theater.

As I read the book, I became aware that in some respects, the South Atlantic theater was a replay of World War I with variations. The first example is the use of the U.S. Navy for conducting Neutrality patrols in both wars, but with a difference. In World War I the Neutrality patrols were enforcing President Wilson's 4 August 1914 Neutrality Proclamation, the principal task being to prevent German agents in the United States, and American sympathizers, from supplying the German surface raiders with coal and other necessities. The three centers of those activities were New York, New Orleans, and San Francisco. In the second war, Neutrality patrols extended from Newfoundland into the South Atlantic, following a 5 September 1939 directive by President Roosevelt and later expanded by the 2 October 1939 Panama Act. The latter was ostensibly a common United States policy to keep the war out of the Americas. But in order to carry out the policy, the Neutrality patrols were after German blockade runners, surface raiders, and U-boats. The similarity between the two wars in this respect is that the Neutrality patrols in both wars were anything but neutral.

Another feature of the conflict in these waters was that the British employed the so-called "Distant Blockade" of Germany as they had in the first war, but this time the British were not concerned with Germany reestablishing trade with the United States as was the case in 1914-1917. In this new war they were stopping German blockade runners making runs between Germany and Japan and Japanese-occupied Asia. Though the Germans were more successful breaking the blockade in the second war, the losses among their blockade runners were enormous.

Another similarity, but one with a difference, was Germany's use of a fleet of cargo submarines to run the blockade, carrying war materials to and from ports in Asia. The Germans pioneered the use of cargo U-boats in World War I when they undertook to build a fleet of eight cargo U-boats to carry pharmaceuticals and dyestuffs to the United States and return to Germany with iron ore, tungsten, rubber and cotton. Only two boats were completed, U-*Deutschland* and U-*Bremen*, with the U-*Deutschland* making two round trips before the Germans reopened the unrestricted submarine warfare campaign in February 1917, thus ending the cargo U-boat operation. In World War II, German cargo U-boats carried freight in both directions between Asian ports and Germany right up to the end of the war.

German front-line U-boats operated in the theater, attacking allied and neutral shipping. Though six U-boat flotillas sent boats into the theater, the undersea war did not match the effort the Germans made in the North Atlantic. This was due in part to the enormous distance involved to reach the operations area, and the limitations placed on time-on-station. Only the bigger, long-range U-boats could effectively operate in the theater. Some of the smaller Type VIIC boats from the 6th, 7th, and 9th Flotillas did show up there, but most of the U-boats encountered there were the Type IXC and XCD2 from the 2nd, 10th and 12B Flotillas.

There is an aspect of the war in the South Pacific that illustrates the most dramatic difference between the two wars with regard to the war at sea—aircraft. The Allies used aircraft for antisubmarine patrols in World War I, but not over the distances that are described in this work. Commander Bruhn clearly shows that by 1943, the Allies had complete air superiority over the Atlantic between South America and Africa. From 1942 to 1944, the Allies sank eighteen U-boats and one Italian submarine in those waters, all but two of which were sunk by aircraft.

Commander Bruhn has described in detail how each one of those eighteen U-boats was caught and destroyed, and wherever possible has included the survivors' narratives of the attacks. Those accounts and the detailed coverage of the destruction of individual German surface raiders and blockade runners make this an action-filled read. The volume of information provided here is supplemented with excellent tables, photographs, and maps, making this book a truly comprehensive study of the war in this theater.

Dwight R. Messimer

Foreword

Ingram's Fourth Fleet by Commander David D. Bruhn, USN (Ret.) focuses the reader on a World War II theater that has received less historical attention, but was vital to Allied operations. The flow of supplies to Great Britain to sustain her ability to fight and later to build up for the invasion of Europe was essential. Additionally, with the Mediterranean Sea closed to the Allies during the early years of the war, a flow of supplies around the Cape of Good Hope to the Near-East, Russia, and Australia was also vital.

From an overall strategic perspective, the Allies imposed a blockade on Germany to prevent war material from reaching her. In the Battle of the Atlantic, the Germans sought to impose a counter-blockade on the flow of supplies to the European and other theaters by the use of submarines, German surface warships of the Kriegsmarine, and aircraft of the Luftwaffe. Because of the ranges involved and aircraft limitations, German aircraft played no part in their South Atlantic effort. By default, the Allies had total control of the air.

Two factors that were crucial to successful Fourth Fleet operations were geography and politics. Brazil was the only South American country to actively support the Allied war effort. U.S. Navy ships gained basing access to Brazilian ports during the Neutrality patrol period prior to U.S. entrance into the war, and U.S. patrol aircraft began operating out of Natal, Brazil, in December 1941. If Brazil had not made the decision to allow the stationing of American ships and aircraft at bases in Brazil, the United States would have been severely constrained in its ability to keep the South Atlantic sea lanes open. Basing at Natal in December 1941 and Ascension Island after July 1942 gave Fourth Fleet patrol aircraft access to the entire area of operations assigned to Fourth Fleet.

Ingram's South Atlantic Force began Neutrality patrol operations as a Cruiser Division, augmented by a destroyer squadron in April 1941. Additional surface combatants and support ships were added over time as they could be made available from Atlantic Fleet assets. They were not available in large numbers and were never intended for offensive operations. They were sufficient for use against blockade runners, auxiliary cruisers, and convoy escorts, but their coverage was limited. The primary asset employed against German naval units and available in much greater relative strength were long range Navy and Air Force patrol squadrons. The Allies had total Air Superiority in the South Atlantic and had the range and depth for complete coverage of the operational area. As Commander Bruhn thoroughly documents in his book, all but two of the German submarines sunk between 1942 and 1944 were aircraft kills.

Another important factor that contributed to Fourth Fleet success was Ingram's performance in a diplomatic capacity. In May 1941 he entered Recife, Brazil, in command of two cruisers ordered to Neutrality patrol. Local officials wanted to know why he was there. He, being the representative of a country at peace, groped to explain. Within a year, after a crucial meeting in April 1942 with Brazilian President Vargas, the president charged him with the protection of Brazilian shipping. After Brazil declared war on Germany in August 1942, President Vargas placed the Brazilian Navy and Air Force under Ingram's operational control. Additionally, Ingram established informal but effective control over U.S. Army and Air Force units in Brazil by telling them he was in charge. These diplomatic and command qualities, as described in Commander Bruhn's book, illuminate the breadth of Ingram's leadership and organizational abilities. In short order he produced a cohesive command structure that lead to operational successes—enemy ship kills and successful convoy transits.

It's also noteworthy that when Ingram first arrived in Brazil as the commander of Task Force 3 (later Fourth Fleet) there was no logistical infrastructure present, other than Panair do Brasil—an Brazilian airline—facilities and fledgling U.S. Army sites in the early stages of construction. As a result of his negotiation with Brazil and under his direct supervision, air fields, and naval stations with support facilities for task force ships were operational even before Brazil declared war.

A very interesting aspect of German operations in the South Atlantic was the success of German auxiliary cruisers/raiders against allied merchant shipping. Germany's principal strategic concept behind these heavily-armed ex-freighters was to force the allies to divert assets to hunt them and thus dilute concentration of Allied forces in European and North Atlantic areas. The large number of sinkings the cruisers achieved was an important collateral benefit. Factors that contributed to cruiser success included: 1) the Germans expended considerable effort to provide the cruisers with the means to disguise themselves, particularly through the use of false superstructures; 2) their operational control came under the same command that controlled the German submarine force, allowing close employment coordination; 3) the Germans used VLF broadcast communications that required minimal response from cruisers or submarines and could not be intercepted; 4) senior Naval officers, considered too old for U-boats, commanded the cruisers and exercised great ingenuity under near autonomous conditions; 5) a global logistics network embedded in almost every important seaport of the world successfully arranged for covert resupply of both submarines and cruisers at remote locations; and 6) the German's broke the British merchant marine code giving them access to sensitive routing information. By way of comparison in all theaters (not just the South Atlantic), nine auxiliary cruisers accounted for 141 (872,891 tons) merchant vessels sunk or captured, while the eighteen U-boats sunk by Allied forces in the South Atlantic were responsible for 104 (561,075 tons) merchant vessels sunk or damaged. Unfortunately for the Germans this success could not be sustained in the face of rapidly expanding patrol by radar equipped aircraft.

Commander Bruhn describes in great detail, Germany's concerted effort by the use of auxiliary cruisers and submarines to disrupt and destroy shipping in the South Atlantic. They failed. By August 1943, Fourth Fleet had accomplished its mission of defeating the submarine threat. In his comprehensive analysis of the many engagements between Allied and German units, consistent lessons emerge:

1. Long range patrol aircraft were essential, but airborne radar was crucial. Without it, the number of aircraft required for effective search would have been much greater.

2. High-Frequency Direction Finding (HF/DF), both ashore and afloat, were very effective for initial detection and cueing of enemy threats. In particular the coordination between shore, surface, and airborne units in Fourth Fleet was very strong.

3. The Germans were at a huge technical disadvantage against airborne radar. At the outset they had no detection capability. Early in the war they had some success with Metox, a receiver that could detect longer wave length radars. However, when the Allies shifted to shorter wave lengths, they were once more defenseless. When they deployed a receiver that could detect shorter wave length radars, the limited sensitivity only gave the German submarine about 1 minute warning, insufficient to the need. The submarine's goal was to remain invisible. Radar defeated this goal.

Ingram's Fourth Fleet is extremely well-researched and delivers an engrossing history that informs the reader on many levels. Historical context is excellent. Higher level strategic concepts that are essential to an understanding of operations at the theater level and interservice contributions are thoroughly evaluated. Descriptions of engagements between individual units are presented in intimate detail. Supporting material in the form of personnel diaries, tables, and photographs provide excellent summaries and reinforce the text.

There is also a wealth of reference material to direct readers to greater detail. This is a scholarly work that carries the reader forward through page after page. I think the book does an excellent job of supporting important theses associated with naval warfare:

1. A country with the necessary resources for wartime production of necessary equipment and the training and equipping of necessary forces can be pivotal if equipment and personnel can be delivered to where it's needed.
2. Protection of merchant shipping and sea lanes.
3. Effective planning and execution of cooperative force employment.
4. Control of air, sea, and land space.
5. Courage and perseverance.

Capt. Steven C. Saulnier, USN (Retired)
Senior Advisor River Assault and Interdiction Division 44,
   Hai Quan Viet Nam, 1970-1971
Commanding Officer, USS *Fletcher* (DD-992), 1980-1982
Commander, Destroyer Squadron Thirteen, 1988-1991

Acknowledgements

I am grateful to the brilliant and prolific maritime and aviation artist Richard DeRosset for creating the stunning cover art for this book. His painting depicts the German blockade runner MV *Karin* aflame, after being stopped in the South Atlantic by two units of the United States Fourth Fleet—the light cruiser USS *Savannah* (CL-42) and the destroyer *Eberle* (DD-430). Before abandoning, her crew had set scuttling charges, which exploded, killing all but three members of a boarding party from the *Eberle* attempting to salvage the ship.

Rob Hoole, a former Royal Navy mine clearance diving officer and commanding officer of HMS *Berkeley* (M40)—a *Hunt*-class mine countermeasures vessel—reviewed the portions of the manuscript relating to the Royal Navy. Hoole is a long-standing member of the Ton Class Association and a regular contributor to its publications. He is also founding Vice Chairman and Webmaster of the Royal Naval Minewarfare & Clearance Diving Officers' Association, and holds key positions in related organizations.

University lecturer, and acclaimed military historian and author, Dwight R. Messimer, was kind enough to pen a foreword for the book. A specialist on the German Navy and U-boats, he has written nearly a dozen books published by the U.S. Naval Institute on this subject and on naval aviation covering the period 1925-1942. His work has also appeared in many periodicals, including *The American Neptune*, *The Quarterly Journal of Military History*, *War Revolution and Peace*, and *Naval History*.

Retired U.S. Navy Captain Steven C. Saulnier also reviewed the book and wrote a foreword. Possessing much knowledge of fleet operations as a result of diverse experience gained during a very distinguished career, his perspective was particularly useful. Saulnier's operational experience included service aboard cruisers, destroyers, submarines, and aircraft carriers, and in the Republic of Vietnam. His sea duty began following graduation from the U.S. Naval Academy with service aboard the USS *Irex* SS-482 (which, commissioned on 14 May 1945, was the Navy's first snorkel submarine) and culminated with his command of Destroyer Squadron 13. In the interim, Saulnier earned two masters degrees from Stanford University, served in a variety of assignments at sea and ashore, including Pentagon duty, and commanding the destroyer USS *Fletcher* (DD-992).

I am particularly indebted to Lynn Marie Tosello for her work as the editor of this text. In addition to the style, eloquence, and proper syntax she lent to the work, she also brought a discerning eye and humor regarding the subject of the book as a whole, and rightly highlighted nautical terms or "fleet shorthands" requiring more explanation.

Preface

This force is averaging about 24 days at sea out of 30. At all advance bases, liberty is restricted to sundown. Living conditions aboard ship in the tropics are not good. The food is excellent. Liberty in Recife, Bahia and San Juan is poor. There is little time for recreation. In spite of the above, the Force morale is high. The mental attitude of all hands is pitched to a winning tempo and is perfect. The men are healthy, brown and look like veterans. Their conduct ashore is exemplary. This condition will be retained by hard work and keeping the sea habit. Holding out a ten day overhaul in Miami at periods from four to six months helps greatly. The ships that have visited there carry a smile for months.

—Observation by Vice Adm. Jonas H. Ingram, regarding the cruiser
Memphis (CL-13) and the destroyer *Winslow* (DD-359) being due
for overhaul and crew rest after strenuous months of duty as
a part of the South Atlantic Force (later the Fourth Fleet).[1]

The Royal Navy had been engaged in war at sea in the South Atlantic (and other theaters) for over two years when the U.S. Navy began to relieve the British of some of their duties in the narrows between the "bulge of Brazil" and West Africa. This action occurred after America entered the war on 11 December 1941, following the Japanese attack on Pearl Harbor. Task Force 3, under American Rear Adm. Jonas Ingram, had already been conducting Neutrality patrols in South Atlantic waters and had captured a "blockade runner." Prior to formal American intervention, the Royal Navy's South Atlantic Station at Freetown, Sierra Leone, on the west coast of Africa was singularly responsible for all naval operations in South Atlantic waters. In addition to its headquarters at Freetown, the Station had bases near Cape Town, South Africa, and at Port Stanley in the Falkland Islands.

Ingram's small South Atlantic Force would, throughout the war, retain this administrative title and remain a subordinate unit of the U.S. Atlantic Fleet, while having a series of concurrent operational designations. The first was Task Force 3, then Task Force 23 and later Fourth Fleet, before downgrading near war's end, from fleet status to Task Force 27. Ingram commanded the South Atlantic Force/Fourth Fleet until 11 November 1944, when, following his relief by Vice Adm. William R. Munroe, USN, he assumed the duties of commander-in-chief Atlantic Fleet.

While Ingram and his Fourth Fleet were synonymous during the war (like Halsey's Third Fleet, Spruance's Fifth Fleet, and Hewitt's Eight Fleet), he was lesser known to the public than other fleet commanders. A brief overview of his naval career follows.

ADMIRAL JONAS H. INGRAM, U.S. NAVY

Photo Preface-1

Seated: Lt. Gen. Hunter Leggett, Adm. C. S. Williams, and Lt. Jonas H. Ingram. Officer standing is General Liggett's aide. Naval Reserve Force Day in San Francisco, California, 27 March 1920.
U.S. Naval History and Heritage Command Photograph #NH 119816

Jonas Howard Ingram was born in Jeffersonville, Indiana, on 15 October 1886, and graduated from the Naval Academy in 1907. Prior to World War I he served aboard several cruisers, destroyers, and battleships. On 22 April 1914, while assigned to the battleship *Arkansas* (BB-33), he landed at Vera Cruz, Mexico, with the Arkansas battalion and was awarded the Medal of Honor for "skillful and efficient handling of the artillery and machine guns and for distinguished conduct in battle." During World War I, Ingram was on the staff of commander, Battleship Division Nine. Comprised initially of four dreadnought battleships of the Atlantic Fleet—coal burners *Delaware* (BB-28), *Florida* (BB-30), *New York* (BB-34) and *Wyoming* (BB-32)—the division constituted the American contribution to the British Grand Fleet. Two other battleships later joined BatDiv 9 in Europe;

Texas (BB-35), and *Arkansas* (BB-33) which replaced *Delaware*.
Following the signing of the Armistice on 11 November 1918, the
division was present for the surrender of the German High Seas Fleet
on 21 November 1918.[2]

Photo Preface-2

Battleship Division 9 arriving off Scapa Flow, Scotland, in December 1917.
Painting by Bernard F. Gribble, 1928; U.S. Naval Historical and Heritage Command
Accession #28-003-A

Between the wars, Ingram served in a variety of important
assignments, earning promotion to rear admiral on 10 January 1941. A
short time later, he turned over the Caribbean Patrol to Rear Adm.
Raymond A. Spruance, USN (commandant of the Tenth Naval
District at San Juan, Puerto Rico) and received orders in March 1941
to take Task Force Three to the South Atlantic on Neutrality patrol.
His force consisted of the four units of Cruiser Division 2; the flagship
Memphis (CL-13), *Cincinnati* (CL-6), *Milwaukee* (CL-5) and *Omaha* (CL-
4). Later several destroyers and auxiliary ships joined the group, which
operated in the South Atlantic for a year before its designation was
changed to Task Force 23 in February 1942. Concurrent with this
change, Ingram received a third star, promoting him to vice admiral.[3]

In March 1943, the vastly expanded task force gained additional
prestige when it became the U.S. Fourth Fleet. The responsibility of
the existing organization to protect vital Allied shipping in the U-boat-
infested South Atlantic, and to combat raiders and runners in these

same waters, did not change. Admiral Jonas H. Ingram completed his tour as commander-in-chief, U.S. Atlantic Fleet, on 26 September 1946. He retired from active duty on 1 April 1947, and died a little over five years later at San Diego, California, on 9 September 1952.[4]

GERMANY'S DEFEAT IN WORLD WAR I, AND LOSS OF HER HIGH SEAS FLEET

I personally think the maritime contribution was our most important one, but not in battle. It was the quieter strangulation by blockade.

—Historian Andrew Choong opining that the strategic defeat of Germany at sea in World War I was an even greater British contribution to victory than the battles fought on land.[5]

The strategy Germany pursued in World War II, regarding her efforts to force Britain to capitulate, resulted from bitter experience in World War I. A sea blockade of the Deutschland by the Royal Navy's Home Fleet helped facilitate Germany's loss of the war and her High Seas Fleet as well. The lessons learned shaped her conduct of naval warfare in World War II and, by extension, that of opposing Axis and Allied forces in the South Atlantic. As such, a short review of the British and German navies in the early 1900s will help to provide context for the book.

In the early 1900s, following a period of expansion, the Imperial German Navy was second in strength only to the British Royal Navy. The two nations had been locked in a naval race since 1898 when Germany embarked on the construction of a blue water navy that Britain viewed as a very significant threat to her well-being. Being an island nation, dependent on imports for food, fuel, and other vital supplies and materials, Britain had to rule the waves. Should she find herself at war with Germany, defeat at sea could lead to blockade, possible starvation, and surrender.[6]

To avoid this possibility Britain pursued building greater numbers of, and more powerful, warships than Germany. By 1914, the Royal Navy was the largest in the world, and the German Navy, though quite powerful, was numerically inferior to the British. When World War I broke out, Britain had over twice as many battleships, and other types of large combatant ships and submarines as did Germany.

British and German Navies in 1914
Numbers of Major Combatant Ships

British Royal Navy		Imperial German Navy	
Pre-dreadnought Battleships	40	Pre-dreadnought Battleships	22
Dreadnought Battleships (13 under construction)	22	Dreadnought Battleships (5 under construction)	15
Battle Cruisers (1 under construction)	9	Battle Cruisers (3 under construction)	5
Cruisers	121	Cruisers	40
Destroyers	221	Destroyers	90
Submarines	73	Submarines	31
Total	486	Total	203[7]

Photo Preface-3

Surrender of German High Seas Fleet off the Firth of Forth, Scotland, 21 November 1918. Vice Adm. William S. Sims, USN, and Rear Adm. Hugh Rodman, USN, observe from aboard the battleship *New York* (BB-34).
Painting by Bernard F. Gribble, 1920; U.S. Naval History and Heritage Command Accession #NH 58842-KN

With superior naval forces, the British were able to rid the seas of German merchant ships by early 1915, effectively blocking Germany's trade routes. The *Deutschland's* increasingly desperate need for food and other supplies, contributed to her surrender. On 11 November 1918, World War I ended with Germany signing an armistice. While peace arrangements were being worked out, the Allies interned the German High Seas Fleet at Scapa Flow, a natural anchorage amid the Orkney Islands of Scotland.[8]

On 21 June 1919, under the mistaken belief that peace talks had failed, Rear Adm. Ludwig von Reuter gave the order to scuttle the entire High Seas Fleet. The crews of all the ships in the Flow (now totaling fewer than 2,000 men) then raised the German flag, and opened seacocks, portholes, watertight doors, hatches, and torpedo tubes. As German sailors took to their lifeboats, ships began to sink with tremendous hissings of steam, spouts of water, and finally sucking and gurgling sounds as they slipped below the surface. A total of fifty-two ships went to the bottom, and this act remains the greatest loss of shipping in a single day.[9]

GERMANY'S GRAND STRATEGY IN WORLD WAR II

Germany's strategy to defeat Britain in its simplest form involved blockade and counter-blockade. Having experienced the effectiveness of the sea blockade imposed by the British in World War I, it decided these roles should be reversed. This could be accomplished, the German Navy believed, by coordinated action between scores of heavy ships (battleships and battlecruisers), commerce raiders, hundreds of U-boats, and thousands of aircraft. With these military forces acting in concert, Germany would impose a strangle-hold on the sea lanes to the British Isles, and force its people and their leaders into submission.[10]

While the British Home Fleet tried to cope with such a blockade, Germany intended to send a steady stream of her own Axis blockade runners—the counter-blockade portion of its strategy—out of French and African ports to the Far East. Germany and Japan planned to exchange strategic war materials/technology on a large scale, by using merchant shipping to run the Allied blockade. Germany's deficiencies included rubber, tin, tungsten, molybdenum, hemp, hides and vegetable oils, all possessed in abundance by Japan and her newly conquered territories. Japan in turn lacked certain essential metals, as well as manufactured articles and technical processes which Germany and, to a lesser degree, Italy possessed.[11]

ENEMY BLOCKADE RUNNERS GENERALLY AVOID ALLIED FORCES DURING THE EARLY WAR YEARS

The German Naval High Command was responsible for the blockade runner program, which utilized, with few exceptions, ships either of German registry or German prizes of war. A few Italian ships were also put into service, under German control. Japan's limited amount of shipping prohibited the assignment of any of her merchant vessels for running the blockade. In 1941 and 1942, Germany sent a total of forty-nine supply ships and tankers out of French ports to run the Allied blockade, proceed around Africa and across the vast Indian

Ocean to Japan and back. Of these, forty runners made the round-trip voyage successfully, carrying precious cargo both ways. Of the nine ships intercepted by the Allies in that period, only three were caught prior to November 1942. One, the German freighter *Odenwald*, was apprehended in November 1941 by two units of Ingram's force—the cruiser *Omaha* and destroyer *Somers*—while conducting Neutrality patrols.[12]

Not until the winter of 1943-44 did the coordinated activities of the British, United States, and Free French naval forces significantly degrade German and Japanese attempts to exchange strategic raw materials across 16,000 miles of water. The desperate persistence in carrying out these activities on the part of the Axis powers was due, in part, to the exceptional degree to which the economic structure of the two nations complemented each other. The other reason for their persistence was the relatively successful manner in which the exchanges occurred under the very noses of the two navies who reportedly ruled the waves.[13]

COORDINATED GERMAN NAVAL OPERATIONS

Although the blockade runners generally made their long cruises independently, their operations were integrated with those of German Navy surface raiders (battleships and battlecruisers), commerce raiders and U-boats. Although the use of battleships and battlecruisers as surface raiders proved ineffective, "top brass" determined that it could still achieve a blockade victory—via the destruction of Allied shipping—by combining the operations of U-boats and commerce raiders. Commerce raiders (formally titled auxiliary cruisers) were non-descript ex-freighters, whose benign appearance disguised the fact that they were "wolves in sheep's clothing" with guns, torpedoes, and scout aircraft cleverly hidden from view until put into action against their victims. The Germans also believed they could continue to outwit the Allies by constantly changing the routes of runners filtering monthly through the Allied blockade.[14]

Raiders, Runners, Supply Ships, and Submarines

Country	Function	Description
Germany	Surface raider	Battleships, and battlecruisers (also called "pocket battleships") used to attack merchant shipping
Germany	Commerce raider	Auxiliary cruisers; ex-freighters fitted with hidden guns/torpedo tubes/scout aircraft—enabling them to prey on shipping
Germany	Blockade runner	Merchant vessels transporting vital war materials
Italy	Blockade runner	Merchant vessels transporting vital war materials
Germany	Supply ships	Navy tankers and merchant vessels. Blockade runners and, less frequently, U-boats were also used for this purpose
Germany	U-boats	Used for anti-shipping warfare, and occasionally as supply vessels
Italy	Submarines	Anti-shipping warfare

Some blockade runners functioned as supply ships for raiders and U-boats, to extend the length of their cruises. German and Italian submarines sank considerably more Allied merchant ships than did naval combatants and auxiliary cruisers, and thus might be considered "raiders" as well. *Raiders of the Deep* was the title of a 1928 best seller by Lowell Thomas which offered a sympathetic account of the crews of U-boats that prowled the Atlantic, Mediterranean, and English Channel during World War I. Despite this lineage, "raider" was not an Allied term associated with German and Italian submarines.

CAPITAL SHIPS PROVE INEFFECTIVE AS RAIDERS

An impediment to Germany's blockade of Britain during the first three years of the war (autumn 1939-autumn 1942) was the inability of her battleships and battlecruisers to evade the Royal Navy long enough to carry out protracted periods of hit-and-run attacks on merchant ship convoys. However, German minelayers, aircraft, and particularly U-boats were having success in interdicting much shipping bound for sea ports in the British Isles.

The first major setback to Germany regarding the use of capital ships against merchant shipping was the loss of the battlecruiser *Admiral Graf Spee* off Montevideo, Uruguay, on 17 December 1939. After she had terrorized sea lanes between 30 September and 7 December, sinking nine Allied vessels, the Royal and French navies deployed massive naval forces to locate and destroy the "pocket battleship." In the Battle of the River Plate, two British and one New Zealand cruiser inflicted sufficient damage on *Graf Spee* to force her to enter Montevideo for repairs. The government of Uruguay directed that she leave port before all necessary repairs were completed, and her commanding officer scuttled the ship a short distance off shore. Having determined that *Graf Spee* was not battle ready, he chose this action in lieu of the possibility of encountering superior Royal Navy forces that he believed lay in wait out to sea.[15]

The second major setback was the loss of the battleship *Bismarck* in the North Atlantic before she could even find a convoy to attack. She was scuttled by her crew following incapacitating battle damage from the guns of a British fleet on 27 May 1941.[16]

The battlecruiser *Scharnhorst* was sunk off North Cape, Norway, on 26 December 1943, by a much stronger British naval force. By this point in the war, Adolf Hitler had become disillusioned with his capital ships. The navy's ambitious pre-war plans for a fleet with impressive large ships had produced the battleships *Bismarck* and *Tirpitz* and a number of smaller battlecruisers. Germany had powerful ships, yet not so overwhelming a force that they could escape containment by the Royal Navy. Because these capital ships posed such a threat if allowed to roam the oceans, the Royal Navy put to sea in force to sink them whenever they ventured out of port.[17]

In addition to monitoring the activities of Germany's capital ships by various means—including military surveillance and human intelligence—the British had been deciphering German naval codes for some time. Thus, the sortie from port in late December 1943 of *Scharnhorst* and the 4th Destroyer Flotilla—*Z29, Z30, Z33, Z34*, and *Z38*—was no surprise. Additionally, the Royal Navy had two strong forces ready to engage the enemy, one sailing from Murmansk in the Soviet Union and the other from Scapa Flow, which included the battleship HMS *Duke of York*—also known as "the Duke."[18]

Following Hitler's latest tirade about the uselessness of his navy, *Scharnhorst* and the destroyers had been ordered out from Altafjord, Norway, on Christmas Day to do their best against a Russia-bound-Arctic convoy (JW55B) of nineteen ships. In a battle fought amidst snow storms in the freezing seas north of Norway, it took the combined firepower of several ships to sink the *Scharnhorst*. That evening, Vice Adm. Bruce Fraser, commander-in-chief of the British Home Fleet, praised the performance of the vanquished battlecruiser:

> Gentlemen, the battle against the *Scharnhorst* has ended in victory for us. I hope that any of you who are ever called upon to lead a ship into action against an opponent many times superior, will command your ship as gallantly as the *Scharnhorst* was commanded [by Capt. Fritz Hintze] today.

Fraser made this declaration to officers aboard his flagship, HMS *Duke of York*—one of the units of the Royal Navy's Force I and Force II that had disposed of the enemy with gunfire and torpedoes.[19]

GERMAN COMMERCE RAIDERS SINK SCORES OF VESSELS UNTIL THE FORTUNES OF WAR CHANGE

While seizure of the runner *Odenwald* on the high seas had set an example for U.S. naval forces, and while the Royal Navy had succeeded in sinking sixteen runners even before that date, German armed commerce raiders achieved much greater success on the other side of the ledger. Between 24 April 1940 and 30 September 1942, nine armed converted freighters—the auxiliary cruisers *Atlantis, Komet, Kormoran, Michel, Orion, Pinguin, Stier, Thor,* and *Widder*—sank 103 Allied ships and captured another thirty.[20]

This great success was not without a cost to the enemy, which increased over time as Allied aircraft and ships hunted the raiders on the seas. *Pinguin, Kormoran, Atlantis, Stier,* and *Komet* were sunk, in that order, between 8 May 1941 and 14 October 1942. *Thor* was destroyed by fire on 30 November 1942, while at Yokohama, Japan. *Michel,* the only raider to send any Allied ships to the bottom after 30 September 1942—a total of eight—was sunk east of Yokohama, by the submarine *Tarpon* (SS-175) on 17 October 1943. The only raiders to survive, *Widder* and *Orion,* were not ordered to make any additional war cruises following their safe return to Germany on 31 October 1940 and 23 August 1941, respectively.[21]

GERMAN BLOCKADE RUNNING CAMPAIGN ALSO SUFFERS INCREASED SHIP LOSSES BEGINNING IN LATE 1942

After autumn 1942, there was an abrupt shift in the fortunes of war, for runners as well as raiders. There were many reasons for this. One was the loss of African harbors, following the Allied landings in North Africa in November 1942, depriving German ships of convenient and valuable hiding places. Another was quite by accident; Allied patrols flown against U-boats in the Bay of Biscay netted runners again and again. An important factor in the South Atlantic was the expansion of combined forces, via the assignment of more U.S. Navy destroyers to the theater and the transfer of patrol vessels to Brazil on lend-lease. Allied tactics and operations were also enhanced by the temporary loan of the auxiliary aircraft carrier *Santee* (ACV-29) to Admiral Ingram's forces. *Santee* quickly became the centerpiece of a hunter-killer group, formed of the carrier and destroyers to aid her embarked aircraft in searching for runners, raiders and submarines. Prosecution of the enemy by planes and combatant ships working in concert, was now possible in mid-ocean and other remote areas that lay beyond the range of shore-based patrol aircraft.[22]

In addition to danger posed to them by Allied forces, runners also faced the possibility that German or Italian submarines might fail to recognize the camouflage (false names, national flags and ship colors) in which they cloaked themselves to escape unwanted attention. One accident of mistaken identity occurred on 31 January 1942 when *U-333* sent the *Spreewald* to the bottom. Kapitänleutnant Peter-Erich Cremer, the submarine commander, could not identify her as German because she was disguised as the Norwegian motor ship *Elg*. At the time of her loss, *Spreewald* was transporting eighty-six prisoners from vessels sunk by the German raider *Kormoran*.[23]

Another such incident took place on 3 March 1943, when *U-43* sank the German auxiliary minelayer *Doggerbank* with a spread of torpedoes, believing her to be a steamship of the *Dunedin Star* type (a refrigerated cargo liner). The ill-fated ship was the former British freighter *Speybank*, which the German raider *Atlantis* had captured on 31 January 1941 in the Indian Ocean. After a prize crew brought the ship to Bordeaux, France, the Kriegsmarine had converted her for naval use. Aboard *Doggerbank* were many crewmen of the German supply tanker *Uckermark* and the raider *Thor*. The two ships had been destroyed by fire on 30 November 1942, while moored alongside one another at Yokohama, Japan. Explosions aboard *Uckermark* set *Thor* on fire, and the two ships were quickly engulfed in flames. Fire then spread across the oil-covered water of the basin and also destroyed the German supply ship *Leuthen* (former British liner *Nankin* captured by *Thor*) and the Japanese freighter *Unkai Maru*.[24]

BLOCKADE RUNNING CAMPAIGN COMES TO AN END IN DECEMBER 1943-JANUARY 1944 PERIOD

The climax to the demise of Germany's blockade running campaign occurred in late December 1943 and the first week of January 1944, in a series of widely separated actions in the North and South Atlantic. On 18 December, aircraft of the British Coastal Command attacked and wrecked the Italian motor vessel *Pietro Orseolo* as she rode at anchor in Concarneau Harbor, Brittany, in northwestern France. A week later, British planes sufficiently damaged the *Orsono* that she was forced to beach in shallow water off Le Verdon-sur-Mer, France.

Finally, on 27 December, aircraft of the Coastal Command sank the *Alsterufer* in the North Atlantic off the Bay of Biscay.[25]

The coup-de-grace was administered by Admiral Ingram's forces in a "triple play" in the South Atlantic against three outbound German blockade runners. The action began when a bomber from Ascension Island in the mid-South Atlantic sighted the *Weserland*. The destroyer *Somers* sank the German ship on 3 January. At the same time, other planes were shadowing *Rio Grande*, which the cruiser *Omaha* and destroyer *Jouett* polished off with naval gunfire on 4 January, aided by scuttling charges set by the ship's crew. The following day, a third runner, the *Burgenland*, was similarly sunk by scuttling charges and gunfire from *Omaha* and *Jouett*. Thereafter, German blockade running dwindled to insignificance.[26]

Between November 1942 and February 1944, the German Naval High Command used twenty-three ships for a total of thirty-four runs attempted. These numbers include five ships that were loaded and ready to sail from France in January 1944, but whose departure was cancelled. Six successful runs were made to the Far East, with losses of four ships sent out from Europe on the long voyage; *Anneliese Essberger*, *Cortellazo*, *Germania*, and *Portland*. Casualties were much higher for ships trying to make the run from the Far East back to Europe. Only four ships were successful, while ten—*Alsterufer*, *Burgenland*, *Doggerbank*, *Hohenfriedburg*, *Irene*, *Karin*, *Regensburg*, *Rhakotis*, *Rio Grande*, and *Weserland*—were not.[27]

During the war, Allied intelligence identified idle merchant ships that Germany might employ as runners. Some of these ships were under the oversight of the German Naval High Command. Others not under the control of the German Navy might also be considered "blockade runners" whether trying to escape internment and/or bring cargos owned by private interests back to Europe. Once leaving port, they had to run the Allied blockade to make it safely to an Axis port.

TIDE TURNS AGAINST U-BOATS IN 1943

> *The only thing that ever really frightened me during the war was the U-boat peril.*
>
> —British Prime Minister Winston Churchill

The destruction of enemy submarines by allied naval and air forces in the South Atlantic increased dramatically in 1943, when thirteen U-boats and one Italian submarine were sent to the bottom. A mere two enemy submarines had been sunk the preceding year. Only three would be destroyed in 1944, and none the following year. A combination of aircraft depth-charge attacks and gunfire from the destroyers *Jouett* and *Moffett* dispatched one of the U-boats in 1943. Patrol aircraft depth-charges were responsible for sending the remaining U-boats and Italian submarine into the abyss.

In the Atlantic generally, "hunter-killer" groups played a key role in turning the tide against enemy submarines. Such groups were comprised of a handful or less of anti-submarine warships (corvettes, destroyers, destroyer escorts, frigates) formed around an escort carrier to actively hunt U-boats in the Atlantic. The fight between an escort ship of one of these groups, the destroyer *Borie* (formerly of the Fourth Fleet) and *U-405* formed the basis for the acclaimed and Oscar-winning film *The Enemy Below* released in 1957, starring Robert Mitchum and Curt Jürgens.

1944 BRINGS VICTORY IN THE SOUTH ATLANTIC

Victory came to the South Atlantic by October 1944 with the sinking of the final three U-boats in that theater. The most hard-fought battle with a German submarine came on 15 June, when Avenger torpedo bombers and Wildcat fighters from the escort carrier *Solomons* (CVE-67) sent *U-860* to the bottom. Losses to the Fourth Fleet were two torpedo bombers and their three-man crews. A little later that same month, a visit by Comdr. Gene Tunney, the former world heavyweight boxing champion, boosted morale. As the director of physical training for the entire Navy, his role was to help ensure that the men of the fleet were in shape for arduous duties they might later be called upon to perform. (Presumably, this was in reference to a possible invasion of the Japanese home islands. Many fleet units were shifted from the Atlantic and European theaters to the Pacific, after it became apparent that Germany's defeat was inevitable.)

On 11 November, Vice Adm. Jonas H. Ingram was relieved by Rear Adm. William R. Munroe as commander Fourth Fleet. Ingram became commander-in-chief Atlantic Fleet with the rank of Admiral. Allied forces then had control of the Mediterranean, and had liberated France, Belgium, and part of Holland. It thus became almost a certainty that Germany, no matter how long she might postpone her ultimate defeat, could no longer send submarines to a theater as distant as the South Atlantic. As a result, on 22 November all escort vessels except four DEs were ordered detached from Fourth Fleet to return to the United States for further assignment to the Pacific.

WANING MONTHS OF THE WAR

Between mid-December 1944 and V-E (Victory in Europe) on 8 May 1945, the transfer of ships by the Fourth Fleet along with its aircraft squadrons, continued.   During this period the Fourth Fleet was downgraded to Task Force status on 15 April 1945. The bulk of the downsizing/departure of naval forces from Brazil occurred on 27 June 1945 with the decommissioning of Fleet Air Wing Sixteen.

NAUTICAL/NAVAL TERMS

Some readers may find the following terms useful as they progress though the book:

- Abaft: Toward the stern, relative to some object ("abaft the deckhouse").
- Armada: A large fleet of warships, though the term may be used symbolically to signify any sizable group of vessels.
- Barbette: A fixed armored housing at the base of a gun turret on a warship.
- Broach: To turn the ship broadside to heavy seas, or lose control of steering in following seas so that the ship is turned broadside to the waves. An extremely dangerous situation in steep seas since the ship may roll over and capsize.
- Caliber: The bore to barrel length ratio of a naval gun, obtained by dividing the length of the barrel (from breech to muzzle) by the barrel diameter to give a dimensionless quantity. For example, a 3-inch/50-caliber gun has a barrel length of 150 inches.
- Davit(s): A crane made of a swinging boom together with blocks and tackle, usually mounted in pairs, which may be swung over the side of a ship to lower and recover the launch or lifeboats.
- Dead in the water: Not moving (used only when a vessel is afloat and neither tied up nor anchored).
- Deckhouse: An enclosed structure built on the ship's upper or main deck, usually the navigating station though the term can refer to any simple superstructure on deck.
- Fathom: A unit of measurement equal to six feet, used to measure water depth.
- General Quarters: Battle Stations.
- Gun(s) opened: To begin firing a gun or guns.
- Gunnel (gunwale): The upper edge of the side of a vessel.

- HF/DF: Land and shipboard high-frequency, radio direction finding equipment.
- Imperial German Navy: Existed from 1871 to 1919.
- Jacob's ladder: A flexible, hanging ladder consisting of vertical ropes or chains supporting wooden rungs that allow people to board a ship from a small boat.
- Kriegsmarine: Navy of Nazi Germany from 1935 to 1945, which superseded the Kaiserliche Marine (Imperial German Navy) of World War I and the inter-war Reichsmarine (Navy of the Realm).
- Land: To put ashore. Disembark.
- Lighter: Flat-bottomed barge.
- Master: The commander of a non-military ship.
- MS (motor ship) interchangeable with MV (motor vessel): Designation for a merchant vessel propelled by diesel engines.
- Prize Crew: A detail of officers and men placed on board a captured ship to bring it into port.
- Rating: The rating of a sailor is a combination of rate (pay grade, as indicated by the number of chevrons he or she wears) and rating (occupational specialty, as indicated by the symbol just above the chevrons).
- Sea anchor: Any device, such as a bucket or canvas funnel, dragged in the water to keep a vessel heading into the wind or reduce drifting.
- Sortie: Deployment or dispatch of a military unit(s) from a strongpoint, usually on a specific mission. For Navy ships, it refers to departure (sometimes very sudden) from a seaport.
- Split plant: Aligning a ship's support systems, engines, pumps, and other machinery so that two or more propulsion plants are available, each complete in itself. Each propulsion plant operates its own propeller shaft. If one plant were to be put out of action by explosion, battle damage, or flooding, the other plant could continue to drive the ship ahead.
- SS: Steamship (sometimes denoted S.S.), a designation that commonly precedes the name of a merchant ship propelled by steam power.
- Stand (past tense stood): Of a ship or her captain, to steer, sail, or steam, usually used in conjunction with a specified direction or destination, e.g., "stand into port."

- Task Force (TF): Temporary naval organization composed of a group of ships. A task force can be assembled using ships from different divisions and squadrons, and can be easily dissolved following completion of the operational task.
- Task Group (TG): A component of a naval task force.
- Vessel: Any craft (from largest ship to smallest boat) that is capable of floating and moving on the water.

GERMAN AND ITALIAN NAVAL OFFICER RANKS EQUIVALENT TO THOSE OF THE U.S. NAVY

German Navy	U.S. Navy	Italian Navy
Kapitän zur See	Captain	Capitano di Vascello
Fregattenkapitän	Commander	Capitano di Fregata
Korvettenkapitän	Lieutenant Commander	Capitano di Corvetta
Kapitänleutnant	Lieutenant	Primo Tenente di Vascello Tenente di Vascello
Oberleutnant zur See	Lieutenant (junior grade)	Sottotenente di Vascello
Leutnant zue See	Ensign	Guardiamarina

USE OF THE BOOK'S INDEX

Former sailors picking up a book such as this one often want to ascertain whether or not it contains any references to a ship(s) in which they served. In acknowledgement of this fact, an extensive index is included. To reduce its size, multiple ships listed on the same page or pages in the text are combined into a single entry. Entries for American ships are located under their associated ship type headings. For example, the battleship *Arkansas* can be found under Ships and Craft, and the sub-categories: United States, Navy, combatants, and battleships. A reader searching for a particular foreign ship should review all entries under the heading for that country.

Since a good portion of this book is devoted to U.S. Navy and Army Air Corps aviation, some readers will likely be most interested in searching for references to a particular Aviation Wing, Squadron, or type of aircraft. This information may be found near the end of the index under the entry United States, and within the sub-categories Army, Navy, or military aircraft.

The names of United States and Royal Navy personnel that are provided in Appendices A (Organization of the Fourth Fleet) and C (HMNZS *Achilles*, HMS *Ajax*, and HMS *Exeter*'s Casualties) are not included in the index.

1

Sailing under False Colors

It must be assumed that blockade runners will attempt to scuttle. Ensure that boarding party includes someone who will be able to recognize and know where to search for data concerning or evidence of navigation routes taken by runners. This information [is] highly important and will require quick action to obtain.

—Commander Task Group 23.1 report of the interception and destruction of the German blockade runner *Karin*.[1]

Photo 1-1

German blockade runner MV *Karin* aflame from fires, set by her crew before they abandoned ship, after being stopped in the South Atlantic by two units of the United States Fourth Fleet—the light cruiser USS *Savannah* (CL-42) and the destroyer *Eberle* (DD-430). A short time later, delayed-detonation scuttling charges exploded, killing all but three members of a boarding party from the *Eberle* attempting to salvage the vessel. The painting is by Richard DeRosset.

Adolf Hitler invaded Poland in September 1939, following which Britain and France declared war on Germany, and established a sea blockade of that country. Because the German Navy initially lacked the strength to challenge the combined British Royal Navy and French Navy for command of the sea, it adopted a strategy relying on commerce raiding using capital ships, armed merchant cruisers, submarines and aircraft. The German ships used to prey on merchant shipping became known as "raiders." These ships interdicted Allied commerce and denuded the British and French fleets of the many warships needed to try to locate and destroy them on the world's oceans.

As the sea blockade continued, Germany became increasingly desperate to obtain badly needed raw materials, such as rubber, tin, tungsten, molybdenum, hemp, animal hides and vegetable oils. These resources were possessed in abundance by Japan and her newly conquered territories. Conversely, Japan was deficit in certain metals, manufactured goods, and technical processes, which Germany and, to a much lesser degree, Italy enjoyed. To help meet their mutual needs, Germany, Italy, and Japan signed a Tripartite Pact on 27 September 1940, which required military and technical cooperation, including reciprocal exchanges of raw materials, equipment and personnel.[2]

This exchange program was dependent upon a sizable fleet of merchant ships which only Germany had available. Accordingly, she assumed the initiative in developing collaboration between the Axis powers—and in particular, between Japan and herself—via the use of blockade runners. Ships of German registry and German prizes of war, as well as a few Italian ships pressed into service under German control, made runs between Germany and the Far East. These ships were referred to as "runners" by Allied navies.

During the first two years of the war as the Royal, French, and German navies battled in the South Atlantic, German U-boats and commerce raiders tried to stop the flow of raw materials to Britain and the United States by attacking Allied merchant shipping. At the same time, Britain and France endeavored to destroy German raiders, runners and submarines. The U.S. Navy assisted in this effort on 6 November 1941, when the cruiser *Omaha* (CL-4) and destroyer *Somers* (DD-381) captured the blockade runner *Odenwald*.

Photo 1-2

Crewmembers of the cruiser *Omaha* (CL-4) pose with U.S. and German flags, on board the German blockade runner MV *Odenwald*. The runner was disguised as the American merchant ship SS *Willmoto* when she was captured by the cruiser *Omaha* and the destroyer *Somers* (DD-381) on 6 November 1941.
U.S. Navy Photograph #80-G-464023, now in the collection of the National Archives

On the German side, blockade runners strove, for the most part unsuccessfully, to dodge the ubiquitous presence of United States and Royal Navy ships in the South Atlantic, and elsewhere in the world. As a part of the desperate cat and mouse contest, runners in port tried to avoid prematurely disclosing their movements to Allied spies ashore by leaving port only under the cloak of darkness during the period of a new moon. Once clear of their berth, another German ship would often shift into it, so that when morning dawned, it would appear to observers that the runner was still present. Runners needed to be both clever and resourceful, because one caught by a warship out at sea was unlikely to survive. Napoléon Bonaparte once stated that he could make men die for the multicolored bits of ribbon he pinned on their chest. Along these same lines, Germany began awarding Blockade Runner badges on 1 April 1941 to the crewmembers of ships that attempted or successfully managed to break the Allied sea blockade.[4]

SEARCH FOR GERMAN RUNNERS AND RAIDERS

On 10 March 1943, Cruiser Division Two, under Rear Adm. Oliver Middleton Read Jr., USN, was at sea in the South Atlantic with orders to patrol in the area bounded by the Equator and fifteen degrees south Latitude, between eighteen and twenty-four degrees west Longitude. Read's primary mission was to search for and capture or destroy enemy raiders and blockade runners. Task Group 23.1 was comprised of a cruiser, two destroyers, and an auxiliary aircraft carrier.

Task Group 23.1 (Cruiser Division Two)		
Ship	Commissioned	Commanding Officer
Savannah (CL-42)	10 Mar 1938	Capt. Robert W. Cary, USN
Santee (ACV-29)	30 Oct 1940	Capt. William D. Sample, USN
Eberle (DD-430)	4 Dec 1940	Comdr. Karl F. Poehlmann, USN
Livermore (DD-429)	7 Oct 1940	Lt. Comdr. H. E. Seidel Jr., USN[5]

As the formation proceeded east on course 087°T, aircraft launched from the carrier conducted search operations for a distance of 180 miles on either side of, and 200 miles along, the base course. In mid-afternoon, *Santee* reported at 1545 that a plane had sighted a solitary ship to the northeast of the "Peter and Paul Rocks" (St. Peter and St. Paul Archipelago) on a north-northwest course at 12 knots. The unidentified vessel was flying Dutch colors aft and another Dutch flag was laid out on deck.[6]

The flagship *Savannah* with Admiral Read, accompanied by *Eberle*, left the formation ten minutes later, turned north and proceeded at 27 knots to intercept the vessel, seventeen miles distant. The warships altered course at 1605 to 027° true. Nine minutes later, a ship "hull-down" came into view broad on their starboard bow at a distance of fifteen miles. The term hull-down means that the upper portion of a ship (its masts) is visible on the horizon, but its lower body (hull) is not.[7]

Photo 1-3

Light cruiser *Savannah* (CL-42) making a full power run off Rockland, Maine, in February 1938.
U.S. Naval History and Heritage Command Photograph #NH 82110

Photo 1-4

Destroyer *Eberle* (DD-430) underway at sea, circa 1940-1941.
U.S. Naval History and Heritage Command Photograph #NH 73451

At 1617, Read ordered the *Eberle* to "Fly WBA, close ship close aboard at high speed, fire across bow and stern. Board quickly, this may be a runner." (The meaning of the International Code flag hoist signal WBA was, "DO NOT LOWER BOATS.   DO NOT SCUTTLE. DO NOT USE RADIO. IF YOU DISOBEY, I SHALL OPEN FIRE.") With the crews of the *Savannah* and *Eberle* at battle stations, and two *Savannah* planes in the air for scouting, the ships came right to course 030°T and increased speed to 31 knots. Several minutes later, it was possible with binoculars to clearly see the ship's masts, painted in a spiral camouflage pattern, suggesting the vessel was likely a blockade runner.[8]

Read directed *Eberle*, "Never mind Dutch flag, pile in there. This is a runner." *Savannah*, in turn, having reached a point about 6,500 yards from the ship, began maneuvering on various courses to circle and inspect her from a distance.[9]

PEDIGREE OF THE BLOCKADE RUNNER

The as yet unidentified runner was the former Dutch motor vessel *Kota Nopan*, a 7,323-ton passenger/cargo ship built for Rotterdamsche Lloyd of the Netherlands in 1931. Ten years later, on Sunday, 17 August 1941, she had been en route from New Zealand to Panama, in the vicinity of the Galapagos Islands, when the First Officer on watch sighted an unidentified ship. The *Kota Nopan* was at prayer, and the officer did not want to interrupt the service to inform the captain. The German auxiliary cruiser (raider) *Komet* drew near and fired a warning shot. As *Kota Nopan* started to transmit an SOS message, the raider (commanded by Konteradmiral Robert Eyssen) opened fire. These shots were intended to cause intimidation but not damage the ship. They served their purpose; clearly outgunned, *Kota Nopan* surrendered to *Komet* after only firing two rounds herself.[10]

Photo 1-5

German auxiliary cruiser *Komet*, one of nine converted freighters which, heavily armed with hidden guns and torpedoes, prowled ocean waters and preyed on Allied shipping. Raider Supplement to the Weekly Intelligence Report No. 64, of 30 May 1941, issued by the Naval Intelligence Division, Navy Staff, Admiralty

The *Kota Nopan* then made passage to Bordeaux, France, with her Dutch crew under German officers. Following a decision to put her in service as a blockade runner, her new master Werner Gippe reported aboard in early 1942. By April, a majority of her new crew had arrived. Renamed *Karin*, she proceeded in early May to St. Nazaire for a thorough refit, including the overhaul of her engines, enlargement of her galley, renewal of her cook ranges, and installation of new reefers (refrigeration machinery).[11]

In consideration of her new role as a runner—and if necessary, support ship for U-boats and raiders—shipyard workers built quarters for possible prisoners on the first "tween deck aft," and fitted her with one 105mm gun and four 20mm guns. The large gun was mounted aft, and below it, two smaller guns protected by splinter shields. The remaining two 20mm guns were mounted forward, one on either side of the bridge. The ship was painted grey, with white spiral stripes on her masts the only camouflage scheme. Four drums of acid were carried aft to enable *Karin* to create a smoke screen. The most ominous additions to the ship were three 50-kilogram and one 25-kilogram explosive charges fitted in the most convenient places in the engine room; one being in the shaft alley. The charges utilized a fuze, with a delayed action of seven-to-nine minutes, activated by manual lanyards. As a safety measure, two separate lanyards had to be pulled to activate each demolition charge.[12]

Before *Karin* left Bordeaux to attempt to run the blockade off Germany, Konteradmiral Heinz-Eduard Menche, chief of the German Navy Service Office, Bordeaux, came aboard to address the composite crew of merchant seamen and naval personnel. He spoke about the importance of the ship's mission—which singularly failed to impress the seamen—and stressed the necessity for keeping silent under interrogation if captured.[13]

Karin successfully reached the Far East on her first outbound voyage as a blockade runner, and spent a week alongside Swettenham Pier at Penang, loading 2,000 tons of tin and 2,000 tons of rubber. The island, located at the northern entry to the Straits of Malacca off the Malay Peninsula, was under Japanese occupation and would soon serve as a German Far-Eastern U-boat base. *Karin* was equipped to refuel U-boats in an emergency and to accommodate prisoners transferred to her by raiders—but would have no occasion to exercise these capabilities.[14]

In early morning on 4 February, the *Karin*, heavily laden (attesting to the critical importance of her cargo to Germany), put to sea. After passing through the Straits of Malacca, she crossed the Indian Ocean and rounded the Cape of Good Hope. From there, *Karin* proceeded westward until roughly in the center of the South Atlantic and then turned northward. On 10 March, she was sailing under the Dutch flag with the signal flags for letters PFLX (those of the Dutch ship *Kota Tjandi*) hoisted aloft. As the *Santee* plane approached and challenged *Karin* by flashing signals, crewmen manned the ship's guns, but waved as the aircraft circled, to indicate friendly character.[15]

Photo 1-6

The German blockade runner *Karin*, sailing under false colors, is caught by the cruiser *Savannah* (CL-42) and destroyer *Eberle* (DD-430) on 10 March 1943.
CTG 23.1 Report of Interception and Destruction of the German Blockade Runner "*Kota Nopan*" (ex-Dutch "*Kota Pinang*"). (The title of the report containing this photograph is incorrect; the *Kota Nopan* and the *Kota Pinang* were two different ships.)

POTENTIAL PRIZE SHIP SCUTTLED BY CREW

> *Blockade runner sank following explosion. Nine men of boarding party from* Eberle *lost in valiant attempt to obtain vital evidence. Further information to [be sent to task] group tomorrow.*

> —Message sent by Rear Adm. Oliver Middleton Read Jr., USN,
> to the four ships comprising his Task Group 23.1,
> on the evening of 10 March 1943.[16]

Closing on the unknown ship, *Eberle* and *Savannah* fired warning shots at 1633 and 1635, respectively, across the suspect blockade runner's bow as she had failed to stop for inspection. After the second shot, *Karin* backed her engines, coming to a stop, and almost immediately hoisted "FM," meaning: "I am sinking, send boat to pick up crew and passengers." Despite a warning by *Eberle* to not use her radio, she also transmitted a distress signal:

1708 RRR de KOTA TJANDI PFLX PSN 7.10 South 20.4 West
ordered to stop by warship unknown" on 500 kcs [khz].

Admiral Read, suspecting that *Karin*'s crew would try to scuttle the
ship to prevent its capture and any intelligence aboard, signaled the
Eberle: "Grab a lifeboat and personnel and board."[17]

As soon as *Savannah* was sighted, the crew of the German vessel
had made their way to "abandon ship" stations, and at 1638 began to
enter and lower boats. There were four at the rail, two on each side of
the vessel. The men carried suitcases, kept packed for such an
eventually. Meanwhile, the chief and second engineers activated the
scuttling charges and set fire to the engines. The master threw the
confidential papers overboard, while the radio officers attempted to
set fire to the radio shack with gasoline and incendiaries. Other sailors
set fire to the cabins on the upper deck. In an effort to keep *Karin*'s
crew on board and, by this action, hopefully prevent the activation of
demolitions, the pilot of *Savannah*'s plane, Lt. C. A. Anderson, directed
steady fire from his fixed machine gun at the water under the boats,
until the gun jammed. He then continued to circle the ship at a very
low altitude, and the gunner in the after cockpit was able to get a few
rounds off in the direction of the boats with his unmounted gun.[18]

Photo 1-7

Curtiss SOC-3 scout observation floatplane similar to those carried aboard the
Savannah (CL-42). Note the .30-cal. machine gun in the after cockpit.
U.S. Naval History and Heritage Command Photograph #NH 80523

At the same time, smoke began to issue from canvas-covered engine room spaces, located just aft of the stack, and a wisp from the poop-deck at the stern. Aboard the cruiser, Read ordered *Eberle* to, "Get in there at high speed, close aboard." At 1643, *Karin*'s four lifeboats (carrying most of her crew) cast off, rapidly cleared the vessel, and proceeded initially in the direction of her stern.[19]

Eberle's motor whaleboat made *Karin*'s side at 1649, as heavy flames enveloped her amidships structure. The boat coxswain came alongside in this area, so that the boarding party could utilize a Jacob's ladder hanging over the side at that location to board the ship. As the men reached the main deck, the last of the Germans dove over the stern, and were recovered by the ship's lifeboats. At 1651, the boarding officer, Lt. (jg) Frederick Edwards—having made a hurried inspection of the bridge, where he found nothing of interest except for a chart of the Black Sea, and having thrown overboard several incendiaries—requested more men to fight the fire. Comdr. Karl Poehlmann, *Eberle*'s commanding officer, upon receiving this request, decided it prudent to get the boarding party off the ship instead. He requested permission from the flagship to recall the men, which was immediately granted.[20]

The boarding and salvage party began leaving *Karin* at 1654. Two minutes later, there were two heavy explosions amidships and one aft on the vessel. The explosions, originating deep within the ship, blew out the port side of the vessel just aft of the bridge structure, and resultant smoke billowed about two hundred feet into the air from the bridge structure and after deckhouse. The force of the blast also destroyed *Eberle*'s boat, killing nine men in the boat, or on the ladder preparing to board it. *Karin* sank stern first, one minute later at 1657.[21]

Savannah had launched a whaleboat (with a boarding party aboard should it be needed) at 1653. The boat, which was nearby, found Seaman Second Louis J. Doll stretched out atop a floating wooden hatch. He was dazed and the bones in his left leg appeared to be broken. After crewmen carefully lifted Doll aboard over the gunnel, the boat made *Eberle*'s side and transferred the injured man to the ship. Leaving the destroyer's side, the boat continued to search amidst floating debris (which included large numbers of bales of rubber and empty 50-gallon oil drums) and found Lt. (jg) Edwards and Seaman First Alexander Bisheimer clinging to a wooden locker. After taking them to the destroyer as well, *Savannah*'s boat joined *Eberle*'s remaining boat and planes from the cruiser in combing the area for any other survivors. Admiral Read ordered the search abandoned at 1830, and directed that the flags of both ships be "half-masted" in reverence for

Eberle's dead and missing. After *Savannah* recovered her planes, the ships sank the German lifeboats with gunfire, and then left the area to rejoin *Santee* and *Livermore*.[22]

Savannah had recovered the entire crew of *Karin* (11 officers and 61 men; made up of 21 regular navy and 40 merchant marine) from the four boats a short time earlier. As the cruiser had approached the lifeboats, men in them were seen to throw navigational instruments and weapons over the side. The prisoners and most of their luggage were taken from the boats, but an assortment of fine food, drink, and other articles was left behind. These items included Japanese rice beer, French champagne, canned salmon and sardines, oranges, bread still warm from the oven, and women's shoes with Hong Kong labels.[23]

Orders from higher authority directed the *Savannah* to hold the prisoners incommunicado, separate the officers from the men, keep them under strict surveillance, and under no circumstances question or solicit any information from them. The Germans behaved well and were landed in the United States on 28 March. The naval prisoners, with the exception of the doctor and two pharmacists, were taken to an Interrogation Center (likely Fort Hunt in Washington, DC) for questioning. The merchant seamen were interrogated on Ellis Island.[24]

AWARDS FOR VALOR; MOST POSTHUMOUSLY

Eleven of the twelve members of the boarding party received medals for valor, nine of them posthumously. The associated award citations may be found in Appendix A. (Louis Doll was recommended for the Silver Star and he likely received it. The author was, however, unable to verify this action.)

Name	Medal
Lt. (jg) Frederick L. Edwards Jr., USNR	Navy Cross
Seaman First Alexander Joseph Bisheimer, USN	Navy Cross
Signalman Third William Joseph Pattison, USN	Navy Cross (posthumously)
Fireman First Dennis Joseph Buckley Jr., USN	Silver Star (posthumously)
Seaman Second Wilbur Gaylord Davis, USN	Silver Star (posthumously)
Watertender Second Alex M. Diachenko, USN	Silver Star (posthumously)
Fireman First William J. Jones, USN	Silver Star (posthumously)
Coxswain Joseph E. H. Metivier, USN	Silver Star (posthumously)
Carpenter's Mate First Robert Merrill Shockley, USN	Silver Star (posthumously)
Motor Machinist's Mate First Merton B. Myers, USN	Silver Star (posthumously)
Seaman Second Carl Welby Tinsman, USN	Silver Star (posthumously)
Seaman Second Louis J. Doll, USN[25]	

2

Commencement of the
Battle of the Atlantic

The Fuhrer's call has gone out to us. In this hour of crisis we are ready to answer for the honor, rights and freedom of the Fatherland. Mindful of our glorious traditions, we shall fight this war with unswerving faith in our Fuhrer, and a firm belief in the greatness of our people and our Reich. Long live the Fuhrer.

—Commander-in-chief German Navy, Adm. Erich Raeder's, Order of the Day to the Navy, on 1 September 1939.[1]

The Battle of the Atlantic was the longest military campaign of World War II. It began immediately upon England and France's declaration of war against Germany on 3 September 1939, following Adolf Hitler's invasion of Poland, and ended with the surrender of Germany to the Allies on 7 May 1945. During the six long intervening years, thousands of ships were sunk and tens of thousands of Navy sailors, Merchant Mariners, other servicemen and civilians in passage aboard them were killed in the Atlantic Ocean. The battle pitted Allied merchant ship convoys and their naval escorts—and single vessels or convoys sailing without escort—against German submarines, aircraft, and surface raiders. British Prime Minister Winston Churchill later said of the Battle of the Atlantic, "Everything elsewhere on land, sea and air, depended ultimately on the outcome of this battle." The Allies required use of the Atlantic sea routes in order to blockade Axis countries in Europe, to enable its own sea movements, and to project military power across the seas. The Axis powers, in turn, wanted to preclude Allied use of the Atlantic to wage war. A portion of the Battle of the Atlantic took place in the narrows of the South Atlantic between South America and Africa, to which this book is devoted.[2]

THE ROYAL NAVY'S SOUTH ATLANTIC STATION

Following the advent of war, as a part of the blockade of Germany, British and French warships began patrolling South Atlantic waters searching for German merchant ships, which, under threat of capture or destruction, were anxiously trying to reach home or neutral ports. The Royal Navy's South Atlantic Station was responsible for naval operations in South Atlantic waters. The former Africa Command (with the 6th Cruiser Squadron as its main component) was retitled South Atlantic Station in September 1939. As part of this change, the headquarters of its commander, Vice Adm. George H. D'Oyly Lyon, RN, was moved from Simon's Town, South Africa, to Freetown, the capital of the British West-African colony of Sierra Leone on the west coast of Africa. Later in the war, upon the establishment of the West Africa Command in August 1942, the South Atlantic Station was transferred back to Simon's Town.[3]

Photo 2-1

View of the entrance of the Sierra-Leone River on the west coast of Africa, on the voyage of John Matthews to this continent in 1785. Engraving by Y. Le Gouar. Freetown is sited at the mouth of the river.
U.S. Naval History and Heritage Command Photograph #NH 1480

Freetown would serve as a convoy station during the war, with up to two hundred cargo and military vessels moving in and out of its well-protected harbor at the height of activities. The South Atlantic Station had been created from the previous Africa Station. Its area of responsibility was quite large: South Atlantic waters south of a line drawn between the northern French West African border and French

Guiana in South America, and the South Atlantic and Indian Ocean east of a line drawn south from the western entrance to the Magellan Strait and west of a line drawn south from the South African/Mozambican border.[4]

Map 2-1

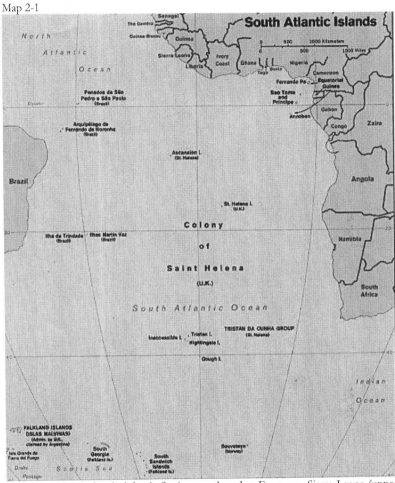

The Royal Navy's South Atlantic Station was based at Freetown, Sierra Leone (upper center), and the South American Cruiser Division to the southwest at Port Stanley, Falkland Islands (lower left).
www.lib.utexas.edu/maps/islands_oceans_poles/southatlanticislands.jpg

In addition to its headquarters at Freetown, the South Atlantic Station had bases at Simon's Town, near Cape Town, South Africa, and at Port Stanley in the Falkland Islands, three hundred miles east of the southern end of South America.   When war broke out in

September 1939, the Royal Navy had sixty-six cruisers. Many of these ships dating back to World War I, were best suited for escort duties, and were at distant stations maintained by the Royal Navy. At Freetown, four old light cruisers and a newer one, four destroyers, two submarines, three sloops, and two minesweeping trawlers constituted the South Atlantic Station.[5]

Five Royal Navy vice admirals served as commander-in-chief of the South Atlantic Station during the war. These individuals were: George H. D'Oyly Lyon (1939-1940), Sir Robert Raikes, (1940-1941), Sir Algernon Willis (1941-1942), Sir Campbell Tait (1942-1944), and Sir Robert Burnett (1944-1946).

South Atlantic Station
Vice Adm. George H. D'Oyly Lyon, RN
(Freetown, Sierra Leone)

Ship or Submarine	Date Commissioned	Commander or Commanding Officer
6th Cruiser Squadron		Vice Adm. George H. D. Lyon, RN
light cruiser *Neptune* (20)	23 Feb 1934	Capt. John A. V. Morse, RN
9th Cruiser Squadron		Capt. Allan Poland, RN
light cruiser *Despatch* (30)	2 Jun 1922	Capt. Allan Poland, RN
light cruiser *Dauntless* (45)	26 Nov 1918	Capt. George Dunbar Moore, RAN
light cruiser *Danae* (44)	18 Jun 1918	Capt. Alfred Creighton Collinson, RN
light cruiser *Durban* (99)	1 Nov 1921	Capt. Alexander Maxwell-Hyslop, RN
Destroyer Division 4		
destroyer *Havock* (43)	8 Jan 1937	Comdr. Rafe Edward Courage, RN
destroyer *Hotspur* (01)	29 Dec 1936	Comdr. Herbert F. H. Layman, RN
destroyer *Hyperion* (97)	3 Dec 1936	Comdr. Hugh St. L. Nicolson, RN
destroyer *Hunter* (35)	20 Sep 1936	Lt. Comdr. Lindsay De Villiers, RN
7th Submarine Flotilla		
submarine *Clyde* (12)	12 Apr 1935	Comdr. William Eric Banks, RN
submarine *Severn* (57)	12 Jan 1935	Lt. Comdr. Bertram W. Taylor, RN
Other Ships		
sloop *Bridgewater* (01)	14 Mar 1929	Comdr. Roy Carlton Harry, RN
sloop *Milford* (51)	22 Dec 1932	Capt. Robert L. B. Cunliffe, RN
sloop *Londonderry* (76)	20 Sep 1935	Comdr. Sir Thomas L. Beevor, RN
MS trawler *Maple* (38)	Feb 1939	J. T. Watson, RNR (as of 18 Sep 39)
MS trawler *Redwood* (86)	Mar 1939	Ch.Skr. James Hay, RNR (14 Mar 40)

A very small South Atlantic cruiser squadron, under Capt. Henry H. Harwood, was based at Port Stanley. Its members—heavy cruisers HMS *Cumberland* (57) and HMS *Exeter* (68), and light cruiser HMS *Ajax* (22)—operated along the South American coast; provisioning as necessary at friendly ports.

**South American Cruiser Division
Capt. Henry H. Harwood, RN
(Port Stanley, Falklands)**

Ship or Submarine	Date Com-missioned	Commander or Commanding Officer
heavy cruiser *Exeter* (68)	23 Jul 1931	Capt. Frederick Secker Bell, RN
light cruiser *Ajax* (22)	12 Apr 1935	Capt. Charles H. L. Woodhouse, RN
heavy cruiser *Cumberland* (57)	23 Feb 1928	Capt. Walter H. G. Fallowfield, RN[6]

BRITISH WARSHIPS SWEEP GERMAN MERCHANT VESSELS FROM THE SEAS

With the sinking of the German liner Columbus *(32,565 gross tons)—one of the most beautiful ships in the world—by its own crew, the number of German ships scuttled has risen to 23. The total tonnage amounts to 139,423. In addition, 19 ships with a total tonnage of 88,128 have been captured by the Allies.*

—The Scuttling of German Ships, report by the *Havas* Agency, 20 December 1939, London.[7]

Photo 2-2

Engraving by Bennett of Rio de Janeiro, Brazil; published in the Naval Chronicle, vol. 19, by J. Gold in London, 1808.
U.S. Naval History and Heritage Command Photograph #NH 67096

On 3 September 1939, the British Admiralty broadcast the signal: "11 AM COMMENCE HOSTILITIES AT ONCE AGAINST GERMANY" in plain language to all home commands and ships. Three hours later, the light cruiser HMS *Ajax* became the first warship to intercept and sink a German merchant ship in World War II. She had been at Rio de Janeiro, when Capt. Charles H. L. Woodhouse, RN, decided that if events in Europe reached a climax and war broke out, his ship should already be at sea. *Ajax* had stood out of port, and was ideally situated when conflict began.

Upon receiving the Admiralty signal, Woodhouse had set the cruiser on a course for the River Plate area, a funnel-shaped indentation on the southeastern coastline of South America. The River Plate formed part of the border between Argentina and Uruguay with the major port and capital cities of Buenos Aires and Montevideo sited on its western and northern shores, respectively. As such, it was a busy area for ships, including those of Allied countries now vulnerable to attack by German ships and submarines, and Axis warships and merchant vessels being hunted by the Royal Navy.[9]

Map 2-2

Port Stanley, the home base of the Royal Navy's South America cruiser division, lay about 300 miles east of the southeast tip of South America in the Falklands. The River Plate is to the north between the borders of Argentina and Uruguay.
Source: http://www.lib.utexas.edu/maps/americas/south_america_pol98.jpg

HMS *Ajax* struck the first blow when she intercepted the German merchant ship *Olinda* in late morning that same day, 3 September, bound for Germany with a valuable cargo of grain and hides. The vessel was fifty miles north of Montevideo and within sight of the Uruguayan coastline. Her crew was taken off, and since it was not practical to make a prize of her, she was sunk by naval gunfire at position 33°50'S, 53°30'W. *Ajax* transferred the forty-two prisoners of war to the British tanker *San Gerardo*, which turned them over to Uruguayan authorities at Montevideo on 5 September. The men were later released in custody of the German consul.[10]

As England and France's declaration of war brought naval action within sight of South American shores, the continent's Atlantic republics of Uruguay, Brazil and Argentina formally announced their neutrality on 4 September. Chile on the Pacific coast also declared her neutrality. German ships at sea in South Atlantic waters, including the valuable ocean liner *Cap Norte*, immediately raced for the shelter of neutral Brazilian, Uruguayan and Argentine ports, seeking to evade HMS *Ajax* and the heavy cruiser HMS *Exeter*. In addition to the *Cap Norte*, these ships included the liner *General Artigas*, operating in the same vicinity as the *Olinda*, and the *Schawaden Afrika*, *Antonia Delfino* and *Madrid*, reportedly along the coast between Montevideo, Uruguay, and Pernambuco, Brazil.[11]

Photo 2-3

Light cruiser HMS *Ajax* at Coco Solo, Canal Zone, in 1939, prior to the outbreak of World War II, while serving with the 8th Cruiser Squadron. U.S. Navy History and Heritage Command Photograph #NH 50344

Ajax found another German merchantman, the *Carl Fritzen*, off Uruguay the following day. Before the ship could be boarded, she was scuttled by her crew and sank. On the 5th, *Ajax* and the heavy cruiser HMS *Cumberland* intercepted the German passenger ship *Ussukuma* off Bahia Blanca, Argentina. She too was scuttled by her crew.[12]

Photo 3-1

German pocket battleship *Admiral Graf Spee* during the opening phases of the Battle of the River Plate. The two water spouts off her starboard bow (left of the painting) are from 6-inch gunfire from the light cruisers HMS *Ajax* and HMNZS *Achilles*. Painting by Richard DeRosset

3

Battle of the River Plate

When you came up the river this morning, when you entered the harbour and saw the crowds cheering on the banks, one may almost think that there were other spectators in the great shades of the past, carrying us back to the days of Drake and Raleigh, to the great sea dogs of the olden times. If their spirits brooded on this scene you would be able to say to them, "We, your descendants, still make war and have not forgotten the lessons you taught."

—Winston Churchill address to the crew of the light cruiser HMS *Exeter*, upon her arrival at Plymouth, England, on 15 February 1940. During comments made, he proclaimed that the Battle of the River Plate "will long be told in song and story."

The first major naval battle of World War II, the Battle of the River Plate, took place on 13 December 1939 when three cruisers of the Royal Navy's South American Division encountered the much heavier-armed German pocket battleship *Admiral Graf Spee*. Commanded by Capt. Hans Langsdorff, *Graf Spee* had been functioning as a commerce raider since 26 September, when Adolf Hitler authorized the Kriegsmarine (German Navy) to commence attacks against Allied merchant ships. During a nine-week period between 30 September and 7 December 1939, she had sunk nine British merchant ships. The British and French had responded to the commerce raiding by German warships with a massive deployment of naval forces. During October, seven hunting groups were active in the Atlantic, most in areas well to the north of *Graf Spee*. (In this account, the *Admiral Graf Spee* is referred to, in different usages, as *Graf Spee*, pocket battleship, and raider.) [1]

ENEMY COMMERCE RAIDER *ADMIRAL GRAF SPEE*

The *Admiral Graf Spee* had put to sea from Wilhelmshaven, Germany, on 21 August 1939, bound for the South Atlantic. By the time the war started, she had crossed the North Atlantic trade route unnoticed and reached the South Atlantic. Major German warships were fitted with radar code named "Seetakt" (sea-beat) that supplied the ships' guns with target data. Use of the radar also helped German raiders to avoid the Royal Navy, and to find/rendezvous with their supply ships.[2]

Photo 3-2

Pocket battleship *Admiral Graf Spee* in European waters in mid-1939, prior to her departure for the South Atlantic.
U. S. Naval History and Heritage Command Photograph #NH 80897

On 1 September, *Graf Spee* refueled from the 13,580-ton German tanker/supply ship *Altmark* southwest of the Canary Islands, just off the southern coast of Morocco. The tanker, under the command of Capt. Heinrich Dau, had obtained its fuel at Port Arthur, Texas, in August. On the 11th, eight days into the Battle of the Atlantic, *Graf Spee* obtained provisions from *Altmark*. Following receipt of orders on 26 September to commence raiding operations, Langsdorff set a course for the Brazilian coast. The order was apparently prompted by a communique the British Admiralty had issued that day, reporting that shortly all British merchant ships would be armed. This declaration, even though it related largely to obsolete guns dating from World War I, was quickly seized upon by Hitler as a justification to attack all armed vessels without warning.[3]

The pocket battleship, disguised as the German heavy cruiser *Admiral Scheer*, found the British merchant ship *Clement*, under the command of Captain F. C. P. Harris on 30 September, fifty miles southeast of Pernambuco, Brazil. The passengers and crew were taken off, and the abandoned freighter sunk by gunfire. The master, chief engineer, and an injured seaman were taken prisoner, and the remainder of the crew was left to make their way in lifeboats, after being given the course to the Brazilian port of Maceió. They all reached Maceió safely on 1 October. The *Graf Spee* later stopped the neutral Greek merchant *Papalemos*. Her master promised not to transmit a message reporting the German ship's presence in the area until reaching the Cape Verde Islands, a Portuguese colony off the northwest coast of Africa. Langsdorff, believing this pledge (which was not kept), let the ship proceed after transferring the three British mariners to her.[4]

Eight powerful British and French battle groups were formed on 1 October to hunt for the *Admiral Graf Spee* and other German commerce raiders. This action displeased Winston Churchill, due to the disparity between the enemy forces and the countermeasures to which he was forced to commit. Churchill was then First Lord of the Admiralty. After being selected for this position on 4 September, he had declared, "The first hours of a war can be a vital consequence for a navy. I therefore informed the Admiralty that I would immediately take up my duties and be in my office at 6 A.M."[5]

Graf Spee captured the cargo ship *Newton Beech* (Capt. Jack Robison) on 5 October, 480 miles east-southeast of Ascension Island, and two days later, the cargo ship *Ashlea* (Capt. Charles Pottinger) between Cape Town and Freetown. The *Ashlea* was sunk after her crew was put aboard *Newton Beech*, and the latter ship sent to the bottom on 8 October, off the coast of Angola, after the combined crews were transferred to the pocket battleship.[6]

Two days later, *Graf Spee*, flying the French tricolor at her masthead, captured the British steamship *Huntsman* on 10 October. The merchantman had been on passage to Liverpool from India and East Africa. Her master, Capt. Albert H. Brown was convinced that *Graf Spee* was the French battleship *Dunkerque* until her flag was replaced. Found aboard *Huntsman* were documents which gave precise details of the routes taken by merchant shipping. The German prize crew that had located this intelligence remained aboard the British ship, and *Graf Spee* headed southwest to rendezvous with *Altmark*, from which she refueled on 14 October. All British seamen aboard the pocket battleship were transferred to *Altmark*. *Graf Spee* would later sink *Huntsman* on 5 December, after all desired supplies had been removed from her, about 650 miles southwest of the island of St. Helena in the South Atlantic.[7]

In the afternoon of 22 October, *Graf Spee* found the motor vessel *Trevanion* (Capt. J. H. Edwards) midway between St. Helena and the west coast of Africa, and sank her. Her crew was initially taken aboard the German warship, then transferred to *Altmark* on 28 October, which already had the crews of *Newton Beech*, *Ashlea* and *Huntsman* aboard her. (*Altmark* later sailed for Germany with 299 British merchant seamen. They were rescued on 16 February 1940 by a boarding party from the destroyer HMS *Cossack*, while the tanker was in Norwegian waters. This action, termed the "Altmark Incident," helped precipitate Germany's invasion of neutral Norway.)[8]

Graf Spee retained the officers of *Trevanion* as prisoners on board, along with those of the other three ships. These men were soon joined by the officers of *Africa Shell*, *Doric Star*, *Tairoa* and *Streonshalh*— which also had the misfortune of encountering the German raider. The officers of these eight ships remained aboard *Graf Spee*, until they were released at Montevideo, following the Battle of the River Plate. Edwards described the loss of his ship and his subsequent captivity:

> We were off the coast of South West Africa when we sighted a warship flying a large French Ensign. When the warship was two miles away, we were told to heave to, and the German Ensign was run up instead of the French. Our wireless operator transmitted our position, and the warship started to open fire.
>
> The order had been given to us, not to use our wireless, but I had given our operator orders to transmit our position. The warship started firing, and inflicted some damage on us, and our operator had just finished his message when a fragment of shell hit the apparatus. I dumped the ship's papers into the sea as the German party arrived, armed with revolvers and fixed bayonets.
>
> A party of twenty Germans then came aboard the *Trevanion*, and the whole of my crew was transferred to the *Graf Spee*. Six days later we were transferred from the *Graf Spee* to a Hambourg ship [*Altmark*], which was disguised as a Norwegian vessel. On board this vessel I found members of the crew of the *Newton Beech* and the *Ashlea*, both of which had been sunk earlier by the *Graf Spee*. This boat [ship], as well as taking over prisoners, was supplying the *Graf Spee* with provisions.
>
> Sometime later with the other officers of the British steamers, I was taken on board the *Graf Spee* again.[9]

During the ensuing battle between *Graf Spee* and the British cruisers, Capt. Edwards was a prisoner below decks, and therefore saw nothing of the action. After the pocket battleship anchored off Montevideo just after midnight on 14 December, an officer told them "Gentlemen, for you the war is over. We are now in Montevideo Harbour. Today you will be free." That afternoon, they were freed.[10]

Photo 3-3

Montevideo, Uruguay. President Franklin D. Roosevelt (not visible) and his staff are under a canopy during a visit on 3 December 1936. Roosevelt had just left the cruiser *Indianapolis* (CA-35), which was carrying him on an earlier "Good Neighbor" cruise to South America.
U.S. Naval History and Heritage Command Photograph #NH 68162

GRAF SPEE SINKS FOUR MORE MERCHANT SHIPS

After sending *Trevanion* to the bottom, *Graf Spee* had steered a course to the southwest away from the trade routes. On 28 October, she met *Altmark* near Tristan da Cunha; a remote group of islands in the South Atlantic approximately midway between the Cape of Good Hope and the east coast of South America. After fueling and transferring the crew of *Trevanion* to the tanker, *Graf Spee* set a course for the Indian Ocean.[11]

On 15 November, she sighted the tanker *Africa Shell* (Capt. Patrick G. G. Dove) off the northern approach to Delagoa Bay, an indentation on the southeastern African coast. After stopping the ship, the master was taken prisoner, the crew allowed to get away in boats, and the vessel sunk northeast of Lourenco Marques. Following her foray into the Indian Ocean, the pocket battleship returned to the South Atlantic. At month's end, Langsdorff changed the appearance of *Graf Spee* through the use of a false gun turret made of wood and sail canvas on the foc's'le to complement a second funnel (stack), similarly made of wood and sail canvas, already fitted. A new coat of dark green paint and this changed silhouette gave *Graf Spee* the appearance of the British battle cruiser HMS *Renown*.[12]

Graf Spee's next victim was the passenger ship *Doric Star* (Capt. William Stubbs). She was sunk on 2 December south of St. Helena, after her passengers and crew, and some provisions were taken off. Unfortunately for *Graf Spee*, her radio operator had transmitted a MAYDAY call giving the *Doric Star*'s exact position, which was picked up by the small freighter *Port Chalmers* near St. Helena. The British Admiralty, upon learning that *Graf Spee* had returned to South Atlantic waters, immediately advised Allied units in the area of this fact, including Commodore Henry H. Harwood at his Port Stanley base in the Falklands. Harwood commanded the Royal Navy's South American Division, comprised of the heavy cruisers *Exeter* and *Cumberland*, and light cruisers *Ajax* and *Achilles*.[13]

Early the next morning, *Graf Spee* sank the *Tairoa* (Capt. William B. Starr) off the coast of Southwest Africa. Langsdorff had hoped to capture the cargo ship for use as a tender. However, after warning gunfire damaged her rudder, he torpedoed *Tairoa* after taking off her crew. Her radio operator had been able to get off a MAYDAY, reporting that the ship had been attacked by the German heavy cruiser *Admiral Scheer*. Based on *Graf Spee*'s position (then believed to be the *Admiral Scheer*) and her estimated average speed, Harwood calculated the raider would likely reach the River Plate by dawn on 13 December. Once there she could prey on British merchant shipping.[14]

On 6 December, *Graf Spee* rendezvoused with *Altmark* for the last time, transferring most of the prisoners to her, and taking on fuel. The next day, *Graf Spee* stopped the cargo ship *Streonshalh* (Capt. J. J. Robinson) about a thousand miles east of São Francisco, a port city on the easternmost part of the bulge of Brazil. As a boat from the *Graf Spee* approached the ship, her captain threw two sacks overboard. The boat crew was able to retrieve one before it sank, which contained a detailed plan of Allied shipping routes from the River Plate to Great

Britain. Langsdorff took off the ship's crew, and sank her. After reading the documents, he set a course for the River Plate where he expected to find large numbers of merchant vessels.[15]

Ships Sunk by the *Admiral Graf Spee*

Date	Ship	Location and Disposition
30 Sep 39	SS *Clement*	Sunk 50 miles southeast of Pernambuco, Brazil
5 Oct 39	SS *Newton Beech*	Captured 480 miles east-southeast of Ascension Island in South Atlantic
7 Oct 39	SS *Ashlea*	Captured between Cape Town and Freetown. Sunk at position 09°52'S, 03°28'W. *Newton Beech* sunk the following day after all prisoners were taken aboard *Graf Spee*.
10 Oct 39	SS *Huntsman*	Captured while en route to Liverpool. Used as a supply ship by *Graf Spee*; sunk on 5 December about 650 miles southwest of St. Helena.
22 Oct 39	MV *Trevanion*	Sunk about midway between St. Helena and the west coast of Africa
15 Nov 39	MV *African Shell*	Sunk 160 miles northeast of Lourenco Marques
2 Dec 39	SS *Doric Star*	Sunk about 500 miles west of Damaraland, off Southwest Africa
3 Dec 39	SS *Tairoa*	Sunk off the coast of Southwest Africa
7 Dec 39	SS *Streonshalh*	Sunk 1,000 miles east of São Francisco, Brazil

EVE OF THE BATTLE

Earlier, following prolonged operations, *Graf Spee* had begun on 24 November to experience difficulties with her diesel propulsion engines, and Langsdorff had informed his officers that the ship would need to return to Germany for an overhaul. This degradation did not, however, alter Langsdorff's plans. With the end of the cruise drawing nearer, he wanted more success, and reasoned that even if an Allied cruiser inflicted damage on his ship off South America, he was about to return to Germany anyway.[16]

Unbeknownst to Langsdorff, at the same time the pocket battleship was heading to the River Plate, so too was the British Hunting Group G under Commodore Harwood. Harwood had decided to take three of his four cruisers—HMS *Exeter*, HMS *Ajax* and HMNZS *Achilles*—to the River Plate while his fourth cruiser, HMS *Cumberland*, underwent a refit at the Falklands. On the night of 12 December, *Graf Spee* arrived off the South American coast and took up position to begin searching at daylight for a four-ship convoy—escorted by an auxiliary cruiser—she expected to find.[17]

COMPARISON OF THE OPPOSING NAVAL FORCES

Harwood had correctly guessed Langsdorff's intentions, and on 13 December he closed in with the heavy cruiser *Exeter* and light cruisers *Ajax* and *Achilles*. None of these three ships could outgun *Graf Spee* or had sufficient armor to face the pocket battleship's 11-inch shells with impunity; all they had was speed and agility. *Graf Spee* boasted six 11-inch guns mounted in two three-gun turrets, with another eight 5.9-inch guns in single turrets, and side armor 2.4-3.1 inches thick. Her only shortcoming was her diesel engines, which gave her greater range (fuel economy), but less speed and reliability than steam propulsion.[18]

Exeter carried six 8-inch guns, and *Ajax* and *Achilles* eight 6-inch guns. All three ships were capable of over 30 knots. They would be outgunned, but not outmaneuvered. The Royal Navy had a tactic for engaging a pocket battleship in battle using two 8-inch cruisers. It involved attacking from different directions to confuse the enemy's gunfire. Harwood would try to employ "flank marking," which involved using the superior speed of his ships, split into two divisions, to shadow *Graf Spee* on each side/flank instead of in a stern chase. This way, they could remain in contact and possibly open fire on her with broadsides, whichever way she turned. Gaining a position which would allow the maximum number of guns to bear on the target was referred to as "Opening 'A' arcs"—with the 'A' as a vector symbol and the gun(s) at its apex."[19]

However, in the absence of reduced visibility, or land masking—geographic features behind which to hide—ships with shorter range guns usually lost, and were often sunk in battle. This was true because the ship with the biggest guns could open fire at maximum effective range and score debilitating hits before adversaries could close enough to employ their guns.

BATTLE JOINED

My policy with three cruisers in company versus one pocket battleship. Attack at once by day or night. By day act as two units, 1st Division (AJAX and ACHILLES) and EXETER diverged to permit flank marking. First Division will concentrate gunfire. By night ships will normally remain in company in open order...

My object in the signal ZMM [ships are to turn to course, starting with the rear ship] is to avoid torpedoes and take the enemy by surprise and cross his stern. Without further orders ships are to clear the line of fire by hauling astern of the new leading ship. The new leading ship is to lead the line without further orders so as to maintain decisive gun range.

—Signals sent by Commodore Henry H. Harwood, RN, to his force
of three cruisers at 1200 and 1813 on 12 December 1939;
the day preceding the Battle of the River Plate.[20]

As dawn broke on the morning of 13 December the British and German ships were approaching one another on converging courses. *Graf Spee* was to the north, sailing southeast, with the British cruisers to the south, proceeding northeast. At 0552, a lookout aboard the pocket battleship reported two masts, then three, on the port bow at a range of approximately seventeen miles. He was higher above the water than his counterparts aboard the cruisers—making his visual range to the horizon greater—so for some time, the British were unaware they were about to meet the German raider.[21]

Langsdorff believed that he had found the convoy for which he was searching, and proceeded toward the unidentified ships. As the range to the ships decreased, a positive identification of *Exeter* was made at 0600, but *Ajax* and *Achilles* were misidentified as destroyers. The order "Action Stations" was given aboard *Graf Spee* in preparation for battle, and Langsdorff increased speed, resulting in dark smoke issuing from the stacks—which was spotted by the light cruiser *Ajax*.[22]

Following the sighting of smoke trails to the north-northwest, Harwood, embarked in *Ajax*, ordered *Exeter* to close and investigate the source, which he expected to be a merchant vessel. This illusion was quickly shattered. At 0616, *Exeter* reported: "I think it is a pocket battleship." Two minutes later, *Graf Spee* opened fire from a range of eleven nautical miles with one 11-inch turret trained toward *Exeter* and the other at *Ajax*. The 1st Division (*Ajax* and *Achilles*) immediately altered course to the north-northwest to close the range. *Exeter* hauled out of the formation, and altered course to the west in order to attack the enemy from a widely different bearing. Harwood's plan was for his ships to close the enemy ship at high speed in order to bring the shorter-range guns of the light cruisers into action. *Graf Spee's* largest guns had a range of some 8,000 yards greater than those of the British ships. Thus, their best chance was to attack the pocket battleship from different directions to prevent her from concentrating her gunfire on one cruiser at a time. *Exeter* opened fire on *Graf Spee* at 0620, *Achilles* a minute later, and *Ajax* at 0623.[23]

Langsdorff had to quickly decide whether he should concentrate his two main turrets on a single target, or split his fire. At 0617, he opened fire on *Exeter* with all his 11-inch guns, straddling her at 0623 with his third salvo. One shell burst short amidships, killing the starboard torpedo tube's crew, damaging communications and riddling the searchlights and aircraft. Meanwhile, to the northeast, *Ajax* and *Achilles* had opened fire on *Graf Spee*. From this point until the action was broken off, *Achilles* maneuvered as necessary to clear her line of fire, remaining close to the flagship *Ajax* and conforming to her movements. *Exeter* acted independently, after initially changing course to the west.[24]

Photo 3-4

Watercolor by Edward Tufnell, RN (Retired), titled *Battle of the River Plate*, 13 December 1939. The painting depicts the cruisers HMS *Exeter* (foreground) and HMNZS *Achilles* (right center background) in action with the armored ship *Admiral Graf Spee* (right background).
U.S. Naval History and Heritage Command Photograph #NH 86397-KN

At 0624, *Exeter* received a direct hit on the front of "B" turret. The 11-inch round burst on impact, knocking the turret out of action. Shrapnel swept the bridge, killing or wounding all personnel there with the exception of the commanding officer and two others, and wrecked steering control from the helm. Her commanding officer, Capt. Frederick Bell, decided to fight his ship from the secondary conning position. However, owing to communications degradation, the ship could be controlled from that position only by messengers physically carrying orders to the after steering position. Lt. Comdr. C. J. Smith succeeded in getting word through to the conning position to turn the ship to port. By this action, her 8-inch guns would be "unmasked" (all of the ship's main armament able to fire simultaneously at the enemy). During this phase of the battle *Exeter* received two more 11-inch hits in the forward part of the ship, causing fires along the deck of the heavy cruiser.[25]

Ajax and *Achilles* concentrating their fire on *Graf Spee* seemed to be scoring hits, and were closing the range rapidly to the enemy. The pocket battleship shifted one 11-inch turret to the 1st Division and *Ajax* was straddled three times at about 0631. The two cruisers turned slightly away to throw off her fire, than turned back to port in order to close the range. *Graf Spee*'s secondary armament was firing alternately at *Ajax* and *Achilles*, but with no effect, though some salvos fell close. *Ajax* catapulted her aircraft, piloted by Lt. E. D. G. Lewin, at 0637; a very fine evolution because the ship's "X" and "Y" turrets were at that time firing on a forward bearing. Owing to a delay in establishing communication, the first air spotting report of the effect of the cruisers' fire was not received until 0654, but this method was then employed for the remainder of the battle.[26]

Though damaged, *Exeter* was still in action and in position to use her starboard torpedoes. She fired a salvo of three at 0632, but missed *Graf Spee*, which made a turn northwestward under the cover of smoke. *Exeter*, steering a westerly course, came right in an effort to engage with her port torpedo tubes. In response to this new threat, Langsdorff directed the fire of both his 11-inch turrets at the heavy cruiser.[27]

At 0639, an 11-inch round hit *Exeter*'s navigator's station, followed by another which knocked out "A" turret and a third which knocked out most of her electrical power. Only the rear "Y" turret was still firing, aimed manually by the gunnery officer, Lt. Comdr. Richard Jennings. Eventually all power was lost to "Y" turret, due to seawater entering a hole in the ship's hull, and Harwood ordered *Exeter* to withdraw from battle at 0730. The heavy cruiser was still seaworthy, but badly damaged. All of her guns were out of action, and she had suffered 61 men killed and 23 wounded. She could no longer fight and, at about 0740, steered southeast at slow speed. Following the arrival of *Cumberland* in the area, she would leave for the Falklands. While there, undergoing necessary repairs, two injured men who died en route were buried in Stanley Cemetery.[28]

A list of *Exeter*'s casualties, as well as those of *Ajax* and *Achilles* may be found in Appendix B.[29]

LIGHT CRUISERS CONTINUE THE FIGHT

Graf Spee had turned to the south at 0716, apparently to finish off *Exeter*. In response, Harwood had ordered the light cruisers to close with the pocket battleship, in order to protect the badly damaged heavy cruiser. As they approached *Graf Spee* on a westerly course, she turned northwest and opened fire on the light cruisers with both her primary and secondary armament. *Ajax* was straddled three times by 11-inch rounds at a range of 11,000 yards, but the fire from *Graf Spee*'s 5.9-inch guns appeared ragged, and landed between *Ajax* and *Achilles*. The two cruisers turned to starboard at 0720 to bring all their guns to bear on the pocket battleship, and their shooting appeared to be effective; flames were observed amidships aboard *Graf Spee*.[30]

Photo 3-5

Light cruiser HMNZS *Achilles* in 1944.
U.S. Naval History and Heritage Command Photograph #NH 79158

However, any damage vested on the German ship by the cruisers' 6-inch guns apparently did not appreciatively reduce her firepower. An 11-inch round hit *Ajax* at 0725; striking her after superstructure, and passing through various cabins and the "X" turret trunk (wrecking the turret machinery below the gun house), before exploding in the commodore's sleeping cabin. A fragment of the projectile struck "Y" barbette and jammed the turret. This single hit killed four and wounded six members of "X" turret's gun crew, and knocked both "X" and "Y" turrets out of action. One of *Graf Spee*'s last salvos brought down *Ajax*'s top mast, destroying all her aerials (radio antennas). Makeshift aerials were soon rigged.[31]

At 0732, *Graf Spee* turned to the west, away from her adversaries, and made much smoke and zigzagged to throw off the 1st Division's gunfire which, particularly from *Achilles*, appeared to be very accurate. *Ajax* was also making good use of her three available guns. However, *Graf Spee* was not done. After altering course to the southwest at 0736, she once again brought all her guns to bear on the cruisers.[32]

By 0738, the pocket battleship had closed to within 8,000 yards of the light cruisers. Harwood received a report about this time that *Ajax* had only twenty percent of her ammunition left, and three guns still in action. *Graf Spee*, on the other hand, was apparently undamaged—with all of her main armament still operable and shooting well. With his ships badly outclassed, Harwood decided to break off the action and renew the fight after dark. Directed to retire, *Ajax* and *Achilles* turned away to the east under the cover of smoke.[33]

Langsdorff now made his most crucial decision of the battle. *Graf Spee* had been hit several times, but had lost the use of only two of her secondary guns, and her only apparent serious damage was a six-foot hole in her bow, well above the waterline. Despite his ship still being in fighting form, Langsdorff decided to proceed west and seek safety in the Port of Montevideo—instead of turning back to finish off the badly mauled British cruisers. This decision may have been based on his understanding that *Graf Spee* needed repairs before she would be fit for the return voyage to Germany. Langsdorff had already forced *Exeter* out of the battle, and badly damaged one of the two remaining ships. It was unlikely the light cruisers could prevent him from leaving Montevideo following repairs, if he decided to fight his way out. Conversely, a lucky shot or torpedo hit now could result in critical damage to the pocket battleship.[34]

The battle thus developed into a long stern chase, as the cruisers followed *Graf Spee* at a safe distance, to make sure she was indeed heading into port. At 1010, *Achilles* came dangerously close to the German warship, and was nearly hit by an 11-inch salvo. The three ships exchanged fire a number of times thereafter, although the only effect was to create sufficient smoke to shield *Graf Spee* from view for some time. At 2317, when it became apparent the enemy was about to enter Montevideo, the two cruisers took up position off the River Plate, and began a watch over the estuary. Both ships were damaged and with casualties; seven men were dead or dying aboard *Ajax*, and four members of *Achilles'* crew had been killed. In accordance with the custom of the Royal Navy, the dead were buried at sea.[35]

British/New Zealand Casualties

Ship	Officers Killed	Officers Wounded	Ratings Killed	Ratings Wounded
HMS *Exeter*	5	3	56	20
HMS *Ajax*		1	7	14
HMNZS *Achilles*		2	4	7
Total casualties	5	6	67	41

Although *Graf Spee* had received some twenty hits, and suffered one officer and thirty-five crewmembers killed, her fighting ability was not seriously impaired. The German seamen who lost their lives were buried the following morning in a communal grave under a cross in the Cementerio del Norte.[36]

Photo 3-6

Admiral Graf Spee anchored off Montevideo, Uruguay, in mid-December 1939, following the Battle of the River Plate.
U.S. Naval History and Heritage Command Photograph #NH 59657

MONTEVIDEO, URUGUAY

The most important figures over the next few days would be Sir Henry McCall, the British Naval Attaché to Uruguay, Argentina and Brazil (the head of British Intelligence in the area), and Capt. Rex Miller, whose office overlooked the harbor at Montevideo. On 14 December, the two men rowed around *Graff Spee* to inspect the ship. The only damage visible was the hole in her bow and some minor damage to the superstructure. They assumed that she must have suffered some hidden damage to cause her to break off the battle—perhaps to her fire-control system—or that she was very short on ammunition. Believing this, they spent the remainder of that day attempting to make sure that *Graf Spee* could only remain in port for the 24 hour-period she was allowed under international law.[37]

The following day, McCall and Miller learned from Harwood that the German ship was intact, and now sought ways to keep her in port, in order to allow sufficient time for other Royal Navy ships en route to Montevideo to arrive there. Ironically, Langsdorff was attempting the exact same thing. He convinced the Uruguayan authorities to allow him to stay for another seventy-two hours and would have liked to remain longer to carry out the repairs he believed needed. Ultimately, Langsdorff received instructions from the government of Uruguay that *Graf Spee* must leave Montevideo by 1700 on 17 December.[38]

Harwood's fourth cruiser, *Cumberland*, had arrived from the Falklands on 14 December. She carried eight 8-inch guns, giving him a slightly more powerful squadron than he had had during the battle. *Cumberland*, *Ajax* and *Achilles* were the only warships that Harwood could expect to have by 17 December. The battlecruiser *Renown* and the aircraft carrier *Ark Royal* were en route to Montevideo, but still a thousand nautical miles distant, and couldn't arrive before 19 December. The cruisers *Dorsetshire*, *Neptune* and *Shropshire* were also en route, as was the 3rd Destroyer Division, but none could arrive in time should *Graf Spee* chose to fight her way out of port.[39]

It's unlikely that the pocket battleship would have prevailed in battle against the three cruisers, unless she was able to very quickly inflict sufficient damage on them to allow her to gain the open ocean. *Graf Spee* had used 57.5 percent of her 11-inch ammunition—most during the battle in which she had crippled *Exeter*—but both the light cruisers had survived. A second battle with an equally strong cruiser squadron on 17 December would likely have exhausted the remaining ammunition, and left her defenseless against any British ships still in action or that she might encounter. Should *Graf Spee* break out into the South Atlantic, she had nowhere to run with other units of the Royal Navy closing in.[40]

Langsdorff would certainly have considered this possibility, and he had other worries as well—which were actually unfounded. One of his officers had reported on 15 December that he believed he had sighted the *Renown*'s masts and superstructure through the ship's range finders. If *Renown* was present, *Ark Royal* was probably with her and possibly additional Royal Navy ships, as well. Ingeniously, the British had used the BBC to broadcast radio reports of strong naval forces off the Plate estuary. This deception caused Langsdorff to believe that he might be facing a battlecruiser, an aircraft carrier, three or four cruisers and a destroyer flotilla. He asked Berlin for advice, if he could not fight his way out, should the *Graf Spee* be scuttled or interned? He was advised the best option was for him to fight, but if he had no other choice to scuttle the ship rather than risk internment.[41]

Rather than risk *Graf Spee* falling into British hands after she lost in battle with a powerful fleet he believed was nearby, Langsdorff decided to destroy his ship. Delay demolition charges were set and after her skeleton crew had abandoned, she was blown up and scuttled. As thousands of people on shore looked on, *Admiral Graf Spee* weighed anchor—with only Langsdorff, three officers and thirty-eight men remaining on board to take her out—and left port at 1820 on 17 December. Following astern was the German cargo/passenger vessel *Tacoma*, aboard which were some 800 members of her crew, and six dinghies. *Graf Spee* hove-to about four miles offshore, and two Argentine tugs with a lighter, and the dinghies approached the ship. A few minutes later, these vessels drew back and at 1956, smoke began emitting from the pocket battleship. An enormous explosion followed, shaking Montevideo and bathing the area in orange-yellow light. The ship then settled to the bottom in the shallows of the River Plate, with only her superstructure and masts protruding above the water's surface.[42]

Photo 3-7

Wreckage of the *Admiral Graf Spee* in the River Plate, near Montevideo, Uruguay, where she was scuttled on 17 December 1939.
U.S. Naval History and Heritage Command Photograph #NH 51977-A

Tacoma, with *Graf Spee*'s crew aboard, remained off Montevideo rather than proceed into the South Atlantic due to British naval forces offshore. On 1 January 1940, the Uruguayan Government interned the *Tacoma* based on the grounds that she had acted under the orders of the commanding officer of the *Graft Spee*, and was thus considered to be a German naval auxiliary. As such, she had been in a neutral port for a period in excess of that allowed.[43]

The officers and crew of the *Graf Spee* were interned in Argentina. On the morning of 20 December, Capt. Hans Langsdorff was found dead in his hotel room in Buenos Aires. He had committed suicide after communicating in a letter to Hitler:

> I can now only prove by my death that the fighting services of the Third Reich are ready to die for the honour of the flag. I alone bear the responsibility for scuttling the pocket-battleship *Admiral Graf Spee*. I am happy to pay with my life for any possible reflection on the honour of the flag. I shall face my fate with firm faith in the cause and the future of the nation and of my Fuehrer.

Having formally expressing his profound regrets for the loss of his ship, he had in full uniform, lay on *Admiral Graf Spee*'s battle ensign and shot himself in the head.[44]

Photo 3-8

Funeral procession of Capt. Hans Langsdorff at Buenos Aires, Argentina, on 21 December 1939.
U.S. Naval History and Heritage Command Photograph #NH 85636

The destruction of *Graf Spee* was the first real Allied naval success of the war, and was treated as a great triumph in Britain. Hitler was predictably furious with Langsdorff's decision to destroy his own ship. Thereafter, the head of the German Navy, Adm. Erich Raeder, issued orders, which stated "The German warship and her crew are to fight with all their strength to the last shell; until they win or go down with their flag flying."[45]

BATTLE HONOURS

Commodore Henry H. Harwood was promoted to Rear Admiral and knighted. All three cruisers received BATTLE HONOURS RIVER PLATE 1939. *Exeter* would later add MALAYA 1942 and SUNDA STRAIT 1942; and *Achilles* GUADALCANAL 1942-43 and OKINAWA 1945. *Ajax* would see the most combat action during the war; garnering eight addition battle honours: MEDITERRANEAN 1940-41, MATAPAN 1941, GREECE 1941, CRETE 1941, MALTA CONVOYS 1941, AEGEAN 1944, NORMANDY 1944, and SOUTH FRANCE 1944.

Shortly after the Battle of the River Plate, the Royal Navy's South American Division was absorbed into the South Atlantic Station.[46]

4

Neutrality Patrol and the
Two-Ocean Ship Act

This nation will remain a neutral nation, but I cannot ask that every American remain neutral in thought as well. Even a neutral has a right to take account of facts. Even a neutral cannot be asked to close his mind or his conscience.

We have certain ideas and certain ideals of national safety, and we must act to preserve that safety today, and to preserve the safety of our children in future years. That safety is and will be bound up with the safety of the Western Hemisphere and of the seas adjacent thereto. We seek to keep war from our own firesides by keeping war from coming to the Americas.

I have said not once, but many times, that I have seen war and that I hate war. I say that again and again.

—Extracts from a radio broadcast (fireside chat) made by President
Franklin D. Roosevelt on 3 September 1939, warning the nation
of the implications which confronted the United States.[1]

At the outbreak of war in Europe, 3 September 1939, the predominant strength of the U.S. Navy was in the Pacific, as had been the case for over ten years, but a partial shift of forces eastward had begun with the formation of the Atlantic Squadron in January 1939. The first impact of the European War on the U.S. Navy came with an order by President Franklin D. Roosevelt on 5 September 1939 to organize a Neutrality patrol. The object of this patrol was to report and track any belligerent air, surface or undersea naval forces approaching the coasts of the United States or the West Indies. Reliable information indicated that German submarines were set to operate along Atlantic trade routes and that a dozen German merchant vessels would operate as armed raiders. (These merchantmen were in addition to the German warships, such as *Admiral Graf Spee*, functioning as raiders.)[2]

Roosevelt had believed for some time that a need for such a patrol would arise. In fact, he had commented to his staff on 20 April 1939 that he was "going to have a patrol from Newfoundland down to South America and if some submarines are laying there and try to

interrupt an American flag and our Navy sinks them, it's just too bad."
Admiral Harold R. Stark, USN, Chief of Naval Operations, remarking
on implementation of the Neutrality patrol, characterized its intended
function more diplomatically: "A deterrent against embarrassing
situations which might come within our waters."[3]

Photo 4-1

Chief of Naval Operations, Adm. Harold R. Stark, USN, on 1 April 1940. Later,
following President Roosevelt's decision to have a single officer serve as both
Commander-in-Chief, U.S. Fleet and wartime Chief of Naval Operations, Adm.
Ernest J. King, USN, assumed the duties of CNO from Stark on 26 March 1942.
U.S. Naval History and Heritage Command Photograph #NH 49967

The purpose of the patrol was to emphasize the readiness of the U.S. Navy to defend the Western Hemisphere. At the Conference of Foreign Ministers of the American Republics, which opened at Panama on 25 September 1939, the U.S. plan was presented for Pan-American sanction. After considerable debate, this was accorded. The Act of Panama issued on 2 October declared it to be the united policy of the Americas to keep the European War from the New World, and warned the belligerents against conducting warlike operations inside a boundary off North American and the Caribbean. This boundary extended southward approximately down longitude 60°W to latitude 20°N (just north of Antigua and Barbuda, part of the Lesser Antilles), thence east-southeast to a point about 600 miles south of Fogo, Cape Verde Islands (off the coast of northwest Africa), and thence south-southwest, roughly parallel to the South American coast.[4]

Newspaper reporters covering the conference flashed details learned to the United States. At a press conference held at the White House, a correspondent asked how far United States territorial waters or maritime frontiers extended toward Europe. President Roosevelt replied that they extended as far as United States interests required them to go. When asked by another reporter, "Does that reach the Rhine, Mr. President?" Roosevelt laughed and said he was only talking about salt water.[5]

Because no American power except the United States possessed more than a handful of combatant ships capable of performing such an operation, the burden of the Neutrality patrol fell on the U.S. Navy. In early September, Admiral Stark directed commander Atlantic Squadron, Rear Adm. Alfred W. Johnson, to maintain an offshore patrol and report "in confidential system" the movements of all foreign men-of-war approaching or leaving the east coast of the United States and approaching and entering or leaving the Caribbean. U.S. naval vessels were also to report the presence of foreign warships sighted at sea to the district commandant concerned. The patrol was to extend about 300 miles off the eastern seaboard of the United States and along the eastern boundary of the Caribbean.[6]

The Atlantic Squadron at that time consisted of only Battleship Division 5, Cruiser Division 7, Destroyer Squadron 10, Patrol Wing 5, and the aircraft carrier *Ranger* (CV-4). Moreover, several ships were out of service while undergoing scheduled overhauls, or were engaged in fall training with reserve units. Considering the span of the area assigned for patrol, the number of ships and planes was woefully inadequate: eighteen destroyers, four cruisers, four battleships, one carrier and two seaplane tenders. Johnson reported to Stark on 6

September 1939, "I have this day begun to establish an offshore neutrality patrol." The preparation, assignment and disposition of his small force required time but, by 12 September, eight separate patrols were organized.[7]

There were, however, difficulties in the early days before the patrol became a smooth running operation. On 9 October, President Roosevelt, in a memorandum to the Acting Secretary of the Navy, expressed his displeasure with "the slowness of getting the East Coast, Caribbean, and Gulf Patrol under way," the "lag between the making of contacts and the follow-up of the contact," and the weakness of the liaison between the Navy, the Coast Guard and the State Department. He further emphasized that "in this whole patrol business time is of the essence and loss of contact with surface ships will not be tolerated." In furtherance of this last point, Roosevelt urged that patrol planes and naval or Coast Guard ships be allowed to report the sighting of any submarine or suspicious surface ship in plain English. This order was quickly implemented. Commander Atlantic Squadron directed his ships on 20 October to use plain language radio reporting of contacts, in order to eliminate the delays caused by coding and decoding messages.[8]

It soon became apparent that the only practical way to cover vast stretches of offshore waters was by means of planes. Before many weeks of operation the Neutrality patrol became predominantly an air patrol, with Patrol Wing 5 the nucleus of such air coverage.[9]

SOUTHERNMOST PATROLS

Rear Adm. Andrew C. Pickens, USN, commanded Patrols 7 and 8, assigned to the southern areas. The below listed ships and patrol squadrons that comprised the patrols, operated at their commanding officer's discretion in the eastern Caribbean, south of latitude 23°10'N.

Ship	Type	Commanding Officer
San Francisco (CA-38)	heavy cruiser	Capt. Charles M. Yates, USN
Tuscaloosa (CA-37)	heavy cruiser	Capt. Harry A. Badt, USN
Borie (DD-215)	destroyer	Lt. Comdr. Joseph W. McColl Jr., USN
Broome (DD-210)	destroyer	Lt. Comdr. Henry E. Thornhill, USN
Simpson (DD-221)	destroyer	Lt. Comdr. Richard H. Cruzen, USN
Truxtun (DD-229)	destroyer	Lt. Comdr. Harry B. Heneberger, USN
Gannet (AVP-8)	seaplane tender	Lt. Comdr. Jack P. Monroe, USN
Lapwing (AVP-1)	seaplane tender	Lt. Comdr. Richard W. Ruble, USN
Thrush (AVP-3)	seaplane tender	Lt. James J. McRoberts, USN
Patrol Squadron 33	PBY-3 aircraft	Lt. Comdr. H. B. Miller, USN
Patrol Squadron 51	PBY-3 aircraft	Lt. Comdr. Stephen B. Cooke, USN[10]

These patrols operated in the Caribbean and on the Atlantic side of the Lesser Antilles, a group of islands that formed the eastern boundary of the Caribbean Sea with the Atlantic Ocean. Patrol Squadrons 33 and 51 were supported by three seaplane tenders. *Gannet* and *Thrush* sailed for San Juan, Puerto Rico, in early September 1939 to establish a seaplane base in support of VP-51. *Lapwing* similarly operated with seaplanes in the Caribbean; at the outbreak of the war, she was based at Trinidad, British West Indies. Patrol Squadron VP-33 operated from Guantanamo Bay.[11]

Photo 4-2

Seaplane tender *Gannet* (AVP-8), a former minesweeper, at sea on 4 May 1937. U.S. Naval History and Heritage Command Photograph #NH 53818

On 4 November, the Neutrality Act of 1939 became law. It repealed the existing arms embargo and substituted a policy of "cash and carry," prohibited U.S. vessels and citizens from entering combat zones, and established a National Munitions Control Board composed of the Secretaries of State, Treasury, War, Navy and Commerce. That same day, President Roosevelt declared the area around the British Isles a combat zone.[12]

Navy ships periodically joined or departed the Neutrality patrol. The heavy cruiser *Wichita* (CA-45) arrived at Guantanamo Bay, Cuba, on 8 December 1939, and her commanding officer, Capt. Thaddeus A. Thomson Jr., USN, assumed command of the newly formed Caribbean Patrol. Comprising the patrol were heavy cruisers *Wichita* and *Vincennes*, destroyers *Borie*, *Broome*, *Lawrence*, *King* and *Truxtun*, and Squadrons VP-33 and VP-51. All units were based at Guantanamo Bay or San Juan, Puerto Rico. In late January 1940, *Wichita* left Cuban waters to serve as the flagship of the newly constituted Antilles Detachment, which included *Vincennes* and Destroyer Squadron 10.[13]

ROOSEVELT'S ADVOCACY FOR NAVAL STRENGTH

President Roosevelt was cognizant of the American people's general aversion to entering into the war in Europe, or even supporting allies, should such action draw the United States into the hostilities. He was also mindful that war with Germany and/or Japan might be largely unavoidable. As such, he worked ceaselessly to prepare the country for war, while reassuring the public that everything possible was being done to avoid it.

As a long-serving former Assistant Secretary of the Navy (1913-1920), Roosevelt was devoted to the Navy and its power, and the writing of naval historian Alfred Thayer Mahan was influential for him. Mahan (September 27, 1840 – 1 December 1, 1914) was a U.S. Navy admiral, geostrategist, and historian. His supposition that countries with greater naval power will have greater worldwide impact was presented in *The Influence of Sea Power Upon History, 1660–1783*, published in 1890. To celebrate the one hundredth anniversary of Mahan's birth—and presumably to emphasize to the American people the linkage between military strength and the avoidance of war—Roosevelt wrote a public letter to the Secretary of the Navy on 27 September 1940, in which he noted in part:

> To this great strategist and statesman, America owes a lasting debt of gratitude. I, for one, trust that the broad lessons of preparedness he deduced so soundly for our benefit will never be neglected. He reaffirmed that the American Fleet must be built and forever maintained in order that the United States could at all times protect American safety. He wrote that to all intents and purposes, America, separated from Europe and Africa and Asia by wide oceans, is insular in geography and that, therefore, threats of aggression can best be met at a distance from our shores rather than on the seacoast itself. Translated into terms of the whole American Hemisphere, this is equally true today.[14]

Roosevelt well knew that the average tax-paying citizen was not familiar with Mahan's broad lessons of preparedness and strategy, and supported only the maintenance of a small standing army and navy. The public generally liked to believe that the Minuteman formula of their forefathers had been good enough for the past and would be sufficient for the future; "In time of war, take the musket down off the wall and fight; in time of peace, put the musket back on the wall and forget about it." Over the course of the nation's relatively short existence, the onset of hostilities had often found America's preparedness for national defense wanting. Necessary and hurried expansion of military forces followed, and after peace ensued, the contraction of these forces. Most recently, an American "preparedness" movement spurred by World War I, had quickly lost favor with the public once the armistice had been signed.[15]

GERMANY WARNS OF AMERICA'S INVOLVEMENT

Roosevelt's guidance that patrol planes and naval or Coast Guard ships be allowed to report the sighting of any submarine or suspicious surface ship in plain English resulted, either by design or as a consequence of such action, in the destruction of scores of German vessels by British warships. Most German ships could not understand these transmissions, but British warships in the area certainly could. Thus, American sighting reports undoubtedly directed the Royal Navy to enemy prey. Only thirty-two of eighty-five German merchant vessels found their way home from the Western Hemisphere in late 1939, while nearly 100 of 126 merchant ships made it back to German waters from other areas of the world.[16]

This fact did not escape notice by Germany. In summer 1940, the commander-in-chief of the German Navy, Adm. Erich Raeder, declared that the Neutrality patrol system was aggressive in character, and he denounced the use of an American naval patrol for the purpose of tipping off the British on the position of German ships.

> Nobody can expect a German warship to look on, while an American warship communicates the position of a German man-of-war to the British Admiralty. Such procedure must be regarded as an act of war which justifies the German commander to act in accordance with the rules of naval warfare and force the ship in question to cease hostile activity.

He stated that such actions had been responsible for the loss of a number of German vessels, including the *Columbus*. (The ocean liner was scuttled by her crew on 19 December 1939, off the coast of Virginia, in lieu of capture by the British destroyer HMS *Hyperion*. The heavy cruiser USS *Tuscaloosa* was also in the area.)[17]

TWO-OCEAN NAVY ACT

As Raeder was protesting the actions of "neutral" American warships, measures were being taken to dramatically increase the size of the U.S.

Navy. Roosevelt and the top leadership of the Sea Service well understood in mid-1940, that with the United Kingdom facing a potential German invasion, the Royal Navy could no longer blockade German and Italian naval movement westward. Following preparation of a Two-Ocean Navy Bill, Admiral Stark appeared before the House Naval Affairs Committee on 18 June and recommended a four billion dollar naval expansion. The request startled all official Washington; but within six hours, the committee by unanimous vote sent the bill to the House, which passed it on 22 June.[18]

On 19 July 1940, the U.S. Congress passed the Vinson-Walsh Act (better known as the "Two-Ocean Navy Act"). The Act allocated the requested monies over the following six years for the construction of combatant ships (including, but not limited to: 7 battleships, 6 battlecruisers, 18 carriers, 27 cruisers, 115 destroyers, and 43 submarines), construction of 15,000 aircraft, conversion of auxiliary ships, construction and renovation of facilities, and manufacture and procurement of various munitions and equipment. After noting that "Dollars cannot buy yesterday," Stark added that the time lost by the U.S. Navy over the past fifteen or so years could not be truly remedied, but the allocation of funding was a step in the right direction. The Congress and the American people generally regarded the Two-Ocean Navy Act as deterrence to any German or Japanese consideration to wage war against the United States.[19]

That same month, Roosevelt accepted the nomination of his party for a third term as president. In a direct and straightforward speech at the Democratic National Convention on 19 July 1940, he said in part while explaining why he wished to continue to lead the nation:

> If our Government should pass to other hands next January—untried hands, inexperienced hands—we can merely hope and pray that they will not substitute appeasement and compromise with those who seek to destroy all democracies everywhere, including here.
>
> I felt it was my duty, my simple plain inescapable duty, to arouse my countrymen to the danger of new forces let loose in the world.
>
> So long as I am President, I will do all I can to insure that that foreign policy [actions by his administration during the past seven years] remain our foreign policy.
>
> All that I have done to maintain the peace of this country and to prepare it morally, as well as physically, for whatever contingencies may be in store, I submit to the judgment of my countrymen.[20]

5

Royal Navy Hunting Groups
Seek Out Runners/Raiders

German merchant ships are being steadily driven from the seas. They are using every artifice and every expedient of concealment to avoid capture, and are taking refuge in neutral harbours.

It is reported that 54 German merchant ships, totaling more than 180,000 tons, are now in the port of Vigo [Spain]. Nine German ships, totaling more than 50,000 tons, are in Japanese ports.

—Article "Driving German merchant ships from the seas."
Daily Telegraph, Sept 8, 1939.

Photo 5-1

French warships in port circa 1939, possibly on the French Mediterranean coast. A 2,400-ton destroyer is in the foreground; beyond her, to the left, is the battleship *Courbet*; while a *Duguay-Trouin*-class light cruiser is to the right. U.S. Naval History and Heritage Command Photograph #NH 110742

In the latter part of 1939—as the U.S. Navy began its fledgling Neutrality patrol—the Royal Navy continued its efforts to find, and bring to battle, German raiders such as the *Admiral Graf Spee*. A concurrent Allied mission was to deny passage of German shipping between Europe and the Far East, and return delivery of war materials to Germany.

Map 5-1

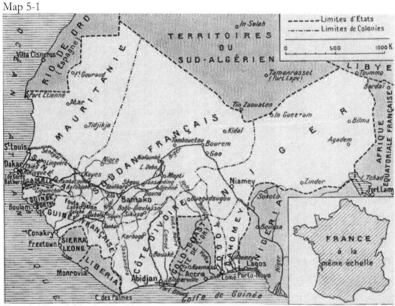

French West Africa in World War II

During the first three days of the war, 3-5 September 1939, warships of the Royal Navy caught the German merchant vessels *Olinda*, *Carl Fritzen*, *Ussukuma* and *Inn* unprotected and alone out at sea. Enemy merchantmen were then desperately trying to find safe haven in a neutral port, or make it home to Germany in one piece. The crews of the aforementioned ships scuttled them to prevent their boarding and capture by the British. This practice would continue throughout the war, although Royal and U.S. Navy ships were occasionally able to capture enemy vessels.

Allied interdiction of shipping was not limited to German vessels. Merchant ships belonging to other Axis powers, and those of neutral countries suspected of carrying minerals, metals, food and textiles Germany needed to sustain its war effort were subject to stopping, and being forced into port for inspection, and/or internment.

FORCE K FORMED, AND ORDERED TO FREEPORT, SIERRA LEONE, ON THE COAST OF WEST AFRICA

In the early hours of 1 October 1939, the Admiralty received a signal from the Naval Control Staff Officer at Pernambuco, Brazil, informing it that the British ship *Clement* had been sunk by a surface raider (*Admiral Graf Spee*) seventy-five miles southeast of Pernambuco, the previous afternoon. The Royal Navy immediately formed several hunting groups to try to track down the pocket battleship.[1]

The aircraft carrier *Ark Royal* (91) and battlecruiser *Renown* (72) received orders on 2 October to sail for Freetown, Sierra Leone, where they were to comprise Force K. That same day, *Ark Royal*—with Vice Adm. Lionel Victor Wells ("Vice Admiral, Aircraft Carriers") embarked—and the destroyers *Ashanti* (F51) and *Foresight* (H68) sailed from Loch Ewe, in the Northwest Highlands of Scotland, and steered for the Butt of Lewis. This headland marked the most northerly point of Lewis, the largest island of the Western Isles (Outer Hebrides) of Scotland. The group rendezvoused at sea with *Renown* and the destroyers *Bedouin* (F67) and *Tarter* (F43) ten minutes past midnight on the 3rd. The force of ships then headed out into the Atlantic before turning south for Freetown. The destroyers detached on 4 October and returned to the Fleet Anchorage at Scapa Flow.[2]

On 9 October, as *Ark Royal* and *Renown* passed east of the Cape Verde Islands, a Swordfish from the carrier sighted an unknown tanker to the west of the islands. (This type aircraft was a biplane torpedo bomber used by the Fleet Air Arm of the Royal Navy during World War II.) When the ship was challenged, her commanding officer, Capt. Heinrich Dau, identified his vessel—the German supply tanker *Altmark*—as the American tanker *Delmar*. Wells decided not to investigate as he had no destroyers with him and he was eager to press on to Freetown. The carrier and battlecruiser arrived at Freetown on the morning of 12 October, in company with the *Hardy* (H87), *Hasty* (H24) and *Hostile* (H55). The destroyers had joined them at sea the previous day to serve as an escort into port.[3]

On the evening of 28 October, Force K—*Ark Royal*, *Renown*, *Neptune*, *Hardy*, *Hasty*, *Hero*, *Hereward* and *Hostile*—left Freetown to patrol to the south as far as Ascension Island. *Hero* detached from the group on the 1st of November to take up escort duties.[4]

BLOCKADE RUNNER *UHENFELS* CAPTURED

On 5 November, a Swordfish from *Ark Royal* sighted the German freighter *Uhenfels*, 300 miles west-southwest of Freetown. The ship had left Lourenco Marques (today Maputo), the capital and largest city of Mozambique, on 13 October, disguised as the Dutch motor merchant *Aagtekerk*. Aboard the 503-foot vessel was a cargo of opium, cotton and hides. The destroyer *Hereward* (H93), commanded by Lt. Comdr. Charles Woollven Greening, RN, was detached from the screen to investigate.[5]

Upon sighting the destroyer churning toward his vessel, the master of *Uhenfels* tried to evade with maximum speed. Seeing that he could not outrun the British warship, Capt. Schuldt ordered lifeboats lowered in preparation to abandon, and seacocks opened to scuttle. Quick action by a boarding party from *Hereward*, in starting pumps aboard the *Uhenfels*, prevented her from sinking. The destroyer brought the blockade runner to Freetown on 6 November.[6]

Uhenfels was taken for British service and, in April 1940, renamed *Empire Ability* by the Ministry of War Transport (MoWT). MoWT was a department of the British Government created early in the war to control transportation policy and resources. It was formed by merging the Ministry of Shipping and the Ministry of Transport. This action centralized the responsibility for shipping and land transport; thereby improving coordination of transport in wartime.[7]

Empire Ability was sunk by *U-69* later in the war. In early morning darkness on 27 June 1941, the German submarine torpedoed two ships sailing as units of convoy SL-78, about 200 miles southeast of the Azores. The British merchant vessel *River Lugas* broke in half and sank within seconds after being hit by a torpedo at 0149. Less than an hour later, *Empire Ability* was hit by a torpedo, caught fire and sank after 21 minutes. Twenty-five merchant ships had sailed from Freetown on 18 June 1941. Eight would be sent to the bottom by *U-66*, *U-69* and *U-12*, before the convoy reached Liverpool on 12 July.[8]

GERMAN CREW SCUTTLES CARGO SHIP *HALLE*

On 16 October 1939, the French light cruiser *Duguay-Trouin* (Capt. J. M. C. Trolley de Prevaux) intercepted the German cargo ship *Halle* about 200 nautical miles southwest of Dakar, Senegal, in French West Africa. *Duguay-Trouin* was a unit of the 6th Cruiser Division, based at Dakar, whose duty was to patrol waters of the Atlantic. The crew of *Halle* scuttled the ship before a French party could board her.[9]

BLOCKADE RUNNER *ADOLPH WOERMANN*

On 18 November 1943, as part of the Royal Navy's continuing effort to locate the *Graf Spee*, Vice Adm. George Lyon dispatched Force K— the aircraft carrier *Ark Royal*, battlecruiser *Renown*, light cruiser *Neptune*, and destroyers *Hardy*, *Hasty*, *Hero* and *Hostile*—on patrol. The ships sailed from Freetown, headed south for the Cape of Good Hope. Two hours after leaving port, the destroyers detached from the group to take up a patrol between Freetown and Pernambuco. By the morning of 21 November, Force K was 150 miles east of Ascension Island. At 0842, it intercepted a signal from the British freighter *Waimarama* reporting a sighting of the German passenger/cargo ship *Adolph Woermann*, 250 miles north of St. Helena Island.[10]

Force K altered course and *Neptune* was sent ahead at full speed to close the position given by *Waimarama*, who was shadowing the *Adolph Woermann*. *Neptune* (Capt. John A. V. Morse, RN) intercepted the 433-foot blockade runner the following morning 366 miles north of St. Helena. On sighting the cruiser, the master of the *Adolph Woermann*, Otto Burfeind, ordered his crew to abandon after engineers opened seacocks to flood the ship. Despite efforts to save her, the ship sank, and *Neptune* returned to Freetown with 162 prisoners. Vice Admiral Lyon subsequently expressed the view that Force K likely missed the *Altmark*, which was awaiting *Graf Spee* away from the Cape shipping routes, an area through which Force K would otherwise have passed.[11]

The passengers and crew of the German ship were taken by the cruiser to England, and interned in a camp near Seaton, Devon. (The site had been a holiday camp before the war, and would revert to this usage afterward.) In 1940, most of the internees from the camp were put aboard the British passenger ship *Arandora Star*. Among the group were Capt. Otto Burfeind, master of the *Adolph Woermann*, and his crew. The ship departed Liverpool, in northwest England, on 2 July 1940, bound for St. John's (the capital and largest city in Newfoundland and Labrador) and Canadian internment camps ashore. Aboard her were nearly 1,500 German and Italian internees, including 86 POWs being transported from Great Britain. The *Arandora Star* bore no Red Cross sign, which might have indicated she was carrying prisoners, and especially civilians.[12]

That morning, while off the northwest coast of Ireland, she was struck at 0758 by a torpedo from the German submarine *U-47*, commanded by Kapitänleutnant Günther Prien. It is assumed that Prien mistook her grey wartime livery for that of an armed merchant cruiser. All propulsion was lost, and thirty five minutes later, *Arandora Star* sank with over eight hundred casualties. The master of the ship, 12 officers, 42 crewmen, 37 guards, 470 Italians and 243 Germans were lost. Among them was Otto Burfeind, who stayed aboard the sinking ship to help with the evacuation. The Canadian destroyer HMCS *St. Laurent* (H83) retrieved 119 crewmen, 163 guards and 586 Italians and Germans and landed them at Greenock, Scotland, a town located west of Glasgow on the southern shore of the Firth of Clyde. (Greenock would become a Free French naval base later in the war, and be heavily damaged by bombing. Today, a huge granite Cross of Lorraine on Lyle Hill above the town, serves as a memorial to the French sailors who lost their lives in the Battle of the Atlantic.)[13]

Less than nine months earlier, Günther Prien and *U-47* had audaciously sunk the battleship HMS *Royal Oak* (08) in the heavily defended British Home Fleet main harbor at Scapa Flow (in the Orkney Islands, Scotland) on 14 October 1939. For this action, Prien became the first U-boat commander to receive the Knight's Cross. He had previously been awarded the Iron Cross 2nd Class, and 1st Class, and later would add the Knight's Cross with Oak Leaves. Winston Churchill described the sinking of *Royal Oak* as "a remarkable feat of professional skill and daring."[14]

"SPECIAL OPERATION P" AGAINST SCAPA FLOW

Kapitänleutnant Prien had been summoned on a peaceful Sunday afternoon on 1 October 1939, at Kiel, Germany, to a meeting with Commodore Karl Dönitz, commander of U-boats. Dönitz had an idea for a daring submarine attack on the British naval base at Scapa Flow, and believed Prien the perfect officer to execute it. Scapa Flow (from Old Norse Skalpaflói meaning "bay of the long isthmus") was a deep-water anchorage in the Orkney Islands off the northeast coast of Scotland, sheltered by the islands of Mainland, Graemsay, Burray, South Ronaldsay and Hoy. The Orkneys comprised in total about seventy islands. Scapa Flow was the northern base of the Royal Navy, from which the mighty warships of Britain's Home Fleet dominated the area through which German ships and submarines passed out of the North Sea into the Atlantic.[15]

Scapa Flow invoked bitter thoughts among German sailors. On 21 June 1919, near the end of World War I, under the mistaken belief that peace talks had failed, Rear Adm. Ludwig von Reuter had given the command to scuttle the entire High Seas Fleet in the Flow. A total of fifty-two ships went to the bottom, and this act remains the greatest loss of shipping ever recorded in a single day. During the 1920s and 1930s a majority of the scuttled ships were raised in one of the largest maritime salvage operations in history. Over the wrecks of the seven remaining German warships floated the British Home Fleet; row upon row of battleships, moored side-by-side at anchor. Even if a submarine was lost executing "Special Operation P," it would be worth it to destroy just one battleship and by such action, greatly embarrass the Royal Navy.[16]

Map 5-2

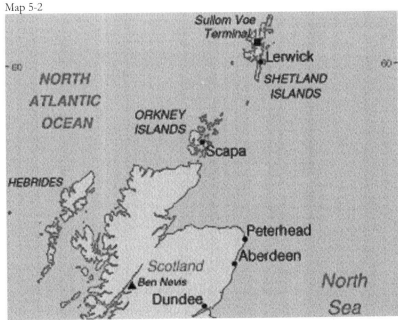

Northern Scotland

Prien, at age 31 was a seven-year veteran of the U-boat service. He had earned his master's papers in the merchant marine at age 24, and joined the Kriegsmarine (German Navy) in 1933. During his first war patrol, he had sunk three ships and been awarded the Iron Cross, Second Class. As he stood before Dönitz aboard the depot ship *Weichsel*, Prien glanced at the charts on the table and saw one of Scapa Flow on top. Dönitz outlined his plan, and then asked, "Do you think a determined commander could get his boat inside Scapa Flow and attack the enemy's forces lying there?" He gave Prien forty-eight hours to look over the collection of charts, photographs and intelligence and give him an answer. Early in the war, German aircraft had reconnoitered the defenses of Scapa Flow, whilst submarines monitored British shipping arriving and departing, and had identified gaps between blockships in Kirk Sound.[17]

Prien considered all the impediments to a successful mission, including strong tides, and anti-submarine booms and sunken ships blocking the bay's seven entrances. After mentally working through the entire problem, he reported to Dönitz a full day ahead of the deadline. The commodore, who was sitting at his desk, fixed his gaze on Prien and asked "Yes or no?" Prien replied, "Yes, sir." "Very well,

Dönitz responded and standing to shake Prien's hand, he ordered, "Get your boat ready."[18]

Photo 5-2

German battleships and cruisers interned at Scapa Flow, 28 November 1918. Note the harbor closure net line at the right.
U.S. Naval History and Heritage Command Photograph #NH 89526

U-47 departed Kiel on 8 October, with no ceremony or fanfare, except for a salute from Kapitan zur See Hans-Georg von Friedeburg. Dönitz would become Reich President much later in the war on 1 May 1945, and Friedeburg would succeed him as commander-in-chief of the German Navy. The submarine proceeded around the Denmark peninsula and into the North Sea, traveling on the surface at night, and lying submerged during the day. Prien had not divulged to his officers (except, presumably the navigator), nor crew, the destination of *U-47*. On the evening of the 12th, having navigated by depth soundings and dead reckoning alone, he brought the submarine to the surface to obtain a celestial fix. Overcast sky and light drizzle obscured the stars but, judging by coastal lights, Prien concluded they were just off the Orkneys, less than two nautical miles from their intended location— no mean feat of navigation.[19]

Prien's navigator during the mission to Scapa Flow was Obersteuermann Wilhelm Spahr. It was his job to work all the navigation problems. It was surely Spahr who accomplished the "no mean feat of navigation," and it is likely he had been with Prien during the forty-eight hours the latter individual was studying the charts and photos that Dönitz had provided, answering questions and offering advice. A unique relationship existed between a U-boat's captain and the Steuermann (navigator). He was a petty officer or chief petty officer who had previously been a boatswain and was hand-picked for training and promotion to Steuermann. The Steuermann never left the captain's side, whether he was in the Central Control Room, in the conning tower, or on the bridge.[20]

When asked by Englebert Endrass, the First Officer, "Are we going to visit the Orkneys, sir?" Prien replied, "Take hold of yourself. We are going into Scapa Flow." To this assertion, the first officer said simply, "That will be OK, sir, that will be quite OK." In early morning darkness, at 0400 on 13 October, Prien set *U-47* down on the seafloor in 45-fathom-deep water. The purpose was to quietly remain stationary, with no propulsion operating, until evening darkness. At 1900, the time of slack water, he ordered the maneuvering watch set. When the submarine surfaced fifteen minutes later, it was night and all clear. With the tide now running northwest, *U-47* proceeded with it toward Holm Sound.[21]

Prien's plan was to make his way into Scapa Flow, via Kirk Sound, on the eastern side of the Flow, through gaps opened after time and tide had shifted the blockships that had sealed it decades earlier during the First World War. Approaching the anti-submarine boom, Prien steered for a gap between the blockships *Thames* and *Soriano*, and eased forward in an effort to ride up over the cable stretched between them under the surface. The wire scraped along the submarine's keel, slew *U-47* hard to starboard, and sent her aground on the Holm shore. Prien had been operating with the sub's ballast tanks partially filled, in order to present a low silhouette to any watchful individuals aboard ship. He now ordered tanks blown and *U-47* floated off the sandbar. Passing into Scapa Flow, Prien was disappointed to find the main Fleet was away at sea. His frustration was partially abated when he sighted a battleship lying under the cliffs at Gaitnip, Holm.[22]

A torpedo struck HMS *Royal Oak* at 0104, which some of her crew dismissed as an internal explosion. Others, fearing it might be due to an enemy air-raid, took cover below the ship's armor-plated deck. This action sealed their fate. Three additional torpedoes hit the battleship, amidships starboard side, sending a pillar of flame as high as the mast. Some of the crew were killed by the warhead explosions, others died when the cordite in one of the magazines ignited, sending flames through the ship. Seawater rushed in through rents in her hull; causing *Royal Oak* to roll over, and drag the drifter *Daisy II* up her side. The mooring lines were cut, and the 86-foot herring drifter (employed as a tender for the battleship) slid back into the water. *Daisy II* saved many lives that night, as did boats launched from the seaplane carrier *Pegasus* and destroyers arriving on scene. The skipper of *Daisy II*, John Gatt, and his crew rescued 386 crew members of *Royal Oak*. Although a civilian, Gatt (from Rosehearty in Aberdeenshire) received the

Distinguished Service Cross for this action—an award for gallantry during active operations against the enemy at sea.[23]

In the icy waters of Scapa Flow, 833 British officers and men perished; some killed outright, others due to being trapped inside the ship, or from hypothermia or injuries sustained. The wreck site of the *Royal Oak* is today an official war grave.[24]

Photo 5-3

U-47 arrives at Kiel, Germany, 23 October 1939, with her crew at quarters. She was returning from a mission in which she sank the British battleship *Royal Oak* inside Scapa Flow on 14 October. The battleship *Scharnhorst* is in the background.
U.S. Naval History and Heritage Command Photograph #NH 97503

As skillfully as he had entered, Günther Prien exited Scapa Flow through Kirk Sound, and the captain and crew of *U-47* returned to Germany for a hero's welcome. They were met at the dock by Dönitz and Grossadmiral Raeder. On the spot, Dönitz awarded Prien the Iron Cross First Class, and everyone else the Iron Cross Second Class; Raeder promoted Dönitz to Rear Admiral. That afternoon the ship's officers and crew flew to Berlin; the following day, Hitler personally placed the Knight's Cross of the Iron Cross around Prien's neck. During the presentation of the award, he called the Scapa Flow raid "the proudest deed that a German U-boat could possibly carry out."[25]

The Knight's Cross was the highest award for extreme battlefield bravery or outstanding military leadership during World War II. Among the military decorations of Nazi Germany, it was second only to the Grand Cross of the Iron Cross, an award given only to Hitler's second-in-command Hermann Göring. The Grand Cross was not an award for bravery. It was reserved for General Staff officers who made "the most outstanding strategic decisions affecting the course of the war." Göring received it for his command of the Luftwaffe during the successful 1940 campaign against France, Belgium, and Holland—at the same time as he was promoted to Reich Marshall of the Greater German Reich. This newly created rank made Göring the senior officer of the military, and confirmed an earlier Hitler decree naming Göring his successor. The Knight's Cross was functionally the highest award that German servicemen of all ranks could obtain.[26]

Over the next seventeen months, Prien took *U-47* on seven more patrols. The submarine left Lorient, France, for her tenth patrol on 20 February 1941. Four days later, Prien attacked convoy OB 290 (bound from Liverpool to North America) and sank four ships—bringing his total to thirty-one ships sent to the bottom, and another eight damaged. *U-47* went missing on 7 March, with the loss of all forty-five members of her crew. The last radio message received from the submarine, sent that morning, reported her position as being south of Iceland in the North Atlantic.[27]

BLOCKADE RUNNER *WATUSSI* SUNK BY CREW

On 27 November 1939, the Admiralty ordered Force K with Force H—the heavy cruisers *Sussex* (96) and *Shropshire* (83)—to patrol south of the Cape of Good Hope, along the meridian of 20°E longitude. *Renown* and *Ark Royal* sailed from Simon's Town—near Cape Town, South Africa, on the shores of False Bay—two days later to commence their patrol between longitude 38 and 40 south. The Royal Navy was then using Simon's Town as an assembly base for ships hunting German raiders and blockade runners in the southern oceans. The most sought quarry being the *Admiral Graf Spee*.[28]

When Force K and Force H rendezvoused in their patrol area on 1 December, they found the weather conditions too adverse for *Ark Royal* to operate aircraft. Only once during the ensuing five-day patrol was flying possible, significantly shrinking the area that could be surveyed. Happily, Force K received a sighting report the following morning from a Junkers Ju 86 bomber (one of three belonging to 15 Squadron, South African Air Force) flying a maritime patrol. The report was of a suspicious vessel in the area south of Cape Agulhas, South Africa. (This rocky headland, whose name means cape of needles, is the geographic southern tip of the African continent, which divides the Atlantic and Indian Oceans. In years past, it was known to sailors as a major hazard along the clipper route around the horn of South Africa.) Force K and Force H, then returning to the patrol area after refueling at Simon's Town, set a course for the position reported.[29]

Force H with *Sussex* leading was the first to intercept the German passenger ship *Watussi*, which had departed Mozambique on 23 November. On the approach of *Sussex* (Capt. Alexander Robert Hammick, RN), the blockade runner was abandoned, set on fire and efforts made to scuttle her. The *Sussex* picked up the 155 members of her crew, and 42 passengers that had been aboard. When Force K arrived on the scene, *Watussi* was aflame but still afloat, and *Renown*, under the command of Capt. Charles Edward Barrington Simeon, RN, sank the hulk with gunfire from her B turret. Force K arrived back at Cape Town on 3 December.[30]

BLOCKADE RUNNER *ADOLF LEONHARDT*

A few days later, *Shropshire* was once again operating with *Sussex* on patrol. On 9 December, her aircraft intercepted the German vessel *Adolf Leonhardt* off the coast of Angola. The cargo ship had sailed earlier from Lobito, a port city sited on one of Africa's finest natural harbors, about midpoint along Angola's Atlantic coast. Her crew managed to scuttle the ship before *Shropshire* arrived on the scene. Brought aboard the heavy cruiser, the Germans were taken to Cape Town and interned there.[31]

6

German Auxiliary Cruisers
Prowl Ocean Waters

If this operational record is impressive, then in economic terms, the figures are even more so, as this outstanding performance was achieved by little more than 3,000 officers and men, in nine second-hand freighters, armed with third-hand weapons, the total cost of which, both in terms of purchase price and the cost of fitting out, represented barely 1% of the cost of the battleship Bismarck!

—Reference to nine former German freighters converted to auxiliary cruisers (commerce raiders) to prey on Allied merchant shipping. These wolves in sheep's clothing accounted for 141 ships sunk or captured in the war.[1]

The first phase of the battle for the Atlantic lasted from autumn 1939 until 22 June 1940, when France surrendered to Germany. During that period the British and French navies drove German merchant shipping from the sea and established a fairly effective long-range blockade of enemy seaports. Meanwhile, the German navy continued inflicting damage on Allied forces at sea (including through the use of converted freighters designated "auxiliary cruisers" employed as raiders to attack Allied merchant shipping). The balance of power between Britain and Germany shifted in May–June 1940, following Germany's conquest of the Low Countries, the fall of France, and Italy's entry into the war on the Axis side. The Royal Navy lost French naval support just when the sea service had suffered ship losses during the evacuation of British troops from Norway and Dunkirk, and was stretched by Italian belligerency.[2]

BLOCKADE RUNNER *WAKAMA* SUNK BY CREW
Throughout 1940, the Royal Navy continued its efforts to interdict German merchant shipping in the South Atlantic. In mid-afternoon on 12 February 1940, the crew of the 3,675-ton cargo ship *Wakama* scuttled their ship to avoid her capture by the British heavy cruiser HMS *Dorsetshire* (40) off Rio de Janeiro.[3]

Wakama, under the command of Bernhard Schacht, had been present at Rio de Janeiro on 1 September 1939, when Germany's invasion of Poland started World War II. Because of the Allied naval blockade, Schacht bided his time in the harbor for six-and-a-half months, until midnight on 12 February 1940. As a new day began, *Wakama* sailed in darkness with a cargo of war materials bound for Germany, including a 150kg piece of crystal and ten tons of nickel. Nickel was particularly critical. Alloyed with steel it yielded high-strength stainless steel for guns, ammunition and vehicles, and could be combined with a host of other transition metals, such as copper, zinc, iron, silver, cadmium and chromium, for other uses.[4]

Photo 6-1

Rio de Janeiro, Brazil; date unknown. Ships include one battleship, either the *Minas Gerais* or *São Paulo*; three destroyers of the *Amazon*-class; and one cruiser, either *Rio Grande do Sul* or *Bahia*.
U.S. Naval History and Heritage Command Photograph #NH42781

Wakama's return voyage to Germany ended less than one hundred miles east of Rio de Janeiro, when HMS *Dorsetshire* (Capt. Benjamin C. S. Martin, RN) stopped her in an area off Cabo Frio, Brazil, after a seaplane from the heavy cruiser found and reported her location. The 46-man crew of *Wakama* was taken aboard the British cruiser and sent to South Africa for captivity.[5]

Photo 6-2

British heavy cruiser HMS *Dorsetshire*, prior to her relief by HMS *Amphion* as flagship on Africa Station, date unknown.
U.S. Naval History and Heritage Command Photograph #NH 60928

Brazil, neutral in the war, was not pleased by this action, nor was Britain by the resultant criticism that ensued. The British maintained that they were protecting Brazilian commerce. "Indeed you are not," the Brazilian Minister for Foreign Affairs, Oswaldo Aranha, retorted, "You are definitely not protecting our commerce by maintaining your warships off our coast. It is apparent to me that your blockade of Germany is plainly ineffective. If it were effective, you could stop the German boats [sic] on the other side before they entered German ports."[6]

HILFSKREUZER (WOLVES IN SHEEP'S CLOTHING)

Up to this point in the war, Germany had employed many of its capital ships as commerce raiders—including the battleship *Bismarck*; pocket battleships *Admiral Graf Spee*, *Admiral Scheer*, and *Deutschland*; battlecruisers *Gneisenau* and *Scharnhorst*; and heavy cruisers *Admiral Hipper* and *Prinz Eugen*. However, with the exception of the success achieved by *Graf Spee* prior to her loss, these warships accomplished relatively little in terms of Allied ships sunk or captured. Considering their enormous cost and firepower, they produced a poor return in this role. *Bismarck* and *Prinz Eugen* had absolutely no effect in interrupting Britain's supply lines, *Deutschland* and *Admiral Hipper* fared only a little better, and the remaining four (with somewhat better results) achieved nothing of significance regarding the blockade of the British Isles.[7]

In support of its goal of starving Britain of the goods and materials needed to survive and stay in the war, Germany introduced the use of Hilfskreuzer (auxiliary cruisers) as commerce raiders in early 1940. These armed ships—nondescript, converted German freighters, disguised as "clapped out" merchantmen of other nations—went to sea and fought as true warships. The 300-plus-man crews of the Hilfskreuzer were led by officers of the rank of captain or commander, all but one having seen active service before the war. For different reasons, they were considered unsuitable for command of a regular navy warship, and either too senior in rank or too old for U-Boat command. Generally, these men were former training ship commanders.[8]

Despite their unglamorous assignments, the commanding officers of the Hilfskreuzer would become among the most decorated in the German military. Eight received the Knight's Cross and four of these men—Kähler, Krüder, Rogge, and von Ruckteschell—received the honor of the oak leaves, as well. This was an impressive achievement, given that only 890 such were awarded during the war; including 8 foreign recipients of the Knight's Cross of the Iron Cross with Oak Leaves.

Commanding Officer	Knight's Cross	With Oak Leaves
Kapitän zur See (Comdr.) Ulrich Brocksien	31 Dec 1942	
Korvettenkapitän (Capt.) Theodor Detmers	4 Dec 1941	
Kapitän zur See (Comdr.) Robert Eyssen	29 Nov 1941	
Kapitän zur See (Comdr.) Otto Kähler	22 Dec 1940	15 Sep 1944
Kapitän zur See (Comdr.) Ernst-Felix Krüder	22 Dec 1940	15 Nov 1941
Fregattenkapitän (Capt.) Bernhard Rogge	7 Dec 1940	31 Dec 1941
Kapitän zur See Helmuth von Ruckteschell	31 Oct 1940	22 Dec 1942
Kapitän zur See (Comdr.) Kurt Weyher	21 Aug 1941[9]	

FIRST AUXILIARY CRUISERS SAIL FROM KIEL

The crews carried are large, at least 300 and probably 400 [officers and men]. They are mainly young regular naval ratings, but some are reservists from the merchant navy who have had peace-time experience of the waters in which the raider is to operate. This is particularly true of the officers, who are in a position to advise the captain of the types and habits of shipping likely to be encountered.

Importance is attached to the nuisance value of minelaying. It is not thought that many mines are ever laid at one time, as the chances of the raider being detected would be too great. It is possible that the ferocity of raiders' attacks on ships are due to their fear of a victim scoring one lucky hit on their stock of mines.

—Raider Supplement to the Weekly Intelligence Report No. 64,
of 30 May 1941, issued by the Naval Intelligence Division,
Navy Staff, British Admiralty

The first three raiders, *Atlantis*, *Orion*, and *Widder*, put to sea from Kiel, Germany (a port city on the Baltic Sea) on 11 March 1940, following the old World War I battleship *Hessen*, being employed as an ice-breaker, through the Kaiser-Wilhelm canal to the North Sea. There, the commanding officer of *Atlantis*, Fregattenkapitän Bernhard Rogge, put his ship through exercises and gunnery practice for several days. On 23 March, he anchored her in Süderpiep Bay, Norway, and his crew went to work disguising the former freighter as the Norwegian motor ship *Knute Nelson*. After this had been accomplished, overflights of British reconnaissance aircraft inspecting the anchored "Norwegian ship," prompted Rogge to change her appearance again.[10]

Posing as the Russian fleet auxiliary *Kim*, complete with Soviet naval ensign, hammer and sickle on the bridge, giant red star on Number 2 hatch, and an indecipherable Cyrillic inscription, *Atlantis* stood out of the bay on 1 April 1940. Under perfect weather conditions to escape notice—wind, rain and zero visibility—and escorted by the torpedo boats *Leopard* and *Wolf*, and submarine *U-37*, she proceeded into the North Sea.[11]

Atlantis traversed the Denmark Strait, evaded the Royal Navy and made it into the Atlantic Ocean on 8 April; beginning a war cruise that would last 622 days, longer than any other raider. During this voyage, she would sink sixteen vessels and capture another six, a tally among the Hilfskreuzer second only to raider *Pinguin* (32) and tied with *Thor*.[12]

REPRESENTATIVE GERMAN RAIDER

Atlantis, the former freighter *Goldenfels* (7,862 tons), was fairly representative of the other Hilfskreuzer—purposefully non-descript—but deadly. Converted at Deschimag-Werft in Bremen in 1939, she was armed with six rapid-fire 150mm guns, one 75mm cannon on the bow, two twin 37mm anti-aircraft guns, and four 20mm guns, all hidden, mostly behind pivotal false deck or side structures. A phony crane and deckhouse on the after part of the ship concealed two of her 150mm guns; the other four were hidden behind flaps in the hull that were raised when action was imminent. *Atlantis* also had four waterline torpedo tubes, two Heinkel He-114C floatplanes in one of her holds (one fully assembled and the other packed away in crates), a high-speed launch, and a supply of mines on board. The Heinkel was later replaced by a smaller and faster Arado Ar-196 floatplane.[13]

Photo 6-3

First Allied published photograph of Raider C (the *Atlantis*).
Weekly Intelligence Report of 31 January 1941, issued by the Naval Intelligence Division, Navy Staff, Admiralty for the information of all officers in H.M. Navy

Photo 6-4

German Arado Ar-196 floatplane on the catapult of a warship in World War II.
U.S. Naval History and Heritage Command Photograph #NH 71324

On 6 April, *Orion*—the former *Kurmark* (7,021 tons)—put to sea from the Elbe River, bound for the South Atlantic. Her armament and ship's complement (377 officers and men) were nearly identical to that of *Atlantis*, but she was fitted with six torpedo tubes.[14]

FIRST SHIP FALLS VICTIM TO HILFSKREUZER

Atlantis crossed the equator on 22 April, after having received orders to proceed into the South Atlantic and attack ships along the Cape Town-Freetown route. In early afternoon on 3 May, she sighted the British freighter *Scientist*, en route to Liverpool from Durban, South Africa. *Atlantis* was now posing as the Japanese freighter *Kasii Maru*, complete with black hull, yellow masts and ventilators (with the ventilator interiors painted red) and her stack black with a red top and a large "K" on its side in white. The letter was a symbol of Koyusai Steamship Company, the owner of the real *Kasii Maru*.[15]

As the two ships drew nearer, the crew of *Atlantis* awaited the order to expose their weapons, and thus reveal their true identity, while watching the British freighter for any attempts at evasion. When the order came, the German ensign was raised, as were signal flag hoists ordering the vessel to stop, and to not use her radio. A warning shot awoke Capt. G. R. Windsor, the master of the British ship, from his afternoon nap. When he realized *Scientist* was being stopped by a German ship, Windsor gathered up the codebooks and other classified documents aboard, placed them in a weighted box and threw it overboard. He then ordered a signal hoisted, acknowledging receipt, and understanding of that of *Atlantis*.[16]

Windsor had no intention of being boarded. Instead, he turned away from the raider and ordered top speed, as his radio room broadcast a warning that the freighter had been ordered to stop by an unidentified merchantman. Aboard *Atlantis*, Rogge took up chase and ordered his starboard guns to fire into the fleeing British ship. The first salvo struck *Scientist*'s stern, starting several fires. When she failed to stop, a second salvo hitting below her bridge resulted in additional fires with grey smoke pouring from holes made by gun rounds. Rogge then held fire, while assessing the damage done his prey. Upon receiving a report that the other ship was continuing to broadcast an alarm, he gave the order to fire at will. Gunfire brought down *Scientist*'s radio aerial and following additional direct hits, Windsor finally ordered "all stop" and directed his 29-man crew to abandon.[17]

A demolition party from *Atlantis* boarded the freighter, and emplaced delayed-action explosives. Rogge had hoped to save the ship, but quickly determined that with fires raging aboard her, this was not possible. After the German party had left the ship's side by boat, the charges blew, but *Scientist* refused to sink. Gunfire directed at her waterline was similarly ineffective and, as *Scientist* continued to burn brightly, Rogge became concerned that the pyre might call attention to *Atlantis*. To prevent this possibility, he reluctantly expended one of his valuable torpedoes to send her to the seafloor.[18]

On the night of 10 May, *Atlantis* seeded the waters near Cape Agulhas at the tip of South Africa, with her entire inventory of ninety-two moored mines. This made the crew very happy, having feared that gunfire from an enemy might detonate them aboard ship. The raider was so close to shore during this operation, that sailors on deck could see the headlights of cars on the coastal road. At completion, *Atlantis* headed into the Indian Ocean in search of prey. There, she would sink or capture thirteen vessels by year's end. The mines laid by the raider off Cape Agulhas were discovered and cleared before they could do any damage to shipping in transit around the horn.[19]

SOUTH AFRICAN NAVY ESTABLISHED

At the outbreak of World War II, there was no South African Navy, only men of the Royal Naval Volunteer Reserve (SA) and former cadets of the South African training ship *General Botha*. This vessel, the former British cruiser HMS *Thames* commissioned in 1888, was used exclusively for the nautical training of British and South African boys, so that they could subsequently serve in ships of the British Empire. The prime minister of the Union of South Africa, Gen. Jan Christiaan Smuts, asked Rear Adm. Guy Waterhouse Hallifax to form a South African naval service. Hallifax, who was retired from the Royal Navy and living in South Africa, agreed, and on 15 January 1940, a new naval unit titled the Seaward Defence Force (SDF) was formed.[20]

Hallifax took charge of the seaward defenses at Cape Town, and arranged for the purchase/chartering of suitable whalers and trawlers of the South African harbors, for employment as minesweepers and anti-submarine patrol vessels. These ships were armed with available guns of the arsenal at Simon's Town. In a related action, the SDF installed a base in each South African harbor. A group of converted trawlers formed a fledgling minesweeping flotilla. These ships began work in May 1940 to clear the mines laid by *Atlantis*. The ex-steam trawler HMSAS *Aristea* had the honor of being the first to cut a moored mine in an effort that would last six months.[21]

Diagram 6-1

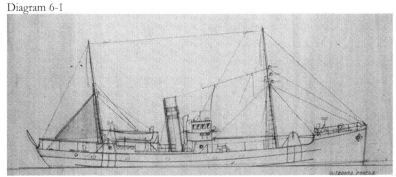

Drawing of *Aristea*
Aberdeen Built Ships, www.aberdeenships.com

Four 125-foot steam trawlers; built by Hall Russell, Aberdeen, Scotland, and requisitioned from Irvin & Johnson—a South African fishing company—comprised the *Bluff*-class minesweepers:

Ship	Commissioned	Decommissioned	Year Built	Disposition
HMSAS *Aristea*	28 Nov 1939	27 Dec 1944	1935	Returned to owners Dec 1944; wrecked 3 miles south of Hondekip Bay, South Africa, on 4 Jul 1945
HMSAS *Babiana*	18 Sep 1939	27 Dec 1944	1934	Returned to owners 1944; broken up in South Africa, 1967
HMSAS *Bluff*	12 Sep 1939	27 Dec 1944	1934	Returned to owners 1944; wrecked 30 Jan 1966
HMSAS *Crassula*	17 Oct 1939	25 Oct 1944	1935	Returned to owners 1946; scrapped 1968[22]

THIRD GERMAN AUXILIARY CRUISER PUTS TO SEA

On the night of 5 May 1940, the auxiliary cruiser *Widder*, under the command of Kapitän zur See Helmuth von Ruckteschell, sailed from Hamburg, Germany. She was a former freighter, the *Neumark*, and shared with *Orion* the same type propulsion system—second-hand boiler-turbine engines that would prove to be both very thirsty and unreliable. Operational experience soon showed that diesel engines, like those of *Atlantis*, were essential for raiders. *Orion* and *Widder* lost many a prize that simply outran them, and suffered oil-replenishment problems.[23]

Photo 6-5

German raider *Orion*
Raider Supplement to the Weekly Intelligence Report No. 64, of 30 May 1941, issued
by the Naval Intelligence Division, Navy Staff, Admiralty

THOR DEPARTS KIEL, GERMANY

On 6 June 1940, the auxiliary cruiser *Thor* stood out of Kiel, Germany,
on her first cruise. She was the former 3,862-ton freighter *Santa Cruz*,
now under the command of Kapitän zur See Otto Kähler with a crew
of 345 officers and men. Propelled by oil-fired steam turbines, she
had been launched in 1938 for intended service as a banana boat. Of
the raiders, only *Komet* was smaller. After sinking the 7,032-ton British
freighter *Delambre* in the South Atlantic on 7 July 1940, Kähler asked
her master, Capt. Pratt, why he had not used either his deck gun or his
wireless radio. *Delambre* had been en route to Freetown from Rio de
Janeiro when approached by the *Thor*. Pratt replied that he hadn't for
one moment considered that "such a midget" could possibly be a
German raider.[24]

Although only 400 feet in length, *Thor* was formidable, boasting
six 150mm guns, two 37mm and two 20mm anti-aircraft guns, and
four torpedo tubes in two twin-mounts. She carried no mines, nor E-
boats (the German equivalent of a U.S. Navy PT boat), but did have
an Arado Ar-196 floatplane for reconnaissance. Discussion of raider
operations in following chapters focuses on action in the South
Atlantic, where *Thor* would enjoy much success.[25]

Because the scope of this book does not allow for more than a
passing reference to these ships, I have provided, in the following
table, for interested readers, summary information about the total
number of ships sunk or captured by the auxiliary cruisers, along with
the ultimate fate of the raiders. The cost of their success would be
high—only two Hilfskreuzer returned safely to Germany from their
last war cruises. In deciphering the information in the Prizes Taken
column, the entry for *Atlantis*, for example, 16/6 denotes sixteen
vessels sunk and six captured by her.

German Navy's Auxiliary Cruisers (Commerce Raiders)

Auxiliary Cruiser	Commanding Officer	Prizes Taken	Fate of Raider
HK *Atlantis*	Fregattenkapitän (Capt.) Bernhard Rogge	16/6	Sunk in the South Atlantic on 22 November 1941 by 8-inch gunfire from HMS *Devonshire*
HK *Komet*	Kapitän zur See Robert Eyssen, Kapitän zur See Ulrich Brocksien	9/1	Torpedoed (sunk) by the British motor torpedo boat *MTB 236*, off Cherbourg, on 14 October 1942
HK *Kormoran*	Korvettenkapitän Theodor Detmers	11/1	Sunk off the northwest coast of Australia on 19 November 1941, by gunfire and a torpedo hit from the light cruiser HMAS *Sydney*
HK *Michel*	Kapitän zur See Helmuth von Ruckteschell, Kapitän zur See Günther Gumprich	17	Torpedoed (sunk) on 17 October 1943 by the submarine USS *Tarpon*, east of Yokohama, Japan
HK *Orion*	Kapitän zur See Kurt Weyher	11/1	Safely returned to Germany on 23 August 1941
HK *Pinguin*	Kapitän zur See Ernst-Felix Krüder	16/16	Sunk by gunfire from the cruiser HMS *Cornwall*, on 8 May 1941 near the entrance to the Persian Gulf
HK *Stier*	Fregattenkapitän Horst Gerlach	4	Sunk on 27 September 1942 by gunfire from the Liberty ship SS *Stephen Hopkins*
HK *Thor*	Kapitän zur See Otto Kähler, Kapitän zur See Günther Gumprich	18/4	Destroyed by fire while in port at Yokohama, on 30 October 1942, as a result of explosions aboard the German vessel *Uckermark*, moored alongside her
HK *Widder*	Kapitän zur See Helmuth von Ruckteschell	9/1	Safely returned to Germany on 31 October 1940
Total Prizes		111/30	

Some sources cite the quantity 142, in reference to total prizes sunk or captured. The 141 (111 + 30) in the table reflects *Michel* having been incorrectly credited with sinking the freighter *Reynolds* on 2 November 1942. The British ship was actually sunk on 31 October 1942 by *U-504*.[26]

PINGUIN SAILS IN JUNE 1940

Pinguin left Sörgulenfjord, a fjord in Norway, on 22 June bound for the Antarctic and Indian Ocean—the last of five auxiliary cruisers Germany would send to sea in 1940. Powered by two six-cylinder diesel engines, she had a top speed of 17 knots and a range of 30,000 miles at 12 knots. Her commanding officer, Kapitän zur See Ernst-Felix Krüder, had placed *Pinguin*—ex-freighter *Kandelfels*—into commission on 6 February 1940 with a wartime complement of 17 officers, 5 prize officers and 398 petty officers and men. She would be the first of the raiders destroyed, sunk less than a year later on 8 May 1941 by the British heavy cruiser HMS *Cornwall* (56) off East Africa. Her many personnel casualties included Krüder, who had amassed a brilliant record with thirty-two ships captured or sunk to his credit. He was the least-known of the Hilfskreuzer top commanders, and the only one to die in action.[27]

Photo 6-6

British heavy cruiser HMS *Cornwall* at Pearl Harbor, 11 August 1928.
U.S. Naval History and Heritage Command Photograph #NH 61359

After encountering HMS *Cornwall* (whose seaplane had located *Pinguin* from forty miles away) near the Seychelles—an archipelago in the Indian Ocean—*Pinguin* fled her pursuer at top speed for hours.

But the distance between the ships gradually lessened, and Krüder opened fire at 8,000 meters in the hopes that a lucky shot might score a fatal hit on the cruiser. His gamble nearly paid off; the first salvo temporarily knocked *Cornwall*'s steering gear out of action, but there was no opportunity for a second one. The cruiser quickly moved outside the range of *Pinguin*'s smaller guns and fired a salvo. A direct hit on the raider's mine storage hold caused a colossal explosion, ripping the ship to pieces.[28]

Within seconds *Pinguin* was gone, taking 341 Germans and 214 prisoners from vessels she had sunk or captured with her. *Cornwall* (Capt. Percival C. W. Manwaring, RN) was able to rescue 24 British and Indian prisoners and 60 German sailors.[29]

ALLIED INTELLIGENCE ON AUXILIARY CRUISERS

From May to September 9 [1940] the total confirmed losses from Raider activities amounted to 16 ships of 108,713 tons, while a further 10 ships of 50,604 tons are also presumed to have been sunk or captured. The largest losses have been incurred in the Atlantic, but recently the centre of activity appears to have shifted to the Indian Ocean. At the beginning of August there appear to have been five raiders operating, but the numbers are now harder to estimate....

The tactics of the raiders appear to have been carefully thought out and probably do not greatly vary. In some cases raiders have been sighted at a considerable distance in the evening and have then disappeared, approaching again during the night or on the following morning to make their attack. They usually seem to approach on a gradually converging course from ahead, so that identification is difficult, and it is impossible for their victims to bring their gun to bear. Fire is opened without warning, shrapnel and pom-poms [anti-aircraft fire] being employed to disable the W/T [wireless telegraphy] gear immediately and prevent the gun being manned. Shooting appears to be very accurate, though H.M.S. Alcantara reported that during the course of her action, it deteriorated when the raider was herself hit.

—Weekly Intelligence Report of 4 October 1940, issued by the
Naval Intelligence Division, Navy Staff, Admiralty for the
information of all officers in H.M. Navy.[30]

At the end of July, 1940, the British Admiralty created a new department charged with matters relating to German commerce raiders. The Admiralty also began assigning a letter designation to individual raiders as they were identified, because the German names of the ships were unknown. *Atlantis*, the first to sail, became Raider C, as the existence of *Orion* and *Komet* was already known.

Each of the raiders now had five identities, of which only four were known to the Allies:

- The original merchant vessel name
- A naval number prefaced HSK assigned during conversion
- A ship number prefaced Schiff—used for signal purposes
- Actual name as a raider—in most cases chosen by her captain
- A distinguishing letter assigned by the British Admiralty

The identities associated with individual raiders are summarized below, as well as their ship length, displacement, and propulsion type. In the table, MS (motor ship) signifies diesel engine, and SS (steam ship) steam turbine propulsion.

Ship Name	Former Name	Length (feet) Displ. (tons)	British ID	HSK No.	Schiff No.
HK *Atlantis*	MS *Goldenfels*	508/7,862	Raider C	II	16
HK *Komet*	MS *Ems*	377/3,287	Raider B	VII	45
HK *Kormoran*	MS *Steiermark*	538/8,736	Raider G	VIII	41
HK *Michel*	MS *Bielsko*	433/4,740	Raider H	IX	28
HK *Orion*	SS *Kurmark*	485/7,021	Raider A	I	36
HK *Pinguin*	MS *Kandelfels*	508/7,766	Raider F	V	33
HK *Stier*	MS *Cairo*	436/4,778	Raider I	VI	23
HK *Thor*	SS *Santa Cruz*	400/3,862	Raider E	IV	10
HK *Widder*	SS *Neumark*	498/7,852	Raider D	III	21[31]

THOR PREVAILS AGAINST HMS *ALCANTARA*

After leaving Germany on 6 June, *Thor* quickly captured or sank six merchant vessels between 1 and 17 July. These were the Belgian *Bruges*; Dutch *Kertosono* and *Tela*; and British *Delambre*, *Gracefield* and *Wendover*. The first to fall prey to the raider was the freighter *Kertosono* on 1 July, aboard which Kähler put a German prize crew and sent her to the French port of Lorient.[32]

Thor sank the other five ships, also freighters, after crossing the equator into the South Atlantic. Having dispatched six Allied ships in a seventeen-day period, Kähler now had 194 prisoners on board to feed. Aboard *Tela*, information was discovered regarding "Route 271," on which the raider's last four victims had been found. This intelligence led Kähler to decide to remain in the same area off the coast of Brazil for ten additional days. During this period, the ship's crew and prisoners settled into a peaceful routine, without any further successes.[33]

Photo 6-7

German Raider *Thor*
Weekly Intelligence Report No. 55, issued by the Naval Intelligence Division, Navy Staff, Admiralty for the information of all officers in H.M. Navy

This changed on 28 July when lookouts spotted a large ship approaching fast, the armed merchant cruiser HMS *Alcantara* (F88). *Thor* was now disguised as a non-existent ship, the 'Yugoslav' *Vir*, from the port of Split, en route to Brazil from Liverpool. Kähler had no desire to seek battle with the 22,209-ton former Royal Mail liner, armed with eight 6-inch and two 3-inch guns. *Alcantara*, commanded by retired Royal Navy captain James Geoffrey Penrose Ingham, was assigned to the South Atlantic Station.[34]

With *Alcantara* still fifteen miles distant, Kähler turned away and increased speed, arousing the suspicions of Ingham, who took up pursuit of the unknown vessel. After three hours, and with the range between the ships now eight miles, Kähler knew that his best hope of escaping the faster ship lay in inflicting sufficient damage on her to slow her down. Following a challenge from *Alcantara* requesting the identification of his ship, Kähler, by way of reply, slowed to fifteen knots, turned hard to starboard, ran up his battle ensign, crossed the cruiser's bow and opened fire with a full four-gun broadside, straddling her with the third salvo.[35]

As *Alcantara* turned, to bring her own full broadside to bear, the German gunners, with the afternoon sun directly behind them, had a decided advantage over their British counterparts, and immediately registered two hits on *Alcantara*, one between the bridge and the stack and one aft. A third salvo scored a hit at the waterline, causing engine-room flooding that significantly reduced the cruiser's speed. Additional hits knocked her fire-control system out of action. This condition further handicapped the British gunners in their targeting efforts, but did not diminish the merchant cruiser's superior fire power.[36]

Photo 6-8

RMS *Alcantara* off Rio de Janeiro between 1934 and 1939, before her conversion from mail liner to merchant cruiser.
Poster by Kenneth Shoesmith

Eight minutes into the action, realizing that he now had the advantage of speed over his adversary, Kähler altered course to move farther away from *Alcantara*, but immediately sustained two hits from the merchant cruiser's 6-inch guns, killing three of his crew. Maneuvering to present only *Thor*'s stern to the British guns, Kähler then resumed firing at *Alcantara*. However, with his adversary shielded by steam and smoke, and in recognition that one lucky hit could knock his ship out of action, Kähler broke off the engagement and left the area. Over the course of the four-and-a-half hour battle, *Thor* expended 284 rounds of 150mm ammunition.[37]

Alcantara, scarred, holed and listing, eventually managed to reach Rio de Janeiro. After burying his dead at sea, Kähler took *Thor* south into calm waters to the north of Tristan da Cunha on 30 July, to carry out repairs. Of the three encounters that would occur between Allied and Axis auxiliary cruisers in World War II, all would involve *Thor*.

The small ship had defeated HMS *Alcantara* in a gun battle, and would later do the same with HMS *Carnarvon Castle* (F25), and sink HMS *Voltaire*.[38]

ROYAL NAVY'S ARMED MERCHANT CRUISERS

The British armed merchant cruisers were passenger ships, acquired by the Admiralty when the war broke out, ranging in size from 6,000 to about 22,000 tons. Armament varied, but the standard was six 6-inch guns and some smaller 3-inch guns. Many of the ships were returned to the Ministry of War Transport relatively early in the war and served as troopships from 1941 onward.[39]

Of the fifty-four ships in the class, three—HMAS *Manoora* (F48), HMAS *Westralia* (F95), and HMNZS *Monowai* (F59)—were units of the Australian and New Zealand navies. A fourth one, *Antonia*, was requisitioned by the Admiralty to be an armed merchant cruiser, and was converted for this role, but then altered again for service as the repair ship HMS *Wayland* (F137). Of the Royal Navy's fifty armed merchant cruisers, eighteen would be lost during the war. Eleven were sunk by German submarines, three were lost to enemy aircraft, three to German ships—the pocket battleship *Admiral Scheer*, battlecruiser *Scharnhorst*, and raider *Thor*—and one due to a fire on board the merchant cruiser, unrelated to combat.[40]

Photo 6-9

Former British passenger ship *Cilicia*, which served as an armed merchant cruiser 1939-1944 and a troop transport 1944-1947, before returning to merchant service. U.S. Naval History and Heritage Command Photograph #NH 91272

MERCHANT CRUISERS IN THE SOUTH ATLANTIC

Twenty-eight merchant cruisers were assigned at various times during the war to the South Atlantic Station, Freetown Escort Force, or West Africa Command. With the Royal Navy stretched thin, particularly before the United States entered the war, the converted passenger liners performed critical patrol vessel and convoy escort ship duties.

Ship	South Atlantic Station	Freetown Escort Force	West Africa Command
Alcantara (F88)	Jan 40-Apr 43		
Arawa (F12)	Nov 40-Jul 41		
Asturias (F71)	Jul 40-Apr 43		May-Jul 43
Bulolo (F82)	Jan-Apr 40 Dec 41-Mar 42	May 40-Nov 41	
California (F55)	Nov 41-Mar 42		
Canton (F97)	Dec 41-Aug 42	Aug 40-Nov 41	
Carnarvon Castle (F25)	Oct 39-Apr 40 Jul 41-Apr 42 Jun 42-Apr 43	May 40-Jun 41	May-Nov 43
Carthage (F99)	Sep-Nov 42 Mar-Apr 43		
Cathay (F05)	Dec 41-Jan 42	Sep 40-Nov 41	
Cheshire (F18)	Nov 39-Apr 40 Dec 41-Apr 43	May-Nov 41	
Cilicia (F54)	Oct 39-Oct 40		May 43-Feb 44
Comorin (F49)	Jan-Apr 40 Feb 41	Mar-Apr 41	
Corfu (F86)	Sep 42-Apr 43	Jul 40-Sep 41	May 43-Feb 44
Derbyshire (F78)	Dec 41-Feb 42	May-Nov 41	
Dunnottar Castle (F34)	Oct 39-Apr 40 Dec 41-May 42	May 40-Nov 41	
Dunvegan Castle	Jan-Apr 40	May-Aug 40	
Esperance Bay (F67)	Dec 39-Apr 40	Nov 40-Aug 41	
Jervis Bay (F40)	Oct 39-Apr 40		
Maloja (F26)		Jul-Oct 40	
Montclare (F85)	Oct 39		
Mooltan (F75)	Oct 39-Apr 40 Jun-Jul 40	May 40 Aug 40-Jan 41	
Moreton Bay (F11)	Sep 40	Oct 40-Jun 41	
Patroclus	May-Jun 40		
Pretoria Castle (F61)	Nov 39-Apr 40 Jun-Jul 40 Jul 41-Jun 42	May 40 Aug 40-Jun 41	
Queen of Bermuda (F73)	Nov 39-Mar 42 Jul-Aug 42		
Ranpura (F93)	Mar-Apr 40		
Salopian (F94)	Oct 39-Jan 40		
Voltaire (F47)	Apr 41[41]		

A complete listing of all fifty of the Royal Navy's armed merchant cruisers is provided in Appendix C. In the interest of keeping the table to a reasonable length, associated information is limited to ships lost, and the identities of commanding officers of the ships assigned to the South Atlantic Station, Freetown Escort Force, or West Africa Command. For the merchant cruisers that served elsewhere in the world, only the name of the ships' first commanding officer is given. With apology to British readers, titles associated with being knighted and references to awards of valor have also been omitted for brevity's sake. For example, Capt. (retired) Sir John Meynell Alleyne, DSO, DSC, RN—one of the commanding officers of *Asturias* (F71)—is cited as Capt. (retired) John Meynell Alleyne, RN.[42]

RENDEZVOUS WITH THE *REKUM* AND *RIO GRANDE*

All the raiders are very well equipped and capable of remaining at sea for at least twelve months. With the possible exception of the Pacific, they do not appear to rely on shore bases, though they probably have definite areas at sea for rendezvous with supply ships and for resting and refits. It is also possible that they make use of islands in the Southern Indian Ocean and of anchorages on the South American coast for more extended self-refits and for a run ashore for their crews.

The lower holds, deep tanks and double bottoms enable them to carry large quantities of fuel, while most, if not all, of them operate in company with tankers, which are relieved from time to time as necessary. An additional but valuable source of supply is provided by their prizes. On the whole, fuel does not present the same problem as it did in the last war, but there have been several reports which show that raiders have run dangerously short of provisions.

Fueling is carried out at sea by means of a length of flexible hose stopped by canvas beckets to a seven-inch manila [rope], the raider usually towing the tanker at slow speed. The system does not appear always to have worked satisfactorily and is in any case a slow one. In consequence raiders take every opportunity of topping up and keeping their tanks full.

—Raider Supplement to the Weekly Intelligence Report No. 64, of 30 May 1941, issued by the Naval Intelligence Division, Navy Staff, Admiralty

After burying his dead (following the battle with HMS *Alcantara*), making repairs, changing *Thor*'s disguise and cleaning her boilers, Kähler rendezvoused with the supply ship *Rekum* on 25 August 1940 and then headed back into Brazilian waters. On 26 September, he sank the Norwegian whale-oil tanker *Kosmos*, en route to Curacao (a small South American island and part of the Netherlands Antilles, located north of Venezuela) from the port city of Walvis Bay (on the bay of this same name) in Namibia, South Africa. The tanker had been located by *Thor*'s seaplane which was used as often as weather permitted.[43]

Two weeks later, while operating from within the Pan-American Security Zone, the raider sank the British Royal Mail refrigeration ship *Natia*, bound for South America. This zone had been established in October 1939 at U.S. behest by the Declaration of Panama, which declared that signatories (representing nations of North and South America), would not tolerate belligerent acts within the zone, which extended between 300 and 1,000 nautical miles offshore.[44]

The survivors from these ships brought the total number of prisoners now aboard *Thor* to 368. With the prisoners out-numbering his crew, plus an urgent need to refuel, and the continuing failure of boiler gauges, Kähler requested a rendezvous with a second supply ship. On 9 November, he transferred all but four of his prisoners to the *Rio Grande*, which had been held in Rio de Janeiro by Brazilian authorities, but had broken out. The crew of *Rio Grande* had changed the ship's name on the hull to that of her sister ship *Belgrano*, and made other modifications to resemble the other vessel, which was well known to the Allies, but at that time was in a German port.[45]

All the prisoners, except for the masters of four British ships, were transferred to *Rio Grande*. These individuals were retained aboard *Thor*, lest they provide leadership necessary to spur the others to try to take over the lightly-armed supply ship. On 16 November, the raider headed south, while "Belgrano" set a course for France, reaching Bordeaux on 13 December 1940.[46]

THOR BESTS HMS *CARNARVON CASTLE*

CARNARVON CASTLE *was in action at 0800 today with a merchant ship raider using complete [gun] director system which escaped behind smoke at 0910 and was last seen in position 31° 0' S., 43° 15' W (500 miles South of Rio de Janeiro) steering 40° at 19 knots.*

CARNARVON CASTLE *is proceeding to Montevideo to make good extensive damage. She has fired 500 rounds and estimates at least 10 hits on the enemy and that the raider, which has two serious fires, was considerably damaged.*

CARNARVON CASTLE *was hit 23 times and will have to undergo dockyard refit before being fit for further service.*

—Admiralty War Diary entry for 5 December 1940.
The estimate of damage to *Thor* was incorrect.

This welcome period of normality ended shortly after dawn on 5 December. That morning, as *Thor* operated southeast of Rio de Janeiro, one of the raider's lookouts spotted a large and powerful ship emerging from a bank of mist four miles away. Kähler recognized her as the *Carnarvon Castle*, the fastest liner on the pre-war South Africa route. The liner had been at Cape Town at the outbreak of the war, and was requisitioned by the Royal Navy on 8 September 1939. Following conversion at the naval base at Simon's Town—which included being fitted with eight 6-inch, and two 3-inch guns—she was commissioned HMS *Carnarvon Castle* on 9 October 1939.[47]

Hoping to avoid the merchant cruiser, Kähler altered course, and for a time outpaced the British ship. With three of *Thor's* six 150mm guns facing aft, Kähler had decided to force *Carnarvon Castle* into a stern chase. By this means, he could minimize his ship's cross section and, if necessary, take the cruiser under fire with half his main battery. The latter course of action loomed closer, when the ponderous yet faster former liner got up to full speed.[48]

Drawing nearer, *Carnarvon Castle* signaled the fleeing raider to identify herself, and to stop engines. When neither action occurred, Capt. (retired) Henry Noel Marryat Hardy, RN ordered his gun crews to fire a warning shot over the unknown ship's bow. Unable to evade, Kähler ran up the German battle ensign, abandoned *Thor's* disguise by exposing his guns, and returned fire. As the German gunners found their target, Kähler changed course to turn the chase into a circular fight against the much less nimble *Carnarvon Castle*—and by this means, to engage her with a full broadside.[49]

While laying down smoke to shield his ship from the view of the British gun crews, Kähler fired two torpedoes at the cruiser. Both missed, but it hardly mattered as *Thor* circled and fired without pause, pounding *Carnarvon Castle*. But then the guns of the raider—obsolete even before World War I—began to malfunction as a result of the sustained action. Gun recoil systems overheated and gun barrels went out of train. Suddenly, as the possible ramifications of this catastrophe became evident aboard *Thor*, the battered merchant cruiser ceased firing, turned and withdrew at top speed.[50]

Thor emerged from the lengthy battle, in which she fired 593 rounds of 150mm ammunition, undamaged, and with no casualties. *Carnarvon Castle* limped into Montevideo harbor on 7 December, with a ten-degree list. She had taken twenty-three hits, suffered four dead, and thirty-two wounded as a result of battle damage. Repairs to her riddled hull were made using plates salvaged from the wreck of the pocket-battleship *Admiral Graf Spee*.[51]

Thor rendezvoused with the 5,947-ton supply ship *Eurofeld* on 21 December and refueled from her the following day. Four days later the raider met up with the *Admiral Scheer* at point "Andalusia"—a rendezvous position in the South Atlantic, between Trinidad and Tristan da Cunha, at which raiders and U-boats could meet their supply vessels. There was some discussion between Kähler and Kapitän zur See Theodor Krancke about the possibility of the two ships hunting together, but the idea was rejected due to the vast difference in their respective speeds, and Kähler's fear that *Thor* would simply become a tender and prison-ship for the heavy cruiser.[52]

Photo 6-10

German heavy cruiser *Admiral Scheer* at sea in mid- to late-1930s.
U.S. Naval History and Heritage Command Photograph #NH 45566

TALLY FOR GERMAN AUXILIARY CRUISERS

Merchant Raider Badge given for acts of valor in the face of the enemy. Some 1,500 were awarded during the war. A version with diamonds was given only once, to Fregattenkapitän Bernhard Rogge, the commanding officer of the raider *Atlantis*.[53]

The year 1940 ended with the five raiders that had sailed from Germany—*Atlantis*, *Orion*, *Pinguin*, *Thor*, and *Widder*—having achieved great success on their maiden cruises. In attacks on Allied merchant shipping, the converted freighters collectively sank forty-three vessels and captured eight. Additionally, *Thor* bested HMS *Alcantara* and HMS *Carnarvon Castle* in battles at sea. There were no ship losses resulting from these actions, but much damage was done to the two British merchant cruisers (ex-ocean liners).

These victories by German auxiliary cruisers helped offset the gains made by Allied navies in blockading Axis merchantmen in port, and sweeping many of those that ventured from harbor sanctuaries, from the seas.

War in the Atlantic in Early 1941

In the longest campaign of the war, the British merchant fleet, with its naval escorts, struggled to bring food, fuel, equipment and raw materials from America and elsewhere across the Atlantic, while Germany mobilized U-boats, battleships, aircraft and mines against them in an attempt to sever Britain's supply lines.

—Reference to the Battle of the Atlantic, the most significant and crucial conflict in which merchant seamen were involved in World War II.[1]

DORSETSHIRE CAPTURES VICHY FRENCH VESSEL

On 8 January 1941, HMS *Dorsetshire* left Freetown with the aircraft carrier HMS *Formidable* (67) and sister ship, heavy cruiser HMS *Norfolk* (78), on an interception patrol and to cover the passage of Convoy WS5A to the Cape of Good Hope. On the 15th, as the latter ships continued to provide convoy coverage, *Dorsetshire* began a patrol. Nearly two weeks into it, she intercepted the Vichy French freighter *Mendoza* on 21 January and put a prize crew aboard which sailed the captured ship to Freetown.[2]

Dorsetshire resumed her patrol until the 25th, when she called at St. Helena Island, where a tanker was stationed to support ships operating in the South Atlantic. The heavy cruiser returned to Freetown on 29 January, where her prize crew rejoined the ship.[3]

THE WS ("WINSTON'S SPECIAL") CONVOYS

Convoy WS5A had already achieved some notoriety before arriving at Freetown the first week in January. The Convoy Code WS meant "United Kingdom to Middle East to India." However, many people believed that these initials, which bore no relationship to convoy origin or destination(s) as convoy codes usually do, was a shorthand for "Winston's Special" as the first convoy was organized on the explicit orders of the Prime Minister. The ships of the convoy's slow section had sailed from Liverpool, England, and the Firth of Clyde (the largest and deepest coastal waters in the British Isles, sheltered from the

Atlantic by the Kintyre peninsula) on 18 December 1940, followed by the fast section from these same departure points the following day.[4]

The objective of the convoy was to carry troops and their equipment to the Suez for British general Archibald Percival Wavell's Desert Army, and to deliver supplies to Malta and Greece via the Straits of Gibraltar. Once formed on 23 December, twenty-six ships comprised the convoy with the commodore (retired Rear Adm. Cecil Nugent Reyne, RN) embarked in *Tamaroa*—a passenger liner converted for use as a troopship. The vice commodore was aboard the minelayer *Atreus*, a former steam cargo vessel launched by Scotts Greenock, Yard No 432, Liverpool, on 27 January 1911.[5]

Convoy WS5A: Great Britain to Straits of Gibraltar/Middle East (Escorts listed are those attached on 24 December 1940)

Slow Section	Slow Section	Fast Section	Escort Ships
Anselm	*Empire Trooper*	*Barrister*	HMS *Clematis* (K36)
Arabistan	*Ernebank*	*Clan Cumming*	HMS *Cyclamen* (K83)
HMS *Atreus* (M.44)	*Leopoldville*	*Clan MacDonald*	HMS *Geranium* (K16)
Bhutan	*Menelaus*	*Empire Song*	HMS *Jonquil* (K68)
City of Canterbury	*Neuralia*	*Essex*	HMS *Berwick* (65)
City of Derby	*Rangitiki*	*Northern Prince*	HMS *Bonaventure* (31)
City of London	*Settler*	*Orbita*	HMS *Dunedin* (D93)
Costa Rica	*Stentor*		HMS *Argus* (I49)
Delane	*Tamaro*		HMS *Furious* (47)[6]
Elisabethville			

Convoy escort was provided by the corvettes *Clematis*, *Cyclamen*, *Geranium* and *Jonquil*, which were on passage to Freetown themselves, and by the destroyers *Bath* (I17) and *St. Albans* (I15) from 18-20 December, and *Harvester* (H19), *Highlander* (H44) and *Vesper* (D55) from the 19th thought the 21st. Light cruiser *Bonaventure* served as an ocean escort. Two aircraft carriers, *Argus* and *Furious*, ferrying crated aircraft for delivery to Egypt, joined the convoy at sea.[7]

Six other destroyers: *Kelvin* (F37) and *Kipling* (F91), the Canadian HMCS *Ottawa* (H60) and HMCS *St. Laurent* (H83), Polish ORP *Piorun* (G65), and Free French FR *Le Triomphant* provided anti-submarine coverage from 19-22 December, while the light cruiser *Naiad* (93) functioned as heavy escort. Following the arrival and departure of various ships on Christmas Eve, the convoy escort consisted of three cruisers—*Berwick*, *Bonaventure* and *Dunedin*—and the four corvettes *Clematis*, *Cyclamen*, *Geranium*, and *Jonquil*.[8]

CRUISER *ADMIRAL HIPPER* ATTACKS CONVOY

25 Dec, convoy dispersed. 28 Dec convoy re-assembled.

—Understated report by Rear Adm. Cecil N. Reyne, RN,
commander Convoy WS5A, regarding an attack by
the German heavy cruiser *Admiral Hipper.*[9]

The *Admiral Hipper*—whose armament included eight 8-inch, twelve 4.1-inch, and twelve 1.5-inch guns, and torpedoes—found WS5A the night of 24 December. Kommodore Wilhelm Meisel aboard the heavy cruiser initially believed it a normal trade convoy. Not wishing to attack in the dark when destroyers with torpedoes might be present, he decided to shadow the convoy until daybreak. Closing from the west in early morning on Christmas Day, he ordered an immediate attack on the convoy to take advantage of the prevailing mist and rain. While the severely restricted visibility helped to prevent alerting his prey— the troopships in convoy—it also kept Meisel from realizing they were so heavily escorted.[10]

Photo 7-1

German heavy cruiser *Admiral Hipper* at sea in 1941
U.S. Naval History and Heritage Command Photograph #NH 81102

At 0808, *Admiral Hipper* fired on the *Empire Trooper*—killing sixteen soldiers—and the freighter *Arabistan*. (*Empire Trooper* was the ex-German 13,942-ton passenger ship *Cap Norte* built in 1922 at Hamburg. While attempting to return safely to Germany from South America in the early days of the war, she had been captured in the North Atlantic on 9 October 1939 by the light cruiser HMS *Belfast*. *Cap Norte* was subsequently renamed *Empire Trooper*, and served Britain throughout the rest of the war.) As the ships of the convoy scattered, per orders of Commodore Reyne, the escort ships searched for the enemy in the gloom. A half hour after *Admiral Hipper* had initiated the attack on the convoy, the heavy cruiser *Berwick* sighted the German heavy cruiser at 0842 and opened fire with her 8-inch guns.[11]

Photo 7-2

British heavy cruiser HMS *Berwick* (65) at Shanghai, China, in 1932.
U.S. Naval History and Heritage Command Photograph #NH 52100

Berwick (Capt. Guy Langton Warren, RN) had reported at 0642, a capital ship of the *Deutschland*-class bearing 290°T from her at a range of twelve miles, but had lost sight of her in the poor conditions; visibility was estimated to be only one-half mile. In the ensuing short action with the *Admiral Hipper*, *Berwick* received the brunt of damage. She was hit four times by gunfire, including a direct hit on her forward turret which killed five Royal Marines. The damage to the ship would require repairs lasting until June 1941. An entry in the Admiralty War Diary for 25 December 1940 briefly addressed her post-battle condition:

BERWICK claimed one hit certain on the enemy abaft the funnel, possibly more. Her own damage included "X" turret out of action, a hit below the water line on starboard side, a shell through forward boiler room, one 4-inch gun out of action, and the midship funnel holed. Four marines were killed and one dangerously wounded.[12]

At 0915, *Berwick* sent a report identifying the enemy as a cruiser carrying 8-inch guns, and an hour later an update that the cruiser had disappeared to the west in thick weather. The position of the convoy was then 660 miles west of Cape Finisterre, Spain. *Admiral Hipper*, upon sighting the elderly cruiser *Dunedin*, mistaking her for a destroyer and fearing a torpedo attack, had broken off the action and retired into the Atlantic mist. She eventually reached the safety of Brest, in northwestern France.[13]

HMS *Cyclamen* escorted *Empire Trooper* to Ponta Delgada, Azores, where they arrived on 28 December. The other three corvettes concentrated on reassembling the convoy. *Bonaventure*, while going to the aid of the damaged *Arabistan*, intercepted and sank the German passenger/cargo ship *Baden* about 325 nautical miles northeast of Ponta Delgada. A boarding/capture of the ship was not possible due to the bad weather, and Capt. Henry Jack Egerton, RN, dispatched her with a torpedo. The *Arabistan* would not survive the war. She was sunk by the German auxiliary cruiser *Michel* on 7 August 1942, south of St. Helena with 6-inch shells and machine gun fire from pointblank range. Twenty-three British crewmen and forty-three Indian Lascars were killed; one survivor, Chief Engineer Edwin Goodridge, was picked up the next morning clinging to wreckage.[14]

The term Lascar referred to a sailor or militiaman from South Asia, the Arab world, or other areas to the east of the Cape of Good Hope, who were employed on European ships from the 16th century until the middle of the 20th century. The word derived from al-askar, Arabic for a guard or soldier.

Clan Cumming, *Clan MacDonald*, *Empire Song*, *Essex*, and *Northern Prince* made their way to Gibraltar, their initial destination. *Empire Trooper*, escorted by the four corvettes and light cruiser *Kenya* (14)—which had been ordered to the area—later called at Gibraltar to disembark her troops, and to effect temporary repairs. Thereafter, she retired to the UK for a lengthy refit. *Leopoldville* proceeded independently, and the remainder of the convoy, once formed again, made its way to Freetown, arriving on 6 January 1941. WS5A was the only WS convoy to be located and attacked by a large German warship during the war, fortunately with only minimal damage.[15]

NETWORK OF SUPPLY SHIPS AND TANKERS

German raiders were able to survive for months in the open seas, while preying on allied merchant ships operating alone, not in convoy. Since Germany did not have any overseas bases, extended operations required a network of supply ships and tankers. An exception was raiders operating in Nipponese waters, where Japanese bases and facilities were used extensively.[16]

Within Germany's naval intelligence was a shadowy special unit called the Etappendienst, established in 1897 following Germany's seizure of Tsingtao to provide the Imperial German Navy with commercial-intelligence in peacetime. Its most important mission in wartime was to provide the German fleet with fuel and supplies. The Etappendienst was also tasked with the responsibility of ensuring that Germany received the raw materials it needed for its war effort, and it cooperated with the German diplomatic corps to establish and run POW escape routes in China and the United States.[17]

To accomplish these missions, the Etappendienst established districts throughout the world, each centered on a major port and controlled by a naval officer assigned to the embassy or consulate in that port. These districts (Etappes) often had sub-cells within their regions that drew on the combined resources of the German diplomatic corps, the international German business community, and German sympathizers. The result was a complex, international network of part-time agents who were sympathetic to Germany, together with dummy companies and bank accounts located in virtually every country in the world.[18]

In addition to the use of former merchant tankers, five specialized supply ships, the *Dithmarschen*-class, were part of the Etappendienst wartime supply system that provided stores, fuel, and spare parts to Germany's raiders, both warships and auxiliary cruisers. The Etappe districts related to the subject of this book were the Etappe Nordamerika (New York City), Etappe Brasilien (Rio de Janiero), Etappe Westindian (West Indies), and Etappe Mittel-und Südamerika that included Etappe Peru and Etappe Valpariso.[19]

Nine *Dithmarschen*-class supply ships were ordered, but only five— *Dithmarschen*, *Ermland*, *Franken*, *Westerward* (*Nordmark*), and *Altmark* (*Uckermark*)—were commissioned. These vessels combined the roles of tanker, repair ship, ammunition ship and dry cargo ship. They were able to supply warships with fuel, ammunition, supplies and spare parts, and were equipped with towing gear to aid damaged vessels. The capacity of the *Dithmarschen*-class replenishment oilers was 7,933 tons fuel, 972 tons ammo, 790 tons supplies and 100 tons spare parts. Other ship characteristics included:

- Length: 584 feet
- Displacement: 8,962 tons
- Propulsion: four MAN nine-cylinder diesel engines, two shafts, 22,000 shaft horsepower
- Speed: 23 knots
- Range: 12,500 nautical miles at 15 knots
- Complement: 284[20]

The most famous of these ships was the *Altmark*, which provided support for the *Admiral Graf Spee*—before and after her scuttling—and was involved in the "Altmark Incident." *Altmark* was subsequently renamed *Uckermark* during the war. Similarly, the *Nordmark* originally went to sea as *Westerward*.[21]

SUPPLY SHIP SUPPORT OF RAIDERS

Between 26 December 1940 and 7 January 1941, the raider *Thor* met up with the pocket-battleship *Admiral Scheer* (Kapitän zur See Theodor Krancke), the 5,947-ton supply ship *Eurofeld*, (Kapitän Blessin), the tanker *Nordmark*, and raider *Pinguin*'s prize ship—the 8,998-ton former Norwegian tanker *Storstad*. *Thor* transferred a prize crew to the *Scheer*, for use aboard a fleet of Norwegian whalers captured by *Pinguin*, and transferred her prisoners from Allied ships to the *Nordmark*.[22]

Photo 7-3

Replenishment fleet tanker USS *Conecuh* (AOR-110) in 1953-1956. She was originally the German navy replenishment oiler *Dithmarschen*, built in 1938. U.S. National Archives Photograph #80-G-678092

USE OF *STORSTAD* AS A GERMAN MINELAYER

Pinguin had captured the motor-tanker *Storstad* off Christmas Island—a 52-square-mile flat summit of volcanic origin located about 300 miles south of Java in the Indian Ocean—on 7 October 1940. The island had been so named by William Mynors, the captain of the British East India Company ship *Royal Mary*. Sailing by it on 25 December 1643, he named it after the day of its discovery. *Pinguin*'s commanding officer, Ernst-Felix Krüder, had previously conceived of a plan to lay mines in six Australian and Tasmanian shipping channels, but believed he would need two ships to accomplish this task. *Storstad*, which had been en route to Melbourne from British North Borneo, appeared to be quite suitable for use as an auxiliary minelayer.[23]

Krüder transferred some of his crew to her, who took *Storstad* to a remote area between Java and northwest Australia. There, they converted her into an auxiliary minelayer by transforming her after accommodation space into a mine deck, complete with launching rails. One hundred ten mines were transferred from *Pinguin* to her, while 1,200 tons of the *Storstad*'s diesel oil went in the opposite direction.[24]

The minelayer *Passat* (ex-*Storstad*) departed on 12 October under the command of Kapitänleutnant Erich Warning, bound for Banks Strait separating Tasmania from the southeastern Australian mainland. All shipping to the busy ports of Melbourne, Stanley, Burnie, Devonport, Bell Bay and Launceston passed through this sea strait. Aboard *Passat* were three other German officers, eight petty officers and nineteen ratings, plus five members of her original Norwegian crew who volunteered to work in the engine room. *Pinguin* headed for the ports of Sydney, Newcastle and Hobart, and later laid mines off Adelaide as well. The two ships planted their deadly minefields off the unprotected ports with ease, with plans to meet up 700 miles west of Perth on 15 November.[25]

Following this operation, *Passat*'s name was changed back to *Storstad*, and she was used as a supply ship, until sent with a prize crew to try to run the Allied blockade and make it to Bordeaux, France. She was successful and arrived in the Gironde estuary, located down the Garonne River from Bordeaux, on 4 February 1942.[26]

CAPTURE OF A NORWEGIAN WHALING FLEET

Late the preceding year, the German Seekriegsleitung (Naval Warfare Command) had signaled *Pinguin* on 17 December 1940 that a Norwegian whaling fleet was in the Antarctic herding grounds around South Georgia. This South Atlantic island, located south of the Antarctic Convergence (a transition region where cold, northward-flowing Antarctic waters meet the relatively warmer waters of the sub-Antarctic) had been named by Captain James Cook in 1775. Landing there, he claimed the territory for Great Britain, and named it "the Isle of Georgia" in honor of King George III. The signal identified the Norwegian factory ships as the *Harpon, Ole Wegger, Pelagos, Thorshammer* and *Vestfjord*, all under British charter.[27]

On Christmas Eve, Ernst-Felix Krüder, the *Pinguin*'s commanding officer, intercepted radio chatter between the *Ole Wegger* and *Pelagos*, and learned that the whalers were awaiting a supply ship; that *Pelagos* was short of fuel; and that *Ole Wegger*'s whale oil tanks were filled to capacity. Upon its arrival, the Norwegian whale-oil tanker *Solglimt* first attended to *Thorshammer*, operating 400 miles to the southwest. She was then to meet up with *Ole Wegger*, and take off some of her whale oil, before refueling *Pelagos* further to the east. *Solglimt* carried supplies for the whaling fleet as well as guns that were to be installed on the factories, though nobody really expected there would be a need for them in this remote area.[28]

Photo 7-4

Norwegian whale factory ship *Thorshammer* at San Francisco, California, about 1943. U.S. Naval History and Heritage Command Photograph #NH 89867

Ernst-Felix Krüder realized the *Solglimt* was armed, and he decided to not attack until she and *Ole Wegger* were moored together for the transfer of whale oil. Neither of the ships would be able to maneuver and the presence of the factory ship would prevent *Solglimt* from using her guns. In early morning darkness on 13 January 1941, the supply ship made up alongside *Ole Wegger*. As *Pinguin* approached them from the west late that night, the lights from the factories and the contours of some of the catchers were clearly visible at 2320.[29]

A heavy snow then set in, forcing the raider to proceed more slowly, but allowing for a completely unseen approach. *Pinguin* reached the Norwegian ships at 0015 on 14 January. Five minutes later her floodlights illuminated the *Solglimt* and *Ole Wegger*. The raider slipped alongside *Solglimt*, ordered the two ships to maintain radio silence, and launched two prize crews in boats. Both ships were quickly captured. *Pinguin* then dispatched a motorboat to round up the whalers. Three managed to escape, but the remaining vessels—*Torlyn, Pol VIII, Pol IX* and *Pol X*—were seized without incident. The Norwegian captains were told to continue with their whaling and that Germany would pay them for their work.[30]

Following this rapid success—the taking of a whaling supply ship, whaling factory ship, and four whalers—*Pinguin* sailed in the opposite direction from that of the remaining factory ship. Once out of sight, she reversed course and approached the brightly lit vessel in dense fog. After closing to within 200 meters, the raider signaled warnings and dispatched prize crews. The factory ship *Pelagos* was captured within minutes. Her captain was instructed to recall his catchers, and the seven whalers, *Star XIV, XIX, XX, XXI, XXII, XXIII* and *XXIV*, were taken as well.[31]

The operation was the single most successful performance by a German auxiliary cruiser during World War II. A supply ship, two factory ships, eleven whalers, whale oil with a value of over four million U.S. dollars, and 10,000 tons of fuel oil were captured—all without a single shot being fired and without any resultant casualties. The Norwegian crews continued to work as if nothing had happened and made no effort to resist.[32]

Pinguin set off on an easterly course, with the fourteen ships in trail astern of her. She did not have enough crewmen to put a prize crew aboard each one. *Solglimt* and *Pelagos*, under German control, departed on 25 January for France. *Pelagos* reached Bordeaux on 11 March and *Solglimt* five days later. Seekriegsleitung directed Krüder to bring the *Ole Wegger* and all eleven catchers to Point Andalusia, located north of the island of Tristan da Cunha in the mid-South Atlantic. There *Pinguin* was to meet the tanker *Nordmark*, bringing prize crews for the remaining whalers.[33]

Pinguin rendezvoused with the *Nordmark* on 15 February, which had in tow the refrigerator ship *Herzogin* (former British ship *Duquesa* captured by the *Admiral Scheer* in December). Three days later, the supply ship *Alstertor* arrived on the 18th with a fresh supply of torpedoes, mines, a crated Arado Ar-196 seaplane, and mail for *Pinguin*'s crew. The ships then proceeded with the whaling fleet to the Kerguelen Islands, where replenishment could take place in safety. Also known as the Desolation Islands, this island group in the

Southern Indian Ocean lay over 2,000 miles southeast of the southern tip of Africa in one of the most isolated areas on Earth.[34]

Pinguin was restocked with 360,000 eggs, 47 sides of beef, 410 sheep and 17 sacks of oxtails from *Herzogin* before the former British ship, depleted of fuel and supplies, was sunk with scuttling charges. The whaling factory ship *Ole Wegger* and ten of the eleven catchers departed for Europe, manned with skeleton crews of armed Germans. The newest whaler, *Pol IX*, was retained as an auxiliary minelayer and renamed *Adjutant*. Two of the catchers, the *Star XIX* and *Star XXIV*, were intercepted by the British sloop HMS *Scarborough* (L25) off Cape Finisterre on the west coast of Spain, on 13 March. The German crews scuttled the ships and were picked up by the British. The *Ole Wegger* and eight remaining whalers arrived at Bordeaux on 20 March.[35]

8

Ingram's Task Force Three

The President of the United States of America, in the name of Congress, takes pleasure in presenting the Medal of Honor to Lieutenant, Junior Grade, Jonas Howard Ingram, United States Navy, for distinguished conduct in battle during the engagement of Vera Cruz, Mexico, 22 April 1914. During the second day's fighting the service performed by Lieutenant, Junior Grade, Ingram was eminent and conspicuous. He was conspicuous for skillful and efficient handling of the artillery and machineguns of the Arkansas Battalion, for which he was specially commended in reports.

—Citation for Medal of Honor awarded to Lt. (jg) Jonas H. Ingram, for heroic actions, in which, as an officer aboard the battleship *Arkansas* (BB-33), he landed at Vera Cruz, Mexico, with the Arkansas landing force.[1]

In early 1941, as British naval forces continued to battle those of Germany at sea, the U.S. Navy increased its presence in the Caribbean, and within months, in the South Atlantic, as well. On 11 January 1941, Rear Adm. Jonas H. Ingram, USN, hoisted his flag in the light cruiser *Memphis* (CL-13) at Guantanamo Bay, Cuba. This action signified his assuming command of Cruiser Division Two, with the associated designation, commander Task Force Three, and additional duty as the commander of the Caribbean Patrol.[2]

The patrol had been conducted for months only by the ships of Destroyer Squadron 2, under Capt. Walden L. Ainsworth embarked in the destroyer *Moffett* (DD-362), and by Patrol Squadron VP-51, twelve PBY Catalina seaplanes under Comdr. W. J. Mullins, based at San Juan, Puerto Rico. In addition to beefing up ship patrols through the assignment of Cruiser Division Two, thirty-six seaplanes operating from both San Juan and Guantanamo Bay were now assigned to reconnoiter Caribbean waters from Key West, Florida, to Trinidad. As part of this effort, patrol aircraft also maintained surveillance on Vichy French naval forces based at Martinique Island, a French territory in the West Indies.[3]

Cruiser Division Two consisted of the *Memphis*, *Cincinnati* and *Milwaukee*, all light cruisers, to which the *Omaha* was later added. Ingram soon saw the advisability of turning over the Caribbean Patrol to the commandant of the Tenth Naval District at San Juan, Puerto Rico, Rear Adm. Raymond A. Spruance. He suggested this action to Adm. Ernest J. King, commander-in-chief Atlantic Fleet, who readily accepted it. Ingram's release from this responsibility gave him a freer hand for operations in the South Atlantic, to which he was soon assigned.[4]

Photo 8-1

Light cruiser *Memphis* (CL-13), looking aft from the bow, circa 1941-1942.
U.S. Navy Photograph #80-G-10535, now in the collection of the National Archives

Ingram visited King in the United States in March 1941. At a meeting on the 24th, Ingram received orders to take Cruiser Division Two to the South Atlantic, on Neutrality patrol. The division was to base at San Juan and Guantanamo, and to utilize Recife and Bahia in Brazil as replenishing ports. The area for patrol included the triangle formed by Trinidad, the Cape Verde Islands 350 miles off the northwest coast of Africa, and the hump of Brazil. The old fleet oiler *Patoka* (AO-9), originally commissioned on 13 October 1919, would serve as tanker, tender and supply vessel for the force.[5]

Admirals King and Ingram both had doubts concerning Brazil and the reception American warships would receive there. King stressed to Ingram that he would have to use initiative and shift for himself in the South Atlantic. The only arrangement made in advance was with the oil companies that would provide his warships with fuel. Ingram commented that so long as there were ships coming out of the Argentine (Argentina) with plenty of foodstuffs, his crews would never starve. King replied that he had always known that Ingram was a pirate.[6]

MAIDEN U.S. NAVY SOUTH ATLANTIC PATROL

Memphis and *Cincinnati* were the only members of Cruiser Division Two immediately available, but since it was deemed necessary to get a patrol into the assigned area at once, Ingram left Newport, Rhode Island, with these ships on 25 April 1941. On 4 May, they reached a point designated as "A"—latitude 20°N, longitude 30°W—located a little to the northwest of the Cape Verde Islands. The two cruisers then steamed due south to Point "B" which, located on the equator at Longitude 30° west, was off the São Paulo (St. Paul) Rocks belonging to Brazil. They reached this group of small islets and rocks on 8 May. Two days later, the ships entered Recife, a port city in northeast Brazil where the confluence of the Beberibe and Capibaribe Rivers flow into the Atlantic.[7]

Ingram would depart Recife with his two ships the following day, after but a single night in port; but he and other officers were able to learn much about the port during their brief visit. Recife was the third largest city in Brazil, with a population estimated at 400,000. The harbor, though protected by a fine breakwater, was small and narrow, requiring both a pilot and tug for mooring and unmooring. The pier space was good, though restricted to vessels with drafts of twenty-five feet or less. Ships could not enter the harbor at night and, unless moored with their bows toward the entrance, had to leave on a flood tide. Warehouses were available for stores of all kinds, but only limited fresh provisions could be had, chiefly fruits, and there were no dry provisions. On a much brighter note, the fueling facilities proved excellent.[8]

The Americans observed, with considerable interest, seven Italian merchant ships, which had been moored inside the harbor with crews aboard since June 1940, to avoid the possibility of capture at sea. One vessel had a cargo of coal, another grain. The other five were empty.[9]

Photo 8-2

Adm. Ernest J. King, USN, commander-in-chief, U.S. Fleet and chief of Naval Operations, on a visit to Recife, Brazil. He is flanked by Vice Adm. Jonas H. Ingram, USN, and Lt. D. Frost, USNR, to his left, and an unidentified lieutenant (junior grade) to his right.
U.S. Navy Photograph #80-G-44061, now in the collection of the National Archives

Admiral Ingram also took the opportunity, while at Recife, to learn as much as possible about Bahia, which lay approximately 400 miles to the south. Although Bahia has an excellent natural harbor compared to the poor one at Recife, it was situated a little too far below the shoulder of Brazil to be the best base for patrol work against Axis submarines. It would be developed as a U.S. naval facility, but would remain of secondary importance during the war in comparison to Recife.[10]

Following a reception aboard the *Memphis*, given by Ingram for Brazilian officials on the morning of Sunday, 11 May, the ships sailed for Port of Spain, Trinidad. They arrived there on the 18th, a day ahead of schedule, having been aided by a 2-knot current off Cape São Roque—the point on the bend of the Brazilian coast closest to the continent of Africa.[11]

Photo 8-3

Port of Spain, Trinidad.
Photo from a USS *Indianapolis* (CA-35) scrapbook of President Franklin D. Roosevelt's cruise aboard the cruiser in 1936

AXIS CREWS SCUTTLE SHIPS TO AVOID CAPTURE

Earlier, while Ingram was in the United States to meet with King, the U.S. government had in late March, taken into "protective custody," Italian, German and Danish ships in American ports. That action followed a report that Italian crews were systematically destroying shipboard machinery. When boarded by U.S. Coast Guard teams, many of the Italian ships were found to have been made ready to be set on fire, or to already have damaged engines. The master of one ship stated that he had received orders from the Italian Naval Attaché in Washington, to destroy his machinery. In U.S. ports, there were twenty-eight Italian ships, two German, and thirty-five Danish. No damage had been done to the Danish ships, but the German tanker *Pauleine Friedrich* at Boston had been damaged.[12]

In a separate, but related action, three Danish ships were seized in Chile, and one in Peru, to prevent the possibility that the German-directed Danish government of occupied Denmark might order their use as blockade runners.[13]

Following this action by the U.S. government, the crews of several German and Italian ships in ports in neutral South American countries scuttled them by setting them on fire. Many, if not all, of these vessels had been lying idle for quite some time to avoid the possibility of their being captured or destroyed by Allied warships if they left port. Apparently, Germany and Italy directed the scuttling of the vessels in anticipation that South American countries might follow the example of the United States and seize them.

Country	Port	German Ships	Italian Ships
Costa Rica	Punta Arenas	cargo ship *Eisenbach*	vessel *Fella*
Ecuador	Guayaquil	cargo ship *Cerigo*	
Peru	Paita	cargo ship *Friesland*	
	Callao	passenger ships *Leipzig* and *Montserrate*	
	In Pacific waters off Callao	passenger ships *Hermonthis* and *München*	
Venezuela	Puerto Cabello	cargo ship *Sesostris*	
	Caracas		tankers *Joli Fascio*, *Teresa Odero*, and *Prottera*[14]

ENEMY SHIPS SNARED BY HMCS *PRINCE HENRY*

Two of these vessels, the German passenger ships *Hermonthis* and *München*, had slipped out of Callao in darkness the night of 31 March 1941 in a desperate effort to escape to sea. Their freedom was short-lived; the Canadian merchant cruiser HMCS *Prince Henry* (F70) intercepted them relatively quickly in Pacific waters off the Peruvian seaport. *Prince Henry* (Capt. Ronald Ian Agnew, RCN) had in February and early March, patrolled off Peru with the British light cruiser HMS *Diomede* (D92), before the latter ship was called away.[15]

Of particular interest during this period, were four large German merchant ships at Callao, *München*, *Hermonthis*, *Leipzig* and *Monserrate*. *Prince Henry* entered Callao harbor on 24 March ostensibly to receive fuel, but in reality to size up her prey, and dropped anchor near the German ships. Agnew's officers made the rounds of the harbor to glean information, and learned the ships intended to try to escape to Japan, and to use scuttling charges if intercepted. *Prince Henry* then stood out of port, but lingered nearby, over the horizon and out of sight. Agnew hoped to convince the German skippers that the cruiser had left the area. The ploy worked. On the evening of 31 March, he received a report from British officers in Callao that *Hermonthis* and *München* had cleared the harbor.[16]

Prince Henry was seventy miles south of Callao, and proceeded at 18 knots to intercept. She sighted the *München*, fifteen miles distant, a little before dawn on 1 April. As the German ship altered course in an attempt to evade, *Prince Henry* fired one round at 0700 (ahead of her and at a range of 12,000 yards) in an attempt to get her to stop. It was unclear where the round hit, but most likely in the water. Within minutes *München* was billowing smoke, presumably as a result of demolition charges. As the German crew took to lifeboats, fire leapt from the ship's hatches and, with seemingly no further action required to ensure her demise, the *Prince Henry* went in search of *Hermonthis*.[17]

Photo 8-4

Peruvian Cruiser *Coronel Bolognesi* in 1942
U.S. Naval History and Heritage Command Photograph #NH 45591

The second German ship was sighted at 1225, aflame, with her crew piling into boats. Determined to salvage the *Hermonthis*, Agnew ordered some of the German crew back aboard and sent a firefighting party from the cruiser aboard her. As they began to battle the blaze, Agnew laid the *Prince Henry* alongside the *Hermonthis* so that the cruiser's fire hoses could also be employed. These efforts came to naught. In late afternoon, as fires aboard the *Hermonthis* continued to burn, the *Prince Henry* left her side and recovered the remaining German crewmen in life boats—who had tried unsuccessfully to reach the safety offered by the Peruvian coast—before returning to sink the *Hermonthis* with gunfire. An ensuing search for the *München* and her crew ended when the Peruvian light cruiser *Almirante Grau* reported that she had sunk the burning wreck and recovered the survivors.[18]

The *Leipzig* and *Monserrate* tried to leave harbor shortly before midnight on 31 March, some hours after the *München* and *Hermonthis* departed Callao. The Peruvian cruiser *Coronel Bolognesi* stopped them by firing warning shots, and they returned to port, where their crews set them afire.[19]

ROYAL NAVY SEARCH FOR ENEMY SUPPLY SHIPS AND BLOCKADE RUNNERS

> U 38 *reported that the "Egerland" sank at supply rendezvous red. She did not refuel and has been obliged, therefore, to return. Since, through the loss of the "Egerland" refueling for the South boats is questionable for some time, the boats have been ordered to return to the supply point "Culebra", and therefore to leave the operational area.*

—Befehlshaber der Unterseeboote (BdU), Commander of the U-boats, (Adm. Karl Dönitz) War Log 1-15 June 1941, describing the detrimental effect of the loss of the German tanker *Egerland* on U-boat operations in the South Atlantic.

In early 1941, as Allied forces continued to seize in port, capture or destroy Axis blockade runners trying to escape internment in South American ports, German supply ships provided support at sea to enemy raiders and submarines. The following is a sampling of such activity in the South Atlantic during the first four months of the year. Normally, supply ships provided fuel, food, and other assistance to raiders and submarines, and accepted the transfer of any prisoners they might have aboard. On occasion, the roles of vessels were dictated by necessity. A U-boat might provide support to a raider, or a raider to a submarine. One good example of interaction between a raider, supply ships, submarines and other raiders occurred in January 1941. Over the course of the month, *Kormoran* sank four British merchant vessels, furnished supplies for several U-boats at prearranged rendezvous points on the high seas, replenished herself from two supply ships, and exchanged intelligence with two other raiders.[20]

The following table of summary information does not include an accounting of the activities of raiders and Axis submarines receiving logistics support at sea. As readers likely surmise, they were either sinking or capturing Allied ships or attempting to do so. In response to these actions, a pair of Royal Navy warships—the heavy cruiser HMS *London* (69) and destroyer HMS *Brilliant* (H84)—were sent in early June to search for supply ships in the South Atlantic. This tasking followed the decryption of German Enigma signals by Britain's Government Code and Cypher School (sited at Bletchley Park in present-day Milton Keynes, about forty-five miles northwest of London), which provided location information. (The name of this clandestine organization was changed after the war to its present title, Government Communications Headquarters).[21]

Date	Raider/ Submarine(s)	Support Ship(s)	Rendezvous Action
2 Jan 41	Raider *Thor*	*Nordmark*	Replenishment
7 Feb 41	Raider *Kormoran*	*Nordmark*	Transfer of prisoners from *Kormoran* and captured ship *Duquesa*
14 Feb 41	Raider *Thor*	*Eurofeld* and *Alsterufer*	Replenishment
15 Feb 41	Raider *Pinguin*	*Nordmark*	*Pinguin* and captured Norwegian whaling vessels rendezvous with *Nordmark* and *Duquesa*
17 Feb 41	Raider *Pinguin*	*Nordmark*	German vessel *Alstertor* joins above group; *Pinguin* sails for the Indian Ocean with *Alstertor*
15 Mar 41	Raider *Kormoran*	*U-105*	Following mechanical problems, *Kormoran* meets the submarine to trade parts and torpedoes
29 Mar 41	*U-105* and *U-106*	*Kormoran*	Raider refuels submarines
3 Apr 41	*Kormoran*	*Rudolf Albrecht*	Replenishment
16 Apr 41	Italian submarines *Archimede*, *Guglielmotti*, and *Ferraris*	*Nordmark*	Resupplied while en route to France from Eritrea
19 Apr 41	*Atlantis*	*Dresden*	Captured passengers and crew of the Egyptian ocean liner *Zamzam* transferred to supply ship
20 Apr 41	*Atlantis*	*Nordmark*	Replenishment
23 Apr 41	Italian submarine *Perla*	*Nordmark*	Resupplied while en route to France from Eritrea[22]

On 4 June 1941, HMS *London* and HMS *Brilliant* intercepted the German tanker *Esso Hamburg* off the Freetown-Natal route. The

tanker's crew scuttled the ship upon the approach of the Royal Navy. All eighty-seven German officers and men making up the ship's complement were retrieved from lifeboats and taken prisoner. *Esso Hamburg* had been en route to join the German tanker *Egerland*.[23]

The warships found the *Egerland* west of Freetown, Sierra Leone, in late morning the following day. When challenged, the German ship replied that she was the Panamanian vessel *Gallia* from Colon in order to gain time, and her crew promptly ignited scuttling charges and abandoned ship. Suspecting the possibility of such action, *London* had opened fire at 1010 with her A and B turrets at a range of 21,000 yards, with the objective of forcing the crew into their boats as soon as possible. The gunfire did not deter the Germans from setting their ship ablaze. After a boarding party from the *Brilliant* reported that the *Egerland* could not be saved, *London's* commanding officer (Capt. Reginald Maxwell Servaes, RN) ordered the destroyer to sink her.[24]

This task proved difficult. Following ineffective naval gunfire by the destroyer, she then fired six depth charges (set to detonate at a depth of 50 feet) from throwers, while making 24 knots as she passed the *Egerland* close aboard. This action injured the enemy ship but did not sink her. With lesser measures having failed, *Brilliant's* commanding officer, Lt. Comdr. Francis Cumberland Brodrick, RN, ordered that one torpedo be fired. It struck *Egerland* about fifty feet abaft amidships, and as seawater poured into her hull through the resultant hole, she settled by the stern. A depth charge, which had landed aboard the ship, but not detonated, now rolled aft on the slanted merchant ship, and exploded; finishing her off by cracking the upper deck down the centerline. The tanker sank stern first at 1530. There were no casualties among her ninety-four officers and men.[25]

In June 1941, British ability to break German naval codes led to the sinking of no fewer than nine supply-ships, three in the South Atlantic. *London* found the third one on 21 June, when she intercepted the tanker *Babitonga* near the St. Paul Rocks off the Brazilian coast. As was common practice, her crew scuttled *Babitonga* to prevent capture by the Royal Navy. The Germans were then picked up by the *London*. *Babitonga* had been the support ship for the raider *Atlantis*. The risk to German vessels was increasing due to greatly diminished supply ship support. Conversely, with fewer and fewer allied ships now sailing outside the Allied convoy system, the number of vessels falling prey to German raiders and U-Boats was slowly decreasing.[26]

In July and August 1941, Royal Navy ships intercepted three more supply ships in the South Atlantic. The crews of each scuttled their vessel, despite the use of naval gunfire on at least one occasion to try to prevent such action. Although blockade runners and supply ships are described in this book as separate and distinct entities, runners might be considered "supply ships" if used to refuel or replenish raiders or U-boats, versus only carrying cargos of vital war materials home to Germany from the Far East.[27]

On 10 July, the merchant cruiser HMS *Canton* (F97), a unit of the Freetown Escort Force, intercepted the German merchant vessel *Hermes*. In hopes of preventing her crew from sinking their ship, *Canton* riddled the *Hermes*' port lifeboats, which were unmanned and still in davits, with machine gun fire and directed six-inch fire from her starboard guns at the port side of the enemy's bridge, radio room, stack, and antennas. The merchant cruiser then swung around to engage her starboard side but, by then, two of *Hermes*' starboard boats were in the water with most of the crew in them. Scuttling charges then went off, terminating her employment as a supply ship.[28]

Two weeks later, the light cruiser *Newcastle* (76) intercepted the *Erlangen* on 25 July southeast of the River Plate. Before the ship could be captured, she was set on fire by her crew. The chronicles of the *Erlangen* prior to her destruction, and similar scuttling of *Norderney* on 15 August, follow the summary information, below.[29]

Supply Ships/Blockade Runners Scuttled at Sea in the South Atlantic, in Summer 1941

Date	German Ship	Royal Navy Ship(s)	Commanding Officer
4 Jun 41	tanker *Esso Hamburg*	heavy cruiser HMS *London* (69) and destroyer HMS *Brilliant* (H84)	Capt. Reginald Maxwell Servaes, RN; Lt. Comdr. Francis Cumberland Brodrick, RN
5 Jun 41	tanker *Egerland*	same as above entry	same as above entry
21 Jun 41	supply ship *Babitonga*	heavy cruiser HMS *London* (69)	Capt. Reginald Maxwell Servaes, RN
10 Jul 41	merchant ship *Hermes*	merchant cruiser HMS *Canton* (F97)	A/Capt. Charles Alfred Godfrey Nichols, RN
25 Jul 41	*Erlangen*	light cruiser *Newcastle* (76)	Capt. Edward Arthur Aylmer, RN
15 Aug 41	*Norderney*	cruisers *Despatch* (D30) and *Pretoria Castle* (F61)	Capt. Cyril Eustace Douglas-Pennant, RN; A/Capt. (retired) Arthur Vernon Hemming, RN[30]

MOST FAMOUS BLOCKADE RUNNER OF THE WAR

> *On the highest tide in that last week, it was with a great cheer, the chains were released that held the ship and as to plan, with no problems at all, it rolled with a great splash backward into the ocean once more. It took some time to fire up enough steam to drive the ship, and during this time we spent some energy to conceal our well-worn tracks as best we could. By the time this was finished, the ship had steam up and we were under way for Chile, safe at last.*

> —Excerpt from "1939 A Saw Cut," one of the Codes of Survival Scripts, short factionalized stories based on historical events in the sub-Antarctic Islands written in 1993 by Lloyd Godman, a former Chinese crewman of the German ship *Erlangen*.[31]

In late August 1939, just prior to the outbreak of war, the 6,100-ton *Erlangen*, of the North-German Lloyd Shipping Company, was moored at Dunedin Harbour, New Zealand. Comprising her crew of sixty-three was the master, Capt. Alfred Grams, twelve other German officers and fifty Chinese seamen. The ship then had only five days of coal supplies remaining on board, and was scheduled to coal in Port Kembla, located just south of Sydney on Australia's east coast. Grams' receipt of a telegram from Berlin ordering him to seek a neutral harbor presented him a particularly tough challenge because the nearest neutral harbor was in Chile, approximately 5,000 nautical miles from New Zealand.[32]

Following careful consideration of this dilemma, Grams quietly steered *Erlangen* from her berth on 26 August, and out of the harbor. A coil of black smoke from her stack was the only trace in the evening sky, and she proceeded without any alarm or problems out into the vast safety of the southern ocean. After making the open sea, *Erlangen* initially steered a northwesterly course before, under the cover of darkness, changing course and proceeding 200 miles south to Carnley Harbour in the uninhabited Auckland Islands; a sub-Antarctic part of New Zealand's Outlying Islands.[33]

Upon reaching her destination, *Erlangen* took shelter in a wide, open harbor at the southern end of Auckland Island. From anchorage in an arm of this large inlet, an abundant forest of large trees was visible, which it appeared could provide fuel the ship would need to leave this sanctuary. With this in mind, the crew began the arduous task of felling and splitting timber to fill the bunkers. The raita trees, which were called "iron wood" because of difficulty associated with cutting them, lived up to this reputation. Based on careful calculations that three tons of wood would be needed to replace each ton of coal, the crew spent five weeks of backbreaking labor, using only primitive tools, to obtain 400 tons of firewood.[34]

The ship's engineers fabricated a toothed saw from a curved winch cover, with each tooth filed out separately by hand and adjacent teeth sprung in opposition direction with a strong pair of pliers. In order to harden the saw, a large wood fire was lit on the beach to heat the blade to red hot, after which it was rushed to the ocean's edge and plunged deep into the water "with a bang, and great hiss and smell of steam." The saw proved much better than axes to cut through the trunks of trees, and Grams had the officers and engineers fabricate addition blades from other winch covers. As more saw blades became available for use, German crewmen joined their Chinese counterparts in felling trees, except for those men whose task it was to continually sharpen and set the blade teeth.[35]

Meanwhile, the ship's chief officer and the Chinese quartermasters fabricated two improvised sails from heavy tarpaulins used to cover deck cargo. The sails were rigged, with derricks serving as yard arms, in such a way that it was hoped, when winds permitted, they would augment the use of the wood for propulsion. The transportation and loading of the timber aboard ship proved more difficult than cutting it. Being newly cut, most of the wood was wet and heavy. Moving it was so painstakingly slow that Grams decided to risk beaching the ship to allow easier access to the winches on board. The ship was moved into the shallows near shore, selected round logs were placed under her keel, one or more lines were led to the shore, and *Erlangen* used her winches to pull herself up and onto the beach. Once fully loaded with wood, unnecessary materials were jettisoned into the bay to "lighten ship," while awaiting high tide to free the beach-gripped *Erlangen*.[36]

The ship stood out of the harbor on 5 October 1939, bound for the west coast of South America. The captain and crew had learned from intercepted radio communications during the ship's stay at the island that England had declared war on Germany. New Zealand—and other Commonwealth nations, in addition to England—was now their enemy, and any warship encountered might be a potential adversary. During the long voyage from the eastern to western hemisphere, fuel supplies became scarce, resulting in many of the ship's wooden fittings being fed into the furnace. Food was also in very short supply. However, despite this deprivation and challenges associated with avoiding Allied navies scouring the Pacific for the elusive steamship, *Erlangen* reached Puerto Mott, a port city in southern Chile, on 11 November. Grams released the Chinese crew, providing opportunity for the men to make their way back to Asia.[37]

Erlangen's use of Carnley Harbour to obtain fuel to reach neutral South America identified to the Allies the possibility of the use of sub-Antarctic islands as enemy bases. These fears were heightened in 1940 when German raiders sank three New Zealand ships in waters of that country further north. Raider *Orion* sank the freighter *Turakina* in August, and *Orion* and *Komet* sank the small cargo ship *Holmwood* and ocean liner *Rangitane* in November.[38]

ERLANGEN ATTEMPTS TO BREAK THE BLOCKADE

In mid-1941, following receipt of orders for the *Erlangen* to return to Germany, Grams laid a course for Montevideo on South America's east coast. Sailors/cadets from the German school ship *Priwall*—a four-masted steel-hulled barque—made up his crew. (*Priwall* had been interned at Valparaiso, a Chilean seaport, at the onset of the war. She was deeded as a gift to Chile in 1941, to avoid potential seizure by the Allies, and the Chilean Navy thereafter used her as a cargo carrying training ship.) Grams' luck held during the arduous and treacherous trip around Cape Horn, during which he was able to avoid detection. It ran out on 25 July 1941, when the light cruiser HMS *Newcastle* (76) discovered *Erlangen* off the coast of Montevideo. Grams ordered his crew to set the ship afire, destroying it. He and the other officers and men were taken prisoner and sent to Sierra Leone, and then Scotland. They were later relocated to Canada, and ultimately freed in 1946.[39]

NORDERNEY SCUTTLED BY CREW

> *The German freighter* Norderney *(3,665 tons), fully laden with 72,000 hides and 500 tons of rubber, is about to leave Para Harbour, Brazil, in an attempt to run the British blockade, says the Rio de Janeiro correspondent of the "New York Times." Fourteen Germans, he says, took [a] plane on Sunday to board the* Norderney, *which has sought refuge at Para since the out-break of the war. At present eight German and 20 Italian ships are anchored in Brazilian harbours.*
>
> —Article, German Ship to Run Blockade, published in the newspaper *The Argus* (Melbourne) on 18 March 1941.

The Royal Navy's last interception/destruction of a blockade runner in the South Atlantic in 1941 occurred on 15 August. During operations with the merchant cruiser *Pretoria Castle* (F61), the cruiser *Despatch*

(D30) found the German freighter *Norderney* off the Uruguayan coast, northeast of the Amazon estuary. The ship was scuttled upon the approach of the Royal Navy, and her unharmed fifty-four crewmembers, and six passengers were later rescued.[40]

ATLANTIC CHARTER CONFERENCE, AUGUST 1941

> . . . *[A]fter the final destruction of the Nazi tyranny, [we] hope to see established a peace which will afford to all nations the means of dwelling in safety within their own boundaries, and which will afford assurance that all men in all lands may live out their lives in freedom from fear and want. . . . [S]uch a peace should enable all men to traverse the high seas and oceans without hindrance.*

> —One of the major provisions of the Atlantic Charter, which historians often cite as one of the first significant steps toward the formation of the United Nations.[41]

Photo 8-5

Atlantic Charter Conference, 9-12 August 1941. Destroyer USS *McDougal* (DD-358) alongside HMS *Prince of Wales* (53), in Placentia Bay, Newfoundland, to transfer President Franklin D. Roosevelt to the battleship for a meeting with Prime Minister Winston Churchill.
U.S. Naval History and Heritage Command Photograph #NH 67195

As the battle of the Atlantic continued unabated with no end in sight, British Prime Minister Winston Churchill and President Franklin D. Roosevelt met from 9-12 August 1941 aboard naval vessels anchored in Placentia Bay, off the coast of Newfoundland, Canada. The two leaders discussed their respective aims regarding the war and outlined a postwar international system. The resultant Atlantic Charter included eight "common principles" that the United States and Great Britain would be committed to supporting in the postwar world. The Charter was not an official document, but rather a joint statement expressing the war aims of the two countries—one still technically neutral and the other at war.[42]

Photo 8-6

Principals at the Atlantic Charter Conference, 9-12 August 1941. From left to right, Gen. George C. Marshall, President Franklin D. Roosevelt, Prime Minister Winston Churchill, Adm. Ernest King, and Adm. Harold R. Stark.
Commander in Chief, United States Atlantic Fleet, Atlantic Fleet History, 13 May 1946

The meeting had been called in response to the current situation in Europe. Great Britain had been spared from a German invasion in the fall of 1940 and, with the passage of the U.S. Lend Lease Act in March 1941, was assured U.S. material support. However, by the end of May, German forces had inflicted defeats upon British, Greek, and, Yugoslav forces in the Balkans and were threatening to overrun Egypt and close off the Suez Canal, thereby restricting British access to its possessions in India. While the British Government was focused on dealing with the Germans in Europe, it was also concerned that Japan might take advantage of the situation to seize British, French, and Dutch territories in Southeast Asia.[43]

While the meeting was successful in identifying some common principles to which both countries pledged commitment, it failed to produce the desired results for either leader. Roosevelt had hoped that the Charter might encourage the American people to support United States' intervention in World War II on behalf of the Allies; however, public opinion remained adamantly opposed to such a policy until the Japanese attack on Pearl Harbor on 7 December 1941. Similarly, Churchill's primary goal in attending the Conference was "to get the Americans into the war." Barring that, he hoped that the United States would increase its military aid to Great Britain and warn Japan against taking any aggressive actions in the Pacific.[44]

Both leaders had some trepidation regarding one or more of the provisions of the Charter the other had insisted upon, and how their governments/people might react to these stipulations. For his part, Churchill realized that the joint statement was the most he could accomplish during the Conference. Although the United States would remain neutral, the declaration would raise the morale of the British public and, most importantly, draw the United States closer to Great Britain. While the Atlantic Charter was not a binding treaty, it affirmed solidarity between the U.S. and Great Britain against Axis aggression, and laid out Roosevelt's vision for the postwar world—one that would be characterized by freer exchanges of trade, self-determination, disarmament, and collective security.[45]

CAPTURE OF THE GERMAN RUNNER *ODENWALD*

In mid-autumn 1941, two U.S. Navy ships—the cruiser *Omaha* (CL-4) and destroyer *Somers* (DD-381)—captured the motor vessel *Odenwald*. As it turned out, this event would precede by only five weeks America's formal entry into the war on 11 December 1941. The latter development, one which Britain had long sought (albeit one spurred by the Japanese attack on Pearl Harbor), was fortuitous for the Royal Navy, which would lose the assistance of the French Navy upon the fall of France to Germany in June 1942.

On the morning of 6 November, just as *Omaha* and *Somers* were about to cross the equator at longitude 27°44' west, they came upon a ship midway between the prominences of South America and Africa. The merchantman was ordered to heave to while *Omaha* went to General Quarters and dispatched a motor whaleboat with a boarding party. On the stern of the merchant ship was the name *Willmotto*, of Philadelphia; and she flew the colors of the United States. Just before the boarding party came alongside her, the ship hoisted the international flag signal, "Fox Mike," indicating that she was sinking and in need of lifeboats to pick up her passengers and crew—who were already abandoning the vessel.[46]

Photo 8-7

Light cruiser *Omaha* (CL-4), on right of photo, standing by the German blockade runner *Odenwald*, which has a U.S. boarding party on board, in the South Atlantic, 6 November 1941.
U.S. Naval History and Heritage Command Photograph #NH 49935

Chief Petty Officer Charles J. Martin, a crewman aboard the *Somers*, described in an interview in 1943, the detection of the German merchant vessel by radar, efforts by her crew to scuttle the ship, and salvage of the enemy vessel by *Omaha* and *Somers*:

Well, just prior to the war we captured this ship that was operating under the name *WILLMOTO*.... We picked it up when we were on patrol duty with the USS *OMAHA*. We picked up the contact and the *OMAHA* sent us the usual plan of the day and it was for the USS *SOMERS* to go in and make the attack while she sought a position of safety. That's the usual custom down on patrol lines like that, because the old cruisers are not equipped with sound gear and they sort of don't like submarines.

We went on and challenged the ship and they gave us the registration number of the *WILLMOTO*.... The Chief Firecontrolman ... by the name of Dean, he suspected ... the ship of being a German ... and he informed the captain about it, and during this time we had sent for the *OMAHA*, sent a message that everything was okay, we had the situation pretty well squared away. And they came back and they challenged this *WILLMOTO* ... evidently the *OMAHA* was satisfied because they started to leave the vicinity. And then our Captain re-challenged them and asked for a secret code or something.... And by the way, the *WILLMOTO* started to throw papers and boxes off their bridge.

...There were two or three small explosions on the ship and they began to abandon ship. Well, the *OMAHA* came back and wouldn't let us put a boarding party aboard. They put a boarding party aboard and we had to circle the vicinity to keep submarines off while the *OMAHA* remained alongside of her. Well, this went on for about four or five hours, they were trying to repair damage on this ship and they couldn't make out so they sent over to our ship and got our Chief Machinist's Mate and he went over and repaired the diesel [engine] and got the ship underway.[47]

As *Omaha*'s boat approached the suspect ship, the detonation of explosives aboard the merchant vessel aroused the suspicions of the already wary boarding party. Once aboard, the sailors discovered that their quarry was the German blockade runner *Odenwald*. Only one of the ship's generators was operating and selected watertight doors were open, indicating, in conjunction with the use of scuttling charges, that an attempt had been made to destroy the ship. These efforts were for naught, and *Odenwald* was escorted into San Juan, Puerto Rico, on 11 November for disposition. Aboard her was a valuable cargo including 4,000 tons of rubber bound for Germany from Japan.[48]

CREWMEMBERS AWARDED PRIZE MONEY IN 1947

The awarding of prize money was an ancient naval custom, by which the officers and men of a warship that captured an enemy vessel were allowed to divvy up the loot. Although the formula governing the division of the spoils gave the lion's share to the officers, and particularly the captain, a rich prize could easily leave an ordinary seaman with an extra year's pay. (An admiral embarked aboard, or who was responsible for the warship, might receive considerably more of the spoils than her captain.)[49]

For much of its history the United States Navy had followed the practice of awarding prize. But in 1900 it was decided to abolish this convention, on the grounds that often those who ran the greatest risk had the least chance to claim prize. For example, during the Spanish-American War, the men who served on blockade duty off Santiago and fought the Spanish Fleet on 3 July 1898, received no prize, while the crews of some cruisers that intercepted defenseless merchant ships on the high seas, did quite nicely.[50]

Following delivery of the *Odenwald* to Puerto Rico, an admiralty court ruled that since the German ship had illegally claimed American registration, there were sufficient grounds for confiscation. Lawyers involved argued that the attempt to scuttle the ship was the equivalent of abandoning her, and they claimed that the crews of the two American ships had salvage rights, in the amount of $3 million. This led to a protracted court case, which in 1947 ruled that the members of the boarding party and the prize crew were entitled to $3,000 apiece, and that all the other crewmen of the *Omaha* and *Somers* were entitled to two months' pay and allowances at their then current rate.[51]

9

German Espionage in Latin America

The Abwehr has nothing to do with the persecution of Jews.... No concern of ours, we hold ourselves aloof from it.

—Statement by Admiral Wilhelm Franz Canaris,
chief of the German Abwehr, at a conference
of senior officers in December 1941.[1]

When war broke out in 1939, large groups of German nationals were settled in the various countries of Latin America, particularly Argentina, Brazil, and Chile. Germany maintained close contact with these expatriates through commerce, diplomatic representatives, and pro-Nazi social organizations. Various German business operations in Latin America were also brought into the National Socialist fold by appeals to patriotism and by threats of interruption of trade. This large expatriate community provided a fertile ground for the introduction of German espionage organizations—first the Abwehr, and later on, the Reich Security Administration.[2]

LEADERSHIP/ORGANIZATION OF THE ABWEHR

These two organizations, separately and in combination, were responsible for Germany's espionage operations before and during the war. Latin America was probably the major theater of operations, but similar espionage organizations were established all over the world. Admiral Wilhelm Franz Canaris headed the Abwehr from 1935 to 1944. Initially a supporter of Adolf Hitler, he later was among the military officers involved in clandestine opposition to the Nazi regime. Canaris was executed in the Flossenbürg concentration camp for high treason on 9 April 1945, just weeks before the end of the war. Sited near the small town of Flossenbürg, in northeastern Bavaria near the Czech border, the camp was built in 1939 and run by the German SS (Schutzstaffel).[3]

Comprising the Abwehr organization were Abwehr I (the service espionage groups), Abwehr II (military espionage, sabotage and uprisings), and Abwehr III (counterespionage). Principal posts of the Abwehr located in important cities were called Abwehr Posts (Ast). The Hamburg Ast was concerned chiefly with naval activity against England and America and was active in South America, the Iberian Peninsula, and in Greece. Subordinate and reporting to the Asts were Branch Posts (Nest or Anst) located in less important cities. Commanded by a lieutenant colonel or commander, the two nests concerned with Latin America were Nest Cologne and Nest Bremen.[4]

Abwehr intelligence and smuggling activities in Latin America were under the control of Kapitan zur See Dietrich Niebuhr, the naval attaché in Argentina since 1936. His previous service included duty aboard *U-21* in the First World War. This U-boat sank the British scout cruiser HMS *Pathfinder*—the first ship to be destroyed by a submarine-fired torpedo—on 5 September 1914 off St. Abbs Head, Berwickshire, Scotland. Niebuhr had been posted to naval attaché duty in Argentina owing to his mastery of Spanish, and was also accredited to Brazil, Paraguay, Uruguay and Chile. The outbreak of the war found him scrambling to set up a spy network to provide shipping information to U-boats operating in the Atlantic.[5]

Photo 9-1

British scout cruiser HMS *Pathfinder* prior to World War I.
U.S. Naval History and Heritage Command Photograph #NH 57856

AID FOR GERMAN SHIPS TO ESCAPE INTERNMENT

Upon the outbreak of war Niebuhr arranged for the departure to Germany of as many merchant vessels as possible, with assistance from the shipping agency of Antonio Delfino, and Thilo Martens, the North German Lloyd representative to Argentina. Martens was a veteran of the Kriegsmarine (the navy of Nazi Germany from 1935 to 1945), who had been recruited by the Abwehr sometime before 1935.

Niebuhr used 500,000 pesos (approximately $170,000) to bribe officials and secure passage for the vessels, while shipping agents paid for the supplies, fuel and equipment needed prior to sailing.[6]

ESCAPE OF *ADMIRAL GRAF SPEE*'S CREW FROM URUGUAY, THEN ARGENTINA, HOME TO GERMANY

Niebuhr's next significant contribution to the German war effort came following the Battle of the River Plate when, on 13 December 1939, the pocket battleship *Graf Spee* put into Montevideo, Uruguay, to repair battle damage from its fight with three units of the Royal Navy's South Atlantic cruiser squadron. Per international law, combatant ships of belligerent nations were only allowed to remain in neutral harbors for seventy-two hours. Hans Langsdorff, captain of the *Graf Spee*—unable to persuade the Uruguayans to extend the deadline—determined that his ship would be unable to defeat a British armada he believed lay offshore. On 17 December, Langsdorff sailed *Graf Spee* just outside the harbor, and scuttled her. Several days later, he committed suicide.[7]

The German embassy in Buenos Aires asked the Argentine government to accept the surviving 1,000 German crewmembers. When the government vacillated, claiming it did not have facilities to house the internees, Niebuhr arranged with Rudolf Hepe of the Antonio Delfino Company (a subsidiary of the Hamburg-South America line) for vessels to bring the officers and men to Argentina. Their arrival in that country caused a storm of protest and embarrassed the Argentine government, which interned the crew in camps controlled by the military. Generous bribes by Niebuhr helped to prevent the return of the men to Uruguay.[8]

Niebuhr then set about orchestrating their escape to Europe. He and two assistants, Lieutenants Franz Mammen and Martin Müller, visited the camps several times and ascertained that the guards would do little to stop a determined escape effort. In January 1940, Eugen Langer and Wilhelm von Seidlitz helped arrange for some of the crewmen to be smuggled back to Germany aboard Spanish and Portuguese ships leaving various ports in Argentina. Other men were taken to Chile, for passage to Germany via Vladivostok, Soviet Union, on Japanese flagged ships. The cost to facilitate the escape of nearly 200 sailors was at least 70,000 dollars. Edmund von Thermann, the German ambassador to Argentina, and Niebuhr decided in November 1940 to cease trying to make possible the escape of additional crewmen, because the operation was causing diplomatic problems with other Latin American nations.[9]

COLLECTION OF INTELLIGENCE IN BRAZIL

The largest German population in South America was in Brazil. The espionage/intelligence gathering groups in that country were headed by Albrecht Gustav Engels and Nils Christian Christensen. Working through a variety of organizations (which Germans staffed all or in part), these groups were able to obtain a great deal of valuable information—the most important being British shipping schedules. Intelligence thus gained was secretly transmitted by radio to Germany. Information from the distant River Plate region (Argentina and Uruguay) was obtained in much the same way and relayed to the Brazilian stations for transmission to the Reich.[10]

Fortunately for the Allies, Germany's U-boat fleet was relatively small in 1940-41, and the submarines operating in South Atlantic waters could not exploit all of the information received regarding the scheduled arrivals/departures of British ships at various ports. As the fleet expanded, with builders' yards churning out more and more submarines, there was a corresponding increase in Allied ship losses between January 1942 and May 1943. The numbers of ships sunk then decreased dramatically, as the Allies began to prevail against Germany in the Battle of the Atlantic.[11]

Allied Ship Losses in the South Atlantic

Period	British, Allied, Neutral ships	Gross Tonnage
Sep 1939-Mar 1940	8	49,000
Apr-Dec 1940	8	55,000
Jan-Dec 1941	29	134,000
Jan 42-May 43	97	611,000
Jun 43-May 44	27	147,000
Jun 44-May 45	5	28,000
Total Number:	174	1,024,000[12]

INCREASED EMPHASIS ON SUBMARINE WARFARE AND EFFECT OF BRAZILIAN ENTRY INTO THE WAR

As the war progressed and the U-boat campaign became increasingly important, German spy rings were ordered to concentrate on naval and maritime intelligence. Prior to the entry of the United States into the war, American and Brazilian authorities acquired considerable information on the South American networks (in part because of the radio transmissions), but the Brazilian authorities did not interfere with their operations. After Pearl Harbor, this situation changed somewhat. The United States began to actively collect counter-intelligence, and endeavored to work with South American governments. Argentina was not very cooperative, but Brazil was; it broke off relations with Germany in January 1942, and declared war on 22 August 1942.[13]

Photo 9-2

President Juan D. Perón of Argentina departing the cruiser USS *Albany* (CA-123) at Buenos Aires, on 23 January 1948, after paying a call on Vice Adm. Lynde D. McCormick. With him are Señora Eva Perón, Rear Admiral Fidel W. Anadon (Minister of Marine) and Dr. Juan A Branueglia (Minister of Foreign Affairs). U.S. National Archives Photograph #80-G-392794

In March 1942, Brazilian authorities arrested German agents in that country. In addition to the resulting significant degradation of enemy intelligence-gathering efforts in Brazil, this action also severely restricted the effectiveness of the German spy rings in other South American countries. Unfortunately, Argentina and Chile took no similar actions. These countries had sizeable resident German colonies with strong local connections, and much support for fascism. Colonel Juan D. Perón, who would become the president of Argentina after the war, was drawn to the ideologies of Benito Mussolini and Adolf Hitler while serving as a military attaché in Italy during the early years of World War II. In the years immediately following the war, he secretly ordered diplomats and intelligence officers to establish escape routes, so-called "ratlines," through ports in Spain and Italy to smuggle thousands of former SS officers and Nazi party members out of Europe into South America.[14]

Chile had a small, but influential German colony which supported a spy ring centered in the important port of Valpariso near Santiago. Agents there (like those in Argentina and Brazil) were able to supply the German Navy and its U-boats with valuable information on Allied shipping. After Juan Antonio Ríos was elected president in 1942, the spy ring was finally exposed in 1943. However, Chile never joined the Allies against Germany. The Rios Government did, however, align itself with the United States when it declared war on Japan on 11 April 1945. Three South American countries—Brazil, Bolivia, and Columbia—joined the Allies against Germany, Italy, or the collective Axis powers, relatively early in the war. The other countries that eventually declared war, waited to do so until it became evident that Germany and Japan would be totally defeated.

Declarations of War by South American Countries

Date	Country	Axis Powers and/or Japan
22 Aug 1942	Brazil	Nazi Germany, Italy
2 Apr 1943	Bolivia	Axis Powers
26 Nov 1943	Colombia	Nazi Germany
2 Feb 1945	Ecuador	Nazi Germany, Japan
7 Feb 1945	Argentina	Nazi Germany, Japan
7 Feb 1945	Paraguay	Nazi Germany, Japan
12 Feb 1945	Peru	Nazi Germany, Japan
15 Feb 1945	Venezuela	Nazi Germany, Japan
15 Feb 1945	Uruguay	Nazi Germany, Japan
11 Apr 1945	Chile	Japan
6 Jul 1945	Brazil	Japan[15]

10

United States/Brazilian
Operations Begin

It is easier for a snake to smoke than for Brazil to go to war.

—Popular saying among Brazilians prior to
their country's entry into World War II.[1]

In October 1941, the Brazilian Navy began training merchant ships to
sail in convoy with its new *Carioca*-class minelayers, and sent one of the
vessels, the *Camaquam*, to patrol the northeast coast of Brazil. The six
ships were products of the Arsenal de Marinha do Rio de Janeiro
(AMRJ) shipyard located on the Ilha das Cobras (island of cobras) in
Guanabara Bay, Rio de Janeiro. The AMRJ was then, and it remains
today, the main shipbuilding and maintenance center of the Brazilian
Navy, which provides the country the capacity to design and build its
own ships. With the experience acquired in the construction of the
minelayers, the yard undertook building larger ships, including three
M-class destroyers, the *Marcílio Dias* (M-1), *Mariz Barros* (M-2), and
Greenhalgh (M-3). Ship plans were obtained from the United States, as
were needed materials.[2]

Camaquam was being relieved of her patrol duties by the *Camocim*
when the Japanese attacked Pearl Harbor on 7 December 1941.
Shortly after, Brazil severed diplomatic relations with the Axis powers
and sent *Camocim*, along with a cruiser and three other minelayers, to
patrol the Brazilian coastline. The ships were under orders to repress
any activities in ports or territorial waters by Axis elements or
Brazilians contrary to the interests of the United States.[3]

In a related action in support of American patrol/protection of
South Atlantic and Brazilian territorial waters, Brazil agreed to the
construction/use by U.S. military forces of airfields and naval bases
along its coastline. Natal was chosen as the principal air base due to its
strategic location and favorable winds, but work also continued or was
begun on airfields at Bahia, Belém, Fortaleza, and Recife. Patrol
Squadron VP-52—six Catalina PBY-5 seaplanes—arrived at Natal on

11 December 1941. From its humble beginning, VP-52 would grow into Fleet Air Wing Sixteen later in the war.[4]

Lt. Comdr. Sperry Clark arrived at Natal on 1 April 1942 with Patrol Squadron VP-83 (land-based PBY-5s) to relieve VP-52. After the second section of aircraft joined the squadron on 15 June, VP-83 was able to patrol the coast of Brazil in some fashion. Most of its 475 officers and men were involved with base construction throughout summer and fall 1942.[5]

Photo 10-1

PBY-5 "Catalina" patrol bombers of Squadron VP-52 in flight on 10 February 1944. U.S. National Archives Photograph #80-G-223134

DEVELOPMENT OF ASCENSION ISLAND AIRFIELD

If I don't hit Ascension
My wife will get a pension....

—Opening lines of an airman's ditty, composed by some imaginative pilot on the South Atlantic flight. Actually, the thirty-four square mile volcanic island had a radio beacon on it, and the navigators aboard planes had no great trouble finding it.[6]

The only reason they didn't send Napoleon to this spot is that in all probability St. Helena is worse.

—Vice Adm. Jonas H. Ingram, USN, commenting on difficulties encountered during ship-to-shore movement of materials at Ascension for the development of airfields, and associated concerns about the regular delivery of necessary fuel and provisions to support the island base.[7]

Other actions taken to strengthen Allied anti-submarine efforts included the development of an airfield on lonely Ascension Island, twelve hundred miles east of Recife, Brazil. The insignificant British possession ("rock") was strategically located in the mid-South Atlantic, 840 miles off the West African coast and along the air route from the United States to South Africa. In recognition of the island's potential to host an airfield, the cruisers *Omaha* and *Sands* carried four U.S. Army officers to Ascension in December 1941 to conduct a survey. Following determination that construction of a field was feasible, planning for this action began. Once completed, Ascension would be used both as a stepping stone for Army planes in transit from the United States to Africa and thence to fighting fronts, and as a mid-ocean base from which anti-submarine and anti-blockade runner planes could patrol surrounding waters. The 1,500 mile "narrows" between Brazil and Dakar, West Africa, were not so easily bridged by patrolling ships, but aircraft flying from Recife to Ascension could make the 1,200 mile hop with reasonable ease.[8]

The main body of Task Force 4612 arrived at the island on 30 March 1942 embarked in the Army transport ship USAT *Coamo* and the freighter *Luckenbach* under escort by two cruisers—*Memphis* and *Cincinnati*—and four destroyers, including *Ellis* (DD-154) and *Greer* (DD-145). The freighter *Pan Royal* had arrived earlier. After sailing from the United States with *Coamo* and *Luckenbach*, she proceeded to the island without escort, while the group stopped over in Recife to refuel before continuing on to Ascension.[9]

Embarked aboard the three ships were the U.S. Army's 38th Engineer Combat Regiment, 154 men of the 426th Coast Artillery, eight men of the 692nd Signal Corps Air Warning Detachment, a seventy-seven person medical contingent, nine-man Army Airways Communication section, two-man postal section, and ordnance, finance, and quartermaster detachments of fourteen, eight, and forty-one men, respectively. Following much work, a 6,000 foot runway at Wideawake Airfield became operational on 10 July 1942. The field was named after the sooty tern—a type of seabird, known locally as the 'wideawake"—which migrated to the island to lay their eggs. As intended, the island airbase would serve as a refueling point for planes travelling between the United States and Africa. Patrol aircraft based there would deter U-boat, raider, and blockade runner activity in and across the isolated ocean area.[10]

TASK FORCE 23 BLOCKADES MARTINIQUE

In May 1942, Ingram's Task Force 23 was called upon to blockade Martinique, and six ships of the Force proceeded to the Caribbean, while two task groups consisting of one cruiser and one destroyer each continued ocean patrol in the South Atlantic. The former Task Force 3 (Ingram's South Atlantic Forces) had been re-designated Task Force 23 on 10 February 1942. The island of Martinique, in the West Indies, was a "Vichy" French territory. The French State was the formal title of France's puppet Vichy administration installed by the Nazis after they conquered France in 1940, but "Vichy France," "Vichy Regime," "Vichy Government," or "Vichy" were commonly used to describe the government, which, officially neutral, collaborated with the Axis powers from July 1940 to August 1944.[11]

Three months earlier, on 22 February 1942, a War Department telegram to any or all U.S. Navy ships and to commander, Task Force 2 had conveyed the following guidance regarding Vichy naval forces in the French West Indies:

> Orders issued to destroy or capture French Naval vessels which may leave port in French West Indies, [auxiliary cruiser] *Barfluer* with Admiral Robert and small number of French seaplanes on usual flights excepted. French territorial waters to be disregarded if necessary to destroy enemy ships or submarines.[12]

Vice Adm. Georges A. M. J. Robert, who had arrived at Martinique in 1939 aboard the French cruiser *Jeanne d'Arc*, was Vichy High Commissioner for the Antilles (Martinique and Guadeloupe), Guiana, and Saint Pierre et Miquelon. Martinique was officially pro-Vichy, and America and Great Britain wanted to limit any impact of its stance on the war. After the United States prepared plans to capture the island, Robert had agreed in late 1941 to keep the French naval vessels immobilized in return for the Allies not invading the French Antilles.[13]

In early May 1942, *Cincinnati*, *Somers*, and *Davis* reported to commander Caribbean Sea Frontier, Vice Adm. John H. Hoover,

USN, for duty off Martinique in blocking the French in that area. The flagship *Memphis*, with *Jouett* and *Winslow* soon followed, arriving at Martinique on the 12th. Ingram was present and in command of the Task Force 23 units, plus the destroyers *Blakely* and *Biddle*. He delivered an ultimatum to Admiral Robert, requiring that he make his ships unfit for war. Before the end of May, Robert accepted this demand and disarmed the Vichy warships at Fort-de-France, but meanwhile, German U-boats and at least one Italian submarine penetrated into Brazilian coastal waters and the merchant vessel *Commandante Lyra* became the first Brazilian casualty in the South Atlantic.

Allied fears that the French naval vessels in Martinique might try to slip away to Europe persisted, however, until mid-1943, when Robert returned to France and Free French sympathizers took control of the French fleet.[15]

TORPEDO ATTACK ON THE *COMMANDANTE LYRA*

On 18 May 1942, the Brazilian *Commandante Lyra* was torpedoed by the Italian submarine *Barbarigo* off Cape São Roque, Brazil. *Barbarigo* was one of eleven submarines of the *Marcello*-class, one of the best produced by Italian shipyards. She had left La Pallice, the deep-water port of La Rochelle, France, on 25 April on a patrol to waters off Brazil. Capitano di Corvetta Enzo Grossi was the commanding officer of the submarine. His orders were to patrol off Cape São Roque, where it was expected there would be heavy shipping traffic and minimal anti-submarine activity.[16]

Barbarigo reached her area of operations on 17 May. The next day, she found and attacked the *Commandante Lyra*. The ship's master later indicated they never saw the submarine, which hit the *Lyra* with one torpedo, eight rounds from her deck gun on one side of the ship, and eleven on the other. Grossi, certain that the 400-foot merchant vessel was near sinking, then departed the area, leaving the *Lyra* burning at position 02°30'S, 34°20'W. Her crew escaped the ship in boats, after transmitting an SOS radio transmission.[17]

The emergency signal was picked up by Task Group 23.6 (Patrol Squadron VP-83 unit at Natal), which passed the location of the ship to two task groups, each comprised of one cruiser and one destroyer, operating at sea in the South Atlantic. Task Group 23.2 (*Milwaukee* CL-5 and *Moffett* DD-362) and 23.3 (*Omaha* CL-4 and *McDougal* DD-358) at once turned toward the position of the Brazilian SOS to hunt and destroy the submarine. *Milwaukee* and *Moffett*, being much closer, arrived first, at 0919 the following day. While still forty miles from

Lyra, a sighting was made of smoke emitting from the ship. Closer inspection revealed a large fire burning in her after hold, and evidence of fire as far forward as the bridge. Moreover, as a result of the torpedo strike and flooding via the resultant breech in her hull, she sat deeper in the water and listed about eight degrees to port.[18]

The seaplane tender *Thrush* (AVP-3), at anchor at Natal, also received the SOS. That evening, as much faster combatant ships rushed to the scene to aid survivors and try to salvage *Lyra*, she put to sea at 1840. Her tasking was to try to tow the damaged, sinking vessel to port. An ex-World War I era minesweeper, she was the closest thing to an ocean tug available. Having been designed to pull heavy sweep gear at slow speeds, *Thrush*'s propulsion plant (Two Babcock and Wilcox boilers, triple expansion reciprocating steam engine, and single shaft and propeller) produced the necessary torque to tow other vessels. In fact, some of her sister ships still in service were serving the Navy as fleet tugs in rear areas.[19]

Photo 10-2

Minesweeper *Thrush* (AM-18) circa 1930, while serving as, but not yet designated as, a seaplane tender (AVP).
U.S. Naval History and Heritage Command Photograph #NH 79070

Thrush had arrived at Para, Brazil, from Trinidad on 7 December 1941 for duty with the South Atlantic forces. After performing wartime patrols out of Para for the next two weeks, she relocated on 20 December to Natal, her new base of operations. Thereafter, she served as a "maid of all duties," refueling planes, carrying supplies from port to port, and functioning on occasion as a floating radio station. After clearing Natal on 19 May, *Thrush* proceeded at standard speed, 11 knots (110 shaft RPMs), toward *Lyra*'s position.[20]

Thrush reached the *Commandante Lyra* in early afternoon the following day, 20 May. *Omaha* and *McDougal* were present in the area. At 1425, *Thrush* took the merchant ship in tow, using 120 fathoms of 8-inch manila line and 30 fathoms of *Lyra*'s anchor chain. The heavy chain created a catenary (dip) in the tow line; enabling the line (when the proper length) to act as a shock absorber and help keep the two ships "in step." A towing vessel and tow were said to be "in step," when they met and rode over their respective wave crests at the same time. In the absence of this type of arrangement, a tug might crest a wave top, and accelerate down into the trough, as the tow maintained its speed, or even slowed, while climbing its respective wave; thereby stretching and snapping the tow line.[21]

As the seaplane tender took up slack in the tow line and with her engine ahead (using about 70 RPM), attempted to make good a southerly course; she faced a daunting challenge. The seas were rough with 16 knot winds from the southeast, and her ponderous charge was aflame and heavily laden. *Lyra*'s draft forward was 30 feet, and draft aft, 26 feet, with #1 cargo hold dry, #2 hold flooded, #3 hold burning, #4 hold flooded, and #5 hold burning. Under these conditions, *Thrush* found it nearly impossible to control the tow, and her advance throughout the remainder of the day was negligible.[22]

The following day, winds from the southeast increased to 20 knots and no headway was made. In addition to opposition imposed by the wind, *Thrush* was not able to make much progress because of the weight of the tow due to flooding, and because her rudder was not sufficiently effective to keep the tow on course. *Omaha* and *McDougal* left the area and proceeded to Recife. Later that day, *Milwaukee* and *Moffett* arrived in the area. That night, fires aboard *Lyra* grew larger and her draft forward increased to thirty-two feet.[23]

At sunrise on 22 May, a salvage party from the *Milwaukee*—twenty-six officers and men—boarded the *Lyra* to pump water from the ship and work the fires. They remained aboard her until evening. Meanwhile, *Thrush* replaced the manila tow line with 110 fathoms of one-and-five-eights-inch wire cable, and then went ahead, making 70 RPMs and steering a course of 200 degrees true. That evening, *Heitor Perdigao*, a Brazilian Navy tug, rendezvoused with the group.[24]

"CAT AND MOUSE" WITH AN ENEMY SUBMARINE

An already difficult situation was made worse the following day when, in early morning darkness, *Moffett* detected an enemy submarine. The destroyer had been screening *Thrush* and *Lyra*, maintaining a circular patrol radius of about 3,000 yards around the two ships. *Milwaukee* was in the vicinity and had been sighted periodically throughout the night, which was characterized by overcast sky with frequent rain squalls, swells from the southeast and moderate seas with whitecaps. At 0306, *Moffett* gained a sound contact, went to General Quarters, and dropped three depth charges a few minutes later. She searched the area and, unable to regain sonar contact, secured from battle stations and resumed her patrol.[25]

Photo 10-3

Destroyer *Moffett* (DD-362) in South American waters on 15 January 1943.
U.S. National Archives Photograph #80-G-64929

About 0736, Lt. Comdr. Jesse C. Bowell, USN (*Moffett's* commanding officer) sighted a wake on the starboard beam, about 2,000 yards distant. The destroyer was then positioned 3,500 yards on the port beam of the tow, with the *Thrush* and *Lyra* in sight, but not *Perdigao*. It was first thought the wake might be *Perdigao's*, but it appeared excessive for so small a tug. All guns and a searchlight were trained on the unseen vessel creating the wake, and the destroyer's rudder put over to head toward it. A dark silhouette took shape which looked much like a submarine, but could have been the tug. At 0738, as orders were given to illuminate the unidentified contact, it crash dove. The submarine was on *Moffett's* starboard quarter, some 1,200 yards away, with the destroyer swinging rapidly to the right.[26]

The destroyer gained sonar contact at 0752 on the submerged submarine (bearing 330°T, range 480 yards), and attacked with three six-hundred-pound depth charges. Neither this attack, nor successive ones appeared to have any effect; *Moffett* continued to reacquire the contact, and carry out ineffective depth-charge runs for over an hour:

- 0809: Contact gained; 025° true, 1,100 yards
- 0812: Attacked with six 600-lb depth charges
- 0836: Contact gained; 280° true, 1,375 yards
- 0842: Attacked with three 600-lb depth charges
- 0854: Contact gained; 155° true, 860 yards
- 0859: Attacked with three 600-lb depth charges[27]

Following a run at 0859, the destroyer was unable to regain contact, and began to search anew. Near the end of this unsuccessful endeavor, a sighting was made at 1201 of three small patches of oil each about twenty feet in diameter and separated by about 200 yards. The oil may or may not have originated from the submarine. If so, it may have been due to depth-charge damage or, more likely, have been purposely discharged from a torpedo tube to make searching ships or aircraft believe their quarry was destroyed. At 1250, *Moffett* received a report from a *Milwaukee* scout observation plane, "Submarine on surface, 015° true, distance 35 miles, preparing to bomb, climbing for altitude."[28]

Moffett arrived at the scene of the plane contact at 1345 and began searching, joining *Milwaukee*'s two scout observation planes and a PBY patrol aircraft in the vicinity. Having only eight depth charges remaining, *Moffett* asked *Milwaukee* to transfer some to her. Before such action could occur, the destroyer gained sonar contact at 1400, bearing 090° true, range 1,500 yards. For the next hour and a half, *Moffett* tried unsuccessfully to destroy a very wily and evasive foe, as detailed in war diary entries:

1409 Attacked dropping three six-hundred-pound depth charges. 1419 Contact bearing 306° true, range 1400 yards. Submarine very active, high pitch propeller noises, and groans from rudder and diving planes or shafts plainly heard. Did not attack with charges as submarine turned inside destroyer turning circle. Circled for another approach. 1449 Contact bearing 035° true, range 1750 yards. 1457 Attacked dropping three six-hundred-pound depth charges. 1509 Sighted an oil slick on the port bow bearing 140° true. 1512 Contact bearing 140° true, range 1800 yards. 1519 Lost contact; did not attack because submarine turned inside. 1522

Contact bearing 185 degrees true, range 740 yards. 1529 Attacked dropping last two depth charges. Proceeded at full speed for rendezvous with the USS *MILWAUKEE* to receive depth charges.[29]

After obtaining four three-hundred-pound depth charges from the *Milwaukee* at 1554, *Moffett* returned at full speed to the contact area. She gained sonar contact at 1644, but quickly lost it three minute later. Between 1652 and 1845, *Moffett* reacquired contact several times, and made two depth-charge attacks before losing the submarine for good, with echoes (sonar returns) mushy and fading.[30]

Lt. Commander Bowell later described difficulties encountered in trying, unsuccessfully, to prevail against the enemy submarine. Each time the destroyer gained contact, and then attempted a depth-charge run, his foe was able to escape a devastating attack via use of a false target, or by nimbly maneuvering inside the turning radius of the ship. By such means, the submarine was able to eventually escape.

> The tactics employed by the submarine varied. One of these was making knuckles at high speed, then hiding behind the knuckle and feinting in one direction but turning hard in the opposite, to get inside the destroyers turning circle. Another was running directly away making a sine curve track until the destroyer was at close range, then cutting inside the turning circle. Still another appeared to be the laying of a wake at high speed across the destroyer's advance then sliding behind this screen and stopping until the destroyer was at close range then swinging inside the turning circle. From the varying ranges at which contact was lost, the submarine apparently changed his depth of submergence between the various attacks.[31]

(A submarine could produce a knuckle through the sudden, back and forth movement of its rudder, creating an especially turbulent spot in the water. It would then slip away from this false target while the sonar operator aboard ship was determining whether the contact was the submarine or a decoy.)

While *Moffett* was thus engaged on 23 May, *Heitor Perdigao* came alongside *Lyra* to pump water from her peak tank (storage for boiler feed water), in an attempt to lighten the ship. That evening, the Brazilian tug passed a cable to *Thrush* and the two of them proceeded to tow in tandem, with *Thrush* furnishing the towing power for *Lyra* and the much smaller craft holding the seaplane tender into the wind.[32]

The remaining two days, 24-25 May, proved uneventful as *Thrush* and *Heitor Perdigao* continued to drag their charge toward Fortaleza.

The *Commandante Lyra* anchored in the Fortaleza Roadstead at 1240 on the 25th, and *Thrush* a few minutes later to recover her towing cable. The seaplane tender stood out of the bay that evening to return to Natal, once again making her standard speed of eleven knots.[33]

No lives were lost in the *Commandante Lyra* episode. *Moffett* recovered a boat containing sixteen survivors and *Milwaukee* twenty-five others aboard two boats, including the ship's master. A fourth boat with the remaining nine survivors managed to reach the coast on its own. The rescue and salvage work by the U.S. Navy created much good will with Brazil. Ambassador Jefferson Caffery received a letter of thanks from the Brazilian government, and the Lloyd Brasileiro Company, owners of the ship, donated $50,000 to the Navy Relief Society.[34]

BRAZIL DECLARES WAR ON GERMANY AND ITALY

Brazil's entry into the war on 22 August 1942 was of great importance to the Allies, particularly regarding her role in helping keep open vital South Atlantic air and sea routes necessary for the supply of Allied troops in Africa. Brazil declared war on Germany and Italy following the sinking between 14 and 17 August of five Brazilian ships—the *Baependi, Araraquara, Itagiba, Acara,* and *Anibal Benevolo*—by U-boats, including a troopship with heavy loss of life. These acts outraged the people of Brazil as illustrated by excerpts from an article in the 18 August issue of the *Journal Pequeno*, a Recife afternoon paper:

> Truly monstrous are the acts which the Axis submarines have just perpetrated against helpless Brazilians. The torpedoing and sinking of five of our ships between Bahia and Sergipe, with the attendant loss of life, caused profound indignation throughout the country. And this wave of revolt shaking the Nation from North to South, is already reflected in all the American continent - each government seeking to manifest its solidarity with Brazil.

> At this moment in many Brazilian homes, there is sorrow and tears. But there is also with all of them, as throughout the country, absolute confidence in the government of the Republic. If Rome, Tokyo, and Berlin think that they can intimidate us by such savage acts, they are completely mistaken.

> Our pride will never be beaten down. We will now know how to confront the enemy - when and exactly how, with all the bravery that has always characterized this nation when its honor was affected.[35]

President Getúlio Dornelles Vargas' first measure of reprisal was an amendment to Brazil's constitution, to permit the seizure of property of those whose countries had carried out acts of aggression. His second step was to order the withdrawal of all Brazilian merchant ships from the seas; at the same time he amended the constitution in such a way as to empower himself to declare war without a vote of parliament. In a related action, the government soon announced that Brazilian secret police had smashed a huge spy ring, with the arrest of more than one hundred Axis agents, including both a colonel in the German Army and a Japanese admiral disguised as a farmer. Police also shut down several clandestine radio stations, among them one that had broadcast to Germany the arrival in Rio, and ultimate destination, of RMS *Queen Mary*. The ocean liner was used as a troopship throughout the war, and was known as the "Grey Ghost" during this period.[36]

Photo 10-4

British ocean liner RMS *Queen Mary*, painted grey and employed as a troopship, at sea on 8 December 1942.
U.S National Archives Photograph #80-G-426373

Brazil was the largest of the South American republics, with territorial waters stretching from latitude 5° north to 32° south—a 2,220 nautical mile swath of ocean off her east coast. Of concern to both the Brazilian and American governments was the vulnerability of the country's northeast region, known as "the bulge." Germany was in control of French North Africa, and there was fear that Hitler could invade the bulge via the Atlantic Narrows between West Africa and Brazil. The Brazilian government was well aware that only the United States could provide the necessary forces to protect that area, and security in the South Atlantic for Brazilian merchant shipping. The United States, in turn, required the use of bases and airfields in Brazil to support Army Air Corps and Navy air and sea operations.[37]

In summer 1942, Vice Adm. Jonas H. Ingram's South Atlantic Force was a relatively small light cruiser and destroyer force with a wide field of operations and a variety of duties. Cruiser Division Two included the *Memphis, Milwaukee, Omaha* and *Cincinnati*, to which the *Marblehead* was subsequently added. In addition, there was Destroyer Squadron Nine, made up of the *Davis, Moffett, Somers, McDougal, Jouett, Winslow* and *Green*. The other ships of the Task Force 23 were the auxiliary oiler *Patoka*, the seaplane tender *Thrush* and the auxiliary ammunition ship *Nitro*. Needing all the combatant forces he could muster, Ingram shifted his staff from *Memphis* to the *Patoka* in order to release the cruiser for wider duties. *Patoka* would remain in Recife, serving as Force flagship, from August 1942 to April 1943.[38]

These ships ranged the western South Atlantic escorting convoys, intercepting blockade runners operating from the Far East around Cape Horn to Axis Europe, and searching for enemy submarines and surface raiders. They also provided protection of a sort to the long coastline of Brazil from Bahia northward, as well as to the mid-ocean garrison of American forces established on Ascension Island in 1942. Navy seaplanes had begun operating from Brazilian bases in December 1941. Shortly after, the Navy brought in land-based amphibian planes in April 1942, to conduct patrols from Natal and Recife.[39]

AMERICAN-BRAZILIAN-BRITISH COOPERATION

Following the Brazilian declaration of war, President Vargas directed his Minister of Marine to put Brazilian naval vessels under Ingram's informal operational control. In a meeting with Rear Adm. Neiva of the Brazilian Navy, the two senior officers made tentative plans for combined operations and exchange of information. Within the next few days, arrangements were completed for unified Brazilian-American operations. Captain Dutra, commanding officer of the Brazilian cruiser division flagship, *Rio Grande do Sul*, presented his compliments and stated that he had received instructions from the Brazilian High Navy Command to operate jointly with Task Force 23. The Brazilian Army Commander in the Recife Area agreed that Naval Forces had paramount interests in Northern Brazil. Hence, commander Task Force 23 should take full responsibility for coastal and offshore operations, while the Brazilian general would look out for security measures ashore. Ingram also worked out an arrangement with Brig. Gen. Eduardo Gomes in which Brazilian Air Force operations in the bulge area would be integrated with operations of the United States Navy.[40]

Photo 10-5

Brazilian President Getúlio Dornelles Vargas inspects troop berthing spaces aboard
the transport *General W. A. Mann* (AP-112), at Rio de Janeiro on 20 July 1944.
Accompanying him is the ship's commanding officer, Comdr. Paul S. Maguire.
U.S. National Archives Photograph #80-G-238937

Brazil's navy was then comprised largely of old ships built in the
United Kingdom—two battleships, two light cruisers, one destroyer,
and six torpedo boats.   Rounding out the sea service were four
submarines built in Italy (three relatively new) and six modern
minelayers constructed in Rio de Janeiro, Brazil.   The naval forces
which Brazil had committed to coastal defense under Admiral Ingram
were minuscule, so the next step was to build up the combined forces
by assigning additional U.S. destroyers to the South Atlantic and by
turning over patrol vessels to Brazil via lend-lease. The minelayers and
Brazilian patrol planes pressed into convoy escort duties were
gradually augmented by eight destroyer escorts, eight sub-chasers, and
eight patrol craft obtained from the United States. The Brazilian Navy
was further strengthened by its acquisition of three bright and shiny
destroyers, built in Rio de Janeiro, and eight anti-submarine warfare

trawlers in Niteroi, Brazil. A complete list of the ships of Brazil's navy in World War II is proved in Appendix D.[41]

FOURTH FLEET/ROYAL NAVY RESPONSIBILITIES

Other conferences were held by Ingram to discuss American and British naval cooperation. On 3 September, Rear Adm. Frank H. Pegram, RN, the British West Africa naval commander, visited Ingram's headquarters at Recife. The result was an agreement by the United States Navy and Royal Navy to a geographical division of the South Atlantic, which made the western half, extending from South America out to and including Ascension Island, an American defense responsibility.[42]

Map 10-1

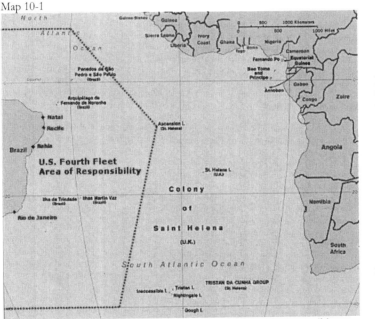

South Atlantic Sub-Area for which the U.S. Fourth Fleet was responsible.

A Fourth Fleet operation plan dated September 1943 defined Ingram's area of responsibility as that part of the Western Atlantic between Latitude 10°N and 40°S, and west of a line from point 10°N, 30°W, to Ascension Island (including that island and its territorial waters), thence to 40°S, 26°W. Simply stated, the Royal Navy was responsible for the eastern portion of the South Atlantic to the coast of West Africa, and the Fourth Fleet, the area between 10°N and 40°S extending west from Ascension Island to the continental land mass of ith America, excluding the territorial waters of South American countries not at war. (The Admiralty retained control of British communications facilities on Ascension, a British possession.)[43]

As practical, the U.S. Fourth Fleet and forces under the command of the Royal Navy's Flag Officer-in-Charge, West Africa (FOCWA), were to render mutual support in the accomplishment of the mission. FOCWA, based at Freetown, desired to know the positions and prospective movements of the Fourth Fleet, particularly in the ocean area adjacent to that for which he was responsible. Ingram was to furnish this information weekly, and by dispatches as changes occurred. The organization of the Fourth Fleet as of 4 September 1943 may be found in Appendix E. Surface ships and aviation squadrons periodically joined or departed the fleet for other duties, but this provides an overview of the force structure.[44]

ORGANIZATION OF THE SOUTH ATLANTIC FORCE

From 1941 to 1945, the South Atlantic Force of the U.S. Atlantic Fleet operated under successive operational designations—Task Force 3, Task Force 23, Fourth Fleet, and finally Task Force 27. Throughout these changes it retained its administrative title, South Atlantic Force. Task Force 3 was re-designated Task Force 23 on 10 February 1942, and Ingram was promoted to vice admiral. His Force continued to grow and was upgraded to the U.S. Fourth Fleet on 15 March 1943. Ingram commanded the South Atlantic Force/Fourth Fleet until 11 November 1944. Following his relief by Vice Adm. William R. Munroe, Ingram assumed the duties of commander-in-chief Atlantic Fleet in the rank of admiral. The Fourth Fleet was downgraded to Task Force on 15 April 1945.[45]

Liberty Ship Sinks German Raider

STEPHEN HOPKINS *overdue at Paramaribo [Suriname] since 9/10 from Capetown. No U/Boats are suspected in this area. Ship may therefore have been attacked by M.T.Bs [motor torpedo boats] from Raider "H" [Michel] or Raider "J" [Stier].*

—Admiralty War Diaries entry of 20 October 1942; highlighting the possible loss of a Liberty ship to a German raider operating in the South Atlantic.

By 30 September 1942, the nine German raiders prowling the world's oceans had collectively sunk one hundred-three ships and captured thirty others, but this impressive record cost them dearly. *Pinguin* was the first auxiliary cruiser to be lost; the heavy cruiser HMS *Cornwall* found her near the entrance to the Persian Gulf on 8 May 1941, and sank her with gunfire. Later in the year, the Australian light cruiser HMAS *Sydney* disposed of *Kormoran* off the west coast of Australia on 19 November 1941, and three days later, *Atlantis* was sunk by the heavy cruiser HMS *Devonshire* in the South Atlantic on 22 November. The fourth casualty was the raider *Stier*. She was sunk in the South Atlantic, nearly ten months later on 27 September 1942. Her loss to *Stephen Hopkins*, in a battle that resulted in the destruction of the Liberty ship as well, symbolized that the reign of terror wrought by the auxiliary cruisers was near an end, and is the subject of this chapter.[1]

Before delving into an account of the battle between the *Stephen Hopkins* and *Stier*, an overview of the final days of other raiders may be in order. *Komet* was sunk by the British motor torpedo boat *MTB 236* off Cherbourg, France, on 14 October 1942. *Thor* was destroyed by fire on 30 November 1942, while at Yokohama, Japan. *Michel*, the only raider to send any Allied ships to the bottom after 30 September 1942—a total of eight—was sunk east of Yokohama, by the submarine USS *Tarpon* (SS-175) on 17 October 1943. The most fortunate of the raiders (and the only survivors), *Widder* and *Orion*, were not sent to sea again after they returned to Germany from war cruises on 31 October 1940 and 23 August 1941, respectively.[2]

Number of Victims of German Raiders

	April 1940 to September 1942		October 1942 to September 1943		
German Raider	Ships Sunk	Ships Captured	Ships Sunk	Ships Captured	Disposition of Raider
Atlantis	16	6			Sunk by HMS *Devonshire* on 22 Nov 1941
Komet	7	1			Sunk by British *MTB 236* on 14 Oct 42
Kormoran	11	1			Sunk by HMAS *Sydney*, 19 Nov 41
Michel	11		6		Sunk by USS *Tarpon*, 17 Oct 43
Orion	11	1			Returned safely to Germany, 23 Aug 41
Pinguin	16	16			Sunk by HMS *Cornwall*, 8 May 41
Stier	4				Sunk by SS *Stephen Hopkins*, 27 Sep 42
Thor	18	4			Destroyed by fire in Yokohama harbor, Japan, 30 Nov 42
Widder	9	1			Returned safely to Germany, 31 Oct 40
Totals	103	30	6		7 of 9 Raiders sunk or destroyed by fire[3]

ENCOUNTER WITH THE ENEMY

On 27 September 1942, the *Stephen Hopkins* was en route from Cape Town, South Africa, to Paramaribo (the capital city of Suriname, on the northeastern Atlantic coast of South America) when two enemy ships suddenly appeared out of the mist and opened fire. *Stier*, the smaller of the two, was heavily armed with six 5.9-inch guns, two 37mm guns, and four 20mm guns, as well as two torpedo tubes and two Arado Ar-231 lightweight floatplanes used to scout for prey. Kapitänleutnant Horst Gerlach also had a large crew at his disposal: eleven officers, three prize officers (to take command of captured vessels) and three hundred ten enlisted men. The larger ship, blockade runner *Tannenfels*, carried smaller-caliber guns.[4]

PREVIOUS RAIDING HISTORY

Stier—the former 4,778-ton freighter *Cairo*—had been fitted out at Szczecin, Poland, near the Baltic Sea in December 1941. Five months later, she proceeded in May 1942 down the Oder River, out the Baltic Sea and on down the English Channel to the Gironde. An estuary in southwest France and the largest in western Europe, the Gironde was formed from the meeting of the rivers Dordogne and Garonne downstream of Bordeaux. After receiving additional supplies there, *Stier* departed for the South Atlantic.[5]

On the forenoon of 4 June, the raider intercepted and sank the 4,986-ton British freighter *Gemstone* in the Atlantic narrows 175 miles east of Brazil's St. Paul Rocks, and took aboard the survivors as prisoners. Her next victim was the U.S. owned/Panamanian-flagged 10,169-ton tanker *Stanvac Calcutta*, which she intercepted on 6 June and sank—after stiff resistance—in the vicinity of 5°S, 28°W. The master of the tanker, Gustaf O. Karlsson, and fifteen of her crew were killed in the furious battle, in which the merchant ship gallantly returned fire with her single 3-inch bow gun and 4-inch after gun. The chief mate, Auge H. Knudsen, and thirty-six mariners abandoned the sinking ship. They were retrieved, oil-soaked, from the Atlantic by the Germans. *Stier* expended 148 gun rounds and a torpedo to destroy the *Calcutta*.[6]

After transferring these prisoners and those taken earlier from the *Gemstone* to the German tanker *Charlotte Schliemann* at a South Atlantic rendezvous, *Stier* continued to search for prey. Her next victim was the 7,072-ton British cargo ship *Dalhousie*, which she came across the morning of 9 August, 250 miles east of Trinidad. After a lengthy chase, the raider caught her quarry at 1248, and sank the cargo ship with gunfire. *Dalhousie*'s thirty-seven crewmen abandoned as the ship settled by the stern, and were taken prisoner. *Stier* rendezvoused with *Charlotte Schliemann* on 27 August, and transferred the latest batch of prisoners to her. That was unfortunate for the beleaguered British mariners; the tanker was on a run to the Far East, and would leave them at Yokohama under Japan's less-than-compassionate care.[7]

Stier met the blockade runner *Tannenfels* (which was on passage from the Far East to Biscay, Spain) 650 miles north-northwest of Tristan da Cunha on 25 September. The purpose of this rendezvous was likely for the raider to obtain supplies from the runner, and then escort her though the "high risk area" of the equatorial Atlantic.[8]

TWENTY MINUTES OF FURIOUS BATTLE

Aboard the Liberty ship *Stephen Hopkins* were a merchant crew of forty-one mariners, a Navy Armed Guard contingent of fifteen sailors, and a passenger, George Townsend, who had come aboard in Durban, a city in eastern South Africa. (A bright and shiny new cargo ship, *Hopkins* had been built at a Kaiser shipyard in Richmond, California, for the U.S. Maritime Commission and delivered on 11 May 1942.) She had encountered a rain squall earlier that morning, 27 September, while steering northwest toward Paramaribo. As a result, despite there being five lookouts on watch topside, no sighting was made of *Stier* or *Tannenfels* until very late. As the German ships appeared out of the mist at 0938, only two miles distant on *Hopkins'* starboard bow, *Stier* commenced firing.[9]

Stier ordered the *Stephen Hopkins* to stop engines. Instead of complying, Paul Buck, the ship's master, ordered hard left rudder and reversed course. By this action, he could bring his 4-inch gun to bear, while presenting only his stern to enemy fire. Buck knew that he did not stand a chance of outrunning the raider (which could make 14 knots in comparison to his top speed of 11 knots). Accordingly, he had previously told his crew that if they found themselves in such a situation they would fight with what they had rather than surrender, and this he intended to do.[10]

As *Stier's* 4-inch guns began shooting simultaneously, under the direction of a fire control system, *Tannenfels* moved in closer, but did not enter the battle except to spray the decks of the *Stephen Hopkins* with machine gun fire. Aboard the Liberty ship, Navy Armed Guard gunners, and mariners assigned as loaders, manned their guns and commenced firing at the German ships. During the battle, Lt. (jg) Kenneth Willett, USNR, the officer-in-charge of the gun crews, was severely wounded in the abdomen by shrapnel, but continued directing the men. Seaman Second Class Moses N. Barker Jr. trained the 4-inch gun directly at the waterline of the raider (about a thousand yards distant), and with his gun crew reloading as fast as possible, he was getting a round off about every forty-five seconds.[11]

Remarkably, two of the first 33-pound projectiles to hit the raider jammed her rudder to starboard, and severed the fuel oil supply to her engines, causing them to stop. With *Stier* drifting in a half circle, Gerlach could now employ his portside armament, but could not fire torpedoes because another hit knocked out electrical power to the ammunition hoists. As the steady fire of *Stephen Hopkins'* stern gun continued, rounds set the *Stier's* fuel bunker on fire, hit the officers' quarters, both hospitals and the bridge. Her crew was then trying frantically to stop the oil fire from spreading toward No. 2 hold and the nineteen torpedoes stored there. A hit on the fire main system had rendered hoses useless, necessitating use of a bucket brigade.[12]

Second Mate Joseph E. Layman, who was in charge of *Stephen Hopkins'* forward 37mm guns, poured rounds into the *Tannenfels* until his ammunition handlers were killed and the gun tub wrecked. Meanwhile, the sailors manning the Liberty ship's smaller armament (four .50-caliber machine guns and two .30-cal. guns) raked the decks of both enemy ships.[13]

Despite the damage inflicted on her by *Stephen Hopkins'* guns, *Stier*'s overwhelming fire power continued to pound the Liberty ship and casualties were heavy.   Salvos from the raider exploded the *Hopkins'* propulsion boiler, demolished the radio shack and mast, wrecked her steering engine room, and sprayed the deckhouse and hull with shrapnel—starting fires and killing merchant mariners and guardsmen.   Most of the 4-inch gun crew were killed or wounded, as well.[14]

LIBERTY SHIP AND RAIDER SINK ONE ANOTHER

We could not but feel that we had gone down at the hands of a gallant foe…that Liberty ship had ended a very successful raiding voyage. We could have sunk more ships.

On the other hand: *She may have sunk us, but she saved most of our lives. We could not have lasted much longer out there those days [with Allied warships finding and sinking raiders] and there would not always have been a* Tannenfels *around to pick us up.*

—Oberleutnant zur See Ludolf Petersen, the *Stier*'s first officer, remarking on the sea battle with the SS *Stephen Hopkins*.[15]

With *Stephen Hopkins'* propulsion lost, superstructure aflame, and the vessel in a sinking condition, Buck gave the order to abandon ship. While the crew was carrying out this instruction, they again heard the harsh bark of the 4-inch gun.   It was being manned by Cadet Midshipman Edwin J. O'Hara, who normally worked in the engine room.   Upon emerging on deck from the burning compartment, he had rushed to the abandoned gun.   Finding five unexpended shells in the ready locker, he loaded and fired them at *Stier*—sinking the enemy ship. (Over the course of the battle, fifteen of the thirty-five four-inch rounds fired at *Stier* hit her; an amazing feat, considering the gun had to be manually trained and elevated, and received no radar-provided target data, as did the raider's guns.)   At 1030, *Stephen Hopkins* sank stern first at position 28°8'S, 11°59'W, taking Lt. (jg) Kenneth Willett and many other dead or wounded men with her.   Willett, despite being gravely hurt, was last seen helping to cast loose life rafts in a desperate effort to save the lives of others.[16]

Stier was in even worse condition, ablaze from stem to stern, and down by the stern.   With no hope of preventing fire from reaching the torpedo warheads, and his ship likely to blow up at any moment,

Gerlach gave orders to set scuttling charges and to abandon ship. Informed of this decision, Kapitän Haase of the *Tannenfels* maneuvered his ship in as close to the raider as he dared in the heavy seas, to take off her crew. After doing so, the blockade runner backed clear of the raider and disappeared in the mist.   A short time later, a heavy explosion was heard at 1157, followed by a second one, two minutes later. *Stier* then disappeared into the abyss, stern first.[17]

Tannenfels, although damaged and encumbered with prisoners and *Stier*'s crew, managed to evade Allied warships and aircraft and reach Bordeaux on 6 November.[18]

THIRTY-ONE DAYS IN A LIFEBOAT

Of the fifty-seven men aboard *Stephen Hopkins*, only fifteen survived. The others were killed in battle, went down with the ship, or perished during thirty-one days at sea in the single surviving lifeboat. When the order to abandon ship was given at 0955, all of the boats except No. 1 had been damaged by enemy fire. As this boat was being lowered, an exploding round hit it, killing two and wounding four of the other men in the boat assisting to put it in the water. However, the survivors succeeded in getting the boat clear of the ship, and men aboard *Stephen Hopkins* able to do so, then jumped overboard and climbed into "doughnut rafts" or swam to the lifeboat.[19]

As the boat drifted near the two German ships, the men in it could see that *Stier* was down by the stern, with huge clouds of smoke emitting from her. When last sighted, the enemy ships were bow to bow, with the mother ship taking off the crew of the raider. As they rowed away, they witnessed their ship, *Stephen Hopkins*, sink by the stern, and moments later heard a large explosion. They inferred the latter event was due to the detonation of the magazine of the raider and were confident that she had sunk.[20]

Hopkins' lifeboat rowed around in the gloom, trying to find survivors from rafts or in the water until decreasing visibility precluded any further efforts. The boat then put out a sea anchor and remained in the area until noon the following day hoping to locate additional survivors. The seas were so heavy there was little chance anyone in the water could have survived the night. No other crewmen were found, and the boat—under the command of the single surviving officer, Second Engineer George S. Cronk—then set off in a westerly direction. Cronk kept a log during the ensuing 31-day journey to South America. The final entry was made on 27 October 1942:

Hurrah; sighted land at 4 a.m. Landed at the small Brazilian village of Barra do Stabapona. Police notified at Rio de Janeiro. Trying to arrange transportation to Rio. G. Cronk, 2d Engineer.[21]

Of the nineteen men in the boat, five were wounded. Four of these men expired during the 2,200 mile voyage, and were buried at sea.[22]

Diagram 11-1

RAIDER "J", 4,778 g.r.t., armed with 6", 4" and 3" director-fired guns.

TANNENFELS, 7,840-ton, lightly-armed runner which fought with RAIDER "J".

HERO SHIP

STEPHEN HOPKINS, 7,818-ton "Victory Ship", armed with one 4", one 37 MM, six mg.

Participants (American and German Ships) in Sea Battle.
Source: Intelligence Division, Office of Chief of Naval Operations Intelligence Report Serial 77-43, of 28 October 1943, Subject: Raider "J" (Case History). (The SS *Stephen Hopkins* is misidentified above as a *Victory*-ship in the diagram; she was a Liberty ship. Moreover, she had two, not one, 37mm guns forward.)

LAURELS FOR *STEPHEN HOPKINS'* CREWMEN

The *Stephen Hopkins* was the only U.S. merchant ship to sink an enemy surface combatant in World War II. For their heroism during this action, six of her crew received Distinguished Service Medals, the Merchant Marine's highest honor. Lt. (jg) Kenneth M. Willett was awarded the Navy Cross Medal. Additionally, *Stephen Hopkins* was designated a Gallant Ship; with presentation of a plaque, and ribbons for crewmen to display on their uniform blouses. Nine ships were thus honored in World War II. Only one other qualifying action took place in the South Atlantic, the battle between the *Stanvac Calcutta* and German raider *Stier*, discussed earlier in the chapter.[23]

Merchant Vessel	Date(s) of Action	Merchant Vessel	Date(s) of Action
SS *Stanvac Calcutta*	6 Jun 42	SS *Samuel Parker*	19 Jul 43
SS *Virginia Dare*	9-21 Sep 42	SS *Cedar Mills*	1 Dec 43
SS *Nathaniel Greene*	12 Sep 42	SS *Marcus Daly*	5 Oct 44
SS *William Moultrie*	12 Sep 42	SS *Adoniram Judson*	24-29 Oct 44
SS *Stephen Hopkins*	27 Sep 42		

Navy Cross Medal   Merchant Marine Gallant Ship Plaque   Merchant Marine Distinguished Service Medal

Vice Adm. Emory S. Land awarded the Distinguished Service Medals (DSM)—four of them posthumously, as was Willett's Navy Cross Medal. Copies of the award citations may be found in Appendix F. Land had retired in 1937; but on 18 February 1938, he became Chairman of the U.S. Maritime Commission, overseeing the design and construction of the more than 4,000 *Liberty-* and *Victory-*class ships that flew the U.S. flag during World War II.

Awardee	Rank	Award
Paul Buck	Master	DSM (Posthumously)
Richard Moczkowski	Chief Mate	DSM (Posthumously)
Joseph Earl Layman	Second Mate	DSM (Posthumously)
George S. Cronk	Second Engineer	DSM
Ford Stilson	Chief Steward	DSM
Edwin Joseph O'Hara	Cadet Engineer	DSM (Posthumously)
Kenneth M. Willett	Lt. (jg), USNR	Navy Cross (Posthumously)

Five ships were named in honor of the crew of *Stephen Hopkins* and of the ship itself:

- SS *Paul Buck*
- SS *Richard Moczkowski*
- SS *Edwin Joseph O'Hara*
- SS *Stephen Hopkins II*
- USS *Kenneth M. Willett* (DE-354)[24]

Anneliese Essberger
Scuttled by Crew

0408: Sighted dark object bearing 306 true, approximate distance 18,000 yards.

0426: Directed SOMERS *to proceed and investigate dark object, which was now seen to be a ship.*

0454: In reply to challenge, strange ship answered "LJPV," the call letters of the Norwegian ship SKJELBRED.

0522: SOMERS *reported strange ship had lowered life boats and was afire. Numerous explosions were observed.*

0542: Member of crew was seen to hoist the German Merchant Marine flag to the mainmast and to lower the Norwegian flag from the staff. Party from SOMERS *boarded and obtained some salvage, but was soon recalled as the ship was down by the stern and obviously sinking rapidly.*

0558: Scuttled ship sank in: Latitude 00-54.0 N. Longitude 22-23.0 W.

—USS *Milwaukee* War Diary entries for 21 November 1942, summarizing the hour and fifty minute period from detection of the German blockade runner *Anneliese Essberger,* to her destruction by her crew via the use of scuttling charges.

In the early months of 1942, intelligence from France indicated that at least one blockade runner had been getting back to German-held ports each month, and it was believed that many of these ships were protected by raiders during parts of their voyages. New raider tactics appeared on 1 May 1942, when the British freighter *Menelaus* was challenged and chased by the raider *Michel*, which used a motor torpedo boat in an unsuccessful attempt to halt and sink the faster merchant ship. These developments led British and American forces to development more effective sweeps in the South Atlantic. Correspondence from Adm. Royal E. Ingersoll, commander-in-chief Atlantic Fleet, to Admiral Ingram on 21 July, included discussion of a plan to use routine Army flights to help scout for potentially enemy ships. Ideally, such location information would include a rough estimate of a suspect ship's course and speed, to assist in its interception by Allied forces.

> I have just recommended to Admiral King that the prospective flights of Army planes to Africa, via Natal and Ascension, or direct, be so organized and scheduled as to provide the maximum air observation of the area, so that your forces can be informed of the locations of suspicious ships, instead of having to rely on what they can see themselves. This should greatly improve the "percentage" performance of the thin line that you can establish. This scheme will require a considerable organization in order to be effective, but it appears well worthwhile.[1]

On 12 November 1942, Task Group 23.2—destroyer *Somers* (DD-381), and light cruisers *Milwaukee* (CL-5) and *Cincinnati* (CL-6)—were on ocean patrol en route to the vicinity of Ascension Island. Aloft *Milwaukee* was the flag of Rear Adm. Oliver M. Read, commander Cruiser Division 2, who was embarked aboard her. Orders were received at noon from commander Task Force 23 directing the ships to proceed to the area of the St. Paul Rocks and intercept the blockade runners *Kota Nopan* and *Anneliese Essberger*. Intelligence indicated the German ships were en route from France to the Far East.[2]

Over the next several days, scout observation planes from the cruisers carried out reconnaissance flights during daylight hours, searching for the runners. By night, the ships relied on radar to detect any nearby ships. Shortly before dawn on 21 November, the *Cincinnati* reported a radar contact bearing 311° true, at a distance of 17,000 yards, upon which the group changed course to intercept the target.[3]

A short time later, a sighting was made at 0541 of a strange ship to the north-northwest, four miles distant, steering a reciprocal east-southeast course. *Somers* was ordered to investigate and maneuvered to do so. When challenged by blinker tube, the suspect ship gave the call letters of the *Skjelbred* (LJPV), Norwegian registry, but no further information. The destroyer then attempted communications by international signals and plain English language. The two cruisers resumed their patrol, and Rear Admiral Read ordered *Somers* to investigate further, then rejoin the group. The destroyer continued to close, and to try to communicate with the ship, to no avail. At 0620, it was possible to make out the Norwegian flag flying from a staff on her stern, and flag hoist LJPV closed up on the port yardarm.[4]

Somers signaled WBA and ordered the ship to heave to. As the destroyer closed to about 1,900 yards astern of the suspected runner, the ship turned hard left and stopped. The destroyer drew alongside it from astern, at which time the ship lowered four lifeboats. *Somers* signaled AJ and also in plain language, "Do Not Abandon Ship." A boarding party had been called away, which ordered the boats to return to their ship. They refused, and fire was observed on the bridge of what would prove to be the *Anneliese Essberger*, followed by three heavy explosions at 0640 in the holds of the ship, one forward and two aft. The German swastika was hoisted on the main mast and the Norwegian flag lowered.[5]

Photo 12-1

Destroyer USS *Somers* (DD-381) in September 1938.
U.S. Naval History and Heritage Command Photograph #NH 66341

The boarding party took a German officer out of one of the boats to serve as a guide, and at 0653 boarded the vessel. Items captured included: both of the flags, one 4-inch shell, a machine gun, the ship's Watch, Quarter, and Station Bill, propaganda booklets, an officers notebook, a helmet, etc. Fires and flooding caused by demolition charges were by then out of control, and the boarding party was unable to reach the bridge. The ship was fitted with one 4-inch gun aft, four 20mm machine guns, and one torpedo boat cutter rigged on a boom for instant lowering. The boarding party was recalled by the *Somers* because the vessel was down by the stern and sinking rapidly. The party left the ship at 0658, returning the officer to the lifeboat before it made the destroyer's side.[6]

At 0711, the *Anneliese Essberger* sank, stern first, leaving all sixty-two members of the crew unharmed and in boats at the scene. The *Milwaukee* and *Cincinnati* departed to search for the other blockade runner. The planes from both ships conducted reconnaissance flights from 0836 to 1245, sighting two British ships which appeared to be corvettes and which made the proper man-o-war to aircraft identification signal. During this activity, the *Somers*, which had remained behind to guard the prisoners in the boats, took up anti-submarine patrol in the vicinity.[7]

Chief Charles J. Martin, a crewman aboard the *Somers*, described the operation during an interview in 1943:

> It seems that the British Intelligence had sent out word that there were two blockade runners trying to get through from Japan to Germany.... There was some talk about ... [their cargo] being machine tools.... They sent us in for the attack at daybreak. As soon as we come upon the ship she started to make about 18 knots, about 15 to 18 knots to run away from us, and we caught her and made her heave to and she immediately began to abandon ship. Everybody on there started to leave and they were flying the Norwegian flag.
>
> We sent a boarding party over there, because these other two cruisers were nowhere in the vicinity, they were well over the horizon then and we sent a boarding party and I don't know, they captured a lot of junk, I guess you'd call it, more or less. It was just, oh, they had one or two old machine guns and stuff like that, and they got a lot of bulletin board data and stuff like that. One or two diaries in German and they went ahead. After our boarding party was taken off there the ship was settling pretty rapidly and ... twenty minutes later the *ANNELIESE ESSBERGER* sank.[8]

The two cruisers rejoined the *Somers* in mid-afternoon, at which time the sixty-two prisoners (14 officers, 13 petty officers, and 35 men) were taken aboard the *Milwaukee*. Eleven of these men were confined as prisoners of war. The three ships set a course for Recife, Brazil. Following arrival there in the mid-afternoon on 24 November 1942, *Milwaukee* delivered the prisoners to the custody of commanding general, 7th Corps Area, Brazilian Army.[9]

13

Losses of Blockade Runners
Prohibitively High

Our blockade runner Osorno *homeward bound today in area (between 11°30'W and 38°50'W at about 45°N). Ship presumably disguised. In the event of meeting her, send report immediately after getting out of sight. Cover name U-1534…Count on deceptive courses of all kinds. Attention is urgently called to prohibition of attacks on unescorted independents…It is your duty to keep (presence of runner) absolutely secret even from crews.*

—German naval message sent to U-boats on 22 December 1943,
warning them that the motor vessel *Osorno* was overdue.
Although, she made it back to Europe from the Far East,
many other such ships were destroyed by Allied forces,
rendering Germany's blockade running campaign
untenable in January 1944.[1]

Between November 1942 and February 1944, the German Naval High Command used twenty-three blockade runners for a total of thirty-four runs attempted. These numbers include five ships that were loaded and ready to sail from France in January 1944, but whose departure was cancelled. Six successful runs were made to the Far East, with losses of four ships sent out from Europe on the long voyage: *Anneliese Essberger, Cortellazo, Germania,* and *Portland.* Casualties were much higher for ships trying to make the run from the Far East back to Europe. Only four of these ships were successful, while ten— *Alsterufer, Burgenland, Doggerbank, Hohenfriedburg, Irene, Karin, Regensburg, Rhakotis, Rio Grande,* and *Weserland*—were not.[2]

At the beginning of the winter of 1942-1943 the Allies were aware of at least twenty-six ships distributed between Europe and the Far East that Germany could employ as blockade runners. Beginning in November 1942, fourteen of them set sail over the next several weeks of which ten were sunk. The first four departures were those of *Karin, Anneliese Essberger, Cortellazo,* and *Germania* from western France. Of these ships, *Karin* would be the only one to elude interception. The

Germans also lost two ships in January and February 1943 of those returning from the Orient, *Rhakotis* and *Hohenfriedburg*.[3] A summary of these and subsequent ship losses follow:

German Blockade Runner Losses November 1942–January 1944

Runner	Date/Location	Route	Disposition
Anneliese Essberger	21 Nov 1942 00°54'N, 22°34'W	outbound	Intercepted by USS *Milwaukee* and scuttled
Cortellazo	1 Dec 1942 500 miles west of Cape Finisterre	outbound	Sunk by British escorts of a convoy off Spain
Germania	15 Dec 42 45°05'N, 15°30'W	outbound	Tanker scuttled and left ablaze after intercepted by sloops HMS *Egret* and HMS *Tanatside*
Rhakotis	1 Jan 1943 45°01'N, 10°50'W	homebound	Intercepted by light cruiser HMS *Scylla* (98); scuttled by crew
Hohenfriedburg (ex-*Herborg*)	26 Feb 1943 41°45'N, 20°58'W	homebound	Intercepted by heavy cruiser HMS *Sussex* (96); scuttled by crew
Doggerbank (ex-*Speybank*)	3 Mar 1943 29°10'N, 34°10'W	homebound	Mistakenly torpedoed and sunk by *U-43*
Karin (ex-*Kota Nopan*)	10 Mar 1943 07°00'S, 21°00'W	homebound	Intercepted by USS *Eberle* and USS *Savannah*; scuttled by crew
Regensburg	30 Mar 1943 Denmark Strait	homebound	Intercepted by light cruiser HMS *Glasgow* (C21); scuttled by crew
Irene (ex-*Silva Plana*)	10 Apr 1943 43°18'N, 14°30'W	homebound	Intercepted by minelayer HMS *Adventure* (M23); scuttled by crew
Portland	13 Apr 1943 06°12'N, 21°45'W	outbound	Intercepted by French light cruiser *Georges Leygues*; scuttled by crew
Pietro Orseolo	18 Dec 1943 Concarneau Harbor, France	in port	Wrecked by planes of the British Coastal Command
Alsterufer	27 Dec 1943 46°32'N, 18°55'W	homebound	Sunk by aircraft of the British Coastal Command
Weserland	3 Jan 1944 14°55'S, 21°39'W	homebound	Sunk by USS *Somers*
Rio Grande	4 Jan 1944 55 miles off Northeast Brazil	homebound	Sunk by USS *Omaha* and USS *Jouett*
Burgenland	5 Jan 1944 07°S, 26°W	homebound	Sunk by USS *Omaha* and USS *Jouett*[4]

The next four runners to sail from Europe were *Portland, Osorno, Alsterufer* and *Himalaya.* Of these, the *Portland* was sunk on 13 April 1943 by the Free French cruiser *Georges Leygues* and the *Himalaya* was forced to turn back. The remaining two made port in the Far East. Four of the five other blockade runners returning from Japan during this same season were sunk as well: *Doggerbank, Karin, Regensburg,* and *Irene*—with *Doggerbank* mistakenly sent to the bottom by the German submarine *U-43. Pietro Orseolo* was the sole survivor.[5]

During the winter of 1943-1944, five more runners attempted to reach Europe from Japan. Of these, *Alsterufer, Burgenland, Rio Grande,* and *Weserland* were sunk en route. The fifth ship, *Osorno,* was attacked and wrecked by planes of the British Coastal Command on 18 December 1943, while riding at anchor at Concarneau Harbor in northwestern France.[6]

The coup-de-grace to the German blockade running campaign was administered by Admiral Ingram's forces in early January 1944 in a "magnificent triple play" in the South Atlantic against three outbound German blockade runners. The action began when a bomber from Ascension Island sighted the *Weserland.* The destroyer *Somers* (DD-381) sank the German ship on 3 January. At the same time, other planes were shadowing *Rio Grande,* which the cruiser *Omaha* (CL-4) and destroyer *Jouett* (DD-396) polished off with naval gunfire on 4 January, aided by scuttling charges set by the ship's crew. The following day, a third runner, the *Burgenland,* was similarly sunk by scuttling charges and gunfire from the *Omaha* and *Jouett.* (These actions are taken up in Chapter 16.) Thereafter, German blockade running utilizing surface vessels dwindled to insignificance.[7]

SEVEN ITALIAN SUBMARINES SERVE AS RUNNERS

Emblem of the Italian Regia Marina ("Royal Navy"); with the birth of the Italian Republic following the war, the Royal Navy (1861–1946) changed its name to Military Navy (Marina Militare).

After Italy fell on 9 September 1943, the Allies learned the Axis had been using Japanese, German and Italian cargo-carrying submarines. Supposedly the idea to transform seven Italian subs into transports originated with Capitano di Vascello Enzo Grossi, commander of the base at Bordeaux, who believed that as a result of battle damage incurred or other considerations, these fleet submarines were not suited for offensive operations. Grossi proposed to Adm. Dönitz that Germany transfer seven newly constructed U-boats in exchange for these seven. Although this proposal might appear laughable, the Germans were producing submarines faster than they could acquire and train crews to man them. Moreover, the Italian boats, being larger, were considered better suited for the long voyage to the Far East and once there, could return with more cargo than the smaller U-boats.[8]

As part of the final agreement reached between the two navies, the Kriegsmarine agreed to transfer ten U-boats of the *VII-c*-class in exchange for the seven boats. The first of these U-Boats (ex-*U-428*) was handed over to the Regia Marina on 26 June 1943 at the Baltic seaport of Danzig (now Gdańsk, Poland) and was designated *S1*. Subsequently, submarine trials and crew training began in preparation for a planned move to an Atlantic base. However, when the Italian Armistice was declared on 9 September 1943, although nine of the ten U-Boats had been turned over by that point, none had left the Baltic. Accordingly, they were immediately taken back into the Kriegsmarine, retaining their original U-Boat numbers.

U-boats Transferred to Italian Navy

U-boat	Italian ID	Date Transferred	U-boat	Italian ID	Date Transferred
U-428	*S1*	26 Jun 1943	*U-748*	*S5*	31 Jul 1943
U-429	*S4*	14 Jul 1943	*U-749*	*S7*	14 Aug 1943
U-430	*S6*	4 Aug 1943	*U-750*	*S9*	26 Aug 1943
U-746	*S2*	4 Jul 1943	*U-1161*	*S8*	25 Aug 1943
U-747	*S3*	18 Jul 1943	*U-1162*	*S10*	not handed over[9]

FIVE ITALIAN SUBS DEPART PORT FOR FAR EAST

The seven Italian submarines of the Regia Marina (Italian Royal Navy) assigned to make the Far East run were titled the Monsun Gruppe (Monsoon Group). The operation was under German control, and the boats were assigned German names, but retained their Italian crews. Only five began the voyage, with the *Torelli* leaving, on 14 June 1943. Of the five boats, the *Tazzoli* and *Barbarigo* were lost within a week of their departure from Bordeaux, believed sunk by Allied aircraft in the

Bay of Biscay. The remaining two, *Bagnolini* and *Finzi*, never left Bordeaux. Summary information about the seven submarines, including class and displacement, launch date at builders' yards, and departure date from Bordeaux for the voyage to the Far East, follows:

Italian Cargo Submarines/Blockade Runners

Submarine	Class/Displacement	Date Launched	Date Sailed
Alpino Attilio Bagnolini	*Liuzzi*-class: 1,187 tons	28 Oct 39	did not sail
Barbarigo (sunk 19 Jun 1943)	*Marcello*-class: 1,063 tons	12 Jun 38	15 Jun 43
Comandante Alfredo Cappellini	*Marcello*-class: 1,063 tons	14 May 39	11 May 43
Giuseppe Finzi	*Calvi*-class: 1,550 tons	29 Jun 35	did not sail
Reginaldo Giuliani (sunk 18 Feb 44)	*Liuzzi*-class: 1,187 tons	3 Dec 39	23 May 43
Enrico Tazzoli (sunk 22 May 43)	*Calvi*-class: 1,550 tons	14 Oct 35	16 May 43
Luigi Torelli	*Marconi*-class: 1,195 tons	6 Jan 40[8]	14 Jun 43[10]

Photo 13-1

Italian submarine at the Bay of Naples, October 1937; probably the *Pietro Calvi*, *Giuseppe Finzi*, *Ostro*, or *Enrico Tazzoli*.
U.S. Naval History and Heritage Command Photograph #NH 111489

When the Italian Armistice was declared, the *Comandante Alfredo Cappellini* was at Sabang (northern Sumatra), the *Reginaldo Giuliani* and *Luigi Torelli* were at Singapore, and the *Bagnolini* and *Finzi* were still at Bordeaux undergoing conversion. All five were then taken over by the Germans and given U-Boat designations: *Finzi* (U-IT-21), *Bagnolini* (U-IT-22), *Giuliani* (U-IT-23), *Cappellini* (U-IT-24), and *Torelli* (U-IT-25). U-IT-23 sailed for France on 15 February 1944 with 135 tons of rubber and 70 tons of tin, and was torpedoed three days later by the British submarine HMS *Tally-Ho* and sunk.[11]

USE OF JAPANESE AND GERMAN SUBMARINES

In addition to the converted Italian craft, at least three Japanese and a considerable number of German submarines were used to carry cargo and passengers to and from the Far East. It is believed that by November 1944, thirty-five submarines had departed Europe for the Far East. This number included the five Italian cargo submarines. During the same period at least eleven submarines were believed to have quit Far Eastern ports bound for Europe.[12]

Although the sailings of surface blockade runners occurred principally in the autumn and winter months (to enable them to negotiate the Bay of Biscay when short days and weather conditions hampered observation), submarines were used in all seasons of the year. Surface blockade-runners utilized French ports exclusively, as did most of the blockade-running submarines, which departed from, or arrived at ports on Bay of Biscay. However, at least seven of the subs used German and Norwegian ports. Submarine voyages between Europe and the Far East required a minimum of two to three months, though frequently, more time was consumed by certain subs carrying small cargos, that engaged in operations in the Atlantic and Indian Oceans while en route.[13]

14

Tide Turns Against U-boats in 1943

The only thing that ever really frightened me during the war was the U-boat peril.

—British Prime Minister Winston Churchill

The destruction of enemy submarines by Allied naval and air forces in the South Atlantic increased dramatically in 1943, when thirteen U-boats and one Italian submarine were sent to the bottom. A mere two enemy submarines had been sunk the preceding year, only three would be destroyed in 1944, and none the following year. A combination of aircraft depth-charge attacks and gunfire from the destroyers *Jouett* and *Moffett* dispatched one of the U-boats in 1943. Patrol aircraft depth charges were responsible for sending the remaining U-boats and Italian submarine into the abyss.[1]

Despite the U.S. Navy having witnessed the devastation wrought by U-boats against Allied shipping, during participation in the Neutrality patrols from September 1939 to December 1941, the Sea Service had been largely unprepared for the submarine threat when it entered the war. However, several initiatives turned the tide against the Axis powers in 1943. These included—beginning in late 1942—the use of long-range Navy patrol aircraft to fly cover over ship convoys. In 1943, there were also sufficient Allied long-range patrol aircraft to cover the mid-ocean air gap, and enough escort carriers to accompany the convoys over their entire routes. However, even with these improvements in anti-submarine warfare, the odds in combat with U-boats were not totally in favor of the Allies. As the war progressed, German submarines became more heavily armed with anti-aircraft defenses, and a larger number of U.S. aircraft were shot down by U-boats than submarines sunk in battle with patrol planes.[2]

Before delving into descriptions of the battles fought between enemy submarines and Allied aircraft and ships in 1943, readers might find useful a tabulation of all such action from 1942 through 1944.

Nineteen enemy submariners were sunk in the South Atlantic during the war. All but three of these kills were due solely to patrol plane depth-charge attacks. In other actions, the British destroyer HMS *Active* (H 14) sank *U-117*; *Moffett* joined with a PV-1 Ventura patrol bomber to send *U-604* to the bottom; and *Moffett* and *Jouett* sank *U-128*, following damage inflicted on her by two PBM-3C Mariner patrol bombers.

German/Italian Submarine War Losses in the South Atlantic
(1942: two; 1943: fourteen; 1944: three; none in 1945)

1942

Date	U-boat	Squadron and/or Ship(s)	Aircraft	Location
2 Oct 42	*U-512*	USAAF 99th Bombardment Group	B-18B bomber	North of Cayenne, French Guiana 06°50'N, 52°25'W
8 Oct 42	*U-179*	British Destroyer HMS *Active* (H 14)		Near Cape Town, South Africa 33°28'S, 17°05'E

1943

Date	U-boat	Squadron and/or Ship(s)	Aircraft	Location
6 Jan 43	*U-164*	VP-83	Catalina *83-P-2*	Northwest of Fortaleza, Brazil 01°58'S, 39°23'W
13 Jan 43	*U-507*	VP-83	Catalina *83-P-10*	Northwest of Fortaleza, Brazil 01°38'S, 39°52'W
15 Apr 43	Italian *Archimede*	VP-83	Catalinas *83-P-5, P-12*	East of Natal, Brazil 03°23'S, 28°W
17 May 43	*U-128*	VP-74 Destroyers USS *Moffett* and *Jouett*	Mariners *74-P-5* and *74-P-6*	South of Recife, Brazil 10°00'S, 35°35'W
9 Jul 43	*U-590*	VP-94	Catalina *94-P-1*	North of Belém, Brazil 03°22'N, 48°38'W
19 Jul 43	*U-513*	VP-74	Mariner *74-P-5*	Southeast of São Francisco do Sul, Brazil 27°17'S, 47°32'W
21 Jul 43	*U-662*	VP-94	Catalina *94-P-4*	Off Dutch Guiana (today Surinam) 03°56'N, 48°46'W
23 Jul 43	*U-598*	VB-107	Liberators *107-B-6, B-8, B-12*	Northeast of Natal, Brazil 04°05'S, 33°23'W
30 Jul 43	*U-591*	VB-127	Ventura *127-B-10*	Southeast of Recife, Brazil 08°36'S, 34°34'W

31 Jul 43	U-199	VP-74	Mariner 74-P-7	East of Rio de Janeiro, Brazil
		Brazilian aircraft	Catalina	23°47'S, 42°56'W
11 Aug 43	U-604	VB-129 Destroyer *Moffett*	Ventura 129-B-8	Scuttled northwest of Ascension Island 04°15'S, 21°20'W
27 Sep 43	U-161	VP-74	Mariner 74-P-2	East of Salvador da Bahia, Brazil 12°30'S, 35°35'W
5 Nov 43	U-848	VB-107 US Army 1st Composite Squadron	Liberators 107-B-12, B-4, B-8 2 Mitchell B-25s	Southwest of Ascension Island 10°09'S, 18°00' W
25 Nov 43	U-849	VB-107	Liberator 107-B-6	West of the Congo Estuary 06°30'S, 05°40'W
		1944		
6 Feb 44	U-177	VB-107	Liberator 107-B-3	West of Ascension Island 10°35'S, 23°15'W
15 Jun 44	U-860	Escort Carrier USS *Solomons* (CVE-67)	seven Avenger and Wildcat aircraft	South of St. Helena Island 25°27'S, 05°30'W
29 Sep 44	U-863	VB-107	Liberators 107-B-9 107-B-7	East-southeast of Recife, Brazil 10°45'S, 25°30'W[3]

VP-83 ARRIVES AT NATAL, BRAZIL, IN SPRING 1942

VP-83, which garnered the first three submarine kills in 1943, had been the first patrol squadron to arrive in Brazil. The squadron was commissioned on 16 September 1941 at Naval Air Station, Norfolk, Virginia. On 30 March 1942, the first of its two divisions (led by the squadron commander, Lt. Comdr. Ralph S. Clarke, USN) and six PBY-5A Catalinas departed NAS Norfolk for advance base operations in Brazil. The aircraft landed at Natal on 7 April, the first military planes to operate from Parnamirim Field. Already present were six planes of VP-52 at the seaplane ramp in the harbor, and a small detachment of U.S. Marines at the airfield.[4]

All six planes of the second division took off from Norfolk for Natal on 8 June. Plane *83-P-12* was lost en route after encountering a severe storm and crashing into the sea five miles northeast of Natal Light. Three enlisted men were picked up by a Brazilian fishing boat; the other seven members of the flight crew perished. The remaining five planes of the division landed at Natal on 13 June, increasing to eleven the squadron's complement of aircraft. VP-83's immediate superior in the chain of command was commander Task Force 44, who worked for commander Fourth Fleet. Both organizations were headquartered at Recife, Brazil, one hundred and forty miles south of Natal.[5]

The airport boasted two macadam runways and U.S. Army Air Force installations recently completed by Pan American Airways. (These type landing strips were constructed of uniformly sized stones rolled or compacted in-place, and sealed with asphalt or coated with tar or bitumen.) Parnamirim Field would soon play a major role in USAAF Air Transport Command ferry operations. During the war, thousands of tactical aircraft of all types stopped at Natal for refueling and crew rest before continuing the journey across the South Atlantic to combat areas. Natal was desert country, with warm weather and 58 inches average annual rainfall. The flying conditions were normally excellent and thunderstorms, while frequent, were of short duration.[6]

The officers and men of VP-83 were housed in Army tents, as were the messing facilities and squadron department offices, such as communications, gunnery, and tactics. The first permanent buildings to be constructed were the mess halls and tactics building, followed by the enlisted men's barracks. Some officers were still living in tents fifteen months later. Recreational facilities and athletic equipment were scarce. As an alternative, ocean swimming was available a few miles from the base at Ponte Negra. Most significantly, due to a lack of maintenance facilities and spare parts at Natal, only minor repairs to aircraft could be made. Planes had to be flown back to Norfolk to have engine changes and major repair work done. These conditions existed until spring 1943, when Air Wing Sixteen arrived at Recife.[7]

U-164 SUNK OFF FORTALEZA, BRAZIL

The first U-boat kill in the South Atlantic by Patrol Squadron VP-83 came on 6 January 1943, when PBY-5A Catalina *83-P-2* (piloted by Lt. William R. Ford) sent an enemy submarine to the bottom off Fortaleza at position 01°58'S, 39°23'W. The squadron had begun systematic patrols of shipping lanes along the 3,800 mile Brazilian coastline— from Rio de Janeiro to Cape Orange—six months earlier on 2 July 1942. (Cape Orange marks the northernmost point of the Brazilian coast, which is separated from French Guiana by the Oyapock River.) During convoy coverage assignments along the 2,000 mile sea route from Bahia to Cape Orange, a squadron aircraft would join a convoy and stay with it for ten to twelve hours. Upon relief by another plane, the aircraft would fly to the nearest Brazilian city to refuel and spend the night. The next day, this same aircraft would relieve the plane on duty and take over the cover. When the aircraft reached the limit of its range from Parnamirim Field, it would depart the convoy and return to base at Natal.[8]

Photo 14-1

Consolidated PBY-5A Catalina patrol bomber in flight, during 1942-43.
U.S. National Archives Photograph #80-G-K-1587

Additional squadrons were subsequently ordered to Brazil to counteract increased enemy submarine activity in Brazilian waters. VP-74 arrived at Natal on 18 December 1942. After receiving new PBM-3S aircraft at Norfolk, Virginia, the squadron was initially assigned to Naval Air Station Floyd Bennett (located in southeast Brooklyn, New York), then was relocated to Elizabeth City, North Carolina. Prior to its arrival at Natal, VP-74 had been under the operational control of commander, Eastern Sea Frontier and assigned administratively to commander, Fleet Air Wing Nine. The next squadron to arrive in theater was VP-94, when the first of its eleven PBY-5As landed at Natal on 18 January 1943.[9]

Meanwhile, following a three-day convoy coverage mission, the PBY-5A piloted by Ford was winging its way back to Natal on 6 January 1943. A little before noon, Aviation Machinist Mate Third Billy Goodall (a flight engineer and gunner) spotted the characteristic wake of a surfaced submarine at a considerable distance. Goodall, who during previous patrols had made two other initial sighting of submarines, was nicknamed "EAGLE EYES." The aircraft was then about sixty-five miles off the northeast coast of Brazil.[10]

Upon receipt of this report, Ford turned ninety degrees to port and pulled the props and throttles all the way back. As he descended at a rate of 2,000 feet per second to make an attack, he tried to keep a small cloud between the U-boat and the plane, and by this action catch the sub unware of the presence of a patrol bomber. Upon the order to drop, the co-pilot who was positioned in the bow, manually released three Mk 17 depth charges simultaneously, and a fourth one a split second later. The attack was made eight minutes after the target was sighted, from a height of only thirty-five feet above the water. The submarine had maintained a steady course and speed, and made no attempt to crash dive, making her an easy target.[11]

After passing over the U-boat, Ford made a steep left turn to view the results, during which two explosions occurred. The first one, about five feet off the portside and abeam the conning tower of the submarine, was quite large; it was believed to have been caused by the first three bombs exploding at the same time. The second smaller blast, about sixty feet starboard of, and slightly abaft the conning tower, was apparently due to the fourth bomb. Following the explosions, the sub rose out of the water and broke into two sections.[12]

Three large tanks were visible as the bow section settled under, and much miscellaneous, nondescript debris appeared momentarily before disappearing below the surface. Amongst the debris were several mangled bodies and three survivors. As a sizable TNT residue stain from the depth charges appeared, with a smaller one about fifty feet away, the stern of the sub breached at the forward edge of the large discoloration. Rising almost vertically, eight-to-ten feet out of the water, it briefly bobbed up and down, then sank straight down.[13]

By the time Ford circled back, one of the men in the water had disappeared, one clung to the top of a tank, and one was still in the water. Two rubber rafts were dropped from the aircraft, and the man in the water climbed into one of them. He paddled it to the tank and took the other survivor aboard. The raft would be home to the Germans for about a week, before they succeeded in reaching a small settlement on the coast of Brazil. There, they received care for a few days and were then taken to São Luiz and delivered to the police. By courtesy of the Brazilian government, the two men were turned over to the U.S. Navy. The prisoners were transported to Natal, than brought to the United States for interrogation. They disclosed that the sunken submarine was the *U-164*.[14]

DETAILS ABOUT *U-164*

The two men, a coxswain and a seaman, yielded a considerable amount of information to interrogators. They had been on deck at the time of the attack, bathing. Upon sighting the plane they dashed up to the bridge, but found it deserted and the hatch already closed. Water was just breaking over the bow as the submarine began to dive. When the bombs exploded, the two men were blown into the water. They identified the objects the plane's crew believed to be tanks as upper deck torpedo containers, and provided additional details about the submarine and her crew.[15]

U-164, a 750-ton submarine built at the Deschimag-Seebeck shipyard at Wesermünde, had been commissioned on 28 November 1941. She was on her second war cruise when she was lost off Brazil. The U-boat had departed Lorient, France—at which the 2nd and 10th Flotillas were based—on 29 November 1942. A minesweeper and a smaller escort vessel accompanied her leaving port and for some time after. Her run on the surface through the Bay of Biscay was enlivened by three nighttime aircraft alarms and crash dives. The GSR search receiver, designed to detect the radar transmissions of aircraft, had provided warning of the approach of the planes.[16]

When *U-164* was on the surface, this gear was used only at night, and lookouts exclusively relied upon by day. In an effort to visually detect approaching Allied aircraft earlier, the watch consisted of a coxswain and two ratings, in addition to an officer. These three individuals were each assigned a sector of 120 degrees to continuously scan. The GSR antenna (known as Kreuz des Südens, meaning the "Southern Cross") was brought up at night. The radioman, who could turn the aerial to any compass bearing, reported contacts to the commanding officer who might order the alarm sounded.[17]

There were fifty-five men aboard *U-164* when she left on patrol: the ship's complement, plus one student commander, one doctor, and two midshipmen. Korvettenkapitän Otto Fechner, age 36, was the commanding officer, with other officers serving as the executive officer, second officer, and engineer officer. Comprising the 47-man crew were sixteen petty officers (two warrant machinists, one warrant quartermaster, seven machinist's mates, three coxswains, two radiomen, and one torpedoman's mate), the remainder being seamen or firemen.[18]

Many U-boats, especially those operating in the North Atlantic, also had aboard a War Pilot (Kriegs-Lotse or Kriegslotse). These were civilians who were peacetime maritime pilots. They were aboard to help the captain to identify ships encountered by their type, owner, and sometimes name simply by observing the vessels. These men were extremely experienced and were very senior. They were also used to pilot the U-boats into foreign harbors, many of them being former merchant officers in addition to being trained and experienced pilots. They were civilians and had no rank other than Kriegs-Lotse, but they were treated as commissioned officers.[19]

All U-boats (750-tonners) leaving on war patrols from Lorient bound for the South Atlantic carried a doctor. Illnesses were frequent because of the heat, long cruises, and infrequent support from supply U-boats. While on patrol, each man was supplied a weekly tinfoil-and-cellophane wrapped package of twelve cream colored vitamins. Schoka-Kola, a chocolate, was available as a stimulant, and black pills for use in strengthening the eyes. There was always plenty of food, but occasionally shortages of water aboard *U-164*.[20]

During the four-to-five-week ocean crossing to the northeast coast of South America, *U-164* proceeded submerged at slow speed, making four knots on diesel-electric power. The survivors indicated that the sub's fuel capacity was 280-300 tons, with consumption about two tons-per-hour at full speed.[21]

She was fitted with one 10.5cm deck gun forward, one 3.7cm anti-aircraft gun abaft the conning tower, and one 20mm anti-aircraft gun on the bridge. The reliability of the latter gun was not trusted, and it was never used. Four MG34 machine guns were also carried. Ammunition for the 10.5cm gun was stored in an ammo locker under the control room (where scuttling charges were also kept), and brought up through the conning tower when needed. Fifteen of the sub's twenty-three 21-inch torpedoes were carried inside the boat, and the remaining eight in containers up on deck.[22]

The submarine celebrated New Year's Day by sinking the Swedish freighter *Brageland* at position 00°19'N, 37°30'W. *Brageland* was en route from Santos, Brazil, to Philadelphia, traveling alone, when a sighting was made of a submarine on the surface one mile off her port quarter. *U-164* overtook the ship in only a few minutes, signaled her to heave to, and ordered the master to board the submarine. The master was interrogated on deck regarding the name of his ship, its destination, cargo, etc. In response to the master's assertion that *Brageland* was a 'neutral' ship, Fechner replied that its cargo was not neutral. After consulting a book containing a list of vessels allowed to "run in trade" without danger of attack, Fechner informed the master that he was obliged to sink his ship.[23]

After the master returned aboard *Brageland*, Fechner in Swedish ordered the ship abandoned. This was done within a few minutes, after which *U-164* maneuvered to a position 500 yards off the port beam of the freighter and fired one torpedo. It struck the ship's hull in the vicinity of the after section of the engine room and detonated, opening a large hole, and rupturing the main deck and plates on the boat deck, causing immediate flooding of the engine room. No distress signals were sent, and the codes and confidential publications on board went down with the ship.[24]

U-164 departed the scene and continued her war patrol, cruising fearlessly on the surface much of the time. The sinking of *Brageland* would be her only success prior to 6 January 1943, when PBY-5A Catalina *83-P-2* sent her down into the depths of the South Atlantic, ending her cruise permanently.[25]

PLANE CREW RECEIVES MEDALS FOR VALOR

The pilot, and crewman of PBY-5A Catalina *83-P-2* who first sighted *U-164*, were awarded the Distinguished Flying Cross. The remaining members of the flight crew received Air Medals.

PBY-5A Catalina *83-P-2* Plane Crew
(for action on 6 January 1943)

Name	Medal
Lt. William Render Ford, USNR	Distinguished Flying Cross
AMM3/c Billy Goodell, USN	Distinguished Flying Cross
Ens. Marion Vance Dawkins Jr., USNR	Air Medal
Lt. (jg) Robert Soule Swan, USNR	Air Medal
ARM2/c Daniel William Dupree, USNR	Air Medal
AMM2/c Sidney Brown Hale, USN	Air Medal
AMM1/c Earl Weathers Luck, USN	Air Medal
ACMM Robert Barker Stamps, USNR	Air Medal

U-507 NEXT SUB TO BE SUNK BY A VP-83 PLANE

In morning darkness on 13 January, another Catalina of VP-83 (piloted by Lt. (jg) Lloyd Ludwig) caught a submarine on the surface north-northwest of Fortaleza. Ludwig and the flight crew of *83-P-10* had taken off from Fortaleza, on the northeastern Brazilian coast, at 0500 to cover a section of the route of Trinidad-Recife convoy TR-1, then passing north of the port city. The plane was on a northwest course at 5,500 feet searching for the convoy, when the co-pilot, Lt. (jg) Mearl G. Taylor, sighted a long white streak forty degrees off the port bow. At first it looked like the wake of a fast boat, such as a patrol craft, but further inspection revealed it originated from a surfaced U-boat.[26]

CATALYST FOR BRAZIL ENTERING THE WAR

Unbeknownst to the plane crew, the enemy submarine was the *U-507*, whose sinking of six Brazilian ships between 16 May and 19 August 1942 had spurred a reluctant Brazilian president, Getúlio Vargas, to declare war on Germany and Italy. In the late 1930s, Vargas had been sympathetic to Nazifascism in Germany and Italy, and the relationship between Brazil and Germany had strengthened year after year up to 1940. During this period, Germany became the second most important trading partner of Brazil, just behind the United States. At the outset of World War II, Brazil was not prepared to give up her pro-Axis stance or neutrality and join the Allies. The reluctance of the Brazilian government to enter into hostilities had given rise to a popular saying among the people, "It is easier for a snake to smoke than for Brazil to go to war."[27]

Photo 14-2

Shoulder patch adopted by the Brazilian Expeditionary Force before its deployment to Europe in 1944. The "smoking cobra" proudly displayed on members' uniforms symbolized that Brazil was able to send troops to fight alongside Allied forces in Italy.

There had been earlier attacks against Brazilian merchant ships, but those by *U-507* in spring and summer 1942 turned Brazilian public opinion against Germany. Demonstrations all over the country finally pressured the president and his government to declare war on Germany and Italy on 22 August 1942. By this action, Brazil became the first South American country to enter the war.[28]

DEPTH-CHARGE ATTACK ON *U-507*

Lieutenant (jg) Ludwig initiated an attack, avoiding detection until nearly on top of the enemy, by approaching out of the blinding light of the morning sun, low on the horizon:

> We proceeded at full speed towards the sub, which was coming in our direction. Although there were a low base and a number of clouds, there were no obstacles to visibility between the plane and the sub; there was no available cloud cover. Air speed was about 160K[nots] indicated and rate of descent about 2000' per minute. Air speed was slowed down to about 140K as we approached sub which, at closer view, was seen to proceed at high speed with deck awash. It left a very large wake. The conning tower was clearly visible, but due to the low haze and large amount of spray (it was quite rough), it was impossible to make out its features. No other part of the sub was seen. The sub continued in this fashion until we were within about two miles, at which time it commenced to dive.[29]

U-507 was steering a reciprocal course (071°T) to that of the aircraft and making 15 knots, apparently trying to catch the convoy, about twenty miles ahead. The Catalina dropped four depth charges, from an altitude of forty feet, about 200 feet ahead of the conning tower; which was then still visible but covered by a wave immediately after. Two 650-lb Mark 29s were followed by two smaller 325-lb Mark 17s. All four bombs hit the water about eighty feet ahead of the conning tower, directly in the path of *U-507*. Although the sub had just gone under, the wake of her sail was still visible.[30]

Ludwig observed oil coming to the surface following the drop, which seemed to evidence damage to the submarine. However, U-boats often purposely released oil and debris in such circumstances to make their adversaries believe they had been destroyed and thus cease any further efforts against them:

> Two large areas of foam and bubbling, caused by the explosions, appeared about five seconds after the bombs hit the water, and merged into one large mass. About four minutes later oil appeared in the bomb residue. It was shining, looked dark, and did not have the appearance of bilge oil (which is a rusty brown color). The oil slick kept growing in size, but was lost from sight

after the plane had circled it five times. It was seen for about 10 minutes. At the time of the attack, the sub was proceeding on the course of [Convoy] TR-1, about 20 miles astern.[31]

Conclusive evidence of the sinking of the submarine with all hands (54 men) at position 01°38'S, 39°52'W, was not obtained until after V-E (Victory in Europe) Day, when it became possible to examine German naval records.[32]

SUBMARINE'S WAR RECORD

U-507 had been built at the Deutsche Werft AG shipyard in Hamburg, Germany. She was commissioned on 8 October 1941 under the command of Korvettenkapitän Harro Schacht. Prior to her loss on 13 January 1943, the submarine had sunk nineteen ships, including six Brazilian vessels.

Victims of *U-507*

Date	Ship	Tons	Nationality
30 Apr 1942	Merchant tanker SS *Federal*	2,881	American
4 May 1942	Merchant vessel SS *Norlindo*	2,686	American
5 May 1942	Merchant tanker SS *Munger T. Ball*	5,104	American
5 May 1942	Merchant tanker SS *Joseph M. Cudahy*	6,950	American
6 May 1942	Merchant vessel SS *Alcoa Puritan*	6,759	American
7 May 1942	Merchant vessel SS *Ontario*	3,099	Honduran
8 May 1942	Merchant vessel SS *Torny*	2,424	Norwegian
12 May 1942	Merchant tanker SS *Virginia*	10,731	American
16 May 1942	Merchant vessel SS *Amapala*	4,148	Honduran
16 May 1942	Merchant vessel SS *Baependy*	4,801	Brazilian
16 Aug 1942	Passenger ship MV *Araraquara*	4,872	Brazilian
16 Aug 1942	Merchant vessel SS *Annibal Benévolo*	1,905	Brazilian
17 Aug 1942	Merchant vessel SS *Itagiba*	2,169	Brazilian
17 Aug 1942	Merchant vessel SS *Arará*	1,075	Brazilian
19 Aug 1942	Sailing vessel *Jacyra*	89	Brazilian
22 Aug 1942	Merchant vessel MV *Hammaren*	3,220	Swedish
27 Dec 1942	Merchant vessel MV *Oakbank*	5,154	British
3 Jan 1943	Merchant vessel MV *Baron Dechmont*	3,675	British
8 Jan 1943	Merchant vessel SS *Yorkwood*	5,401	British[33]

Also lost aboard *U-507*, in addition to her officers and crew, were four prisoners. They were James Stewart, master of *Oakbank*; Donald MacCallum, master of *Baron Dechmont*; Frank Herbert Fenn, master of *Yorkwood*; and Chief Mate John George Swanson, Stewart's trainee aboard the *Oakbank*.[34]

VP-74 PLANE FINDS ENEMY BLOCKADE RUNNER

Conduct sweep followed by ocean patrol with primary mission to search for and capture or destroy enemy raiders and blockade runners.

En route to area of patrol conduct an ocean sweep in a general northeasterly direction from Recife, attempting to intercept Spanish M/V El Saturno. If intercepted, board, examine and take action in accordance with previous instructions.

—Portion of orders given Rear Adm. Oliver M. Read, USN, regarding tasking to search for enemy blockade runners, and specifically the Spanish motor vessel *El Saturno*.[35]

Amidst the ongoing anti-submarine warfare in the South Atlantic, U.S. Fourth Fleet forces continued their efforts to thwart blockade runners. Such endeavors were usually prompted by the receipt of intelligence concerning the anticipated movements of suspect ships through the area. On 21 February 1943, Rear Adm. Oliver Read, departed Recife, Brazil, with four of his ships—the light cruiser *Savannah* (CL-42), auxiliary aircraft carrier *Santee* (ACV-29), and destroyers *Livermore* (DD-429) and *Eberle* (DD-430)—to conduct an ocean patrol and search for blockade runners. Read was "double hatted" as both commander Cruiser Division Two (Task Group 23.1) and commander Ocean Patrol, South Atlantic Force.[36]

Of special interest was the Spanish merchant ship *El Saturno*, described as a 3,450-ton freighter, with a plumb bow, single stack, two masts, split superstructure, and a flush deck, raised forecastle and poopdeck with a counter stern. The freighter had left Montevideo, Uruguay, on 10 February, bound for Las Palmas, one of the Canary Islands belonging to Spain off northwestern Africa. Although Spain officially remained neutral throughout World War II, the country's dictator, Francisco Franco, was ideologically aligned with Nazi Germany and Fascist Italy and provided aid to Germany, including opening ports to its submarines. *El Saturno* was reported to be carrying fifteen kilos of platinum, and a valise containing German official correspondence given to Boatswain Vitturo and now wrapped in a blue paper package, probably safeguarded in an officer's stateroom.[37]

Read conducted the first day's search for *El Saturno* in an area corresponding to an assumed ship's speed of 7.5 to 8.5 knots, and across the usual route of merchantmen bound from South America to Spain. As part of this effort, the group of ships proceeded on a course perpendicular to the assumed track of the freighter, while planes were sent out parallel to this course at intervals based on existing visibility, the speed of the carrier and the hunted ship's assumed speed. Following an unsuccessful hunt on 22 February, the search plan was revised based on *El Saturno* making a slower speed of 6.7-7.8 knots.[38]

In mid-afternoon on 25 February, Lt. (jg) Harold C. Carey, piloting a PBM-3C Mariner of Patrol Squadron 74, intercepted the blockade runner at position 04°08'S, 31°40'W. *El Saturno* disregarded signals to heave to; plane *74-P-11* repeated them and then fired a burst across her bow. Admiral Ingram, upon receiving a report that *El Saturno* had been located and stopped, ordered the seaplane tender *Humboldt* (AVP-21), destroyer *Kearny* (DD-432), and Patrol Squadron 83, then engaged in a submarine hunt near the scene of the sighting, to direct the freighter into Recife.[39]

Photo 14-3

Martin PBM-3 "Mariner" patrol bomber in flight, circa 1942-43.
U.S. National Archives Photograph #80-G-K-13516

Humboldt sighted the blockade runner at 1515, upon which her crew was ordered to battle stations and material condition Able was set. Nearing *El Saturno*, the seaplane tender stopped engines, and a boarding party of two officers and ten men left the ship bound for the freighter. They boarded her at 1550. Following an hour-and-a-half long search, the party departed the freighter at 1725.[40]

Returning aboard *Humboldt*, the officer-in-charge reported to Comdr. George C. Montgomery, USN, that *El Saturno* appeared to be in order. Upon learning that nothing of interest had been found, and that everything appeared to be in order aboard the suspect vessel, Montgomery resumed the anti-submarine operations in which the seaplane tender had been previously engaged.[41]

When *El Saturno* arrived at Recife the morning of 27 February, the Brazilian Minister of Marine advised Ingram that the Spanish merchant vessel could not be searched by U.S. forces inside the continental limits of Brazil. Accordingly a search party left port aboard the minesweeper *Linnet* (AM-76) to board and search the ship at her anchorage, situated three miles offshore in international waters. *Linnet* (commanded by Lt. Merritt Berner, USNR) was based at Recife to perform harbor mine clearance operations, as necessary, to permit the free passage of ships in and out of port.[42]

Photo 14-4

Minesweeper *Flicker* (AM-70) in 1940-41.
U.S. Naval History and Heritage Command Photograph #NH 81360

Unlike in other theaters, minesweeping duty in the South Atlantic was neither dangerous nor particularly arduous, because enemy submarines were preoccupied with sinking ships. As such, they carried a full load of torpedoes on patrol in lieu of replacing some of their "fish" with sea mines necessary to close ports to Allied use. Arnold Lott characterized, in *Most Dangerous Sea*, the duty of the yard minesweeper *YMS-76* and minesweepers *Flicker* and *Linnet*—which served as harbor entrance guard ships while awaiting a call to sweep mines—thus:

> *YMS-76* started off to war June 4, 1942, by way of the South Atlantic. With *Flicker* [AM-70] and *Linnet* [AM-76], she vegetated luxuriously in the Brazilian ports of Bahia, Recife, Belém and Rio, where the weather was mild and the women were not, and convoy escort or sweeping duty came so seldom the helmsman forgot how to steer a straight course.[43]

An inspection of *El Saturno*'s crew, examination of the ship's papers, and a search of officer and crew quarters revealed no partisan service. The freighter was released at approximately 1230, whereupon she proceeded into Recife for coal.[44]

VP-74 DETACHMENTS AT ARATU AND RIO, BRAZIL

> *Natal is a land where we take our last stand,*
> *The climate is simply just grand.*
> *We live in a stable,*
> *And fly when we're able*
> *To dig our planes out of the sand.*
>
> *Aratu is one step in our tour of S.[outh] A.[merica]*
> *Where we found our good neighbors okay.*
> *The swells were most wavy,*
> *But the duty just gravy,*
> *And we plan to return there some day.*
>
> *And now we're in Rio a place of delight*
> *Where we dine, dance, and drink every night.*
> *Spending muito late horas*
> *With bonitas senoras;*
> *You'll admit they're a beautiful sight.*

> —VP-74 ditties addressing the squadron's duty
> at Natal, Aratu, and Rio de Janeiro, Brazil.[45]

Patrol Squadron VP-74 relocated from Trinidad to Natal in December 1942, with the first section of PBM-3 aircraft departing for a naval base on the Essequibo River in British Guiana (today Guyana) and Belém en route to Natal on the 18th. Associated with this action, the seaplane tender *Humboldt* was ordered to Natal for ferrying and maintenance duties. The move of VP-74 was full of difficulty and melodrama. The squadron had previously received word that it was going to Africa. On the night of 15 December, most of its personnel were at the base theater. Suddenly the movie was stopped, and an announcement came over the loud speaker ordering everyone to return to squadron headquarters. Here the men learned that the movement was to be to Brazil. The planes were partially loaded that night, and heavily laden by the time of departure three days later. Everthing they had was piled aboard—office files, personal gear, beaching equipment, and anything else the squadron possessed.[46]

Some patrol bombers had to make five or six runs to get off the water. There was even greater difficulty at U.S. Naval Air Station, British Guiana, where they spent the first night. Forty miles up the Essequibo River, it had a sufficiently long and unobstructed water landing area in a region free from malaria. But the water was dead calm, requiring one plane to run up tide, while two others ran down, to ruffle the surface sufficiently for the planes to be able to break free and spring into the air.[47]

After a relatively short time at Natal, VP-74 established a three-plane detachment on 20 March 1943 at Aratu, 460 nautical miles down the Brazilian coast, preparatory to moving the entire squadron there. Upon arrival, personnel found only the shell of a seaplane base. There were a number of buildings and a nose hangar, but much work remained to put the base into commission. A nose hangar was a rectangular structure with solid walls on three sides, and a roof above it. A sheet of canvas covered the remaining side, allowing the noses of planes to protrude through round openings in the canvas into the structure. By this means, mechanics could work inside engine compartments while sheltered from the environment.[48]

Three months later, there came an assignment for which everyone was eager to volunteer—duty at Rio de Janeiro. Following the establishment of a two-plane detachment there on 25 June, aircraft and personnel, under Lt. J. F. Voorhies, were ordered to Rio for basing at Santos Dumont airport. The detachment was later relocated to Galleo Island in Rio Bay and lived in the quarters of the Brazilian Air Force. While at Santos Dumont, located in the city, the men were housed in the Hotel Pax. Squadron offices were in the Metropol building along with those of the British and American embassies. The squadron history of VP-74 wryly noted, "Rio was a gay and wonderful place, but unfortunately the best stories do not bear printing."[49]

VP-83 PLANE SINKS ITALIAN SUB *ARCHIMEDE*

On 15 April 1943 (while VP-74 was establishing itself at Aratu), PBY-5A Catalina *83-P-5* (piloted by Ens. Thurmond E. Robertson, USN) was on a routine scouting patrol about 350 miles east of Natal, when his lookout sighted a submarine on the surface. By the time this report reached Robertson, he had overflown the sub, which immediately began firing at the plane as it came around to make an attack. Realizing that he had to act fast before his prey slipped into the deep, Robertson dove sharply down at a 6o-degree angle, in the face of steady anti-aircraft fire. This type of dive-bombing maneuver was not something a patrol aircraft was designed to do. Nevertheless, four depth charges dropped from 2,000 feet damaged the sub, preventing it from submerging. With no bombs left, Robertson made two strafing runs for good measure and remained in the area to provide locating information to a second Squadron VP-83 plane en route to the scene.[50]

Photo 14-5

Italian *Brin*-class submarines moored near one another.
U.S. Naval History and Heritage Command Photograph #NH 111495

    The enemy submarine, which the pilot and crew of the Catalina believed to be a U-boat, was actually the *Archimede*. One of Italy's five *Brin*-class submarines, she was of typical Italian design, with a wide beam and deep hull, capable under ideal conditions of making 17 knots on the surface or 8 knots when submerged. Named after the famous Greek mathematician, physicist, engineer, and astronomer

Archimedes, the submarine had been launched on 5 March 1939. Her armament consisted of four 21-inch torpedo tubes at the bow and four at the stern, as well as a single 100mm deck gun near the aft portion of the conning tower, and four 13mm heavy machine guns on her sail. (The forward deck guns shown on the submarines in the photograph, on the previous page, were later removed.)[51]

Operating from the Axis-held city of Bordeaux on the western French coast, *Archimede* had sunk two ships on previous war patrols: the Panamanian freighter *Cardina* off Brazil on 15 June 1942, and the British troop transport *Oronsay* off Liberia on 8 October 1942.[52]

Within an hour, Catalina *83-P-12* arrived, guided by homing signals provided by the patrol plane on scene. Upon sighting the enemy eight miles distant, fully surfaced but down by the stern with her afterdeck awash, Lt. Gerard Bradford Jr. altered course to set up for an attack. Reaching the right position astern of his target, four Mk 44 depth bombs were released from 50 to 100 feet. It appeared that the bombs bracketed the sub's hull just abaft the conning tower, though explosions were observed only along her port quarter. Damaged, the submarine settled gradually by the stern, and her bow correspondingly rose out of the water, higher and higher, until reaching an angle of about 50 degrees.[53]

The officers and crew of *Archimede* did not capitulate. Gun crews exchanged fire with the aircraft throughout the attack, and continued to do so during subsequent strafing runs. Machine gun fire from the sail ceased only as the conning tower slipped slowly beneath the surface, followed by the bow and accompanied by one large burst of bubbles. Only two dozen or so survivors and a large quantity of heavy brown oil remained on the surface. Bradford ordered three life rafts dropped, then departed for base, having reached his PLE (prudent limit of endurance) and with three hits in the starboard wing from enemy gunfire. (PLE refers to the time an aircraft can remain airborne and still retain a certain safety margin of remaining fuel.)[54]

Twenty-five Italian sailors, including the commanding officer, Saccardo, escaped the sinking submarine; but six immediately drowned due to injuries sustained in the attack. Thirteen survivors boarded one of the rafts, and the remaining six men, a second one. The latter raft reached the Brazilian coast nearly a month later with a single occupant still alive, and one or two bodies (accounts vary). Accounts also vary as to the exact number of days spent at sea and the site where the boat made shore. Two Brazilian fishermen found Coxswain Third Class Giuseppe Lo Coco alive, though weakened and delirious, and took him to the nearby island of Brigue.[55]

It was four days before Lo Coco regained consciousness and recovered sufficiently to convey that he was Italian, and a member of the crew of the *Archimede*. He was taken into custody by the police and transported by Brazilian gunboat to Belém. Following arrival there on 6 June, he was interned at the naval base until flown to the United States. After a long convalescence, Lo Coco was sent to a prison camp in Mississippi and later another in New York. He was repatriated on 26 October 1946, and would live a long life. The sole survivor of the *Archimede* died on 30 August 2004 at age eighty-six.[56]

AWARDS FOR VALOR

Ens. Thurmond Robertson and Lt. Gerard Bradford Jr., the pilots of the PBY-5A Catalinas, were awarded the Distinguished Flying Cross for their actions in sinking *Archimede* at position 03°23'S, 28°W. After action reports associated five of the nineteen men comprising the two plane crews with a specific aircraft. The remaining fourteen men were aboard either Catalina *83-P-5* or *83-P-12*.

PBY-5A Catalina *83-P-5*
(for action on 15 April 1943)

Name	Position	Award
Ens. Thurmond E. Robertson, USN	Pilot	DFC
Ens. Eugene Colley Morrison, USNR	Navigator	Air Medal
Sea2/c Earl Joseph Kloss, USNR		Air Medal

PBY-5A Catalina *83-P-12*
(for action on 15 April 1943)

Lt. Gerard Bradford Jr., USNR	Pilot	DFC
Mach. Jesse Wilson Bamber, USN	Bow Gun	Air Medal

Other Crew Members of These Two Aircraft

Ens. George Albert Houchin, USNR	Air Medal
Ens. Boyce Sample McCoy, USNR	Air Medal
Lt. (jg) Carrell Ivan Pinnell, USN	Air Medal
Ens. Richard Morrison Riggs, USNR	Air Medal
Sea2/c Arnold Peter Burggraff, USNR	Air Medal
ARM1/c Thomas Wilson Cowdery, USNR	Air Medal
ARM1/c Solomon Greenberg, USN	Air Medal
AMM1/c William Titus Hamilton, USNR	Air Medal
ACRM Jack Vietch Jenkins, USN	Air Medal
ARM2/c Murray Irving Jorgensen, USN	Air Medal
AM2/c John Wesley Pittman Jr., USN	Air Medal
AMM3/c Raymond Monroe Scott, USNR	Air Medal
AMM2/c Henry Lee Slusher Jr., USN	Air Medal
AMM3/c Carl Nelson Von Buskirk, USN	Air Medal[57]

VP-83 REDESIGNATED VB-107 IN MID-1943

In late April 1943, Squadron VP-83 planes and flight crews began to depart Natal bound for Naval Air Station Norfolk, Virginia, with the last five aircraft arriving there on 15 May. On that date, VP-83 was decommissioned, and Bombing Squadron VB-107 was commissioned with new planes—PB4Y-1 Liberators (ex-Army B-24Ds)—and the same personnel. The first six planes of VB-107 returned to Natal on 20 June. Six days later, the squadron was at full strength with twelve planes. That autumn, a detachment was created at Ascension Island on 30 September 1943, to facilitate the conduct of anti-submarine barriers and sweeps (searches for submarines) in the narrows between West Africa and the "hump" of Brazil.[58]

SHIPS AND PATROL BOMBERS SINK *U-128*

As Fourth Fleet forces continued to hunt enemy submarines in South Atlantic waters, two patrol bombers and a pair of destroyers joined forces to sink *U-128* south of Recife, Brazil, on 17 May 1943. Eight days earlier, Ingram had ordered a sub alert from Recife to Victoria, following an HF/DF detection of a possible submarine within one hundred miles of position 13°S, 36°W. The acronym HF/DF, nicknamed "huff-duff," referred to high-frequency radio direction finding equipment used to detect HF radio transmissions between U-boats and their land-based headquarters. When antennas sited in different geographical areas detected the same signal, the information could be correlated to determine the location of a U-boat sending a short transmission.[59]

The morning of 17 May, a PBM-3C Mariner of Patrol Squadron VP-74 (*74-P-6*) took off from Aratu to patrol a search sector out to a distance of 200 miles. Weather in the vicinity of the base was almost completely overcast, with light rain and visibility of between two and ten miles. Conditions improved to the northeast after forty minutes of flying, with a ceiling of 2,500 feet with cumulus and scattered cumulonimbus clouds, and increased visibility of thirty-five to forty miles.[60]

At 0843, AMM3/c R. F. Foote, who was at the bomber's window, reported a ship one point (11.25 degrees) on the starboard bow. The pilot, Lt. Howland S. Davis, USN, sighted a white wake fifteen miles distant, which inspection with binoculars revealed to be a submarine with decks awash, making about 12 knots. It was steering a north-northwest course, ideal for Davis to attack from out of the sun and astern of the enemy.[61]

The sub was in the process of a slow submergence and, despite Davis increasing plane speed to 180 knots (using 45 inches of manifold pressure and 2,450 rpm), the distance to it seemed to be painstakingly far. While still one mile away, the enemy disappeared; leaving a swirl, 75-100 feet in diameter, as the only evidence of previous presence on the surface. Following a drop of six Mk 44 depth charges from fifty feet above the water, Davis made a sharp turn to port and visually surveyed the scene while climbing to 1,200 feet. No signs of destruction were evident to him or the plane crew.[62]

U-128 DAMAGED BY DEPTH-CHARGE ATTACK

The unknown submarine was the *U-128*, under the command of Kapitänleutnant Hermann Steinert. Her bridge watch had sighted the approaching plane, but when Steinert gave the order to crash dive, nothing happened due to failure of the high pressure air manifold. The indicator board showed that all vents were open—necessary to expel air in ballast tanks, and enable them to fill with seawater—but investigation revealed they were shut. An order was given to open them by hand, and finally the submarine was able to submerge. The depth charges exploded around the forward part of *U-128* rupturing her hull near the forward starboard torpedo tubes. As water poured in through a four-finger-wide gap, men rushed to the aft parts of the boat to obtain the trim necessary to stop the dive, and level out the submarine.[63]

Realizing that he could not remain submerged without grave danger to the crew, Steinert gave the order to blow ballast tanks. About three minutes after the attack, *U-128* surfaced. Both diesel engines were started and at full speed, the sub set a course toward the South American coast, estimated roughly by the stand of the sun. This means of navigation was necessary because seawater entering the boat had caused the gyro to fail. Immediately upon surfacing, Steinert ordered anti-aircraft guns manned.[64]

A SECOND PATROL BOMBER ATTACKS *U-128*

Unfortunately for *U-128*, another patrol bomber was nearby. At 0847, as PBM-3C Mariner *74-P-5* was flying the east leg of a fifty-mile square of ocean, the radar operator reported a contact twenty-eight miles ahead. The weather was good and through binoculars, Lt. (jg) Harold C. Carey, USN, could see a fully surfaced submarine, and initiated an attack. As the submarine started to submerge, the plane crew noticed another aircraft (*74-P-6*) about two miles ahead going in for an attack.

Consequently, Carey withheld releasing bombs when passing over the location where *74-P-6* had just dropped ordnance.[65]

As Carey made a climbing circle to the right, he sighted the sub surfacing about a half mile off the plane's starboard beam, and he immediately began a bombing run:

> A diving attack was launched, and at an altitude of 100 feet, airspeed about 190 knots, and target angle 225°, six Mark 44 bombs with fuses set to function at 25 feet were released, using intervalometer control [a device which timed the release of bombs from the bomb rack] with a 72 foot corrected spacing. The resulting explosions bracketed the submarine just forward of the conning tower, and within a minute a series of 20 coordinated strafing runs was begun. During these runs a flashing explosion lasting about one minute was observed to occur just abaft the conning tower of the submarine. The submarine continued on the surface in a down by the stern condition, maneuvering erratically and leaving a trail of oil. Fifty-six minutes after the bombing attack the submarine stopped [being now quite] low in the water, and its crew started to abandon ship.[66]

GUNFIRE FROM DESTROYERS SINK SUBMARINE

To prevent Germans emerging from the conning tower hatch from manning the guns of the still afloat submarine, planes *74-P-5* and *74-P-6* kept up continuous strafing, until the latter aircraft departed to rendezvous with, and lead, Fourth Fleet warships to the scene. As the last of the survivors were abandoning, the destroyers *Moffett* (DD-362) and *Jouett* (DD-396) arrived and started shelling the submarine. After four direct hits, she nosed over and sank at position 10°00'S, 35°35'W. As *Moffett* began picking up survivors, *Jouett* patrolled nearby, screening her from any other enemy submarines that might be present while rescue operations were in progress. At completion, *Moffett* set a course for Recife to land the fifty-one prisoners she had aboard. A few superficial wounds from machine gun fire, and one inflicted by a shark, were treated aboard the destroyer. Four of the Germans died aboard ship while en route to the Brazilian port, including the chief engineer, Gustaf Stutz. His death was believed due to chlorine poisoning, caused by seawater getting into damaged battery cells (as the U-boat sank) and mixing with acid, forming the lethal gas.[67]

As a matter of interest, the Chief Engineer (Leitenderingenieur) was the second most important officer aboard a U-boat. In addition to his responsibilities associated with the engineering department, this individual was responsible for controlling the submarine when diving, running at depth and surfacing. The captain or the officer of the deck gave the order to dive or crash dive, and specified how deep to go, but the Leitenderingenieur controlled the boat during the dive and while running at depth. He might be a chief petty officer (Obermaschinist), a warrant officer (Obermaschinist mit Portepee), or a commissioned officer (Deckoffizier Maschinist). Regardless of his actual rank, the Leitenderingenieur was considered to be an officer; he ate with the captain and the watch officers, and he slept in the officers' quarters.[68]

AWARDS FOR VALOR

The plane captains of the two PBM-3C Mariners, Lt. Howland S. Davis, USN, and Lt. (jg) Harold C. Carey, USN, were awarded the Distinguished Flying Cross for their roles in the destruction of *U-128*. Carey received his posthumously. His was lost at sea on 3 July along with the plane he was piloting and its entire crew—cause unknown. The only wreckage found was one wingtip pontoon and an unused life raft. At first, it was suggested that pilot error was to blame for the loss. The squadron commander, Lt. Comdr. Joseph C. Toth, USN, did not believe this, and thought it more likely that the plane was lost due to enemy action. It may have been critically damaged in an encounter with *U-199*.[69]

PBM-3C Mariner *74-P-5* Plane Crew
(for action on 17 May 1943)

Name	Position	Award
Lt. (jg) Harold C. Carey, USN	Plane Capt./Co-pilot	DFC (PH)
Ens. Hubert Smolanik	Pilot	
Lt. (jg) Dino Marati	Navigator	
Ens. Dale W. Kelly	Photographer	
AMM2/c W. A. Perisho	Flight engineer	
ARM2/c E. O. Jones	Radio	
ARM2/c W. W. Herlihy	Radar	
AMM2/c P. L. Lyons	Bow gunner	
AOM2/c V. A. Capite	Tail gunner	
AMM2/c H. J. Oleson	Starboard waist gunner	
AMM3/c J. T. Fruend	Port waist gunner	

PBM-3C Mariner *74-P-6* Plane Crew
(for action on 17 May 1943)

Lt. Howland S. Davis, USN	Pilot	DFC
Lt. (jg) William J. Barnard	Co-pilot	
Lt. (jg) Paul D. Fitzgerald	Navigator	
Ens. Donald Osheim	Photographer	
AP1/c E. L. Richoz	Bomber	
AMM3/c R. Bass	Flight engineer	
AMM1/c J. R. Carlin	Turret gunner	

ARM2/c R. M. Fortner	Radioman
AOM2/c R. F. Bradley	Bow gunner
Sea2/c E. M. Hunt	Tail gunner
AMM3/c L. L. Mahoney	Port waist gunner
Sea2/c W. A. Kmieciak	Starboard waist gunner

Six U-Boats Destroyed in July 1943

May of 1943 was the turning point in the Battle of the Atlantic, during which the Third Reich lost 40 U-boats which constituted 25% of its operational strength at the time.

Germany never recovered from this disaster and Dönitz withdrew all but a token number of U-boats from battle. This month has been called "Stalingrad of the U-boat arm" by some.

—The greatest number of U-boats sunk in the South Atlantic occurred in July 1943, two months after the pivotal point in the Battle of the Atlantic.[1]

U-590 SUNK 9 JULY 1943 NORTH OF BELÉM

As 1943 dawned, with enemy submarines making heavy inroads on shipping off South America, the first Trinidad-Bahia, and Bahia-Trinidad convoys were formed. In support of this action, Patrol Squadron VP-94 received orders to Natal, Brazil. With all eleven of its planes loaded with gear and personnel, the squadron took off from Jacksonville, Florida, on 16 January. The PBY-5A Catalinas reached Natal five days later—following stops at Guantanamo, Cuba; San Juan, Puerto Rico; Georgetown, British Guiana; and Belém, Brazil. Almost immediately, the planes began escorting convoys and making sweeps of ocean waters searching for submarines.[2]

VP-94 personnel found the living conditions at Natal primitive at best. A lack of housing was solved via the use of tents but, in spite of ditches and trenches dug at all hours of day and night to try to divert frequent torrential rainfall, wet floors continued to be a problem. The food, consisting of a steady diet of sausage, Spam and salmon, also left a lot to be desired.[3]

The squadron's Catalinas patrolled the coastal waters of Brazil from Amapa to Bahia, a distance of 1,800 miles. There was little time for training as almost every flight was an operational mission. Squadron planes followed their assigned convoys down the coast, landing on primitive fields for refueling and food, with flight crews sleeping in the planes when hotels were full or unavailable.   Each stopping point was earmarked as a place to get beans, or to unload a few dozen cans of Spam, or to get some eggs.   Barter took place with Army cooks, with cans of Spam or sausage exchanged for cans of peas, fresh potatoes, or onions.   Some patrol planes were away from Natal as long as two weeks, making the Amapa-Bahia run south, and returning with a northbound convoy.[4]

Operational tempo increased in May 1943, when VP-83 returned to the United States for new planes, and Patrol Squadron 94 then had the Brazilian coast practically to itself.   VP-83 had operated under even greater makeshift conditions.   Following its arrival in Brazil in April 1942, the squadron utilized existing Panair facilities and those of the U.S. Army, under construction.   (Panair do Brasil was an airline of Brazil.   Between 1945 and 1965, it was considered to be the largest carrier, not only in Brazil, but in all of Latin America.)   VP-83 planes flew up and down the coast, landing on Panair fields and borrowing spare parts from Panair and the Army, while covering convoys as the submarine situation warranted.   When back at their home base, aircraft crews lived in local hotels.[5]

Because Natal was regarded as a possible German stepping stone to the Americas, the U.S. Army was represented in some force at both Natal and Belém.   The U.S. Navy added to its forces in the area with the establishment of Fleet Air Wing Sixteen at Natal in April 1943.   In order to facilitate closer contact with the Fourth Fleet, the wing relocated to Recife in July 1943.   The first Naval Air Facility was established in Recife in October, at Ibura Field.   In December 1943, the estimate of enemy submarines engaged in coastal operations dropped to zero, allowing the Wing to devote greater effort to trying to intercept blockade runners and cargo submarines in the central South Atlantic.[6]

VP-94 DETACHMENTS AT BELÉM, RIO DE JANEIRO, AND AMAPA, BRAZIL

On 18 June 1943, a detachment of six aircraft was moved from Natal to Belém, Brazil—a base destined to be the most active for VP-94 for anti-submarine operations.   Due to renewed activity of enemy submarines (and the necessity to base newer squadrons flying PV-1 Ventura patrol bombers with shorter operating ranges closer to the convoy lanes), VP-94 was further split into additional detachments. When the convoy routing system was extended southward from Bahia to Rio, four planes were ordered to Santos Dumont airport in Rio de

Janeiro. These Catalinas were kept busy flying coverage and anti-submarine sweeps around the clock. Another detachment was sent to Amapa, a small settlement in the northern region of Brazil. Its airstrip was very short, and every landing and takeoff, especially at night, was memorable.[7]

CONVOY ATTACKED, CATALINAS DISPATCHED

On the night of 7 July, a submarine attacked Convoy TJ-1 in the Trinidad area; sinking the Norwegian motor-tanker *B. P. Newton* and American merchant vessel *Eldena*, and damaging the Latvian merchantman *Everagra*. Following this incident, VP-94 planes were dispatched from Belém to operate out of Amapa, and to provide coverage for the convoys. On 9 July, Catalina *94-P-1* was en route to TJ-1 to relieve another plane on convoy duty. Shortly before noon, a sighting was made of the swirl of a submerging submarine. The plane reported the sighting to base and advised that gambit tactics would be employed. "Gambit" referred to a ploy in which an aircraft purposefully flew outside an area where a U-boat was believed to be, inducing the submarine to surface and proceed along the seemingly safest course, that of the disappearing plane. In a countermove, the plane would return, and attack the sub, ideally with the assistance of Navy ships.[8]

At approximately 1230, another plane (*94-P-10*)—sweeping the area immediately east of TJ-1—sighted a surfaced submarine about sixty miles distant from the previous swirl. This sub, which would prove to be the *U-590*, apparently did not see the aircraft until quite late, for it made no attempt to submerge. Alternatively, it may have decided to fight instead of flee. When the Catalina had closed to within a little more than a mile from the submarine, orange flecks disclosed the U-boat's anti-aircraft guns were firing. A round entered the fuselage of the plane, on the port side, forward, and exploded against the instrument panel. Shrapnel struck the pilot, Lt. (jg) Frank F. Hare, USNR, killing him instantly.[9]

The co-pilot took over control of the aircraft and continued the attack. During the run in, the bow gunner kept up continuous .30-caliber fire. Once nearly overhead the target, the two starboard depth charges were released, and the port blister .50-caliber gun was brought to bear. The bombs landed close together, 25-35 feet astern of, and off the starboard side of the submarine. When plane *94-P-10* departed the scene about 20-30 minutes later, the submarine was surfaced and apparently undamaged. Two other aircraft, *94-P-1* and *107-B-5*, arrived in the area around 1300, but found no trace of the U-boat.[10]

U-590 SUNK

While this action was occurring, Catalina *94-P-1* continued its gambit. At 1424, a sighting was made of a submarine surfacing about three miles dead ahead at 03°22'N, 48°38'W. Water was rushing from the decks of the U-boat and within a few seconds it was fully surfaced, cruising at about 15 knots on an east-southeast course. There was no indication that the three or four men visible in the conning tower were aware of the approach of the aircraft. Lt. (jg) Stanley E. Auslander was flying at 3,700 feet over a broken cumulus cloud base, and had just passed through a fairly heavy cloud. He held the plane in a dive directly toward the sub without changing course and after cutting the throttles, obtained an air speed of 200 knots. Depth bombs were released at an altitude of about 150 feet, spaced at seventy-three feet.[11]

Spray from the bombs' blasts was still visible after the plane had pulled up, and made an easy turn to port. When the water plumes subsided, there was no trace of the submarine. Only a greenish-brown slick was visible. In its center, there were two men swimming and some floating debris (a large timber, and two boxes and several smaller articles). A plane crew member reported three additional men in the water, and on the next approach, the co-pilot sighted them as well. Five men were counted at this time, but three apparently slipped below the surface and perished. A life raft dropped by the plane drifted away before the remaining swimmers could reach it, following which four life jackets were then dropped. It appeared from the air that the two survivors were each able to don one. Emergency rations were also dropped. Apparently, the two Germans never made it to shore. Thus, *U-590* (commanded by Oberleutnant zur See Werner Krüer) was lost off the Amazon delta north of Belém with all hands.[12]

AWARDS FOR VALOR

Lieutenants (jg) Stanley Auslander and John Elliott, the pilot and co-pilot of *94-P-1*, received the Distinguished Flying Cross, and the other members of the plane crew, Air Medals. Lt. (jg) Frank Fisher Hare, USNR—killed in action piloting *94-P-10*—was awarded the Distinguished Flying Cross and the Purple Heart posthumously.

PBY-5A Catalina *94-P-1* Plane Crew
(for action on 9 July 1943)

Name	Position	Award
Lt. (jg) Stanley Ernest Auslander, USNR	Pilot	DFC
Lt. (jg) John Milton Elliott, USNR	Co-pilot	DFC
Lt. (jg) Frank Joseph McMackin Jr., USNR	Navigator	AM
AOM3/c Joseph James Mustone Jr.	Tower	AM

AMM2/c Franklin Joseph DeNauw | Port Blister | AM
ARM2/c John Henry Watson | Starboard Blister | AM
AMM3/c Elmer Bryant Smith | Bow | AM
ARM2/c Hoyt Edwin Garren | Radio | AM

PBY-5A Catalina *94-P-10*
(for action on 9 July 1943)

Lt. (jg) Frank Fisher Hare, USNR	Pilot	DFC/PH
Lt. (jg) Jean Price Phelps, USNR	Co-pilot	
Lt. (jg) Michael Carl Argento, USNR	Navigator	
AMM2/c Joseph Lombardo, USN	Tower	
AMM3/c Clifford Emery Eisaman, USNR	Bow	
AOM3/c Andrew Frank Testen, USNR	Starboard Blister	
ARM3/c Thomas Russell Brown, USN	Port Blister	
ARM3/c James Thomas Lack, USN	Radio[13]	

U-513 SUNK SOUTHEAST OF SÃO FRANCISCO DO SOL, BRAZIL

The plane showed great courage in attacking us.

—Statement made by Kapitänleutnant Friedrich Guggenberger to
a medical officer aboard the seaplane tender *Barnegat* (AVP-10),
after he and six members of his crew, the only survivors of
U-513 sunk by plane *74-P-5*, were recovered by the ship.[14]

Ten days after the sinking of *U-590*, Germany lost another submarine
in the South Atlantic. In early afternoon on 19 July, a PBM-3C
Mariner patrol bomber of VP-74 sank the *U-513* southeast of São
Francisco do Sul at position 27°17'S, 47°32'W. This city (situated on
the northern end of the island of São Francisco at the entrance to
Babitonga Bay) was the third oldest in Brazil, having been founded as
a village by the Portuguese in 1658. Lt. (jg) Roy S. Whitcomb, USN,
piloting the so-called "Nickel Boat" (*74-P-5*), located the enemy, which
elected to remain on the surface and fight it out with anti-aircraft
batteries versus trying to escape. Whitcomb's plane was one of two
Mariners of the squadron operating out of Florianapolis, Brazil
(located less than 500 miles south of Rio), supported by the seaplane
tender *Barnegat* (AVP-10). Their presence there was part of the
temporary measures enacted to meet the U-boat threat.[15]

BARNEGAT-CLASS OF SEAPLANE TENDER

Barnegat, the lead ship in a new class of seaplane tenders, had been commissioned on 3 July 1941, at Puget Sound Navy Yard, Bremerton, Washington. The introduction of the *Barnegat*-class ships into the fleet reflected the increased importance of patrol planes in the air arm of the Navy, and recognition that patrol squadrons would have to operate in areas where shore support was not available. Previous small tenders were converted vessels (elderly World War I-era minesweepers and destroyers) not specifically designed for functional tending and not suitable for adaptation to the latest developments in armament and associated fire control. Although the primary function of the AVPs was the operational tending of patrol planes, a good deal of *Barnegat*'s war service would be devoted to transport and anti-submarine patrol. She performed much of this work off the coast of South America between June 1943 and May 1944. During this period, her duties as a transport ship between Recife, Natal, Bahia, and Rio de Janeiro, Brazil, and Montevideo, Uruguay, were interspersed with periodic patrols and maneuvers with the Brazilian Navy.[16]

Photo 15-1

Seaplane tender *Barnegat* (AVP-10) under way off the coast of Brazil on 4 April 1944. U.S. Navy Photograph #80-G-361055, now in the collection of the National Archives

The seaplane tender's armament of three 5"/38 guns, depth charges, and numerous light anti-aircraft guns, plus her inherent capability for handling and carrying large amounts of supplies and personnel, made her especially adapted for a variety of services she was called upon to perform. This included rescuing and transporting the survivors of two German submarines sunk by patrol aircraft.[17]

Following her initial arrival at Natal on 26 June 1943, *Barnegat* had reported for duty with Fleet Air Wing Sixteen, relieving the *Humboldt* (AVP-21) in servicing Fourth Fleet planes assigned to cover convoys from Brazil to Trinidad. Her arrival coincided with the beginning of a German submarine "blitz" against coastal shipping. Dispatched to Florianapolis, located about 1,800 miles down the coast from Natal, the seaplane tender anchored there on 18 July to await her assigned aircraft, which arrived less than four hours later.[18]

FOURTH, AND LAST PATROL OF *U-513*

U-513 had departed Lorient on 18 May 1943, under the command of Kapitänleutnant Friedrich Guggenberger. One of Germany's famous U-boat aces, he had, by this point in the war, already sunk a total of thirteen ships—including the British aircraft carrier HMS *Ark Royal* (on 13 November 1941, while in command of *U-81*). *U-513* was expected to operate in the area of Recife and her patrol to last sixteen weeks. Leaving port, she carried twenty-one torpedoes (six in upper deck containers and fifteen inside the submarine), and was escorted, as was the usual practice, by a minesweeper and a patrol craft until she reached waters deep enough to submerge.[19]

In early June, *U-513* rendezvoused with a supply submarine, *U-460* (Kapitänleutnant Ebe Schnoor), north of St. Paul Rocks. As the two submarines cruised on the surface at slow speed, about 165 feet apart, *U-513* received about thirty cubic-meters of fuel oil from *U-460*. As was common practice, the doctor from the supply submarine came aboard to give the crew a quick medical checkup, and Guggenberger spent time aboard the *U-460* exchanging news with Schnoor. After receiving provisions in canisters via cargo nets, *U-513* resumed her southward trek toward the Brazilian coast, and *U-460* northward, en route to a French base.[20]

Schnoor was one of the oldest U-boat commanders to see active service when he took the "milch cow" *U-460* out from Bordeaux, France, on 27 August 1942. (Milch cow, meaning milk cow, was the German nickname for supply submarines.) He was forty-seven years old, and would make five patrols before *U-460* was sunk on 4 October 1943, thirty-six days into her fifth patrol—by aircraft from the escort carrier *Card* (CVE-11). Only two members of his crew survived; Schnoor was among the sixty-two who did not.[21]

U-513 passed the island of Trinidad off her port beam on 20 June. Later, a brief alarm and dive were occasioned by the sighting of something in the sky, which the quartermaster classified as an airplane, but which Guggenberger believed was only a large seabird. Per his orders, the quartermaster's entry in the log was amended to read, "The commander insists that the cause of the alarm was an albatross, not an airplane." Within a few days, the sub reached her operational area— the stretch of coastline between Rio and Santos, extending for some distance out to sea. The hunting in this area was good; *U-513* sank four ships, and damaged the tanker *Eagle* in less than four weeks.

Victims of *U-513* on her Fourth Patrol

Date	Ship	Tons	Nationality
21 Jun 1943	Merchant vessel MV *Venezia*	1,673	Swedish
25 Jun 1943	Tanker SS *Eagle* (damaged)	6,003	American
1 Jul 1943	Merchant vessel SS *Tutoya*	1,125	Brazilian
3 Jul 1943	Liberty ship SS *Elihu B. Washburne*	7,176	American
16 Jul 1943	Liberty ship SS *Richard Caswell*	7,177	American[22]

OPERATING OFF RIO DE JANEIRO

During *U-513*'s patrol, she was often near enough Rio de Janeiro to see the lights of the city, and one old destroyer patrolling the harbor entrance. Several times it seemed possible for the submarine to get into attack position; however the setup was never perfect. On one occasion, *U-513* inadvertently broached the surface about 1,500 yards ahead of the destroyer. Her crew was quite certain the conning tower was visible. However, after flooding the quick diving tank and submerging, followed by some anxious moments, it became evident that the incident had escaped observation by the warship.[23]

DESTRUCTION OF *U-513*

On 19 July, *U-513* was cruising on the surface south of Santos. The weather was hazy with scattered clouds, and visibility was about twenty miles. The bridge watch consisted of the second watch officer, a petty officer, and two enlisted men. At 1355, as the sub proceeded on a westerly course, a patrol bomber of squadron VP-74 made radar contact on her at a distance of twenty miles. The PBM-3C, piloted by Lt. (jg) Roy S. Whitcomb, had taken off from San Miguel Bay, Florianapolis, at 0702 that morning on an anti-submarine sweep. Taking advantage of cloud patches, Whitcomb remained on course 030°T until he reached a position dead ahead of the U-boat. Then while in a cloud, he turned right to 080°T (the reciprocal course of the enemy) and closed the submarine from out of the sun.[24]

The watch team on *U-513*'s bridge sighted the approaching plane just before it entered the cloud. Guggenberger rushed to the bridge and quickly gave orders to man and fire the anti-aircraft guns. He considered it too late to dive, and could hardly believe that what he thought was probably some "old crate" would be foolhardy enough to attack a U-boat firing both AA guns. He also gave orders for the submarine to start zigzagging, after making a sharp turn to starboard to present her beam to the attacking aircraft.[25]

To readers familiar with naval tactics, this decision might appear imprudent. The commanding officer of a ship would normally try to avoid such action, and would instead maneuver to minimize the vessel's cross section, thereby presenting a smaller target. In the case of a submarine, exposing its beam to an attacking aircraft increased the odds that dropped bombs would land farther away, improving its chances of survival. A plane flying at high speed across the narrow width of a submarine had a more difficult target than if flying down its length.

Whitcomb described the situation, and the forceful maneuvers he made to try to avoid taking fire from *U-513*'s guns during the attack:

> The sub was maneuvering as if to avoid [bomb] drops or give me a beam run. I maneuvered so as to deliver attack as close to a keel run from stern as possible. The fire from sub at this point had become heavier with tracers from deck gun and, I believe, at least one machine gun. Tracers were to port and starboard of us. Past experience in firing free guns from carrier planes had taught me that half deflection shots were most difficult target, so I was skidding first left then right as violently as possible without spoiling the run. This I did without conscious effort as I was using the tactics before I realized it.[26]

The PBM-3C Mariner released six bombs from a height of 50 feet and airspeed of 166 knots while *U-513* was in a slight turn to starboard. The drop straddled the sub, with two bombs striking her deck with a slight delay in detonation. Whitcomb initially remained low with a slight skidding turn to the left. After making a steep turn to observe the results of the attack, he was surprised to see nothing but rising boils and a brown stain on the water. Returning over the drop point, spreading oil, brown discoloration, boiling bubbles, and about fifteen to twenty survivors struggling in the water were visible. Whitcomb slowed, lowered flaps, and dropped two rubber rafts and some life vests to the men in the water. Following this action, he advised *Barnegat* of the position of the survivors. Two of the Germans were able to swim to a raft and succeeded in picking up five of their shipmates. The second raft could not be located, resulting in it being very cramped for the seven men on the only one available. Many were forced to hang their legs over the side with feet in the water; pulling them up only when a large shark came uncomfortably close.[27]

Survivors recounted that bomb detonations had caused the sub's forward compartments to burst open, throwing the men on deck and on the bridge into the water. One or two of the men saw the stern of *U-513* rise up, before the submarine disappeared at a sharp angle into the deep, with propellers still turning. The small quantity of oil on the water was attributed to the outboard fuel tanks being empty. *U-513* had been near the end of her patrol, and had expected to meet a supply submarine on the way home to receive needed fuel.[28]

AWARDS FOR VALOR

For their roles in the destruction of *U-513*, Lt. (jg) Whitcomb, and AP 1/c Donald T. Ward, USN (the second pilot and the individual who dropped the bombs) received the Distinguished Flying Cross. The other officers and men received the Air Medal.[29]

PBM-3C Mariner *74-P-5* Plane Crew
(for action on 19 July 1943)

Name	Position	Award
Lt. (jg) Roy S. Whitcomb, USN	Plane captain/Pilot	DFC
AP1/c Donald T. Ward, USN	Co-pilot	DFC
Lt. (jg) Jordan B. Collins, USNR	Navigator	Air Medal
Ens. Robert M. Sparks, USNR	Bomber	Air Medal
AMM1/c F. P. Green, USN	Flight engineer	Air Medal
ARM2/c J. R. Burleson, USN	Radio	Air Medal
ARM2/c W. S. Stotts, USNR	Radar	Air Medal
AMM3/c T. W. Govern, USNR	Bow gunner	Air Medal
Sea2/c C. L. Mathews, USNR	Tail gunner	Air Medal
AMM2/c G. L. Cole, USNR	Port waist gunner	Air Medal
AOM3/c H. E. Hill, USN	Starboard waist gunner	Air Medal[29]

BARNEGAT PICKS UP *U-513* SURVIVORS

After receiving a report of the U-boat kill, *Barnegat* proceeded swiftly to the scene, arriving there in less than four hours to begin a search. At 1915, she sighted the life raft containing the seven men, and closed to pick them up. The first prisoner boarded the ship at 1930 and the last one twenty minutes later. Among them was the commanding officer, youthful 28-year-old Kapitänleutnant Friedrich Guggenberger. The gathering darkness hindered finding other potential survivors, and the seaplane tender ceased her efforts a little after midnight.[30]

Barnegat returned to San Miguel Bay. Shortly before noon on 22 July, she received a report from her other plane (*74-P-7*) of a sighting of a life raft with survivors on board. With her prisoners still aboard, she put to sea and in late afternoon, located two rafts lashed together. Chief Engineer Harold Van R. Forest, of the recently sunk *Richard Caswell*, along with eleven other members of her crew and six of her Navy armed guard detachment, were in or clinging to the rafts. The Liberty ship, torpedoed on 16 July, had been the *U-513*'s last victim.[31]

Just as the ship broke in two, the submarine had surfaced to question the survivors. Guggenberger told the men that he had lived in Brooklyn, New York, for seven years and asked how the Dodgers were doing. The Germans gave the men cigarettes and then left the area. The individuals in the two rafts comprised only a portion of the surviving crewmen of the *Richard Caswell* (60 of 69 men) who had abandoned ship in three lifeboats and two rafts. Two of the boats, carrying twenty-six men, were picked up on 19 July by the Argentine steam merchant *Mexico*, and landed two days later at Rio Grande, Brazil. The sixteen survivors in the third boat made landfall on their own at Barra Valha, Brazil, on 22 July.[32]

Barnegat returned to San Miguel Bay the night of 22 July, but remained only overnight before getting under way for Rio. Upon reaching there on the 24th, she was held "incommunicado" until her prisoners could be transferred to authorities ashore the following morning. The seaplane tender then disembarked the eighteen men from the *Richard Caswell*.[33]

GUGGENBERGER ESCAPES FROM POW CAMPS, IS RECAPTURED, AND DECADES LATER SERVES AS DEPUTY CHIEF OF STAFF OF A NATO COMMAND

Following surgery and a long stay in a hospital, Friedrich Guggenberger (the holder of the Iron Cross 2nd Class, U-boat War Badge 1939, Iron Cross 1st Class, Knight's Cross, and Knight's Cross with Oak Leaves) was transferred to the Fort Hunt Interrogation Center, New York, on 25 September 1943. From there he was sent first to a Prisoner of War camp at Crossville, Tennessee, and then to the Papago Park POW camp near Phoenix, Arizona.[34]

On 12 February 1944, Guggenberger and four other U-boat commanders escaped from the Papago Park camp. Guggenberger and his companion August Maus (*U-185*) were recaptured in Tucson, Arizona. Guggenberger was also one of twenty-five prisoners who escaped from this same camp the night of 23 December 1944. He and his companion on that occasion, Jürgen Quaet-Faslem (*U-595*), were recaptured on 6 January 1945, less than ten miles from the Mexican border. Guggenberger was transferred in February 1946 to Camp

Shanks, New York, then to a POW compound in Germany in the British Zone near Münster. He was released from Allied captivity in August 1946.[35]

Guggenberger continued his career in post-World War II, joining the Bundesmarine (Federal German Navy) in 1956, and retiring in October 1972 with the rank of Konteradmiral. Late in his career, after graduating from the U.S. Naval War College in Newport, Rhode Island, Guggenberger served for four years as the deputy chief of staff for the NATO command AFNORTH (Allied Forces North Europe). At age seventy-three, he went for a walk in the woods on 13 May 1988, and did not return. His body was found two years later.[36]

PATROL BOMBER *74-P-7* AND BRAZILIAN PBY CATALINA SINK *U-199* EAST OF RIO DE JANEIRO

Attention is invited to the fact that the U/B [U-boat] forced beam attack on 74-P-7; that he pressed home his attack deliberately and vigorously in the face of heavy A/A [anti-aircraft] fire; that his second attack was nearly bow on - both attacks being the most difficult to deliver and that in spite of the above he so crippled the U/B that it was not able to submerge and that it had to stay surfaced and fight it out until the final blow was dealt by the PBY.

The Brazilian airforce is deserving of special credit for the success of this action, especially because of their inexperience and the inferiority of their equipment.

The usual good performance of the BARNEGAT in recovering the survivors is again noteworthy. The complete operation from attack to recovery of survivors took only four hours and 45 minutes.

—Lt. Comdr. Joseph C. Toth, USN, commander VP-74,
in an Anti-Submarine Action by Aircraft Report
describing the sinking of *U-199*.[37]

While *Barnegat* was at Rio de Janeiro, the Trinidad-bound Convoy JT-3 departed there on 31 July 1943 under the protection of both American Navy and Brazilian Air Force planes. A Brazilian PBY Catalina was to cover the sortie (departure) from Rio Harbor, then sweep for submarines ahead of the ship convoy. Meanwhile, a VP-74 Mariner (*74-P-7*), piloted by Lt. (jg) Walter F. Smith, USN, was to make a barrier sweep of the harbor approaches paralleling the convoy route. The patrol bomber took off at 0630, and soon gained a radar contact nineteen miles distant. At fifteen miles, a sighting was made of a faint wake with a black object at the left edge which, when the plane had closed to ten miles, was identified as a fully surfaced U-boat.[38]

When the wake was first sighted, Lt. (jg) Smith had immediately pushed the plane over into a power glide. Now, he took it into a steeper glide at 185 to 190 knots. Concurrently, in preparation for an attack on the submarine, Aviation Pilot First Class (AP1/c) Dalton W. Smith, USN, opened the bomb doors. At about a mile from the U-boat, Lt. (jg) Smith leveled off at 150 feet and 180 knots, gradually decreasing altitude to 75 feet at the time of the bomb release. Seeing that a beam attack was probable, he ordered bomb spacing reduced to 65 feet and made the final approach with a series of skids to avoid anti-aircraft fire; which was heavy, though inaccurate. As the plane crossed the submarine from its port side, just forward of the conning tower, AP1/c Smith released six depth charges. Following this initial drop, Lt. (jg) Smith made a turn to the left before returning to deliver a second attack down the length of the sub from bow to stern, with the last two charges released from forty feet above the water at 160 knots. Bomb detonations enveloped the U-boat in spray.[39]

Having expended all his bombs, Smith then began a series of strafing runs on the submarine, which would prove to be the *U-199* on her first war patrol. Injured by depth charge detonations, smoking heavily, leaking oil, and attempting to return fire, the sub initially made a series of tight circles; suggesting that her rudder was not operating properly. This condition was apparently rectified, because after about fifteen minutes, *U-199* straightened out on a northerly course and maneuvered to use her guns to best advantage, as the patrol bomber came in on a strafing run. At 0804, she made an attempt to submerge, after first clearing her decks of personnel. This effort was for naught. *U-199* appeared to lose control and sink (submerging completely without diving), before resurfacing in the same spot with difficulty, her stern completely awash. After partially regaining correct trim, the desperate sub resumed her gun battle with Mariner *74-P-7* while proceeding along her former course.[40]

FOLLOW-ON ATTACKS BY BRAZILIAN AIRCRAFT

At 0840, a Brazilian Hudson A-28A came in from the northeast. As *74-P-7* drew the sub's fire, the light bomber made an approach to attack. It crossed the *U-199*'s bow from starboard, releasing two Mk 17 depth charges in salvo from an altitude of 300 feet. The drop was short, with the explosions occurring 150 feet away from, and broad on the starboard bow of the submarine. In a seeming avoidance action,

U-119 then made a half-circle to starboard before steadying up on a northwesterly base course.[41]

Photo 15-2

U.S. Navy and Brazilian Air Force officers inspect a flight line of Brazilian PBY-5A patrol planes circa 1945.
NARA Photograph #80-G-K-5258

The Hudson departed the scene immediately, and soon a Brazilian PBY appeared thirty miles away. (Both of these planes had been assigned coverage of the sortie of JT-3, then in progress from Rio Harbor.) The Brazilian Air Force Catalina was piloted by 2nd Lt. Alberto M. Torres. While making 160 knots, the PBY attacked *U-199* from off the submarine's port quarter, and released three Mk 44 depth charges spaced at fifty feet. The sub attempted to dodge the bombs by altering course between 340° and 60° true. One of the bombs exploded tangent to the port quarter of the submarine; the other two depth charges fell short. The PBY then circled sharply to port before returning for the kill, dropping its one remaining depth charge on the submerged stern of *U-199*. (At the time of this attack, only the bow then remained above the surface.) The submarine sank immediately at position 23°47'S, 42°56'W, east of Rio de Janeiro.[42]

RECOVERY/INTEROGATION OF SURVIVORS

After a preliminary interrogation at Recife, all prisoners were brought to the United States for detailed questioning. They were the most security conscious group ever interrogated in this country. While in the water between sinking and rescue, Kraus had given a final warning to his men against giving any information to the enemy.

—Report titled, Interrogation of Survivors from *U-199* Sunk on 31 July 1943, O.N.I. 250 – G/Serial 22, dated 27 September 1943.

After receiving a report at 0958 on 31 July that an enemy submarine had been sunk, *Barnegat* hurried to the scene led by plane *74-P-2*. She spotted life rafts at 1138, and picked up five officers and seven enlisted men, among them *U-199*'s commanding officer, 28 year old Kapitänleutnant Hans Werner Kraus. Kraus was a decorated U-boat commander (who had previously taken *U-83* on nine patrols) and former executive officer to the U-boat ace, Günther Prien.[43]

Photo 15-3

Survivors from *U-199* in life rafts.
U.S. Naval History and Heritage Command Photograph #NH 121234

In his post mortem on the attack, commander VP-74 singled out the seaplane tender for her "usual good performance…in recovering the survivors" of the sunken U-boat. As before, *Barnegat* anchored in the harbor at Rio with the German prisoners held incommunicado until disembarked under heavy guard. They were taken to the airport, for a quick flight to the United States for thorough interrogation.[44]

The primary item of interest gleaned from the interrogation was a description of *U-199*, one of the new 1,200-ton submarines. Built at AG Weser, in Bremen, Germany, and commissioned on 27 November 1942 sporting a coat of dark grey paint, she spanned 290 feet in length with a 22 foot-beam and 14 foot-draft. Her armament consisted of:

- One 105mm gun forward, and one 37mm gun aft
- One 20mm gun on the conning tower platform (and one reserve 20mm stowed below decks)
- Two Type 15 machine guns on the conning tower (and two in reserve), plus a number of G.7.H automatic pistols
- Six torpedo tubes (four bow, two stern) and twenty-seven torpedoes (twelve in upper-deck containers and fifteen inside the submarine)[45]

Following her trials and fitting out, *U-199* had cast off from the pier at Bergen (located up the Weser River from Bremerhaven) in the evening of 17 May 1943 and departed on her first war patrol. She was escorted by one ex-Norwegian torpedo boat until making open water, whereupon she set course 300°T and the escort parted company. While in passage in the North Sea, *U-199* was compelled several times to dive upon sighting aircraft, but one became an attack. Following a late sighting of the plane by the lookout, the sub crash dove. A stick of four bombs or depth charges straddled *U-199* while she was still at periscope depth, but no serious damage resulted. The submarine remained at sixty meters' depth for about one hour, then surfaced and proceeded on her way.[46]

U-199 was fitted with two 9-cylinder main propulsion engines, each rated at 2,400 hp. When surfaced and in fair weather, she could make a top speed of 17.5-18 knots. She also had two 6-cylinder auxiliary diesels used principally for charging batteries. While on ocean passage, *U-199* never made more than half speed (12 knots) in order to save fuel, and once in her operational area never more than 3/4 speed (14 knots). While on patrol, she often ran only a single diesel engine for propulsion, in order to save fuel. She also sometimes utilized diesel-electric power. At other times, she used one diesel for propulsion and operated the other to charge her batteries.[47]

Diagram 15-1

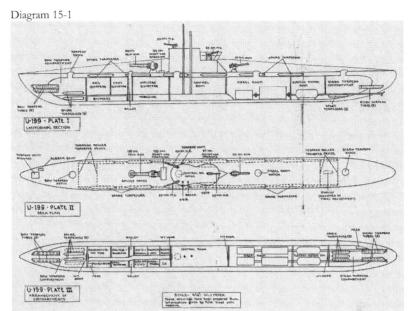

The text at the bottom of these plates warns, "These drawings have been prepared from information given by Ps/W [prisoners of war]. Treat with reserve.
Report on the Interrogation of Survivors from *U-199* Sunk on 31 July 1943, O.N.I. 250 – G/Serial 22, 27 September 1943

After passing from the North Sea into the Atlantic, *U-199* steered a southwesterly course until reaching latitude 47° north. She then changed to a southerly course to pass west of the Azores and crossed from the North Atlantic into the South Atlantic about 10 June. There was no "crossing the equator" celebration, as Kraus considered it unwise to relax his condition of readiness when in the narrows between Freetown and Natal. Continuing her transit, the submarine passed a few miles to the west of the St. Paul Rocks (a part of the Brazilian St. Peter and St. Paul Archipelago) en route to the Brazilian coast, but did not sight them. At about position 03°S, 30°W, Kraus received a signal from Grand Admiral Karl Dönitz, commander-in-chief U-boats, ordering him to proceed to a designated area. Kraus was to patrol this area to intercept and destroy Allied ships proceeding from Rio de Janeiro and points north, to the River Plate and points south.[48]

U-199 arrived in her operational area in mid-June, upon which Kraus adopted a policy of remaining submerged during daylight hours at a depth of twenty meters, occasionally rising to periscope depth for reconnaissance. At dusk, he would generally surface to operate the auxiliary diesels to recharge batteries, and to air out the boat, then not dive again until dawn. In July, he sank two vessels: the Brazilian sailing ship *Changri-Lá* on 4 July and twenty days later, the British steamship *Henzada*.[49]

Kraus used his 105mm deck gun to send the *Changri-Lá* (a small vessel with a sail aft) to the bottom off Arraial do Cabo, Brazil. A search of the area found no survivors. The *Henzada* was hit amidships by one of two stern torpedoes, broke in two, and sank about one hundred miles southwest of Rio de Janeiro. (This success followed a failed attack by *U-199* against the ship a few hours earlier, in which three torpedoes missed the *Henzada*.) Kraus was about to surface and search among the wreckage when there was a loud explosion close at hand, believed to be an aircraft depth charge. He thus remained submerged for a while, and then left the area. Two *Henzada* crewmen were lost. The ship's master, William Innes McIntosh, the remaining fifty-three crewmen, and eight Naval Armed Guard gunners were rescued by the Panamanian tanker *Baltic* and landed at Montevideo on 28 July.[50]

SURVIVORS' ACCOUNT OF THE SINKING OF *U-199*

U-199 had been on the surface, steering a west-northwest course the morning of 31 July 1943. It was Kraus' intention to move nearer to shore into 600 foot-deep water, and then submerge and lie in wait. Immediately after receiving a report of the sighting of a patrol bomber (*74-P-7*), the quartermaster on watch had ordered the helm put hard over to starboard, and speed increased to full. This action was endorsed by Kraus when he came up on deck. The submarine was then steering 090° true. The quartermaster's orders were, however, misunderstood, below. Consequently, alarm bells were rung and some of the forward ballast tanks flooded in preparation for a crash dive before the order, as given, was correctly carried out.[51]

As the patrol bomber closed within range, *U-199* opened fire with all her armament, including the 105mm deck gun firing anti-aircraft rounds. The plane returned fire, scoring several hits on the sub's conning tower, and straddled her with depth-charges, which caused damage below decks and the escape of oil from fuel tanks. (There was one casualty during this action, a man from the upper-deck gun crews.) *U-199*, smoking heavily abaft the conning tower, could not submerge, and could proceed only at a very slow speed, then changed to a westward course. Kraus had decided to close the shore until reaching water shallow enough to permit him to lie on the bottom and effect repairs. He felt that if he remained surfaced, the sub would be subjected to further aircraft attacks. Kraus instructed the quarter-master to monitor soundings until the depth of the water was no more than 135 meters (about 440 feet).[52]

U-199 had just reached this water depth when a Brazilian Hudson arrived on the scene and carried out an attack—which caused no additional damage because its depth charges fell short. A second Brazilian plane, a PBY Catalina, then appeared overhead and delivered two successive attacks, sending the sub to the bottom, stern first.[53]

As the first bombs from the PBY began to fall, Kraus realized that the situation was hopeless and he ordered the crew to abandon ship. Most of the men were already on deck. The remainder of the crew, largely engineers, made a desperate effort to navigate flooded compartments, reach the ladder to the conning tower hatch, climb up, and escape the submarine. Only the quartermaster was successful. When he arrived up on deck, the sea had reached the 20mm gun on the conning tower platform. *Barnegat* picked up the survivors at noon. Patrol bomber *74-P-7* remained in the area during the Brazilian attack to draw the U-boat's anti-aircraft fire and was hit in one engine, but was able to return to base successfully.[54]

AWARDS FOR VALOR

The Mariner's pilot, Lt. (jg) Walter F. Smith, USN, and bomber, AP1/c Dalton W. Smith, USN, were awarded the Distinguished Flying Cross. The remainder of the officers and men received the Air Medal in recognition of their services.

PBM-3C Mariner *74-P-7* Plane Crew
(for action on 31 July 1943)

Name	Position	Award
Lt. (jg) Walter F. Smith, USN	Pilot	DFC
Ens. Claude F. Grotts, USN	Co-pilot	Air Medal
AP1/c Hans K. Kohler, USN	Navigator	Air Medal
AP1/c Dalton W. Smith, USN	Bomber	DFC
AMM2/c T. E. Jarusewicz, USN	Flight engineer	Air Medal
ARM2/c C. R. Wilson, USNR	Radio	Air Medal
AMM2/c W. H. Meadows, USNR	Observer	Air Medal
AMM2/c R. L. Nagel, USNR	Bow gunner	Air Medal
AMM1/c J. J. Smith, USN	Tail gunner	Air Medal
AOM3/c C. H. Hennis, USNR	Port waist gunner	Air Medal
ARM2/c O. L. King	Starboard waist gunner	Air Medal[55]

U-662 SUNK OFF DUTCH GUIANA (SURINAM)

Undoubtedly the submarines have received definite orders to remain surfaced and use their guns. In the past 15 days the submarines, using these tactics, have slightly damaged four planes--none completely out of commission--killed one officer pilot, and wounded one radioman. In return, during the same period, these tactics have afforded the planes the opportunity to make nine sightings, six of which resulted in attacks giving three possible sinkings. Our reaction is that the decision to stay surfaced and shoot it out is hard on submarines. We hope that the submarines maintain their present tactics.

> —Lt. Comdr. Joseph B. Tibbets, USN, commander VP-94,
> describing attacks made by squadron planes between
> 9 and 23 July 1943; one of which sank the *U-662*.[56]

Morale aboard U-662 *was in general bad…. Conversation on board frequently touched upon the prospect of Germany's losing the war and upon the likelihood that, under [Kapitänleutnant Heinz-Eberhard] Müller,* U-662 *would be sunk. The general mood of the crew was pessimistic and depressed.*

> —Interrogation of two enlisted survivors of *U-662* indicated that morale
> aboard the boat had been poor before her sinking. The interrogation
> report stated that the commanding officer, Müller, did not seem to
> have enjoyed the absolute loyalty of his men. As an example of the
> culture aboard, one of the seaman stated that it was the custom on
> board for the officers to smoke the best cigarettes and to drink the
> finest Hennessy [cognac], even though the 2,000 "North State"
> cigarettes, for instance, had been issued to the boat
> for equal distribution to all on board.[57]

In early morning darkness on 21 July, plane *94-P-4* took off at 0230 from Belém to relieve *94-P-7* in providing coverage for Convoy TJ-2, which was then about 300 miles from Belém. The PBY-5A Catalina, piloted by Lt. (jg) Richard H. Rowland, arrived in the area about 0530 and began searching for the convoy in darkness. At 0602, as the plane was flying southward, the bow watch, AMM2/c Franklin J. DeNauw, sighted a submarine thirty degrees off the plane's starboard bow, two to three miles distant. Sporting a coat of grey-green paint, broken up by brown camouflage markings, the sub was paralleling the aircraft's course, steering 180°T at 5 to 7 knots. Due to the slow speed, her deck was only slightly awash and she was producing little wake.[58]

Rowland rolled the plane slightly to bring the enemy into view, and then turned to attack. As the pilot's bombing switch closed, and the warning horn blown, DeNauw attempted to ready the .30-caliber gun, but was unable to free the barrel group to allow the breech lock to disengage. Rowland, aware of the trouble with the bow gun and encountering heavy anti-aircraft fire, veered slightly to port and then started a shallow diving run. While still a mile distant from the target, the plane encountered anti-aircraft fire, wounding ARM2/c John H. Watson, as described by Rowland:

> Gunfire from the sub was persistent, forming a heavy barrage, lying two thirds of the distance from the sub to the plane with some projectiles apparently disintegrating at that point. Others came through to meet the plane and exploded on contact. The rudder fin was hit at the base during final turn. A shrapnel shot was received at the chine of the hull at the radioman's station, when the plane was approximately one mile from the submarine. The path of this shot could be followed by tracer, and the ensuing explosion heard upon contact. Radioman Watson suffered lower leg and ankle injuries from this shot, but managed to pull himself to the blister and ask [ARM2/c Hoyt E.] Garren to relieve him.[59]

As Rowland continued his run in to make an attack on the submarine, the enemy remained on the same course, with the same speed and running condition. Anti-aircraft fire ceased just prior to the plane's bomb drop, made from off the U-boat's port quarter at an altitude of about seventy-five feet with the conning tower visible close by to starboard. Although one of four depth charges failed to release, the remaining ordnance sank the submarine, as described in a report detailing actions by the pilot and other plane crew members:

> Lt. (jg) Rowland pressed the pickle [bomb release], but the inboard starboard [depth charge] hung-up.... From reports of the crew, it seems that charges #1 and #2 landed so close that they exploded almost under [the submarine's] port side just aft of the conning tower. During a shallow pull-out and turn to port, the bow of the submarine was seen by the PPC [patrol plane commander] to be emerging from the geysers of water at a sharp angle.
>
> The port gunner and the tower watch could both see the two port bombs enter the water and viewed the start of the explosions.... The starboard bomb was observed to drop to starboard of and ahead of the bow of the submarine at a distance judged to be about 30'.

The port gun was brought to bear and a full can was fired in long bursts. The pilot continued the turn for approximately one minute in order to remain in the immediate vicinity. Lt. (jg) [Albert C.] Anselmo observed the sinking of the sub while the plane was in this turn...[60]

Rowland, upon reestablishing visual contact with the spot where the submarine had been, saw only an oval oil patch which increased in size to 200 yards in length and 150-175 yards wide. Coming back over the drop point, a definite circular slick was visible in the middle of the increasing pool of oil at position 03°56'N, 48°46'W. The pilot ordered two life rafts dropped, and then departed the area.[61]

Photo 15-4

German submarine under attack by a plane of VP-94 from Belém, Brazil, at 03°33'N, 48°45'W, on 20 July 1943. Submarine is possibly the *U-662*, which was sunk by this squadron the following day.
U.S. National Archives Photograph 80-G-85237

SURVIVORS OF *U-662*

Only four members of the submarine escaped death—Kapitänleutnant Heinz-Eberhard Müller and three seamen—who promptly made use of the two rafts. One remaining survivor, a coxswain, died in the water before he could be pulled aboard. During the ensuing sixteen days at sea, the rafts were constantly followed by sharks. At some point, the survivors consolidated into a single raft, and placed the other one above it to provide shade from the sun, and to collect rain water. A hole made in this makeshift awning enabled water to drain into the raft below. The survivors also rigged a makeshift sail, enabling some headway to be made, at times as much as three knots. The raft capsized on one occasion, and it was only with great difficulty that the men were able to right it again and struggle back aboard.[62]

The four survivors were picked up the afternoon of 6 August at position 09°47.5'N, 57°10.5'W by the sub-chaser *PC-494*; which had been serving as part of the escort for Convoy TJ-4, and been guided to the raft by a patrol plane. *PC-494* later transferred the prisoners to the patrol yacht *Siren* (PY-13) via whaleboat. Seaman Second Willi Lübke, died an hour later of multiple injuries and exposure, leaving Müller, who was also wounded, and Seamen First Hermann Grauff and Ferdinand Marx as the only survivors.[63]

FOURTH AND FINAL PATROL

Prior to *U-662* departing from St. Nazaire in western France on 26 June, Grauff and Marx had said formal farewells to all their friends in port, since South Atlantic patrols were regarded as much more dangerous than those in the North Atlantic. The *U-662* was a 500-ton submarine, with a complement of forty-seven: the commanding officer, a surgeon, an engineer officer, two watch officers, 15 petty officers, and 27 lower ranked enlisted men. According to the prisoners, fifteen other U-boats were then operating in the South Atlantic. Besides *U-662*, these included *U-406*, *U-487*, *U-510*, and *U-614*. Some of the others were *U-199*, *U-591*, *U-598*, and *U-604*.[64]

The prisoners stated that on 20 July, the day before *U-662* was sunk, a four-engine patrol plane had dropped four bombs ahead of the submarine, but no apparent damage resulted. (An attack had been made against a U-boat that day, in which the pilot had reported, "Sub sighted, all bombs short - am circling and firing my guns.")[65]

When Rowland made his attack on *U-662* the following day, all her anti-aircraft armament was brought to bear against the PBY-5A Catalina. However, there was a shortage of ammunition aboard the sub, and (unrelated to this situation) both 20mm guns soon jammed. Earlier in the patrol, Müller had directed that gun crews get some practice in the use of their anti-aircraft armament, using radar decoy balloons carried aboard as targets. One of the prisoners recalled that the gunners had trouble hitting the balloons.[66]

During Rowland's attack, Müller knew the Catalina had been hit, and he commented on the nerve and steadiness of the pilot. The direction of the battle soon changed, when machine gun fire from the plane killed the entire bridge watch on the conning tower and one or two other men on deck, as well. The detonations of depth charges caused an explosion in the control room, fuel oil caught fire, and sea water began to pour into ruptured ballast tanks, the conning tower, and the control room. Müller, thrown into the water by the force of the explosions, received extensive injuries. The bow of *U-662* then rose high in the air, and she broke in two and sank, stern first.[67]

MÜLLER SENT TO FORT MEADE, MARYLAND

When Italy entered the war in 1940 the news was received late at night at Hitler's headquarters. Fieldmarshal [Wilhelm] Keitel went to Hitler, who was asleep and reported: "Mein Führer, the Italians have declared war." Still half asleep, Hitler ordered: "Send three divisions to the Brenner." "No, no", said Keitel, "they have entered the war on our side." "In that event," Hitler replied, "send twenty divisions."

—Story told by Kapitänleutnant Heinz-Eberhard Müller during interrogation, to illustrate the general German contempt for Italy regarding the country's military capabilities.[68]

Kapitänleutnant Müller was flown to the United States, and initially confined in the hospital at Fort Meade, Maryland, by his wounds. During questioning, Müller indicated that since becoming a U-boat captain in February, he had often tuned in "The Voice of America" program (produced by the Office of Naval Intelligence), and that he had particularly enjoyed the broadcasts by Commander Robert Norden and would like to meet him, if possible. Following this request, Lt. Comdr. Ralph G. Albrecht, USNR ("Comdr. Norden") visited Müller and spent a couple of hours with him. During their time together, Müller told Albrecht that he was not inclined to believe what was said as it was pure propaganda. However, he and his officers found the broadcasts highly entertaining by reason of the manner in which they were presented, particularly the use of irony by the speaker and occasional "barbed shafts" directed at particular personalities.[69]

Albrecht suggested to him that even the officers of the German Navy might not be fully informed concerning U-boat losses. Müller readily admitted that the O. K. M. (Oberkommando der Marine, Nazi Germany's Naval High Command) never published such lists, but said that the various naval academy "crews" (classes) kept themselves pretty well informed with respect to what was happening to their own numbers. When he was pressed to estimate the numbers of his "crew" of 1936 who had been killed or captured while in command of their own boats as proof of his knowledge of U-boat casualties, Müller stated that a few less than thirty U-boat captains probably had been lost. Albrecht pointed out to him that the losses must have been high as commanders and even captains had been given U-boat commands. Müller agreed that, for a short while, quite a number of captains had commanded large U-boats for the purpose of gaining experience at sea prior to taking shore appointments, but he believed that these captains were now all in shore billets (jobs).[70]

In discussing recent changes in the armament of U-boats, Albrecht tried to ridicule the theory that approved of U-boats fighting it out on the surface with enemy aircraft. Müller disagreed strongly, but conceded that the anti-aircraft armament of frontline U-boats was still inadequate, and that they should have more effective guns with which to fight off attacking aircraft. He said he spoke with feeling, for during the last few days before it was sunk, his U-boat had been attacked four times from the air. These attacks were very unpleasant, the next-to-last attack had been altogether too close for comfort, and the last one had proven disastrous. The loss of *U-662* had confirmed the premonition of disaster that he had felt when he departed his base for the final patrol.[71]

AWARDS FOR VALOR

The pilot and co-pilot of Catalina *94-P-4* received the Distinguished Flying Cross. The other members of the plane were awarded Air Medals, and ARM2/c John Henry Watson, who was injured in combat with *U-662*, the Purple Heart, as well.

PBY-5A Catalina *94-P-4* Plane Crew
(for action on 21 July 1943)

Name	Position	Award
Lt. (jg) Richard Hoff Rowland, USNR	Pilot	DFC
Lt. (jg) William Henry James, USN	Co-Pilot	DFC
Lt. (jg) Albert Charles Anselmo, USNR	Navigator	AM
AMM2/c Franklin Joseph DeNauw	Bow	AM(2nd)
AMM3/c Elmer Bryant Smith	Port Waist	AM(2nd)
ARM2/c Hoyt Edwin Garren	Starboard Waist	AM(2nd)
ARM2/c John Henry Watson	Radio	AM(2nd)/ Purple Heart
AMM3/c Ernest Wilbur Wood Jr.	Tower	AM[72]

U-598 SUNK NORTHEAST OF NATAL, BRAZIL

Squadron VB-107, having been lately equipped with PB4Y in place of PBY-5A aircraft, has combined operational with training flights during the recent, July 1943, intensification of submarine activity along the Brazilian coast. The action, described in the five reports forwarded herewith, occurred during a persistent hunt lasting 23 hours which resulted in the sinking of the submarine.

—Commander Fourth Fleet endorsement on
Anti-Submarine Action Reports of VB-107
(ASW-6 #2, 3, 4, 5, 6), dated 31 August 1943.

Two days after *U-662* was sunk, the combined efforts of PB4Y-1 Liberator patrol bombers of VB-107 (the former VP-83) sent *U-598* to the bottom on 23 July. Both these submarines had been part of a group of five—*U-406, U-591, U-598, U-604,* and *U-662*—which had sailed from St. Nazaire on 26 June. The *U-598* reached her operating area off the coast of Brazil in the third week of July. On the morning of 22 July, while cruising on the surface, she was detected by a plane from Bombing Squadron 107, which immediately closed in for an attack.[73]

Liberator *107-B-7*, piloted by Lt. Comdr. Renfo Turner Jr, USN, was flying at 8,700 feet when the bombardier, Ens. Rosser, reported a wake at one o'clock, one-and-a-half miles distant. (The term "one o'clock" in this usage refers to the practice of describing the positions of attacking enemy aircraft by reference to an imaginary clock face—in this case, 030 degrees relative bearing.) Closer examination revealed it was from a submarine (which appeared to be a U-boat of the 740-ton class) fully surfaced on a southeasterly course at 8-10 knots. The plane was just emerging from between two cloud layers, heavy cumulous below from 5,500 to 8,000 feet, and stratus above with bottoms at 9,000 feet. Visibility was limited to about five miles due to a surface haze. Turner made an S-turn toward the sub (away along her course line, and back over her into the sun) losing altitude in preparation for an attack run.[74]

This maneuver required a minute or so, at the end of which the plane was above the sub at 3,500 feet. At approximately this time, the enemy (which would prove to be *U-598*) sighted the plane and began a crash dive. Within 85-90 seconds, Turner performed a wing over and attacked the U-boat from her starboard quarter—dropping a stick of six Mk 66 depth bombs from an altitude of 150 feet at 200 knots—

and was again passing over the submarine. Following this attack, Turner remained on scene for approximately twenty minutes, hoping to sight evidence of damage, and because he thought it probable that the sub would be forced to surface very close to her point of submergence. After twenty minutes, Turner abandoned hope of sighting wreckage and began flying a hold-down square, ten miles by ten miles, centered on the attack position.[75]

Photo 15-5

PB4Y-1 Liberator *107-B-7* commences a bombing run.
A History of Patrol Squadron 83 and Bombing Squadron 107, September 15, 1941 to December 31, 1944

PLANE *107-B-8* MISSES CHANCE TO DAMAGE SUB

Meanwhile, *U-598*—which had been forced to surface due to damage suffered—encountered a second Liberator. Plane *107-B-8*, piloted by Lt. (jg) John T. Burton, USNR, had taken off from Natal that morning to make a sweep for a possible sub off the coast. While flying the upper leg of a 25-mile square centered on its believed position, Burton picked up an air contact on radar, turned toward it, and soon sighted the plane piloted by Turner.[76]

The bow lookout, AMM1/c Rodney L. Damiano, USN, reported a wake about ten or twelve miles away, and Burton started descending and heading toward it. A submarine came into view, surfacing, with periscope and conning tower visible—which then starting back down in a shallow dive. Burton's first reaction was to decrease power in order to lose altitude more rapidly, so he momentarily pulled the throttles back. Quickly realizing that he couldn't reach the sub in time to attack, he applied maximum power, and increased the angle of glide. As *U-598* came within range, the bow gun and crown turret opened fire on her still-visible conning tower. *107-B-8* closed rapidly, but the submarine was nearly submerged when the plane passed overhead, fifteen to twenty feet forward of her conning tower.[77]

Burton pressed the throttle button to release depth charges, but the ordnance failed to drop because the bombardier had inadvertently left the select lever on the bombers quadrant in the locked position. After pulling out of sun, Burton observed squadron mate *107-B-7* making a run on the submarine about thirty seconds after his plane's ineffective attack.[78]

PLANE *107-B-7*'S SECOND ATTACK ON U-BOAT

Liberator *107-B-7* had found *U-598* a second time while at 4,300 feet on course 130°T. The sub was on a parallel course, making about five or six knots. Turner increased power and began a straight approach at 210 mph, holding altitude until four miles from the submarine. At this point the co-pilot, Ens. Terry, reported another plane (*107-B-8*) making a run on the same sub, and machine gun splashes appeared around her as she slowly dove. Turner momentarily looked away from the sub to the plane, and never again was able to resight the enemy. Terry began coaching him to the right and, as time was getting short, Turner turned control of the plane over to the co-pilot. Terry completed the run; dropping the remaining three bombs with some of the sub's structure still visible.[79]

Following this attack, *107-B-7* remained in the area for about fifteen minutes, searching for evidence of damage, before turning the "hold-down" over to *107-B-8*, and returning to base to rearm. No swirl had been sighted, only some oil in the water believed to be bomb residue. Plane *B-8* circled the area for fifty minutes then began to fly a twenty-five mile square around the point of attack; remaining in the area until relieved by *107-B-5* and then returning to Natal. Two other planes took off that afternoon and early evening to assist with the hold-down; *107-B-15* and *107-B-14*, piloted by Lieutenants (jg) Hill and Edward A. Krug Jr, respectively.[80]

VB-107'S SEARCH FOR SUBMARINE INTENSIFIES

Beginning shortly after midnight on 23 July, Bombing Squadron 107 dispatched still more planes from Natal to search for *U-598*. The below excerpts are from a summary report of the action:

0035   *107-B-12* Lt. (jg) BALDWIN took off to continue hold-down.
0640   *107-B-6* Lt. (jg) WAUGH took off to search for sub.
        107-B-7 Lt. Comdr. TURNER took off to search for sub.
        107-B-8 Lt. FORD took off to search for sub.
        107-B-15 Lt. (jg) HILL took off to search for sub.
        107-B-1 Lt. (jg) YOUNG took off to search for sub.[81]

LIBERATOR *107-B-12* FURTHER DAMAGES *U-598*

At 0646, *107-B-12* (piloted by Lt. (jg) Charles A. Baldwin, USNR) attacked *U-598* at position 04°04'S, 33°23'W. After taking off shortly after midnight, Baldwin flew at 2,300 feet to conduct a square search and continue to hold down the sub sighted and attacked the previous day by *107-B-7* and *B-8*. At sunrise, he went up to 5,000 feet to increase the "height of eye" of the plane's radar and visual horizon of his crew. Thereafter, Lt. (jg) David M. Davis, USNR, sighted a sharp clearly defined wake, about six to eight miles distant on the beam of the aircraft. After starting a right turn, Baldwin identified a submarine steering an east-southeast course at 8-10 knots. He promptly initiated an attack, which was thwarted by the missteps of two of his crew while trying to ready the bow gun for action:

> Plane started down immediately with throttles all the way back, no power at 250 MPH, downwind, with sun at back of plane. Subsequently turned on power, target angle of 015; course 300 mag[netic], speed about 240 MPH, altitude 75 ft. Plane apparently not sighted by sub until this point. Bow gun and crown turrets started firing, and obtained hits. Pilot pressed pickle [bomb release switch] to release all 6 bombs, with intervalometer set for 60 ft. spacing at 200 knots, but bombs failed to release. Subsequent investigation showed that while ... and ... in the bow compartment were endeavoring to unship [make ready for use] the bow gun, their violent movements inadvertently threw the rack selector switch (a two position switch) on the bomb release panel from B7 (the correct rack) to B5, with the result that the proper racks were not tripped. The switch had been properly set prior to the attack.[82]

Following this missed opportunity, Baldwin started a sharp turn to the left. As he did so, he noted light flak just forward of the bow and just aft of the tail, which be believed to be from a 20mm gun. Undeterred, he directed Davis in the bombardier's compartment to release bombs in salvo on command. As the plane crossed forward of *U-598*'s conning tower (at 220 mph, full power, and 100 feet off the water), the crown turret directed steady fire at the sub to keep personnel from emerging from her conning tower hatch up on deck.[83]

Diagram 15-2

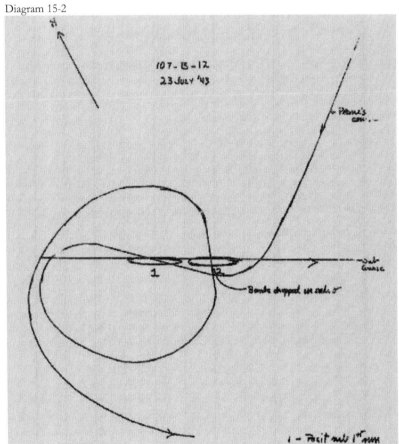

Rough sketch (not to scale) of two depth-charge attacks made by a PB4Y-1 Liberator patrol bomber (*107-B-12*) on *U-598*, which other same type aircraft ultimately sank. VB-107 Report of Anti-submarine Action by Aircraft #2, 22 July 1943

The bombs were dropped as ordered and, although the charges were inadvertently unarmed, two explosions were observed. (Both the pilot and the bombardier had forgotten in the excitement that a salvo release would drop the depth charges unarmed, unlike the convention with PBY-5A aircraft, which the squadron had previously flown.) One of the explosions occurred about thirty feet from the submarine and the other very near to, or underneath her stern, damaging *U-598* sufficiently that she could not dive. Her stern rose from the water, apparently in an effort to submerge, and then settled slowly as a quantity of oil began to emerge from the hull.[84]

Baldwin made another left turn and was able to observe a large depth charge residue stain on the water. While in this turn, *107-B-12*'s port waist gun was making some hits on the conning tower of the sub—which was still putting out a large amount of AA fire, mostly astern of the plane. Baldwin circled the sub out of gun range and began trying to establish contact with other planes in the area. In fifteen minutes, contact was made with *107-B-15*, piloted by Lt. (jg) Hill. Baldwin remained in the area with no bombs remaining; hoping, if the opportunity arose, to aid in a coordinated attack on the sub by drawing some AA fire away from other aircraft.[85]

Photo 15-6

Officers and crew of *107-B-12*; piloted by Lt. (jg) Charles A. Baldwin, USNR.
A History of Patrol Squadron 83 and Bombing Squadron 107, September 15, 1941 to December 31, 1944

LIBERATOR *107-B-6* LOST IN ATTACK ON *U-598*, BEFORE SUBMARINE SUNK BY PLANE *107-B-8*

At 0828, plane *107-B-6* piloted by Lt. (jg) Goree E. Waugh, USNR, attacked and, in coordination with Lt. (jg) William R. Ford, USNR (*107-B-8*), sank *U-598*. However, there was little joy following this action, because immediately after releasing its bombs, *107-B-6* plunged into the ocean with the loss of all hands. Ford dropped his bombs on *U-598* a few seconds later, sinking the submarine. He had followed Waugh over the target so closely that he flew through the spray of *107-B-6*'s bomb explosions, but was able to pull up to safety.[86]

A Navy Department report on the interrogation of survivors from the submarine concluded about the loss of the aircraft: "Probably because of the force of the explosion, the first plane fell into the water out of control and disappeared." The Liberator's flight crewmembers were awarded, posthumously, a Distinguished Flying Cross or Air Medal, and the Purple Heart. Waugh and his plane crew had arrived at Natal from Norfolk, Virginia, just three days earlier. With the loss of *107-B-6*, the complement of VB-107 at Natal stood at thirteen aircraft.

PB4Y-1 Liberator *107-B-6* Plane Crew
(killed in action on 23 July 1943)

Name	DFC	Air Medal	Purple Heart
Lt. (jg) Goree Edward Waugh, USNR	X		X
Lt. (jg) Robert Soule Swan, USNR	X		X
Ens. Donald Russel Besmehn, USNR		X	X
Ens. William Gladfelter Maierhofer, USNR		X	X
ACRM, Edward Lawrence Chapman, USN		X	X
AMM2/c John Daniel Edwards, USN		X (2nd)	X
AMM2/c Daniel Joseph Ford, USNR		X	X
Sea2/c Donald Wallace McLatchie, USNR		X	X
ARM2/c Anthony John Petaccio, USN		X	X
ARM3/c Walter George Seidel, USNR		X	X
AMM2/c, Sterling Francis Seymour, USN		X	X
AOM3/c George John Zukiewicz, USN		X	X[87]

TWO SURVIVORS OF *U-598* PICKED UP BY *SENECA*

Earlier that morning, 23 July, the fleet tug *Seneca* (AT-91) under the command of Lt. Herman B. Conrad, USN, had been ordered from Natal to proceed to the area of the submarine. That evening, following a sighting of a life raft to starboard, *Seneca* picked up two survivors; Oberleutnant Heinrich Huschin and Machinist Second Josef Machenschalk. They were stripped, searched, physically examined by medical personnel, and placed in the custody of armed guards and interrogators. Huschin was found to be suffering from multiple contusions and abrasions, and a sprained right hip with possible fracture. The prisoners were lodged in different parts of the ship, and not permitted to communicate with one another.[88]

On the morning of 26 July, *Seneca* passed to starboard of the channel entrance buoy leading into Recife, Brazil. One minute later, the pilot boat made her side, and pilot Nelson Campos and Lieutenant Hunnicutt (an interpreter) boarded the ship. The tug passed inside the breakwater at 0625 and moored starboard side to Pier 5. The two prisoners were then almost immediately taken off the ship under armed guard; Machenschalk at 0708 and Huschin (in a stretcher) several minutes later.[89]

OTHER AWARDS FOR VALOR

PB4Y-1 Liberator *107-B-12* Plane Crew
(for action on 23 July 1943)

Name	Position	Award
Lt. (jg) Charles Arba Baldwin, USNR	Pilot	Air Medal
Ens. Richard Morrison Riggs, USNR	Co-pilot	Air Medal (2nd)
Lt. (jg) David Meacham Davis, USNR	Bow Gunner	Air Medal
Ens. George McDaniel Shannon, USNR	Bow Gunner	Air Medal
AM2/c Samuel Eugene Nix, USN	Starboard Waist Gun	Air Medal
ARM1/c Harry Adolph Schneider, USN	Crown Turret	Air Medal
ACRM Solomon Greenberg, USN	Radio	Air Medal (2nd)
AMM1/c Stanley Smith Shedaker, USN	Flight Deck	Air Medal
AOM2/c Martin Striano, USNR	Tail Gun	Air Medal
AMM1/c George Ernst, USN	Port Waist Gun	Air Medal
AOM2/c Fred William Stern, USNR	Relief Port Waist Gun	Air Medal[90]

PB4Y-1 Liberator *107-B-8* Plane Crew
(for action on 23 July 1943)

Name	Position	Award
Lt. William Render Ford, USNR	Pilot	DFC (2nd)
Lt. (jg) John Thomas Burton, USNR	Co-pilot	Air Medal
Ens. Norman Frank Paul Butler, USNR	Navigator	Air Medal
Sea1/c Raymond Lewis Bohon, USN	Flight Deck	Air Medal
ARM2/c George Edgar Meyer, USNR	Radar	Air Medal
ARM2/c Daniel William Dupree, USNR	Radio	Air Medal (2nd)
AMM3/c Donald Wilber Carpenter, USN	Port Waist Gun	Air Medal
AMM1/c Rodney Lewis Damiano, USN	Top Bow Gun	Air Medal
ACM1/c Paul George Richter, USN	Crown Turret	Air Medal
Sea2/c Floyd James Rackley, USNR	Tail Turret	Air Medal[91]

16

Four More Submarines Sunk
in Summer and Fall of 1943

Except for the rather unsatisfying consolation of the anti-submarine "warrior"
that he "held them down" [enemy U-boats] the only occasion on which the
operational and training time "paid off" was on 30 July 1943.

—VB-129 Squadron History.[1]

Kapitänleutnant Höltring, the commanding officer, was something of a madcap.
He was ambitious and daring. Drink and firearms seem to have been his
weaknesses. Survivors said he carried a revolver at all times.
According to one tale of Höltring's past, he once was laying drunk in his
bunk at Gotenhafen. Sighting his foot sticking from beneath the covers, he drew
a bead on his big toe and shot it off. This was said to have caused Dönitz to
delay his promotion from Oberleutnant to Kapitänleutnant. His crew
nicknamed him "the gunman."
Survivors from U-604 indicated that they were constantly uneasy under
Höltring's command, particularly after the boat was seriously damaged on the
last patrol, when he was said to have become exceedingly nervous.

—Navy Department, Office of the Chief of Naval Operations,
Report on the Interrogation of Survivors from *U-604*
and *U-185* sunk 11 August 1943 and 24 August 1943.

Four additional German submarines were sunk in the South Atlantic
in the late summer and autumn of 1943. Bombing Squadron VB-129
was responsible for the demise of *U-604*; Patrol Squadron VP-74 sank
U-161; and Bombing Squadron VB-107, *U-848* and *U-849*—bringing
the year's total to thirteen U-boats and the Italian submarine *Archimede*.
Before progressing into these actions, a few pages are devoted to
introducing Bombing Squadron One Hundred Twenty Nine.

VB-129 ARRIVES AT NATAL FOR INITIAL DUTY

Bombing Squadron VB-129 was commissioned at Naval Air Station Deland, located slightly inland from Florida's northeast coast about halfway between Orlando and Daytona Beach, on 22 February 1943. The squadron was allocated twelve Lockheed PV-1 Ventura maritime patrol aircraft. Many features of this plane were entirely new to Naval Aviation at that time, including two powerful 2,000 hp engines (which sacrificed range for speed) and unusually high wing loading. The latter characteristic mandated great care during take-off and landing. Pilots and crews were still involved in "shakedown" training with the aircraft, when demands of the Atlantic Fleet resulted in the squadron receiving orders on 29 May to proceed immediately to Natal, Brazil.[2]

Despite the short notice, all planes were made ready and loaded, and by 5 June the last three-plane element had arrived safely at Natal. Immediately upon reporting to commander Fleet Air Wing Sixteen, VB-129 was pressed into operation. In the coming days, challenges associated with maintenance and the supply of parts proved to be the greatest obstacles. The Wing headquarters squadron (hedron) at Natal had practically no experience in servicing, or parts for, the R-2800 engines, and the existing repair facilities were very limited.[3]

The living conditions were not much better; most of the squadron's officers had to live six deep in "victory huts" (temporary prefabricated housing), and the crew quarters were likewise crowded and inadequate. Duty at Natal also initiated the squadron into the recreation limitations and medical problems associated with Brazilian duty. In addition to the dangers of fungus and infection, the town offered nothing in the way of leisure. What diversion there was came from the facilities of the Army Post Exchange and nightly outdoor motion pictures, which were—more often than not—interrupted by sudden rain squalls.[4]

RELOCATION TO RECIFE

Per orders from Fleet Air Wing Sixteen, VB-129 moved from Natal about 160 miles down the coast to Recife on 15 June 1943. Here maintenance difficulties were even greater. The hedron was still being established, and there were, as yet, no shop or personnel facilities. Squadron office and living facilities were considerably better than at Natal, and the city of Recife offered more in the way of entertainment; local clubs, both Brazilian and British, were very hospitable. However, just like at Natal, the enlisted men were afforded little or no decent recreational facilities ashore.[5]

MOVEMENT DOWN THE COAST TO BAHIA

On 24 July, the Wing moved VB-129 once again, this time to Ipitanga Field at Bahia, down the coast from Recife. The field consisted of a single airstrip, whose seaward and upwind end was bordered by 300 foot high sand hills. The Rio Ipitanga (Ipitanga River) partially bounded the landing field, and swamps existed on nearly all sides of the base. Prevailing winds blew over the field from the southeast and east, temperatures averaged 77 degrees, and the annual precipitation was about 77 inches with a rainy season similar to that in Recife. Transportation between the field and quarters was difficult, and travel from the base to the city of Bahia involved a tortuous thirty-mile road of mud. The city was smaller and more picturesque than Recife with about the same recreational and social facilities. A considerable Navy population was already present at Bahia assigned to the Naval Operating Base. However, except for a handful of officers previously detailed to arrange for base facilities, VB-129 was the first Navy group at Ipitanga (previously used solely by the Army's Air Transport Command and Pan American Airways.)[6]

The headquarters squadron was established without benefit of even a nose hanger, and the first base radio was the Bendix transmitter in the plane of Lt. Comdr. Jamie E. Jones, USN, the squadron commander. The base had no recreational facilities. However, it was not long before some buildings were transformed into an officers' club and an enlisted mans' club, and a warehouse was converted into a movie hall. Additionally, ground was found for a morale-boosting softball diamond. All hands ate at the general mess, which could only provide consistently poor fare, largely due to the difficulties of supply and the inadequacy of existing cooking facilities. The off-duty highlight of duty in Brazil was when VB-129 was able to spare one plane crew at a time on five-day-leave in Rio de Janeiro. Transportation was provided by the Naval Air Transportation Service (a branch of the U.S. Navy from 1941 to 1948) and the Army's Air Transport Command.[7]

FLIGHT OPERATIONS AND MISSIONS AT BAHIA

Since Lieutenant Commander Jones was the senior naval aviator during most of VB-129's Brazil service, he was responsible for planning the daily operations and assigning them to units under his command. These included VP-74 at the Seaplane Base at Aratu in Bahia Bay, and a small group of Brazilians also based at Ipitanga. The Brazilian detachment consisted of three Lockheed Hudson light bombers and their crews.[8]

Jones received daily estimates of enemy submarine positions and convoy position reports from Fourth Fleet headquarters in Recife. He then allocated assignments for convoy coverage or submarine sweeps to meet these demands based on the capabilities of the longer range PBM-3C Mariners and the short-range PV-1 Venturas and Brazilian A-28A Hudsons. For the most part, dawn and dusk coverage was handled by the PV-1s, with the span of midday hours falling to VP-74, the PBM squadron. The Hudsons were usually assigned coverage of inter-coastal shipping. The planning of sweeps varied with the nature of the object of the search. A definite estimate of the location of the enemy, based on good HF/DF bearings, usually resulted in the assignment of a four plane PV-1 sweep of parallel sectors with tracks spaced fifteen miles apart. Often the perimeter of the search area was patrolled by a longer-range PBM.[9]

The PV-1 Venturas were best suited for high-speed striking work. Thus, VB-129, along with the other Ventura squadrons in the area, was tasked to provide mobile detachments on short notice whenever the Wing or Fleet deemed it necessary to change the disposition of anti-submarine air strength along the Brazilian coast. This meant that in addition to maintaining crews in readiness for action in its own sector, VB-129 was continually "on call" to provide planes for Recife or Natal.[10]

The bombing squadron typically assigned a five-man crew to each aircraft, comprised of a pilot, co-pilot, plane captain, radioman, and an ordnance man. Occasionally, a third officer was carried, after VB-129 received three non-pilot navigators. The duty of the PV-1 Ventura maritime patrol planes included routine anti-submarine flights; convoy escort, and associated sweeping of convoy tracks; barrier sweeps; and "hold downs." For the most part, these operations were carried out in daylight; most of the night flying involved dawn or dusk patrols or while proceeding to or from a mission. Operational flights were normally approximately five hours in duration, with an effective patrol range of about 400 miles.[11]

VB-129 AIRCRAFT DAMAGES ENEMY SUBMARINE

Less than a week after arriving at the Bahia base, VB-129 was detailed to fly a four-plane coastal barrier sweep northeastward from Bahia. In the early afternoon of 30 July 1943, while nearing the outboard end of his allocated sector, Lt. Comdr. Thomas D. Davies, USN, piloting *129-B-8* sighted a fully surfaced enemy submarine. Pressing home his attack in the face of 20mm anti-aircraft fire, Davies succeeded in clearing the decks of the U-boat with his bow guns and at 1410, dropped four Mk 47 depth bombs athwart the submarine. The drop was made at position 11°46'S, 34°33'W. The sub submerged following the attack, broached a few minutes later, then went down at a sixty-degree angle with screws and rudder clear of the water. No further evidence of the submarine (*U-604*) was seen, although the plane remained in the vicinity for over two hours until, having reached its PLE, it departed to return to base. Four other aircraft conducted baiting and hold-down tactics until early evening when adverse weather prevented further flying.[12]

Photo 16-1

U-604 under attack on 30 July 1943 by a PV-1 Ventura of Bombing Squadron VB-129. The German submarine was badly damaged in this attack, and eventually scuttled by her crew on 11 August 1943.
U.S. National Archives Photograph #80-G-358477

U-BOAT FURTHER DAMAGED BY VB-107 AIRCRAFT

On the morning of 3 August, Lt. Comdr. Bertram J. Prueher, the squadron commander of VB-107 (piloting *107-B-1*), was sweeping an estimated submarine position, based on HF/DF bearings obtained from shore stations. A sighting was made of a U-boat at 0722 and Prueher immediately pressed home an attack as the enemy crash dove. Following the bomb drop, a large oil slick was observed at 09°33'S, 30°35'W, the position of the attack. Soon, another U-boat was sighted (which may have been the same one) about 10-12 miles away, but it quickly submerged, and *107-B-1* returned to Recife to rearm.[13]

With his plane refueled and rearmed, Prueher took off again at 1345, and made an attack on another submarine at 1735, just as darkness was settling in. Following radar detection, the plane headed toward the suspected enemy contact—whose exact position was ascertained by tracer fire emanating from the U-boat's conning tower when the plane was still four miles away.[14]

The plane's crown turret and lower bow gun opened fire, which was very accurate, once within range. Prueher dropped four bombs on his first run. After the resultant water plume subsided, it was possible to see the U-boat had swerved sharply to starboard. Her bow then rose, before the entire submarine settled back down into the water. The bow then rose again so sharply that the keel was visible for one-third the length of the submarine. With his prey seemingly wounded, Prueher immediately made a second attack, dropping the remaining two bombs. This time, anti-aircraft fire from the sub was very heavy and it hit the plane's starboard wing; damaging the propeller and No. 3 engine and producing twenty-three perforations in the wing itself. As day transitioned to night, the submarine was no longer visible, and a search with the aid of flares was fruitless in locating the enemy.[15]

Two members of the flight crew of *107-B-1* received awards for valor for their actions during the combat on 3 August 1943:

PB4Y-1 Liberator *107-B-1* Plane Crew Members

Name	Position	Award
Ens. George Aaron Wimpey, USN	Co-pilot	DFC
Lt. (jg) Grover Cleveland Hannever, USNR	Bow Gunner	Air Medal

SUB CRITICALLY DAMAGED BY DEPTH CHARGES FROM AIRCRAFT AND THE DESTROYER *MOFFETT*

Attacked with 5 depth charges.... During these runs on the submarine, propeller noises were distinctly heard each time the target was closed. Echos were unquestionably those of a U-boat.... In general, the submarine defense plan was to present its stern toward the attacking vessel without right or left movement until the range had closed to about 600 yards. The submarine would then make a high speed turn in an effort to cut inside the destroyer's turning circle. Several times this was preceded by a faint in the opposite direction. Attack speed of 20 knots was used by the MOFFETT *on the latter runs in an attempt to counter this tactical advantage.*

—Report Covering USS *Moffett*'s Engagement
with Enemy Submarine, August 3-4, 1943.

The submarine attacked and damaged by planes *107-B-8* and *107-B-1* on 30 July and 3 August, respectively, was *U-604*, a 750-tonner under the command of Kapitänleutnant Horst Höltring. The submarine had left Brest on 24 June, headed for the Brazilian coast. During the attack on 30 July, Höltring had been wounded in his left shoulder and chest by machine gun fire from the plane, which mortally wounded the executive officer, Oberleutnant Aschmann, and a coxswain, Herbert Lurz. The explosions of the depth charges dropped by *107-B-8* had jammed a starboard hydroplane, knocked out a motor and punctured several tanks. As a result of the severe damage, Höltring reported to headquarters that he could not bring his submarine back to port. Konteradmiral Eberhard Godt (Karl Dönitz's chief of staff, and commander of the U-boat arm of the German Navy) promised help from another boat. *U-604* then began proceeding with difficulty to a rendezvous with the *U-185*.[16]

The depth-charge attack on 3 August had further damaged *U-604*. Höltring had submerged during this attack, and remained under until darkness before surfacing to charge batteries. While surfaced, the sub's crew heard gun rounds passing overhead which they assumed originated from a ship. Höltring released several radar decoy balloons to divert the attention of the unknown firing vessel, and submerged again. Throughout the night the U-boat crew heard sonar piercing the ocean depths searching, and numerous depth charge explosions.[17]

The following morning, 4 August, *U-604* surfaced, after having been down about twenty hours. The ship that had attacked her was the destroyer *Moffett* (DD-362), commanded by Lt. Comdr. Gilbert Haven Richards Jr., USN. *Moffett* had been en route to Ascension Island the preceding day in company with the cruiser *Memphis* (CL-13) and the merchant vessel *Bohemian Club*. At 1145, commander Task Group 41.5 (aboard the *Memphis*) ordered the destroyer to leave the convoy and proceed immediately to the position where a plane had bombed a submarine.[18]

In mid-afternoon, *Moffett* obtained a radar contact of three planes in the general direction and vicinity of the reported contact. Upon her arrival in the area a short time later, the destroyer established voice communications with the aircraft. After ascertaining that they were unable to provide any additional information, *Moffett* slowed to 15 knots and began a sonar search, covering a front of seven-and-a-half miles working in an east-northeast direction, as it was assumed the submarine would be on such a course. In early evening all planes left the area, and it was not until 1930 that replacements arrived.[19]

At 2000, one of the new arrivals reported an oil slick eighteen miles to the north, and *Moffett* proceeded to investigate. The destroyer sighted the slick at 2030 and then, a smaller slick north of the main one. At almost the same time, there appeared about twenty miles distant on her starboard quarter, anti-aircraft fire from a surfaced submarine, or aircraft fire directed at it.[20]

After changing course to 115°T to head directly toward the target, *Moffett* increased speed to 20 knots, then 25, working up to full power. At 2042, lookouts sighted a submarine ten degrees on the destroyer's starboard bow, and subsequently a plane started dropping flares to illuminate the enemy's position. *Moffett* continued to close the submarine, but very slowly as it appeared to be making about 20 knots. At 2105, the radar operator reported "lost contact"—indicating the sub had submerged.[21]

MOFFETT HIT BY FRIENDLY FIRE FROM AIRCRAFT

Disaster struck at 2122 when, in the dark and confusion of action, a friendly aircraft using the call sign "Baker 5" mistook *Moffett* for the submarine and made a strafing attack on the destroyer. Machine gun fire started a fire in the 40mm ammunition storage, and wounded seven men. While the damage control party worked to extinguish the flames (during which nine cases of ammo were thrown overboard to help prevent the possibility they might explode), medical personnel tended to the injured. In addition to the below listed officer and men—the most grievously wounded—five other individuals received minor wounds from the spray of small metal fragments.

Name	Description of Injuries
F2/c Charles H. Abbott	Gunshot wound to right forearm
FC2/c Clarence H. Kroll	Multiple gunshot wounds to left side of chest
S1/c Stanley J. Ludwinski	Gunshot wounds to middle and small fingers of right hand
CGM Edward A. Riley	Gunshot wounds to both legs just above the ankles
F1/c James C. Sullivan	Gunshot wounds to left hip and buttock, and left leg
RM3/c Walter W. Pilch	Gunshot wounds to both legs and feet
Ens. Kenneth H. Kardon	Gunshot wound to left upper arm[22]

Upon realizing that she was under attack, *Moffett* had flashed recognition signals from both a bright portable searchlight and a blinker tube, but the plane failed to answer. Voice communications were attempted at the same time, but were not established until 2135 when the aircraft reported that she had had the "submarine" under fire! In a report later submitted, Lieutenant Commander Richards recommended actions that he believed would help prevent another such "friendly fire" incident in the future, with the most pointed observation being the final one:

- All planes taking off for joint action be recalled to base if test of TBL voice communication is not satisfactory. This test to be made with base as soon as plane takes the air.

- No more than one plane and one surface vessel be detailed to cooperate in one "Hunter-Killer" group during darkness. With communications established one plane and one ship can positively identify each other by exchanging radar bearings.

- A definite doctrine for plane illumination by flares for the surface ship firing be established.

- That it is standard doctrine for plane making a contact to transmit "MOs" [to home other aircraft to the target] on frequency of 414 kcs [khz] to identify which plane has contact and also to give bearing if plane is beyond radar range.

- Aviators be trained in recognition of surface ships and wakes made by destroyers at high speeds.[23]

At 2155, *Moffett* slowed and began a spiral box sonar search for the submarine. Less than an hour later, she gained contact on a target bearing 080°T, range 2,400 yards, and maneuvered to set up for an attack. After making a depth charge attack on the target at 2252 (with a seven-charge pattern), the destroyer maneuvered to reattack but lost contact and resumed her search. Sonar contact was regained at 2327, with correlating propeller noise, and *Moffett* made another attack with seven charges at 2334. Several minutes later, crewmen on deck smelt a strong odor of oil. Contact was lost, followed by reacquisition and preparation for another attack, during which contact was again lost.[24]

After regaining the submarine on sonar, *Moffett* made a third seven-depth-charge attack at 0039, followed by five depth charges several minutes later. During these runs on the submarine, propeller noises were heard each time the destroyer closed the target. The sonar echoes were definitely those of a U-boat, whose movements indicated that despite any damage incurred, it was still fast and maneuverable. *Moffett* lost contact and then gained possible contact at 0058. As the ship maneuvered to try and hold contact, additional depth charges were brought up from storage below deck and armed.[25]

This game of cat and mouse continued throughout the night until around dawn when at 0625, a plane dropped a flare over a submarine on the surface. *Moffett* fired a spread of star shells from her forward gun mounts illuminating a U-boat, and commenced firing at the target, 7,150 yards distant, with her forward mounts. Five hits were observed by the commanding officer, gunnery officer and other personnel on the bridge. The destroyer then checked fire, turned to port to unmask her after mounts, and resumed fire. At 0635, the target disappeared from the radar scope; having been sunk at 09°18.5'S, 29°42'W.[26]

Moffett expended 132 rounds of 5-inch/38 against the submarine, and would be credited with sinking her. In actuality, *U-604* (though only marginally functional) was still operational.[27]

THREE U-BOATS RENDEZVOUS; LIBERATOR SHOT DOWN BY *U-185*; *U-604* SCUTTLED BY OWN CREW

Word was received from Natal that Lieut. Comdr. Prueher, Commanding Officer of VB-107 is overdue on an anti-submarine sweep. All available planes at Natal have been sent out to search for him. One of these planes sighted a possible submarine at 01-45 South, 22-08 West at 1030 Peter [local time]. The sighting was at a distance of 15 miles and no attack was made.

—Commander Fourth Fleet 12 August 1943 War Diary entry.

After evading her attackers, *U-604* continued slowly to her rendezvous point to avail herself of promised assistance. On the morning of 11 August, she met *U-185* and began transferring her provisions, fuel and equipment to the other submarine. This process took several hours. Near its completion, *U-172* commanded by Kapitänleutnant Karl Emmermann arrived. She was too late to receive any fuel or provisions, but inasmuch as she was to carry half of the *604*'s crew, a number of bunk mattresses were transferred to her.[28]

A short time later, a PB4Y-1 Liberator (believed to be Lt. Comdr. Bertram J. Prueher's *107-B-1*) dove from the clouds in a surprise attack; and Emmermann immediately crash dove. The plane made two runs on the remaining submarines, strafing and dropping a total of four bombs, which caused no damage. As *U-185* began circling *U-604* in an attempt to protect her, the aircraft turned to make another run, wobbled and plunged into the sea. Witnesses aboard the submarines believed that anti-aircraft fire from *U-185* brought down the plane.[29]

Following the air attack, preparations to scuttle *U-604* continued. In the absence of *U-172*, *U-185* had to accommodate all of *U-604*'s crew. These men were ordered overboard, to swim the one hundred yards to the other submarine. Höltring, whose wounds had not yet healed, was rowed over in a rubber boat. *U-604*'s engineering officer was the last to abandon. After setting four detonation charges with 8-minute fuzes, he opened the vents, climbed quickly up through the conning tower hatch, dove overboard and swam to *U-185*. Before he reached her, the charges exploded. *U-604* sank by the stern northwest of Ascension Island. *U-185* and *U-172* met a few days later for the transfer of half of *U-604*'s crew to the latter submarine. Following this action, they parted and *U-185* set a course for home port.[30]

On 24 August 1943, *U-185* was sunk by two aircraft from the escort carrier *Core* (CVE-13)—a fighter and a bomber—southwest of the Azores. Following a strafing run by the fighter, whose machine gun fire wounded the entire bridge watch, the bomber let go its depth charges. A report on the interrogation of survivors from *U-604* and *U-185* includes a vivid account of the final death throes of *U-185*, and the suicide of Höltring, who killed himself after shooting a crewman, who was unable to escape the sinking submarine, and had begged him to do so:

> The tanks on the port side were crushed and the pressure hull cracked. No. 1 battery was damaged. As [the commanding officer, Kapitänleutnant August] Maus shouted down, asking if the boat was in diving condition, the engineer officer shouted back: "Everything's smashed....Batteries....chlorine!"
>
> Maus immediately ordered the crew to put on life belts and come topside. Chlorine gas formed quickly as sea water rushed into the battery compartment under the officers' quarters, forward of the control room. As the Diesels still were running, the gas was sucked through the boat to the engine room. Several men died at their stations. All those who were able climbed to the bridge.
>
> Meanwhile, in the bow compartment, a strange drama was being enacted. According to survivors, Höltring was in his bunk in the officers' quarters, with his pistol, as always, close at hand when the attack began. In the bow compartment lay a member of *U-185*'s crew with a bullet wound in his leg, sustained in a previous action. Unable to walk, he was trapped as chlorine gas began to spread. Seeing Höltring rush into the bow compartment with his pistol in hand, the youth cried to Höltring to shoot him. According to survivors' accounts, Höltring shot and killed the boy, then shot himself through the head.[31]

The destroyer *Barker* (DD-213)—a unit of the *Core* hunter-killer group—retrieved thirty-six survivors and two bodies. Comprising the living were five officers including Maus, one chief petty officer and thirty other more junior enlisted men. Nine were *U-604* officers and men, who provided information about their submarine.[32]

Photo 16-2

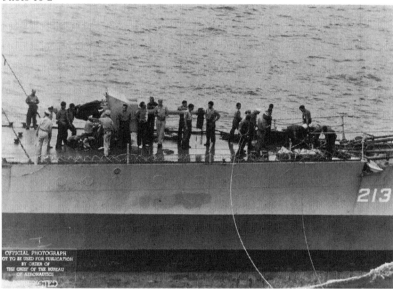

Destroyer *Barker* coming alongside the escort carrier *Core* on 24 August 1943 to transfer prisoners from the German submarine *U-185* sunk earlier that day by aircraft. A group of Germans are near the 4"/50 gun mount.
U.S. National Archives Photograph #80-G-269039

AWARDS FOR VALOR

The entire crew of *107-B-1* was lost at sea. Prueher and his crew had taken off in "the Spirit of 83" (a tribute to the squadron's former designation), from Natal at 0900 on 11 August 1943. It was destined to be the last flight for the squadron commander and the other men. No communications were received from the plane following takeoff. Prueher received the Distinguished Service Medal, and the other nine members of the plane crew the Distinguished Flying Cross. All ten men received the Purple Heart, as well. All awards were given posthumously:

Plane Crew of PB4Y-1 Liberator *107-B-1* ("the Spirit of 83")
(killed in action on 11 August 1943)

Name	Awards
Lt. Comdr. Bertram Joseph Prueher, USN	DSM/Purple Heart Medal (PH)
Lt. (jg) Grover Cleveland Hannever, USNR	DFC/Purple Heart Medal (PH)
Ens. Eugene Louis Coupe, USNR	DFC/Purple Heart Medal (PH)
Ens. Robert Tehan, USNR	DFC/Purple Heart Medal (PH)
ACRM Howard Clifton Brandon, USN	DFC/Purple Heart Medal (PH)
ARM2/c Donald Wayne Gardner, USNR	DFC/Purple Heart Medal (PH)
AOM1/c Gordon Granville Merrick, USNR	DFC/Purple Heart Medal (PH)
S2/c Joseph Mihalsky, USN	DFC/Purple Heart Medal (PH)
ACMM Clyde Albert Smith, USN	DFC/Purple Heart Medal (PH)
AMM1/c John Roy Van Horn, USNR	DFC/Purple Heart Medal (PH)[33]

The plane crew of *129-B-8*, which had damaged the *U-604* on 30 July 1943, also received medals for valor. The pilot and co-pilot were awarded Distinguished Flying Crosses, and the other three members Air Medals:

Plane Crew of PV-1 Ventura *129-B-8*

Lt. Comdr. Thomas D. Davies, USN	30 Jul 1943	DFC
Ens. Walter L. Schenck, USNR	30 Jul 1943	DFC
AMM1/c Edwin I. Casada, USN	30 Jul 1943	Air Medal
ARM1/c Paul Siminuk, USNR	30 Jul 1943	Air Medal
AOM1/c Henry J. Dorman, USNR	30 Jul 1943	Air Medal[34]

U-591 SUNK SOUTHEAST OF RECIFE BY VB-127

On 30 July 1943 (the same day that *129-B-8* attacked *U-604*), a Ventura of VB-127 sank *U-591* southeast of Recife. Around noon, plane *127-B-10* piloted by Lt. (jg) Walter C. Young, sighted a fully surfaced submarine at 08°36'S, 34°34'W. The Ventura was flying at 4,000 feet while on air escort duty with convoy TJ-2. Young immediately started an attack run at the U-boat; located almost dead ahead, twelve miles distant. Three minutes after the initial sighting, six Torpex Mk 44 depth charges straddled the submarine, one landing on her deck just forward of the conning tower, and exploded. (Torpex was a torpedo explosive of RDX, TNT and powdered aluminum, fifty percent more powerful than TNT by mass.) The U-boat made a ninety-degree turn to port, stopped, began to settle by the bow and sank very quickly. From the air, there were no air bubbles or floating debris visible after the attack. A large oil slick on the surface was the only obvious sign of the destruction of the submarine.[35]

It appeared that the submarine had been completely unaware of the plane's approach, as it took no evasive action, put up no anti-aircraft fire or attempted to crash dive. The sky was mostly free of cloud cover, and visibility unlimited, but Young had made his run out of the sun to shield his approach. After the depth charge attack, he made a strafing run using bow and turret guns; expending about 250 rounds of .50-caliber ammunition. Just before the bomb drop, the men topside had run toward the conning tower. They were believed killed by the explosions. Of the estimated thirty survivors in the water following the sinking of U-591, twenty-eight were picked up several hours later by the patrol gunboat *Saucy* (PG-65).[36]

LAST PATROL OF *U-591*

> *Most of the surviving crew showed a rather listless attitude; this was no doubt partly due to the feeling that the famed German U-boat arm was decreasing rapidly in effectiveness; partly due to the fact that their new commander had not lived up to the example set by their old skipper, Kapitänleutnant [Hans-Jürgen] Zetzsche. The most experienced man was Oberbootsmannsmaat Köhnke who had made 15 patrols in all; some of them in a boat [U-47] commanded by Korvettenkapitän [Günther] Prien. A good many of the other members had been on U-591 for several patrols, but on the whole the men were of the same standing and experience as other captured U-boat crews.*

—Office of the Chief of Naval Operations report
on the interrogation of survivors from *U-591*.[37]

The *U-591*, commanded by Oberleutnant zur See Reimar Ziesmer, had left the harbor of St. Nazaire (the site of a heavily fortified submarine base on the west coast of German-occupied France) on 26 June 1943; part of a group of five U-boats sailing at the same time for mutual protection. Unbeknownst to four of the crews, their boats would not be returning home. They would be sunk off the coast of Brazil.

Submarine	Commanding Officer	Date Sunk
U-406	Kapitänleutnant Horst Dieterichs	survived patrol
U-591	Oberleutnant zur See Reimar Ziesmer	30 Jul 1943
U-598	Korvettenkapitän Gottfried Holtorf	23 Jul 1943
U-604	Kapitänleutnant Horst Höltring	11 Aug 1943
U-662	Kapitänleutnant Heinz-Eberhard Müller	21 Jul 1943[38]

Saucy had received orders from commander Task Group 42.5 (aboard *PC-494*) in early afternoon on 30 July, to proceed with *PC-494* to the position of a reported submarine contact, and pick up any survivors. In late afternoon, the patrol gunboat sighted a life raft and took aboard twenty-eight German prisoners. *PC-494* and *Saucy* then set a course for Recife. *Saucy* moored there at 2220, starboard side to the pier with six 5-inch mooring lines. Twenty minutes later, a Marine Guard and naval officers removed the prisoners from the ship. After a preliminary interrogation was conducted, Ziesmer and three ratings were flown to the United States for further questioning at an interrogation center. The following account is based on information the enlisted men provided, and amplifying notes in the Office of Naval Intelligence interrogation report.[39]

Photo 16-3

Patrol gunboat *Saucy* (PG-65) in May 1942, after being taken over from the Royal Navy. She was formerly HMS *Arabis* (K 73), one of a group of *Flower*-class corvettes transferred to the U.S. Navy under reverse Lend Lease.
U.S. Naval History and Heritage Command Photograph #NH 79081

A minesweeper and two patrol craft had provided escort for the U-boats out of St. Nazaire, after which the group sped through the Bay of Biscay before separating after about two days. Aboard *U-591* were four officers, a doctor and forty crewmembers. The commanding officer, Reimar Ziesmer (only about 25 years old) had succeeded the former commander, Kapitänleutnant Hans-Jürgen Zetzsche, just five days before leaving on this patrol. Ziesmer had previously commanded the *U-145* and *U-236*, but these boats had not made any war patrols during his service aboard them.[40]

Three days after leaving St. Nazaire, *U-406* returned to base due to engine trouble. The other four submarines met the "milch cow" *U-487* in early July (at approximately 41°N, 14°W) to top off with fuel oil; each received about 30 cubic meters. *U-591*'s ensuing passage toward the bulge of Brazil was uneventful. Several trial dives were made during the otherwise quiet and enjoyable surface transit.[41]

On 22 July, a sighting was made of a patrol aircraft and *U-591* dove immediately. Once below, bomb explosions were heard but no significant damage resulted. Upon surfacing, *U-591* was the target of a second attack; which she again eluded by crash diving. These attacks were probably delivered by Bombing Squadron 107. (VB-107 aircraft had made an attack in about the same area, and at about the same time on *U-598*. It was probably during subsequent holding-down tactics that *U-591* was sighted and attacked.)[42]

After arrival in her operational area, *U-591* initially patrolled near shore. She was standing out to sea on 30 July, steering an easterly course at moderate speed, when attacked from the air. Her bridge watch consisted of an officer, a petty officer and two seamen. Upon receiving a report of the plane, Ziesmer ordered the 20mm gun manned, but the aircraft's rapid approach left no time to fire it. One of the dropped bombs exploded close aboard the sub, starboard side, tearing a large hole in her pressure hull. Either its blast or the detonation of another depth charge likely tore the vent value off a diving tank, allowing seawater to enter and cause the U-boat to settle and sink so rapidly. Another depth charge hit the 20mm cannon on Platform II, exploded, demolished the gun, pierced the upper deck, and fell inside the hull. It may also have ruptured one or more high pressure air bottles (under the deck grating abaft the conning tower), releasing the air necessary to blow seawater from ballast tanks.[43]

Ziesmer, upon realization that *U-591* was doomed, gave the order to abandon. The depth of water in the control room was about three to four feet, and rising, when the last man able to, climbed up the ladder to the bridge and escaped the submarine. It is unclear whether or not men in the after compartments (largely engineers) heard the order to abandon and, if so, whether they were able to do so. As men were going over the side of the sinking submarine, the attacking plane strafed *U-591*; which sank before the attack was over.[44]

After circling, Ventura *127-B-10* dropped a life raft into which the wounded were placed. The other men took turns hanging on the raft. At one point, a shark brushed against one of the sailors. Ziesmer sighted the frightening predator but told the men it was only a porpoise—an assertion the quartermaster supported, although he was aware that it had been a shark.[45]

Saucy arrived on the scene about five hours later. After retrieving the prisoners, her crew began firing at sharks following the ship. One of the Germans jumped overboard, apparently because he believed the shots were directed at his fellow prisoners aboard the patrol gunboat.[46]

POOR MORALE IN THE U-BOAT ARM OF THE NAVY

Survivors from the *U-591* spoke about the general poor state of morale within the U-boat service. The interrogation report included a summarization of the observations made by a senior enlisted member of the crew, regarding this subject:

> A chief petty officer freely discussed the waning morale of U-boat crews. Although he was convinced that the technical instruction received by U-boat officers and recruits is just as thorough as ever, the attitude towards their branch of the service has changed. No amount of pep talks alters the feeling that generally speaking the fat years are over and the lean and dangerous years have begun for U-boat crews. Officers are now either too cautious, remaining under water at the slightest sign of danger and intent only on bringing the boat back, or they are foolhardy, in which case the chances of survival are greatly reduced. Green crews react badly to either attitude and consequently the strain on them is much greater than in the days when U-boat crews felt they were leading a charmed life. Men who have served in the U-boat arm for a longer time also feel the difference. Their attitude is more fatalistic; nevertheless they know that each patrol may be their last.
>
> It was stated that the offensive weapons of the U-boat have been increased and improved constantly, but that the defensive armament has been neglected. Officially, U-boat men are told that the airplane is not to be feared, but it may be that the knowledge that this is not so makes the men even more wary of airplane attacks. It was felt by many of the crew that the U-boat arm has already lost the war.[47]

AWARDS FOR VALOR

The entire flight crew of the Ventura patrol bomber received an award for valor. Shiell was awarded his medal posthumously. He was injured by shrapnel from an explosion on the deck of *U-591* piercing the plane, as it passed overhead while making an attack, and later died.

PV-1 Ventura *127-B-10* Plane Crew
(for action on 30 July 1943)

Name	Position	Award
Lt. (jg) Walter Chappell Young, USNR	Pilot	DFC
Ens. Calhoun Sterling, USNR	Co-pilot	Air Medal
AMM2/c Willis Reed Shiell, USNR	Plane captain	Air Medal (PH)

| RT1/C Marvin Emery Johnston, USNR | Radioman | Air Medal |
| AOM2/c John Anthony Laury Jr., USN | Ordnanceman | Air Medal[48] |

VB-127'S SHORT DUTY ASSIGNMENT IN BRAZIL

Bombing Squadron 127 had been commissioned on 1 February 1943 at Deland, Florida, and had trained with U.S. Navy SNB-1 Kansan twin-engine aircraft pending delivery of PV-1 Ventura maritime patrol aircraft. The squadron received its allotted twelve planes between 19 March and 12 April. A week later, VB-127 departed Deland for U.S. Navy Auxiliary Airfield Boca Chica on an island in the lower Florida Keys. Following operational training, VB-127 took flight for Natal, arriving at Parnamirim Field on 15 May for duty with Wing Sixteen.[49]

The officers and men were quartered in long one-story barracks that were fairly cool and comfortable, though quite dusty due to the constant winds. The food was good, and there was a small officers' bar at one end of the mess hall with a good supply of liquors. Beer was available for purchase by the men at the ship's service store every afternoon. There was plenty of space and equipment for volleyball and softball, and transportation could be secured for travel to an excellent beach between the base and town of Natal. On the other hand, repair and maintenance facilities left much to be desired. Shortly after the squadron's arrival, it became necessary to strip an operational plane to obtain parts required to keep the others flying.[50]

On 21 June, a detachment of fifteen officers, thirty-two men and eight of the squadron's twelve planes were sent 270 miles up the coast to Fortaleza, to establish an operating base there. There was an Army detachment at the field, and squadron personnel ate at its mess. Like at Natal, the food was good, though the dining was rather crowed at times. There was not an officers' club or a bar, but Brazilian beer could be obtained at the Army Post Exchange. Recreational facilities were adequate and there were numerous volleyball and softball games between the officers and men. There was also a local basketball league in the town of Fortaleza, which the officers joined. The games played between Navy personnel and local civilians helped to promote goodwill. Fortaleza also had a very good, easily accessible beach.[51]

The repair and maintenance facilities were, however, meager; it was necessary, as it had been at Natal, to ground a plane for spare parts. But, VB-127's duty in Brazil would be short. The squadron departed Natal on 2 September 1943, bound for Port Lyautey, French Morocco, and duty with Fleet Air Wing Fifteen.[52]

U-161 SUNK EAST OF SALVADOR DA BAHIA

Two attacks were made in the face of the heaviest A.A. fire yet encountered.... Valuable information was gained from photographs taken, from observation from the pilots and crew, also from survivors of the merchantmen, ST. USK, sunk by this or a similar submarine. Since this was the first submarine of this type, with the added mount aft, seen in this area, the following information is of interest:

The submarine was estimated to be 1200 tons. ST. USK's ... stated that C/T [conning tower] was 36' long (by comparison with their 28 ½' lifeboat) The armament consists of a 4.1 gun forward of C/T, two 37mm guns on fwd. bandstand of C/T, and a quadruple 20mm mount on aft bandstand.

Two 37mm hits on the plane did more damage than many 20mm hits. The guns were manually controlled. The survivors stated the 20mm quadruple mount aft has two wing shields which open out when in use. These protect the pointer and trainer. They are folded back and the ammunition cans are sent below prior to submergence. They also stated whereas the 4.1 gun was rusty, the quadruple mount was shiny and showed perfect care.

The submarine maintained an efficient lookout watch of 4-6 men on C/T watching for aircraft. There was no evidence of radar.

—Comments by Lt. Comdr. Gorman C. Merrick, USN,
commander Patrol Squadron VP-74, regarding attacks
made by plane *74-P-2* on German submarine *U-161*.[53]

In late morning on 27 September 1943, a Mariner of VP-74 (*74-P-2*) was flying a barrier sweep in the vicinity of an HF/DF contact obtained the previous evening. At 1050, the radar operator, ARM1/c D. A. Bealer, reported a contact eight degrees on the port bow, at a range of thirty-eight miles. The plane was flying east at 110 knots, at an altitude of 4,500 feet. The wake of a submarine was sighted visually by the co-pilot, Lt. (jg) Charles M. Fergerson, about ten miles dead ahead, and at a right angle to the aircraft, indicating the sub was steering a southerly course. The pilot, Lt. (jg) Harry B. Patterson, immediately increased speed and made a shallow turn to the left to take advantage of the morning sun, and get in position to make a stern attack.[54]

There were no clouds to hide the aircraft's approach, and the U-boat sighted *74-P-2* at this time. When the plane had closed to about seven to eight miles distant, she opened fire while in a port turn, attempting to bring her after guns to bear on the Mariner. This action was puzzling to Patterson, as U-boats usually maneuvered to present a beam target. The exploding rounds fired by the submarine were short, leaving white puffs in a line across the plane's course. As *74-P-2* closed to within range of its own guns, the bow gunner opened fire at about 3,000 yards. The fire of AOM2/c L. V. Schocklin fell short but then got on target as the range closed. Fergerson dropped a string of six Mk 44 Torpex-filled depth charges as the Mariner (approaching from the sub's port quarter) passed over the conning tower.[55]

Diagram 16-1

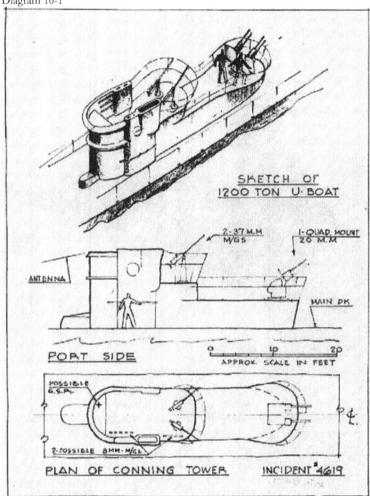

Sketch of a 1,200-ton U-boat made on 13 November 1943, and reproduced at the U.S. National Archives. The fitting of more anti-aircraft guns aft changed the tactics used by these type U-boats against attacking aircraft, which now desired to present their stern versus a beam aspect.

Patterson then made a successive attack, in which the plane took heavy fire and two members of the plane crew were severely wounded:

> I made a sharp left turn. Sub appeared to be just emerging from bomb slick, most of which seemed to be on starboard side of sub's track. The sub started turning right. When the plane was broadside the sub again opened fire, the shells exploding off our port side. After reaching 800' altitude, I gave orders to standby and commenced 2nd attack. During this run, the fire was heavier and more accurate. We were hit just forward of galley door by a shell that exploded just as it struck. Ensign BRETT was emerging from bombing compartment after having reset the intervalometer. He was severely wounded by shrapnel and aluminum from this shell, as was Radioman [ARM1/c D. A.] BEALER. At this time I did not know that BEALER was hit nor where or how badly the plane was damaged.[56]

Fergerson dropped the remaining two bombs as the plane passed directly over the submarine from stern to bow at about 165 knots at 160 feet altitude. Patterson then immediately gained altitude believing there was a possibility that his engines or fuel tanks were damaged. Ens. Ruben D. Larson, the navigator, carried Ens. Oliver J. Brett aft to a bunk where AMM2/c C. V. Hansen administered first-aid. The flight engineer reported to Patterson that they had been hit in many places, and the electric instruments were out of commission.[57]

Patterson witnessed evidence of damage to the submarine, before departing the scene to seek medical attention for his injured crewmen:

> Just before reaching 2500' altitude at which I leveled off, I glanced back and noticed that BEALER was wounded in his right leg. He was still at his station helping Ensign LARSON with the amplifying report and had never reported being hit. After checking Ensign BRETT's injuries and the damage to plane I realized that he needed medical attention quickly. Although we were out of range at this time, the sub kept up a continuous fire. It maneuvered erratically after the 2nd attack and the speed was noticeably reduced. It squared away on straight course of 140°T and submerged at 1122 P [local time]. I flew over the swirl and dropped [a] D/C Marker, and then departed for base.[58]

PLANE CREW AWARDS

Lt. (jg) Harry B. Patterson received the Air Medal for this attack, and Ens. Oliver J. Brett and ARM1/c D. A. Bealer, Purple Heart Medals.

PBM-3C Mariner *74-P-7* Plane Crew
(for action on 27 September 1943)

Name	Position	Award
Lt. (jg) Harry B. Patterson, USNR	Pilot	Air Medal
Lt. (jg) Charles M. Fergerson, USNR	Co-pilot	
Ens. Ruben D. Larson, USNR	Navigator	
Ens. Oliver J. Brett, USN	Bomber	Purple Heart
AMM1/c J. J. McGann, USN	Flight engineer	
ARM1/c D. A. Bealer, USN	Radio	Purple Heart
AOM2/c L. V. Schocklin, USN	Bow gunner	
Sea2/c L. W. Lackey, USN	Tail gunner	
AMM2/c C. V. Hansen, USN	Port waist gunner	
ARM3/c T. E. Hartwell, USNR	Starboard waist gunner	
Sea2/c W. S. Buckhout, USNR	Photographer[59]	

LAST WAR PATROL OF *U-161*

The submarine depth charged by patrol bomber *74-P-2* was the *U-161* which, unbeknownst to the plane crew, sank at 12°30'S, 35°35'W with the loss of all hands.   The submarine had left Lorient on 8 August 1943 on her sixth war patrol.   Korvettenkapitän Albrecht Achilles, her commanding officer since 1 January 1942, had taken *U-161* on the preceding patrols, during which he sank a total of eleven ships, and damaged another seven including one later declared a total loss.[60]

More recently, *U-161* had found the British merchant vessel *St. Usk* a week earlier on the morning of 20 September, about 240 miles north of Martin Vaz Rocks. These rocks—a part of the Trindade and Martin Vaz Archipelago—marked the most eastward point of Brazilian territory, about 700 miles off the mainland. The British merchantman was making 9 knots, when hit port side aft in #5 hold by one torpedo. The after part of the ship flooded rapidly and settled to deck level in a few minutes, forcing her crew of forty-two and six naval gunners to abandon in two large lifeboats. *St. Usk* sank by the stern at 1150 with one casualty, a gunner who suffered a fractured skull (most likely when the mast fell, due to the torpedo's detonation.)[61]

U-161 surfaced, and took the master, chief officer, second officer and radio officer aboard for questioning, and provided hot coffee to the remaining survivors.   Achilles apologized to the mariners for sinking their ship before questioning them.   Before leaving the survivors upon the sea, the Germans gave them extra water, identified their position on a chart, and removed a radio set to prevent them from reporting the position of the U-boat. The German doctor put a dressing on the head of the injured gunner. Upon learning that he was to be retained aboard the sub, the master, George Henry Moss, wrote a message to his wife and handed it to the chief officer before being taken down inside the conning tower. The other three men were allowed to return to the lifeboats and the sub left the area. Moss later perished when *U-161* was sunk by the PBM-3C Mariner.[62]

The twenty-seven survivors in the lifeboat under the charge of the second officer were picked up by the Spanish merchant ship *Albareda* on 25 September and landed at Rio de Janeiro three days later. Brazilian and American patrol aircraft sent out to search for the other lifeboat (containing the remaining twenty survivors), located it on the evening of 26 September about 135 miles south-southeast of Salvador da Bahia. The Brazilian sub-chaser *Juruena* (CS54) was sent from Bahia to pick up the survivors, but returned to port the following day after failing to find them. A Brazilian aircraft spotted the lifeboat that evening, but a thunderstorm prevented any rescue operations.[63]

The boat reached the Brazilian coast on its own at daybreak on 29 September (after a nine-and-a-half-day journey of some 750 miles), and followed the shoreline until sighting the lighthouse of Morro de São Paulo about thirty miles southwest of Bahia. Before long, the lifeboat encountered the Brazilian coaster *Porto-Seguro*, which towed it into an anchorage and took the survivors aboard. The following morning a Brazilian schooner towed the lifeboat to Bahia, arriving the afternoon of 30 September. The survivors were then all flown to Rio to join the remainder of the crew aboard the British passenger ship *Highland Monarch*.[64]

The day before she, herself, would be sunk, *U-161* had sent the Brazilian *Itapagé* to the bottom the evening of 26 September, with two torpedoes. The merchant vessel went down off Lagoa Azeda, about twenty miles south of Maceió, Alagoas, with twenty casualties: sixteen members of the crew and four passengers. The survivors (the master, fifty-four crewmen and thirty-two passengers) abandoned ship in lifeboats and made landfall at São Miguel dos Campos.[65]

U-848 SUNK SOUTHWEST OF ASCENSION ISLAND

In every respect this flight and attack was perfect. The result was inevitable from the start. Lieutenant Taylor used the flight to the scene of action to test his plane and its equipment and to instruct and prepare his crew for every incident which might occur including the relief of the pilot should he be wounded or killed in action. Upon contact he carefully planned and executed his attack to take advantage of the enemy's inaccurate fire during a turn. He placed his first stick of bombs in an exact straddle of the U-boat. He rapidly and skillfully

maneuvered his plane into position for a second attack and delivered it from the
sub's vulnerable bow and this time blasted it to complete destruction (three bombs
were within lethal range). Immediately he set about locating a surface vessel and
directing it to the scene of action to pick up prisoners and gather evidence.

—Lt. Comdr. Renfo Turner, USN, commanding officer VB-107,
describing the final demise of *U-848*. The German submarine
withstood attacks by three PB4Y-1 Liberator patrol bombers of
Squadron VB-107 and two B-52 bombers of the US Army Air
Forces 1st Composite Squadron, before finally succumbing to
patrol bomber *107-B-4*, piloted by Lt. Samuel K. Taylor Jr.[66]

In November 1943, the eleven PB4Y-1 Liberator aircraft of Bombing
Squadron VB-107 were split between two bases. Planes *107-B-1, 2, 5,*
7, 9, and *10* operated from Parnamirim Field at Natal, and *107-B-3, 4,*
6, 8, and *12* from Ascension Island. At 0623 on 5 November, one of
the Liberators at the latter location (*107-B-12*) took off on an anti-
submarine patrol. After five hours of flight and having turned to the
homeward leg, the pilot, Lt. Charles A. Baldwin, decided to transfer
fuel from the outboard wing tanks. At 1110, while on course 068°T at
3,500 feet and passing through a small front, the bow watch reported a
sighting of a ship through a break in the clouds. Baldwin and the co-
pilot, Ens. John Leonard, sighted the same object at about five miles,
two points (22.5 degrees) off the plane's port bow. Balwin's sardonic
comment, "Heck, that's a Nazi Submarine," sent everyone to their
battle stations.[67]

As the aircraft broke through the cloud cover, Baldwin sighted the
sub on his port beam, one-and-a-half miles away, steering course
090°T and making 15 knots or better. After making a diving turn to
port at 250 mph, which brought the aircraft down to 75 feet off the
water, Baldwin dropped six bombs, one just forward of conning
tower. Following this initial attack, he pulled up in a steep port bank
to set up for a second run. However, the submarine made a turn to
starboard and Baldwin was unable to straighten the plane out in time,
and passed her about sixty feet inside of his turn. Turning again to
port, he dropped his three remaining bombs from only twenty-five
feet above the water, which nevertheless fell and exploded short of the
target. Pulling out to port and away, Baldwin looked back and
observed the sub was still in her turn and losing a great amount of oil.
He also saw three puffs of smoke, which he believed were the only
shots fired at the plane during the three runs.[68]

Diagram 16-2

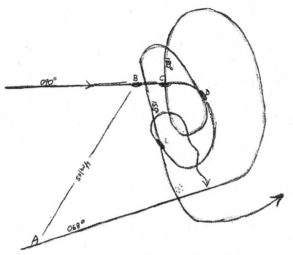

Relative movements of plane *107-B-12* and *U-848* during two attacks made by the patrol bomber on the German submarine. The sketch (from the pilot's "Report of Anti-submarine Action by Aircraft") is not to scale.

A: Position of plane at sighting

B: Position of submarine at sighting

C. First attack (6 bombs dropped)

D. Second run (no bombs dropped)

E. Second attack (3 bombs dropped)

ATTACKS MADE BY SECOND PLANE INEFFECTIVE

Baldwin contacted *107-B-4* (which was then returning to Ascension on the return leg of a 600-mile sweep it had been conducting jointly with Baldwin's plane), and told the other pilot, Lt. William R. Ford, USNR, of the attack and started sending MOs so as to home the plane in on the target. Meantime, the submarine was still losing oil and appeared to be down by the stern, steering an erratic course in a southerly direction making about 4 or 5 knots.[69]

After receiving this report, Ford altered course to 180° magnetic to intercept the target. At 1141 a sighting was made of the submarine, which was twelve miles distant and making a large circling turn. At one to one-and-a-half miles away, the sub opened up with heavy anti-aircraft fire. This was mostly to the portside of, and below the plane. Believing that the enemy would soon correct his aim point and score hits, Ford turned to port and lost altitude until he saw the bomber was within the smoke puffs of the AA fire. Even so, submarine gunfire was taken on the starboard bow and beam of the aircraft. As Ford straightened out for a bombing run, the plane's crown turret and both bow guns opened up with very accurate fire on the conning tower.

Their fire scored very good hits on the sub's gun crews, or scared the hell out of them. In any case, all AA fire ceased.[70]

Photo 16-4

Conning tower of German submarine *U-848*.
A History of Patrol Squadron 83 and Bombing Squadron 107, September 15, 1941 to December 31, 1944

While making 200 knots and from a height of about 150 feet, Ford released six Mk 47 depth bombs—set to explode at a depth of 25 feet and spaced 60 feet apart. The patrol bomber then passed over the sub's conning tower at about 25-30 feet, and the tail turret opened with very accurate fire, but was unable to maintain it due to a sharp pullout. After gaining 500 feet, Ford completed the sharp left turn and made a second run.[71]

While in a dive at 250 mph, and against no opposing enemy fire, he dropped three Mk 47 bombs (same settings) from 100 feet altitude, and once again crossed over the conning tower at about 25 feet. The drop looked fair, but it was estimated the closest bomb was thirty feet short. Ford turned to port in a climb and sent a message to Ascension requesting that a standby plane be sent immediately. As *107-B-12*'s communications were already set up and ready to home relief planes, and the other patrol bomber had more fuel, *107-B-4* departed to return to base.   After landing, refueling and rearming, *B-4* (now under the command of Lt. Samuel K. Taylor Jr.) took off again at 1513.[72]

Photo 16-5

Officers and crew of *107-B-4*, piloted by Lt. William R. Ford, USNR.
A History of Patrol Squadron 83 and Bombing Squadron 107, September 15, 1941 to December 31, 1944

ADDITIONAL PLANES ARRIVE ON SCENE

While *107-B-4* was away, a third squadron plane, *107-B-8*, arrived and initialed an attack from astern of the submarine. However, while still about 1,000 yards from the target, smoke started emitting from "Baker 8's" No. 2 engine and the plane was forced to return to base. In mid-afternoon, the U-boat stopped losing oil and began cruising at speeds of 10 to 12 knots for short periods of time.[73]

Captain Main of the 1st Composite Squadron of the US Army Air Forces based at Ascension, piloting a B-25, arrived at 1545 and carried out two bombing runs from 1,400 feet. The bombs fell short. Major Atkins of the same unit (also in a B-25) arrived at 1635, at which time Baldwin and the plane crew of *107-B-12* headed for base. At 1642, he met Lt. Samuel K. Taylor Jr. in *107-B-4* and directed him to the target. A few minutes later, he encountered Major Orr of the 1st Composite Squadron in a PBY-5A Catalina and also provided him with directions to the submarine. Baldwin landed at Ascension at 1833.[74]

107-B-4 ADMINISTERS THE COUP DE GRACE

Patrol Bomber *107-B-4* had taken flight from Ascension to destroy, if possible, the injured submarine. With the exception of the pilot, Lieutenant Taylor, and third pilot, Ens. Edward Whyte, the crew was the same as before its stop at the base to refuel and rearm. Now, it returned to reengage with *U-848*. On the way out, Taylor was in contact with "Baker 8" (then returning to base), and the two B-25s—whose horizontal drops with 500-lb bombs had been close, but not quite close enough.[75]

At 1650, the sub appeared eight miles ahead and twelve miles west of an oil slick, making 8-10 knots and steering a southwest course. Taylor maneuvered to the right of his adversary and began a wide counter-clockwise circle hoping to attack from her bow. The sub continued on the same course until she and the plane were on parallel, reciprocal courses about five miles apart, and then began a turn to starboard bringing her bow toward the aircraft. Taylor, in response, began turning left to close her, while maintaining 2,000 feet altitude.[76]

As the submarine continued a starboard turn as if attempting to present a beam target, Taylor applied high RPMs and 44 inch manifold pressure and began a dive, turning sharply to the left again. (Gunfire bursts and cannon fire passed over the plane's No. 3 engine while in this turn.) Taylor straightened out of the turn, came in over the bow of the submarine, and dropped five 350-lb flat-nosed, Torpex depth bombs from a height of seventy feet.[77]

Taylor immediately followed up the first drop by pulling up to 400 feet, then whipped around to make a run over the submarine's starboard bow. In this diving attack, he dropped his four remaining bombs along her starboard side. The sub settled straight down and then from the conning tower forward, shot up in the air. A tremendous cone-shaped explosion followed, originating from and surrounding the entire submarine, which rose high in the air. As it subsided, everything seemed to be swallowed by the sea.[78]

The next instant, three life rafts with 25 or 30 men appeared on the ocean's surface in the middle of an oil patch, along with a dark object that looked like submarine wreckage and which soon disappeared below the surface. *107-B-4* dropped one raft, and men were seen to get into it. An Army PBY arrived shortly after and dropped an additional three rafts. The last estimate of the number of survivors sighted by the patrol bomber before departure was fifteen to twenty men; some were in the rafts, others hanging on, swimming, or floating. One of the rafts failed to open and sank.[79]

The German submarine sunk at position 10°09'S, 18°00'W, after an exhaustive fight for survival, was the *U-848*, commissioned on 20 February 1943. Her commanding officer, Fregattenkapitän Wilhelm Rollmann, was lost at sea with the remainder of his crew.

Photo 16-6

U-848 under attack by PB4Y *107-B-12* of Bombing Squadron VB-107 southwest of Ascension Island on 5 November 1943.
U.S. National Archives Photograph #80-G-208282

AWARDS OF VALOR

The pilots and second pilots of three flight crews involved in the destruction of *U-848* on 5 November 1943 received the Distinguished Flying Cross. Ens. Harland Clark served as the second pilot in two different flight crews of *107-B-4*, which returned to Ascension, refueled, rearmed and changed crews before revisiting an area southwest of Ascension and sinking the sub in a second series of attacks.

Name	Plane No.	Award
Lt. Charles Arba Baldwin, USNR	*107-B-12*	Distinguished Flying Cross
Ens. John Michael Leonard Jr., USNR	*107-B-12*	Distinguished Flying Cross
Lt. William Render Ford, USNR	*107-B-4*	Distinguished Flying Cross
Ens. Harland Calvin Clark, USNR	*107-B-4*	Distinguished Flying Cross
Lt. Samuel Kyle Taylor Jr., USNR	*107-B-4*	Distinguished Flying Cross

U-849 SUNK WEST OF CONGO ESTUARY

The attack was excellent in all respects. The pilot retained his advantage of surprise by skillful use of cloud cover and by the swiftness with which he prepared and delivered his attack. The [bomb drop] was extremely accurate and deadly.

—Lt. Comdr. Renfo Turner Jr., USN, commanding officer VB-107.[80]

The last of fourteen enemy submarines sunk in the South Atlantic in 1943, was destroyed on 25 November. That morning, Lt. (jg) Marion V. Dawkins Jr., piloting *107-B-6*, took flight from Ascension Island on an anti-submarine sweep. While flying at 5,200 feet, Dawkins and his co-pilot, Ens. Marvell E. Eide, sighted a surface contact about ten miles distant, thirty degrees off the plane's starboard bow which they readily recognized as an enemy submarine.[81]

The submarine, later identified as the *U-849*, was relatively new. Commanded by Kapitänleutnant Heinz-Otto Schultze, she had been commissioned only a little over eight months earlier on 11 March 1943. Following a training period with the 4th Flotilla based at Stettin (Szczecin), Poland—on the Oder River near the Baltic Sea—*U-849* was transferred to the 12th Flotilla operating from Bordeaux, France. Bordeaux was also an inland port, located on the Garonne River in southwestern France sixty miles from the coast.[82]

The patrol bomber was proceeding on an easterly course and the submarine on a southerly one. After instructing the navigator to check the intervalometer and the sub's position, and the photographer to man his station, Dawkins changed course to 150° true. At about five miles from the sub, he ordered the standard U-boat warning signal "SSS" sent and began a rapid descent through clouds, breaking through at 2,000 feet, one mile astern of his target. He released six bombs from the port pilot's seat in a steep glide with a spacing of 50 feet at 200 mph. The detonations of the bombs enveloped the submarine; two landing close to her starboard quarter, three her port beam, and the sixth possibly striking her deck.[83]

After the drop, the tail turret gunner strafed the conning tower and deck on which a few personnel were seen. The crown turret and nose guns did not fire due to the suddenness of the attack, and chow was being served at the time of sighting, which led to some confusion aboard. Dawkins thought it advisable not to delay the attack until these guns were ready, as the element of surprise might be lost. The enemy was taken completely off guard and did not fire a shot until after the plane had passed over the conning tower.[84]

As Dawkins cleared the conning tower, he felt a loss of control in rudders and the nose dropped badly. As the plane lost further altitude and nearly struck the water, he pulled heavily back on the yoke and climbed slowly to 800 feet where he observed bursts of anti-aircraft fire short and below the aircraft. The damaged sub was motionless and surrounded by a large oil slick. Dawkins climbed up to 1,500 feet out of range of AA fire. He had three bombs remaining, but after observing that the enemy was severely crippled and not knowing the extent of damage to his plane, he decided to delay a second attack until another squadron plane (*107-B-8*) arrived. Meanwhile, he kept within striking distance and ordered the plane crew to watch for any attempt by the U-boat to submerge.[85]

Photo 16-7

Explosions of depth charges during a successful attack made against *U-849* by a PB4Y-1 Liberator aircraft of Bombing Squadron VB-107 on 25 November 1943. U.S. National Archives Photograph #80-G-208592

While circling the submarine, Dawkins was informed by the after station and bow lookouts that her crew was abandoning. He then moved in rapidly to take photographs, but while still one mile distant the submarine exploded, with smoke rising to some 200 feet in the air, and sank. The plane then descended to 500 feet to take pictures of survivors before departing. *U-849*'s entire crew of sixty-three were lost; all were killed in action, or when the sub went down, or made it clear but perished at sea.[86]

A post-action inspection of *107-B-6* revealed that damage suffered by the plane was from fragments of a depth charge which apparently broke up upon striking the water. One fragment lodged in the center leading edge of the starboard vertical stabilizer—evidencing how low over the submarine Dawkins had made his attack. Others produced some small scratches and tears in the fabric of the plane.[87]

AWARDS FOR VALOR

PB4Y-1 Liberator *107-B-6* Plane Crew
(for action on 25 November 1943

Name	Position	Award
Lt. (jg) Marion Vance Dawkins Jr. USNR	Pilot	DFC
Ens. Marvell Elsworth Eide, USNR	Co-pilot	DFC
Ens. Wayne Ambrose Grimm, USNR	3rd Pilot	AM
Ens. George H. Valentine, USNR	Bow Gun	AM
Sea2/c Earl Joseph Kloss, USNR	Camera	AM (2nd)
AMM1/c George Brownlee Jr., USNR	Crown Turret	AM
AOM3/c Richard Deforrest Gilpin, USNR	Tail Turret	AM
AMM3/c Francisco Salvatore Renda, USNR	Port Waist Gun	AM
ARM3/c Joslyn Simpson	Radar	AM
ARM1/c Carl Verner Roberg, USNR	Radio	AM

17

Fight to the Death between
USS *Borie* and *U-405*

The BORIE *rode up and over the forecastle of the submarine. Realizing the situation, we stopped the engines and pinned him there for about the next ten minutes. During this part of the action, all guns that could be brought to bear were used at ranges anywhere from ten feet to forty feet. Number two main battery four-inch concentrated on the after part of the submarine. The two ships were in almost parallel positions now, about 30 degrees being the bearing between them. Number four main battery gun was able to bear on the main deck of the sub just aft the conning tower. Machine guns two, three, four and six were able to bear on the port side, but machine gun number two was blanked off by the main battery gun which was just aft of it on the galley deck-house, therefore it fired very few shots during this part of the action. Machine gun number six, located on the main deck aft, port side, was able to sweep the submarine decks continuously.*

We were deeply impressed by the ruggedness and the toughness of those particular boats. She was almost as long as the BORIE, *painted a very, very light grey, almost an off white. On her conning tower there was a polar bear device. There were three numbers also painted on the conning tower, but they were illegible since the machine guns had so badly shot the bridge structure away.*

—Lt. Comdr. Charles H. Hutchins, former commanding officer of
the destroyer USS *Borie* (DD-215), describing the opening action
of a prolonged battle with the German submarine *U-405*, in
which both antagonists were lost. *Borie* sank the submarine,
but gravely hurt, and unsalvageable herself, she was
abandoned; and later scuttled by friendly forces.[1]

There has been little reference up to this point, regarding the critical role "hunter-killer" groups played in turning the tide against U-boats in the Battle of the Atlantic. The action in this chapter, though it took place in the North Atlantic, provides a vivid example of how hard fought the action was. The fight between the destroyer *Borie* and *U-405* formed the basis for the acclaimed and Oscar-winning film *The*

Enemy Below, released in 1957, starring Robert Mitchum and Curt Jürgens.

The four ships of Task Group 21.14 stood out of Casablanca Harbor, French Morocco, the morning of 20 October 1943 to operate as a hunter-killer group. Such groups consisted of anti-submarine ships (corvettes, destroyers, destroyer escorts, frigates), formed around an escort carrier to actively hunt U-boats in the Atlantic. Comprising Task Group 21-14 were the escort carrier *Card* (CVE-11), and three destroyers assigned to screen and protect her from attack: *Barry* (DD-248), *Borie* (DD-215), and *Goff* (DD-247). Initially, warships had accompanied convoys to help fend off attacks from aircraft and submarines. As numbers of CVEs increased, escort carriers became the center-pieces of hunter-killer groups which had the freedom to seek out enemy submarines instead of remaining tethered to a particular convoy.[2]

Embarked aboard the *Card* was Composite Squadron VC-9, commanded by Lt. Comdr. Howard M. Avery, USN. The squadron had come aboard on 23 September 1943 and would remain until 8 November. Its complement of aircraft was twelve torpedo bombers—a combination of Grumman TBF and TBF-1c Avengers, and the TBM Avenger (same type aircraft but manufactured by General Motors versus Grumman)—and nine fighter aircraft, a combination of Grumman FM-2 and F4F Wildcats. Composite Squadron Nine was commissioned on 6 August 1942 to operate from escort carriers protecting convoys and conducting anti-submarine warfare in the Atlantic.[3]

Photo 17-1

"Baby flattop" USS *Card* (CVE-11) at sea in the Atlantic on 15 June 1943, with F4F Wildcat fighters and TBF/TBM Avenger torpedo bombers staged on her flight deck. U.S. Naval History and Heritage Command Photograph #NH 106564

Escort carriers—commonly referred to as "jeep carriers" or "baby flattops" within the United States Navy, and "Woolworth Carriers" by the Royal Navy—were typically half the length of larger fleet carriers. They were also slower, and carried fewer planes and less armament— causing some crewmen to opine that the designation CVE stood for "combustible, vulnerable, and expendable." However, escort carriers were cheaper and could be constructed quickly. Most often built on a merchant ship hull, they were too slow to keep up with the main forces, fleet carriers, battleships, and cruisers; they were instead used to protect convoys and hunt U-boats.

Photo 17-2

Grumman TBF-1 Avenger torpedo bomber being hoisted aboard the auxiliary aircraft carrier USS *Santee* (ACV-29) at Norfolk, Virginia, in November 1942.
U.S. National Archives Photograph #80-G-469839

The 495-foot *Card* had been built by Seattle-Tacoma Shipbuilding Corp., Seattle, Washington, as a merchant vessel, type C3-S-A1. The Navy acquired her on 1 May 1942 and later commissioned her an aircraft escort vessel (AVG-11). She was reclassified an escort carrier (CVE-11) on 15 July 1943. Her two boilers and steam turbine coupled to a single shaft could propel the ship to a modest speed of 16.5 knots. She had no armor, but was fitted with naval guns for self-defense: two 5-inch/51 gun mounts (later two single 5-inch/38) for surface engagements. For anti-air defense, she had ten twin 40mm/56-caliber mounts and twenty-six single 20mm/70-cal. mounts.[4]

The three destroyers were *Clemson*-class ships, commissioned shortly after the end of World War I. Propelled by two Westinghouse or Parsons steam turbines driving twin screws, the ships were fast and maneuverable, capable of 35 knots. They also packed a punch, boasting four 4-inch/50 gun mounts, one 3-inch/23 anti-aircraft mount, and twelve 21-inch torpedo tubes. The marriage of CVEs and DDs to form hunter-killer groups optimized the strengths of the two types of ship, and compensated for their individual vulnerabilities. Through use of their radar and sonar, the destroyers could screen the "baby flattop" from submarines, and attack them with guns, depth charges, or torpedoes. In turn, fighter and torpedo bomber aircraft from the CVE could provide defense against air attack for both herself and the destroyers.

Task Group 21.14

Ship	Length (ft.) Displ. (tons)	Speed (kts) Crew Size	Builder/Date Commissioned
Card (CVE-11)	495/7,800	16.5/890	Seattle-Tacoma Shipbuilding Corp., Seattle, Washington 8 Nov 42
Barry (DD-248)	314/1,215	35/114	New York Shipbuilding 28 Dec 20
Borie (DD-215)	314/1,215	35/114	Cramp, Philadelphia 24 Mar 20
Goff (DD-247)	314/1,215	35/114	New York Shipbuilding 19 Jan 21[5]

After clearing the harbor on the 20th, *Card* had begun zigzagging along her base course. This defensive measure was commonly used by ships in waters that might contain one or more enemy submarines. After a U-boat located a target ship, it had to get into a torpedo firing position. By making fairly significant turns at irregular intervals, a ship could make it more difficult for an enemy submarine to approach to a good firing position and obtain weapons-release data, based on an accurate estimate of where the ship would be when a fired torpedo reached it. Zigzagging was somewhat analogous to a boxer bobbing and weaving to deny an opponent the luxury of a stationary target.

The three destroyers took up protective positions around *Card*, with the escort carrier in the center of the formation serving as the guide.[6]

Late that afternoon, a sighting was made of Convoy UGS-20—a slow eastbound trans-Atlantic convoy in passage from the United States to Gibraltar—and Task Force 65 at a distance of ten miles on the port bow of the carrier. The convoy passed astern of the group of ships at a distance of five miles. Over the next two days, Task Group 21.14 steered generally a northwesterly course. At 0600 on 23 October, the General Quarters alarm sounded aboard *Card*, calling her crew to battle stations and material condition Affirm was set aboard the ship. Forty-five minutes later, the escort carrier ceased zigzagging and turned into the wind for flight operations. At 0659, four TBF Avenger torpedo bombers were catapulted for anti-submarine patrol. *Card* then secured from General Quarters, set material condition Baker and condition II MS—lesser conditions of shipboard readiness—and resumed zigzagging.[7]

TORPEDO BOMBER PROTECTION OF SHIPPING

Card recovered the torpedo bombers of Group I in late morning and that afternoon, launched a second group of four TBFs on anti-submarine patrol. Group II was recovered in early evening. The same pattern of sending groups of torpedo bombers out on patrol continued the next day, with one deviation. At 1142 on 24 October, the escort carrier catapulted one TBF to provide coverage for the destroyer *Stockton* (DD-646) and Liberty ship *David G. Burnett* en route to Ponto Delgada, Azores, from Convoy GUS-18. (GUS was an acronym for "slow westbound convoy." This convoy, the eighteenth such, had departed Alexandria, Egypt, on 9 October and would arrive at Hampton Roads, Virginia, on 6 November.) At 1400 that afternoon, Task Group 21.14 passed Santa Maria Island of the Azores abeam to starboard at a distance of fifteen miles. That night *Card* gained radar contact on the *Stockton* returning to GUS-18.[8]

On 25 October, the ships of the task group joined the convoy for a time in order that the three destroyers could refuel from the oiler *Kennebec* (AO-36). The routine of the past few days continued with periodic launches of torpedo bombers from *Card* on anti-submarine patrol. In early afternoon on the 27th, a sighting was made of a different convoy (GUS-21) at a distance of nine miles. At 1848 that evening, *Card* gained an HF/DF contact, bearing 000 degrees true, within fifty miles. Invented by the Royal Navy, HF/DF equipment (known as "Huff Duff" to sailors) was designed to detect the bearings of high-frequency radio transmissions of U-boats making reports to headquarters. Initially this equipment was only at shore sites on both sides of the Atlantic and in Iceland, Greenland and Bermuda. In 1942, the Allies began to install HF/DF on some ships. A U-boat might be mere miles from a ship gaining detection with this equipment, yet perhaps be out of radar range. If two or more ships gained HF/DF contact they could calculate a reasonably accurate estimated position of the U-boat, or at least good enough to considerably reduce the area to be searched.[9]

TORPEDO BOMBERS SINK *U-584*

Anti-submarine patrols on 28 October found no U-boats, and the only mildly interesting sighting by a torpedo bomber was of a British corvette escorting a tramp steamer. The following day, as air patrols continued, *Card* refueled *Barry*, *Borie*, and *Goff*. Sailors aboard ship awoke the morning of 30 October to heavy rains and rough seas, which increased over the course of the day. Just before sunset that evening, a TBF out on patrol spotted a U-boat on the surface.[10]

As the pilot, Lt. (jg) Harry E. Fryatt, USN, initiated an attack, the submarine dove and escaped. Fryatt sighted two other U-boats on the surface, descended to 500 feet, reported their position, and then stayed out of range of anti-aircraft fire directed at his aircraft until two other Avengers—piloted by Lieutenants (jg) Letson Balliett and Alexander C. MacAuslan—arrived on the scene. One of the submarines (*U-91*) submerged before the planes got there. The other was not so lucky. Two Mk 23 Fido torpedoes, one dropped by each aircraft on opposite sides of *U-584*, sent her to the bottom north of the Azores, with the loss of all hands.[11]

The latter submarine, not then known to be *U-584*, was the eighth submarine kill by Task Group 21.14 since 27 July. These U-boats were sunk by aircraft (of VC-1 and later VC-9) operating from *Card*. A ninth U-boat would be sunk by *Borie*, the principal subject of this chapter, on 1 November. Before we get to this event, readers might be interested in an overview of *U-584*'s past involvement in landing a team of saboteurs on America's eastern seaboard.

OPERATION PASTORIUS

Nearly a year and a half earlier, *U-584*, then under the command of Kapitänleutnant Joachim Deecke, had participated in in an operation planned by the Abwehr (defense) section of the German Military Intelligence Corps, code named PASTORIUS. The submarine had departed Brest, France, on a very special patrol on 25 May 1942. On 18 June, after crossing the Atlantic (submerged by day, surfaced at night), she had landed a saboteur team of four men at Ponte Vedra Beach, twenty-five miles southeast of Jacksonville, Florida. A second four-man team carried by *U-202* to Long Island, New York, had already landed there six days earlier on 12 June. After discharging her passengers, *U-584* returned safely to Brest on 22 July.[12]

The operation was a complete failure. To field the two teams of saboteurs, the Abwehr had scoured the records of the Deutsches Ausland Institute (which had financed the return of thousands of expatriates from America) to find Germans who had lived in the United States and were familiar with the country, its customs, and its transportation systems. The assignment of the team that landed at Long Island was to destroy the hydroelectric plants at Niagara Falls; the Aluminum Company of America factories in Illinois, Tennessee and New York; as well as the Philadelphia Salt Company's cryolite plant in Philadelphia, which supplied the mineral for aluminum manufacture. The men were also instructed to blow up locks on the Ohio River between Louisville, Kentucky, and Pittsburgh, Pennsylvania.[13]

The job of the team that landed in Florida was to travel north, blow up the Pennsylvania Railroad station at Newark, as well as a horseshoe bend section of the railroad near Altoona, Pennsylvania, and sections of the Chesapeake and Ohio Railroad. Other targets were the New York Central Railroad's Hell Gate bridge; the lock and canal complexes at St. Louis, Missouri, and Cincinnati, Ohio; and New York City's water supply system.[14]

Before either team could carry out any of its assignments, two members of the first team and one of the second went to the FBI, and informed agents of the plan to cripple America's industrial might. All eight men were arrested, and the caches of explosives, large sums of cash, and other items they had brought ashore were seized.[15]

BORIE SENT TO SEARCH FOR OTHER U-BOATS

The sinking of *U-584*, by two of *Card*'s torpedo bombers the evening of 31 October, occurred about thirteen miles from the position of Task Group 21.14. Following destruction of the submarine, the escort carrier and three destroyers steamed on a reciprocal course for a time; then *Borie* was detached from the group and ordered back to that area to conduct a night search alone.[16]

PREVIOUS FOURTH FLEET DUTY

Borie had previously been a unit of Ingram's Fourth Fleet. After reporting for duty in February 1943, she had been assigned duties escorting convoys. This involved her going with a convoy from Trinidad to Recife where Brazilian escorts took over these duties for continued passage to Bahia. In the latter part of June, *Borie* had received orders to report to the New York Navy Yard. After a short period of training, she was assigned to Task Group 21.14. The task group had departed Norfolk, Virginia, on 27 July on a cruise that lasted through 10 September 1943, during which aircraft of Composite Squadron VC-1 destroyed four U-boats. Summary information pertaining to those submarines, and five others sunk on *Card*'s subsequent cruise, follows.[17]

German Submarines Sunk by TG 21.14
(7 August–1 November 1943)

Date	U-boat	U-boat Commander	Location	Task Group Unit
7 Aug 43	*U-117*	Hans-Werner Neumann	39°32'N, 38°21'W	VC-1 from *Card*
9 Aug 43	*U-664*	Adolf Graef	40°12'N, 37°29'W	VC-1 from *Card*
11 Aug 43	*U-525*	Hans-Joachim Drewitz	41°29'N, 38°55'W	VC-1 from *Card*
27 Aug 43	*U-847*	Herbert Kuppisch	28°19'N, 37°58'W	VC-1 from *Card*
4 Oct 43	*U-460*	Ebe Schnorr	43°13'N, 28°58'W	VC-9 from *Card*
4 Oct 43	*U-422*	Wolfgang Poeschel	43°18'N, 28°58'W	VC-9 from *Card*
13 Oct 43	*U-402*	Siegfried Freiherr von Forstner	48°56'N, 29°41'W	VC-9 from *Card*
31 Oct 43	*U-584*	Joachim Deecke	49°14'N, 31°55'W	VC-9 from *Card*
1 Nov 43	*U-405*	Rolf-Heinrich Hopman	49°00'N, 31°14'W	*Borie* (DD-215)[18]

DUTY WITH TG 21.14 IN THE NORTH ATLANTIC

The task group had left Norfolk on its current cruise on 25 September, one that would provide even more promising hunting. Planes of Squadron VC-1 operating from *Card* spotted a nest of four submarines refueling on 4 October and sank two of them, disposed of a third U-boat on 13 October, and a fourth (*U-584*) on 31 October.[19]

Lt. Charles H. Hutchins, USNR, the commanding officer of *Borie*—which sank the fifth submarine of the cruise—later described the general role of his ship in convoy work between Norfolk and Gibraltar, thence Gibraltar to Norfolk:

We left the latter part of July on our first trip of the convoy out of Norfolk with destination of Gibraltar. As soon as the convoy was within range of the shore-based aircraft, we would be relieved from that duty and would proceed to known concentrations of submarines for offensive action. The purpose of the *BORIE*, of course, as well as the other destroyers with the carrier, was merely the role of protector for the carrier. We formed the screen as she and her planes accomplished all the killing.[20]

BORIE FINDS AND ATTACKS ENEMY SUBMARINE

Upon arriving on station on 31 October (where *U-584* had been sunk a little earlier), *Borie* began a search for other U-boats and at about 2000, made her first radar contact. Running down the contact, Hutchins ensured that it was an enemy submarine and prepared to engage it with gunfire. However, the *U-405* (commanded by Fregattenkapitän Rolf-Heinrich Hopman) then dove, necessitating a depth-charge attack, which Hutchins initially believed had destroyed the enemy, as he later described:

> After three attacks, during which time we had seen the submarine rise to the surface with its bow high and appear to settle by the stern, we considered the submarine sunk. Also, a heavy under-water explosion further confirmed this in our minds. However, we conducted a search for about three to three and a half hours in the area to make sure they had no chance to escape. Then upon returning to the point at which we had made that attack, this was marked by the float lights we had dropped, we noted a heavy oil on the surface, the diesel oil fumes were very rank, and we received no further contact in this area.[21]

This belief proved false. In an effort to further eliminate any possibility of the submarine's escape, *Borie* had continued to search to the east. After passing out of the area in which it was believed the U-boat might be, the destroyer got a radar contact, dead ahead at 8,000 yards. Upon receipt of this report, Hutchins initiated another attack:

> We immediately put on all available speed, having four boilers lite, steaming split plant and steamed towards the contact. At about range 2800 yards the submarine submerged and we continued a sound attack picking him up at 2200 yards, tracked him into about 500 yards during which time he appeared to be on an easterly course. But at the 500 yard point the bearing suddenly started to draw right. We, of course, came hard right and steadied up on course 210 and dropped our depth charges on that course.[22]

As *Borie* continued on this course, her radar picked up a contact about 400 yards distant in the area in which she had made the depth charge attack. At about the same time, one of the lookouts spotted the sub on the surface and the destroyer came around hard right and began pursuit using a searchlight to illuminate the enemy. As the range opened up to from 1,200 to 1,400 yards, the destroyer's 4-inch main battery guns opened fire, in local control, as soon as they could bear. The U-boat began returning fire with her anti-aircraft machineguns. She did not fire her deck gun, located forward of the conning tower, because the second or third 4-inch salvo had struck the submarine just under the gun and, when the smoke cleared, it had been carried away without firing a shot.[23]

CLOSE QUARTERS FIGHT

The fight then progressed to the destroyer and U-boat being locked in combat, literally, blasting away at each other from point blank range, which included small arms combat at close quarters. Hutchins explained the events during pursuit of *U-405* that preceded his ship riding up over the bow of the submarine, temporarily immobilizing and clinching them together in deadly combat, as described in the quoted material at the beginning of the chapter:

> The submarine turned and went on a northwesterly course and we closed to ram with our 20mm. guns sweeping their decks completely clear, the four-inch scoring some effective hits during this time. As soon as the situation was favorable we came in from his starboard quarter to ram and, just a few seconds before contact was made, the submarine turned hard left with the result that we struck a glancing blow on his forecastle, rather than a good straight hit.[24]

Although the seas were moderately rough, with waves twelve to eighteen feet high, the submarine was operating low in the water with her decks only just awash, which had allowed *Borie* to ride over her bow. During the next ten minutes, all of the destroyer's guns that could be brought to bear—number two and four main battery 4-inch, and number 2, 3, 4, and 6 machine guns—maintained steady fire from a range of only ten to forty feet away. While gun crews kept banging away, other crewmembers aboard *Borie* broke out small arms carried aboard the destroyer for security in port:

All available small arms were broken out and used. The Executive Officer and a Signalman manned tommy guns from the bridge. We had shot-guns, which were kept on board as riot guns, those were broken out and used, rifles and pistols, one person even firing a very pistol [flare gun] down into the conning tower of the sub from the bridge. Others, not otherwise engaged, threw whatever was at hand. Kurtz, the gun Captain of Number two main battery, picked up empty shell casings and heaved those over onto the sub's deck striking one man and knocking him overboard. Another member of the crew pulled his pocket knife threw that and was able to stick it in the stomach of one German, knocking him overboard. The Germans, during this time, attempted to man their gun—their machine gun. However, none of them could get close. It is estimated up to this time that there had been about 30 to 35 casualties in the crew of the submarine. None of the bodies were left lying on deck—all fell overboard and were never seen again.[25]

BORIE AND *U-405* BOTH SEVERLY DAMAGED, BUT BREAK APART AND COMBAT ACTION CONTINUES

After about ten minutes of the hammering, the destroyer and U-boat broke apart, whereupon Hutchins learned the submarine's hull had inflicted grave injury to his ship:

> It was then we realized aboard ship that we were seriously damaged ourselves. The submarine's hull had cut a serious hole along our entire port side. The forward engine room was flooding badly where plates were opened up at the joints and frames crushed in. The after engine room was flooding but we were able to control that water. However, the damage in the forward engine room was beyond control and it was later necessary to abandon the engine room. The crew of that particular engine room maintained flank speed on that engine, even though they were standing in water up to their necks with the turbines operating underwater. After the two ships broke apart, the submarine got under way at a speed of about 15 knots and, just as we fired a torpedo at him, he turned left to avoid the torpedo and then went into a tight left hand circle. The *BORIE*, of course, all this time was pursuing and firing every gun available.[26]

U-405, apparently unable to submerge, circled in an effort to prevent her pursuer from ramming her. *Borie* could not turn as sharply and thus circled her prey in a larger turning circle. During this maneuvering, the submarine's stern pointed directly at the destroyer, and Hutchins rightly worried about the possibility of harm from her "stinger," a single torpedo tube located at her stern. Since Hutchins had radar contact on *U-405*, he ordered *Borie*'s search light doused to shield the destroyer from view, and encourage the submarine to try to escape in the darkness.[27]

This eventually occurred and, as distance between the antagonists increased and with the U-boat no longer an immediate threat, the destroyer once again turned on the searchlight and continued the action. With the submarine now positioned on her starboard bow, *Borie* closed at 27 knots in an attempt to ram again. However, just prior to making contact, *U-405* turned hard left, leaving her bow pointed at the destroyer's after engine room—"turning the tables" so to speak. Hutchins "backed hard on the port engine, threw the rudder hard left and stopped the starboard engine." This swung *Borie*'s stern toward the U-boat on a nearly parallel course, enabling the destroyer to fire her three depth charge projector guns, starboard side, aft:

> These had been set at 30 foot depth with 50 yard impulse charges in the forward and after guns and 75 yard impulse charges in the center gun. When the submarine was within range these guns were fired, resulting in a perfect straddle around his conning tower. One depth charge landed just over the conning tower, the other two landed just short. This explosion stopped the submarine dead in the water with his bow about 6 feet from the side of the *BORIE*.[28]

U-405 SUNK

Hutchins, mindful of the possibility of damage to the destroyer's screws with the submarine so close to her stern, went ahead to gain a more favorable position. Fregattenkapitän Hopman, in turn, came left and *U-405* passed under the destroyer's stern; escaping destruction yet again. An ensuing chase lasted several minutes, during which *Borie* fired a torpedo that missed the submarine's bow, before her guns scored a hit on the starboard diesel exhaust. The sub immediately slowed almost to a stop, and crewmen poured up on deck from below. Although they had their hands up in surrender, the men continued to run toward the topside guns, and B*orie* continued to fire, until the word "kamarade" (German for surrender) was yelled.[29]

When the order "cease fire" was given aboard the destroyer, all guns stopped except No. 1, which scored a hit on the conning tower with several men still inside it. When the flash subsided and the smoke cleared, most of the tower was gone. However, despite the loss of her sail, the submarine was still making way and steering evasive courses. Hutchins believed *U-405* communicated with another U-boat nearby, before she ultimately sank or was scuttled by crewmembers abandoning the submarine:

> The submarine fired several white [Very pistol] stars interspersed with green and red. We assumed that the white star indicated that they were attempting to surrender but could possibly be a signal to any submarine which might be in the area. Keeping a sharp lookout for any answering signals, we saw a Very star fired on bearing 220. The distance to that star was indeterminate, but it appeared to [originate] short of the horizon. The submarine's crew then abandoned ship. The submarine was dead in the water, about 15 men went over the side, five of whom, it is estimated, were lowered in yellow inflated rafts. They were obviously injured and had to be strapped to the raft and then lowered. The balance of the ten or twenty men got into the water in their rafts and were very quick in doing so. The submarine submerged stern first, at a very sharp angle, and exploded just under the surface as the last man got off the sub.[30]

When *U-405* slipped beneath the surface, *Borie* was steering a course of 240° true, with the survivors about 50 to 60 yards on her port bow. With the hope of picking them up, she was moving in to rescue when the sound operator picked up the noise of a torpedo coming from 220° true—the same bearing as the flare seen previously. The destroyer then increased speed to flank, came hard left to parallel the course of that torpedo, and unfortunately had to pass through the group of survivors. As the ship cleared the group, the torpedo passed down her port side about thirty yards away. Maneuvering on zigzag courses, with only a single engine still operating, *Borie* cleared the area to avoid any other contact, since the destroyer was not in condition to press any further attack. Hutchins' hope was to draw the submarine with the ship, and by contacting the task group have the other destroyers attack this third U-boat. As *Borie* departed the area, Very stars were seen coming from the group of survivors.[31]

BORIE ABANDONED AND SCUTTLED

The ruined and sinking destroyer was just able to make progress toward a rendezvous with Task Group 21.14. Just before noon the following day, 1 November, she was sighted by the carrier group. Later, following completion of a detailed survey of the damage to *Borie* begun earlier at daylight, Hutchins ordered the ship abandoned:

> We were badly holed all along the port side, fuel tanks contaminated, fresh water gone, the turbines locked, the main

deck was broken across just forward of the forward bulkhead of the forward engine room, she was wallowing heavily and the bulkheads themselves surrounding the flooded engine room showed signs of giving away, the stern was completely underwater and other compartments were flooded. Since the Carrier could not provide escort for the ship back to port, and New York at that time was 2200 miles distant with submarines surrounding the area, with a bad weather front approaching, it was considered absolutely impossible under the circumstances to run the ship back to port under her own power. The only alternative was to lie to and wait for a tug to come from port. In view of the fact that the radio by this time was absolutely inoperative, the chances of a tug locating the ship at sea were considered very small.[32]

Just prior to sunset, Hutchins gave the order to abandon ship and after doing so, the officers and crew were picked up by the *Goff* and *Barry*. Tragically, this evolution resulted in the loss of 24 men and 3 officers due to the prevailing conditions. The water temperature was forty-four degrees Fahrenheit with very cold air, the seas were high and, although the operation was very orderly, when rafts got alongside *Goff*, the pitching and rolling of the ship tossed fatigued men into the frigid North Atlantic. At times, the bilge keel of *Goff* was visible and, at other times, the seas were over her main decks as she rolled. Some of the men who had had no sleep since the previous night, who had fought the action all night, and had then spent the balance of the night and next day in controlling damage, were unable to make it from their rafts up over *Goff*'s violently moving side to her deck.[33]

Borie had begun launching life rafts at 1644, and *Goff*, standing by to provide assistance, began rescue operations at 1705. By 1819, when these efforts ceased, she had taken aboard 104 survivors, including the commanding officer, five other officers, and ninety-eight enlisted men. *Goff* then began a patrol and search of the surrounding area and at 2105, sighted a life raft on her port bow. She came alongside the raft fifteen minutes later and picked up three men. Meanwhile, *Barry*, which had arrived in the area at 1720, located a raft containing four survivors and one deceased crewmember.[34]

Lt. Comdr. Charles H. Hutchins, USNR (who was promoted to this rank following the battle), later described in an interview the pride his crew felt following the triumph of their antiquated World I vintage destroyer over a modern German submarine commissioned in 1941. (*U-405* spanned 220 feet, displaced 871 tons, and could make 17.7 knots on the surface or 7.6 submerged. Able to fight on or below the ocean's surface, she boasted five 21-inch torpedo tubes—four bow, one stern—one 3.46-inch deck gun, and various anti-aircraft guns.):

> The complete pleasure of the crew in having accomplished the sinking was visible all over the ship. When the submarine sank there was a yell that went up from all hands—it probably could be heard in Berlin. The men were clasping each other and patting each other on the back and all during the action there were times when it was actually comical to observe the situation, particularly with the submarine pinned underneath. Bearing in mind that this crew has been together a long time and have received many compliments from many different sources as a crew, and the fact that heretofore their one dream had been to catch a submarine, depth charge him, bring him to the surface and then to sink him with gun fire, this particular action more than justified their hopes.[35]

Photo 17-3

Destroyer USS *Borie* (DD-215) abandoned and sinking on 2 November 1943, following her victory over *U-405* in early morning darkness the previous day. U.S. National Archives Photograph #80-G-85280

Daybreak on 2 November revealed the abandoned *Borie* was stubbornly still afloat. Ordered to sink the derelict ship, *Barry* opened fire at 0905 with her "A battery." Seven minutes later she fired a torpedo prematurely, which missed the destroyer. A second torpedo at 0925 likewise missed, and a third at 0935 passed under the bow of *Borie*, failing to hit. *Barry* ceased fire at 0939, having set *Borie* aflame but not having sunk her. At 0944, a torpedo bomber from *Card* (TBF

#1) dropped four depth charges, one at a time, on the destroyer, which sank eleven minutes later, at position 50°28'N, 30°35'W. *Barry* and *Goff* then took up positions to screen the *Card* as she zigzagged and the task group resumed its patrol.[36]

Task Group 21.14 returned to Norfolk, Virginia, on 9 November. The following morning, a party of "top brass" arrived aboard *Card*, moored starboard side to Pier 5 at the Naval Operating Base. At 0953, Adm. Royal E. Ingersoll, commander-in-chief Atlantic Fleet, accompanied by Vice Adm. Patrick N. L. Bellinger, ComAirLantFlt; Vice Adm. Alexander Sharpe Jr., ComServForLant; Rear Adm. David M. LeBreton, commandant 5th Naval District; Rear Adm. Gerald F. Bogan, ComFltAir Norfolk, Va.; and Rear Adm. Calvin T. Durgin, ComFltAir Quonset, made an official call to present the Presidential Unit Citation to the USS *Card*, USS *Barry*, USS *Borie*, and USS *Goff*. As indicated in the below citation, Composite Squadrons VC-1 and VC-9 were also recipients of this award.[37]

TASK UNIT TWENTY-ONE POINT FOURTEEN
Consisting of the
U.S.S. *CARD*, U.S.S. *BARRY*, U.S.S. *BORIE*, U.S.S. *GOFF*
And VC SQUADRONS ONE AND NINE
for service as set forth in the following

Citation:
For extraordinary performance during anti-submarine operations in mid-Atlantic from July 27 to October 25, 1943. At a time when continual flow of supplies along the United States-North Africa convoy route was essential to the maintenance of our established military supremacy and to the accumulation of reserves, the *CARD*, her embarked aircraft and her escorts pressed home a vigorous offensive which was largely responsible for the complete withdrawal of hostile U-boats from this vital supply area. Later, when submarines returned with deadlier weapons and augmented anti-aircraft defenses, this heroic Task Unit, by striking damaging blows at the onset of renewed campaigns, wrested the initiative from the enemy before actual inception of projected large-scale attacks. Its distinctive fulfillment of difficult and hazardous missions contributed materially to victorious achievements by our land forces.

PERSONAL AWARDS FOR VALOR

Every officer and sailor within the task group was authorized to wear the Presidential Unit Citation ribbon on their uniform blouses. Several men also received medals—the Navy Cross, Distinguished Flying

Cross, or Legion of Merit—for personal heroism. The associated medal citations for the four officers and men of USS *Borie* may be found in Appendix G.

USS *Borie* (DD-215)

Individual	Award	Award Date(s)
Lt. Charles Harris Hutchins, USNR	Navy Cross	1 Nov 43
Lt. Morrison Ropes Brown, USNR	Navy Cross (PH)	1 Nov 43
Machinist's Mate Second Class Irving Randolph Saum Jr., USNR	Navy Cross	1 Nov 43
Lt. Philip Bausche Brown, USNR	Legion of Merit	Jun-15 Nov 43

USS *Barry* (DD-248)

Individual	Award	Award Date(s)
Lt. Comdr. Herbert D. Hill, USN	Legion of Merit	27 Jun-9 Nov 43

USS *Goff* (DD-247)

Individual	Award	Award Date(s)
Lt. Comdr. Hinton Ira Smith, USNR	Legion of Merit	

Composite Squadron Nine (VC-9)

Individual	Award	Award Date(s)
Lt. Comdr. Howard Malcolm Avery, USN	Legion of Merit	24 Sep-10 Nov 43
Lt. (jg) Letson Samuel Balliett, USN	Distinguished Flying Cross	31 Oct 43

Photo 17-4

Officers of Task Group 21.14 hold the Presidential Unit Citation flag during awards ceremonies held aboard USS *Card* on 10 November 1943. From left to right: Lt. Comdr. Herbert D. Hill, commanding officer, USS *Barry*; Lt. Comdr. Howard M. Avery, commanding officer, Squadron VC-9; Lt. Charles H. Hutchins, commanding officer, USS *Borie*; and Lt. Comdr. Hinton Ira Smith, commanding officer, USS *Goff*. U.S. Navy Photograph #80-G-43652, now in the collection of the National Archives

18

Fourth Fleet's "Triple Play"
Against Blockade Runners

Target, having fired on two planes and having refused to obey orders, was definitely enemy.

Exact nature of target was unknown. If blockade runner, armament was probably light. If raider, target might carry guns up to five point nine inches, torpedo tubes, and possibly motor torpedo boats. Target might be radar equipped.

Since both planes fired on had been hit, personnel appeared to be well trained.

Since flare had been dropped target must suspect, or know, that a surface vessel was in the vicinity and therefore the target was probably on alert.

—Report by commanding officer, USS *Somers* (DD-381)
on the pursuit and sinking by gunfire of the
German Blockade Runner MS *Weserland*
on 3 January 1944.[1]

On 1 January 1944, the Fourth Fleet received information that northbound blockade runners, returning to Germany from Japan, would soon be transiting western South Atlantic waters. Intelligence on enemy vessel movement came from many sources. Earlier, a report had been received by a U.S. Military Attaché from a passenger aboard the Swedish ship *Gripsholm*, that three German merchant ships were ready to sail from Saigon on 15 October 1943 with cargos of rubber, bound for Germany. The French were reportedly trying to delay their departure by use of sabotage. This report was passed to the British Admiralty, which assessed it as probably true, and identified candidate vessels: blockade runners *Rio Grande*, *Osorno*, *Weserland*, *Burgenland*, and *Navelland*; tankers *Brake*, *Madrono*, and *Charlotte Schliemann*; and U-boat supply ship *Alsterufer*.[2]

In response to this information, Fourth Fleet established an air blockade barrier intended to deny to enemy ships practically the whole extent of the South Atlantic narrows between Africa and Brazil. Eleven PB4Y-1 Liberator patrol bombers and fifteen crews of VB-107 were assigned to the patrol. Six planes and nine crews operated from Ascension Island, and five planes and six crews from Parnamirim Field at Natal. The bombing squadron was to maintain a barrier patrol approximately 600 miles west of Ascension Island.[3]

A PB4Y-1 Liberator (*107-B-9*) flown by Lt. Mearl G. Taylor, sighted a ship on 1 January at 9°35'S, 23°45'W. The vessel, steering course 060° true at speed 10 knots, was not on the friendly merchant ship plot for the day. Taylor circled the suspect vessel to investigate, and challenged it by blinker. The ship hoisted a four letter call sign, but then hauled it down before it could be read. As the patrol bomber drew closer it was possible to read "Glenbank" on a small nameplate on the bridge. When, after several additional challenges by the plane, the ship failed to hoist either a call sign or authenticator, Taylor fired warning shots across her bow.[4]

Photo 18-1

PB4Y-1 Liberator patrol bomber flies out from the British coast for a Bay of Biscay anti-submarine patrol in November 1943.
U.S. National Archives Photograph #80-G-407692

In response, the ship opened anti-aircraft fire (believed to be from 37mm guns) in continuous bursts. The enemy gunners knocked out the Liberator's No. 3 engine, registered several hits on its fuselage, and inflicted shrapnel wounds on the arms and legs of a member of the plane crew photographing the ship. Taylor jettisoned his nine bombs, notified his home base of damage received, and departed to return to the landing field at Ascension Island. Lt. William Ford was dispatched in *107-B-12* to renew contact. He made contact by radar, reported it to both the surface ship support force, and base, and the destroyer *Somers* (DD-381) was assigned to intercept the target.[5]

The ship that had fired on the plane was obviously an enemy, identity unknown, and the signboard displaying "Glenbank" a ruse. The British freighter *Glenbank* had sailed from Cape Town, South Africa, on 24 December for Montevideo, Uruguay, and was estimated to be in the vicinity of 25° south, 12° west; hundreds of miles away.

Photo 18-2

USS *Somers* (DD-381) at anchor in September 1938.
U.S. Naval History and Heritage Command Photograph #NH 66340

After reaching the location of the enemy in the early hours of 3 January, Comdr. William C. Hughes Jr. determined that the darkness warranted caution. If the enemy was a blockade runner, her armament would probably be light; if a raider, she might carry guns up to 5.9-inches, have torpedo tubes and motor torpedo boats, and possibly radar. Hughes decided to attempt surprise by maneuvering *Somers* so as to place the target "down moon," then close to within effective gun range and open fire. Should the enemy be armed with large caliber guns and return fire, he intended to press home a torpedo attack. If not, he would sink the ship with gunfire. Making 25 knots, the destroyer quickly narrowed the range to 7,000 yards. At 0223, Hughes gave the order to "commence firing," with instruction to use a modified down ladder; first salvo to hit, second up 500 yards, third down 1,000 yards. (The classic "ladder" method involved deliberately opening fire short, thereafter firing salvos as quickly as possible at small increments in range until the target had been crossed, then reversing so as to re-cross the target in the opposite direction.)[8]

Diagram 18-1

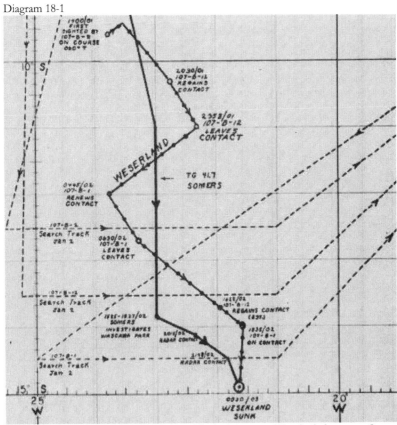

Plot chart of the movement of German blockade runner *Weserland*, destroyer *Somers*, and VB-107 patrol bomber.
Source: Fleet Air Wing 16, War History 2/16/43 to 6/27/45

Survivors from the blockade runner *Weserland* later said that the first gun salvo scored, one round killing four men on the bridge. At that moment the order was given to abandon ship. Meanwhile, the *Somers* closed the range to 6,000 yards and continued firing until fifty flashes from hits and two explosions in the center of the ship had been observed. The order was then given to cease fire, but since no flames were visible, and the enemy ship did not appear to be sinking, firing resumed at 5,000 yards. Every salvo struck, producing what appeared to be five to six explosive flashes. *Weserland* sank at 0300, about 550 miles southwest of Ascension Island, at position 4°55'S, 21°39'W.[9]

Somers set about picking up the survivors, but after one boat of prisoners was recovered, it seemed wisest to move off for a bit, and return after daylight. Beginning at dawn, the destroyer collected seven lifeboats, and one life raft, containing 17 officers and 116 men, which she landed at Recife two days later on 6 January. Personal papers and belongings taken from the survivors established the vessel's identity as the *Weserland*, en route from Japan to Germany. Survivors stated that her cargo had consisted of rubber, tin, and wolfram (tungsten).[10]

Photo 18-3

German prisoners from the MV *Weserland* aboard the destroyer USS *Somers* (DD-381). A History of Patrol Squadron 83 and Bombing Squadron 107, September 15, 1941 to December 31, 1944

OMAHA AND *JOUETT* SINK THE *RIO GRANDE*

The following day, 4 January, Task Group 41.1—consisting of *Omaha* and *Jouett* with Rear Adm. Oliver Read in command—sank a second blockade runner, later determined to be the *Rio Grande*. The group had departed Recife on 2 January on an ocean patrol with the primary mission being support of the barrier sweep between Natal and

Ascension Island. By the 4th, the two ships were operating in the vicinity of 06°11'S, 25°57'W, conducting an air search with *Omaha*'s planes. At 1025, the *Omaha* sighted a ship almost dead ahead on her port bow, about twenty miles distant. At about the same time, the planes sighted the contact; whereupon the *Omaha* directed one to investigate the contact and the other to go on with routine patrol. Thirteen minutes later, *Omaha* and *Jouett* proceeded at 20 knots to intercept the runner.[11]

Photo 18-4

Steamship *Rio Grande* during the 1930s.
U.S. Naval History and Heritage Command Photograph #NH 60528

While the two ships were reducing the range, the vessel started to send a message. Very little of this could be made out, because *Omaha* jammed it on 500 kcs (khz) in accordance with doctrine. Meanwhile, the blockade runner was not displaying her flag of nationality, nor her flag hoist call sign. She offered no identification when challenged. By 1107, with the range to her now about 20,000 yards, it was possible to see smoke aft on the ship. Also, the *Omaha* aircraft reported that explosions had occurred aft and amidships, and that the crew had abandoned ship in lifeboats. The task group opened fire for the purpose of forcing the boats back to the ship, then began firing at the target itself. At 1114, *Omaha* and *Jouett* ceased firing on orders from Read. When it became apparent that the boats had no intention of returning to the ship, they reopened at a range of 7,600 yards and continued until the target sank, from a combination of gunfire and demolition charges set by the crew before abandoning ship.[12]

As *Omaha* and *Jouett* cleared the area at high speed, they passed four lifeboats containing the runner's crew; an estimated fifty men. In one boat there appeared to be officers in white uniforms. The group made no attempt to recover the survivors. The following day, 5 January, the two ships passed through a large oil slick, near the area of the sinking, presumably from the runner. It had a distinct odor of vegetable oil. *Jouett* was ordered to collect various items of cargo still afloat and did so. The most important was crude rubber, in bales of 245 kilograms, with French Indochina markings.[13]

From observations of the ship's characteristics the previous day, it was believed that the sunken ship could be the *Rio Grande*, if she had been northbound, or the *Elsa Essberger*, if southbound. The nature of the cargo found definitely established the runner as the *Rio Grande* northbound from the Orient.[14]

THIRD RUNNER, *BURGENLAND*, SUNK

Task Group 41.1 also accounted for the *Burgenland*, the third of the German runners. On 5 January, a few hours after investigating the floating cargo of the *Rio Grande*, *Omaha* and *Jouett* resumed their primary mission of supporting the barrier sweep and intercepting blockade runners. In early afternoon the ships intercepted a message from plane number 5 of Patrol Squadron 203, addressed to the senior naval aviator, Natal. The message reported that the pilot was investigating a ship (at position 08°38'S, 25°43'W, on course 085°T at 12 knots) believed to be the American freighter *Floridian*.[15]

Read consulted his plot for the day and ascertained that the *Floridian* did not belong in the position reported. This made the contact suspicious, and at high speed *Omaha* and *Jouett* changed course to intercept the ship. A message was sent to plane number 5, instructing the pilot to keep the admiral informed of the ship's speed and direction. At 1626, Read sent a message to commander Fourth Fleet and the senior aviators at Ascension and Natal, requesting them to take immediate steps to keep the ship under vigilance. A short time later, plane number 5 informed Natal that it had reached its limit of endurance, and that it could not remain on the scene.[16]

A relief plane departed from Natal, and *Omaha* and *Jouett* split up to broaden their search, and cover any dramatic course change by the suspect ship. At 1853, *Omaha* gained a radar contact and altered course to investigate. Eight minutes later, the mast of the ship was sighted, and 20 minutes after that, the *Omaha* challenged, receiving no reply. When the range had closed to 22,000 yards, the cruiser fired a shot across the runner's bow. Minutes later, smoke began emitting from amidships, and then the deck house burst into flames. Information held by *Omaha* made the ship's identification as the *Burgenland* possible without delay.[17]

Jouett had arrived to join *Omaha* and the cruiser and destroyer both commenced firing at 1933 and continued to fire for ten minutes, hitting the target heavily. At 1952, an explosion took place on board the runner, as well as explosions from small caliber ammunition. Five minutes later, the *Burgenland* settled rapidly, and within a moment or two, sank at 07°29'S, 25°37'W. Task Group 41.1 did not attempt to rescue the four boatloads of survivors; *Omaha* and *Jouett* instead cleared the area, retiring eastward.[18]

Other ships picked up survivors of the *Rio Grande* and *Burgenland* and put them ashore in installments. The destroyer *Davis* (DD-395) picked up twenty-one of the *Burgenland*'s crew on 7 January, and the next day *Winslow* (DD-359) rescued thirty-five more. Seventy-two men from the *Rio Grande* were recovered by the cruiser *Marblehead* (CL-12), also on 8 January. Twenty-two survivors of the *Rio Grande* reached Fortaleza in a whaleboat on the 11th, and were taken into custody by the 10th Brazilian Military Region Commander. Finally, on 13 January, the Brazilian minelayer *Camocim* (while escorting a Rio-Trinidad convoy) picked up a whaleboat with twenty-five Germans and nine Italians. These were the final survivors recovered from the triple-sinking. All of the prisoners were subsequently taken to the United States for interrogation.[19]

Floating rubber cargo of the sunken ships was too precious to be allowed to drift idly in the South Atlantic. Two fleet tugs—*Carib* (AT-82) and *Seneca* (AT-91)—spent a week collecting the scattered bales, salvaging a quantity of rubber enough to make tires for 5,000 bombers. The rubber floated only two or three inches out of the water, and lay widely scattered, necessitating that it be found and handled bale by bale. The poorest hunting netted twenty-two bales for one ship in a day; the best brought 226 aboard. The crewmen that did this work had to use hooks and tongs, because the rubber was difficult to hook fast (hang onto). The total salvage came to 1,996 bales.[20]

AWARDS FOR VALOR

The commanding officers of the *Omaha* and *Jouett*—Capt. Charles D. Leffler, USN, and Cdr. John C. Parham Jr., USN—were awarded Legion of Merit Medals for their actions on 4-5 January 1944 against the blockade runners in the South Atlantic. Comdr. William C.

Hughes Jr., USN, commanding officer of the *Somers*, received this same award for his actions on 3 January 1944. The associated citation for Commander Parham, which is representative of those of the other two men, follows:

> The President of the United States of America takes pleasure in presenting the Legion of Merit with Combat "V" to Commander John Calhoun Parham, Jr., United States Navy, for exceptionally meritorious conduct in the performance of outstanding services to the Government of the United States as Commanding Officer of the U.S.S. *JOUETT* (DD-396) during action against German blockade runners in the South Atlantic Area. Determined and aggressive in carrying out a vital mission, Commander Parham boldly intercepted a hostile vessel on 4 January and on 5 January 1944, engaging the enemy with devastating fire on both occasions and enabling the *JOUETT* to score accurate hits on the German ships, thereby contributing materially to their destruction. Commander Parham's forceful leadership, his superb ship-handling and fearless devotion to duty were essential factors in the success of the campaign against German blockade runners and raiders in this important area.[21]

19

1944 Brings Victory
in the South Atlantic

With the capture of the blockade runners in January, every reasonable indication existed that the battle of the South Atlantic had been won. From then on, although U-Boats appeared at intervals, the intervals became rarer. Finally, the Allied invasion of Continental Europe, commencing in June, soon wrested from the Nazis the western French ports in which so many of their subs had been based. As 1944 swung into its last quarter, the Mediterranean, France, Belgium, and part of Holland, had been liberated. It thus became almost a certainty that Germany, no matter how long she might postpone her day of collapse, could no longer send submarines to a theater as distant as the South Atlantic.

—United States Naval Administration in World War II, Commander South Atlantic Force, Commander-in-Chief, Atlantic Fleet, Volume XI

Following the conclusion of the Fourth Fleet's "Triple Play," operations in the South Atlantic reverted to routine, unbroken save for occasional intervals. On 9 January 1944, a boarding party from the fleet tug *Carib* (AT-82) took a German stowaway off the Spanish merchant ship *Monte Anniboto* outside Bahia. This man was an alleged internee in Argentina from the *Graf Spee*, sunk off Montevideo by the British late in 1939. The purpose of his removal was interrogation.[1]

U-177 SUNK WEST OF ASCENSION ISLAND
On 6 February, a PB4Y-1 Liberator based at Ascension Island attacked and sank *U-177* at position 10°35'S, 23°12'W. Plane *107-B-3*, piloted by Lt. (jg) Carrell Pinnell, took off that morning to conduct a sweep to include a Commander Fourth Fleet estimate of an enemy submarine plotted in the general area of 10°S, 24°W. The clouds were mostly cumulus with bases at 2,000 feet, and visibility was good.[2]

The Liberator was flying west at 2,500 feet, making a speed of 145 knots when the bow lookout reported a contact twelve miles away, off the aircraft's starboard quarter. Pinnell immediately turned toward the contact and all hands manned battle stations. Drawing closer, it was seen the contact was a submarine creating a heavy wake in a moderate sea. The U-boat was steering a southerly course making approximately 10 knots. Pinnell described taking fire during his attack run:

> When plane was approximately two miles from sub a moderate amount of heavy anti-aircraft fire was noticed approximately 100 yards in front and slightly to port. Still having two miles to close target and believing that the AA fire would become more concentrated, put the plane into a power glide for a few seconds then pulled up for a short space. Then being at 1000' and having a range of about 3/4 of a mile went into attack run. During this maneuver the bow gun was brought to bear upon the C/T and no further AA fire was observed near the plane.[3]

The plane dropped six bombs from an altitude of 100 feet, just forward of conning tower. There were no sightings of anyone on deck and the submarine gave no indication of even attempting to crash dive. Just before passing over the U-boat, there were gun flashes (probably machine guns) from a position near the conning tower. The aircraft was at full power with an indicated air speed of 210 knots. Immediately after passing over the enemy, the tail gunner commenced firing, expending 400 rounds of .50-caliber ammunition.[4]

After climbing to 800 feet and making a sharp bank to port to observe the results, Pinnell noted that the submarine had completely disappeared from the surface, but a large disturbance and her conning tower were still visible a few feet under the water. She appeared to be turning to starboard. Pinnell immediately pressed home a second attack by dropping his remaining three depth bombs well ahead of the estimated position of the conning tower.[5]

Coming back over the scene of the attack, after initially leveling off, before regaining attitude, and then making a slow turn to the left, Pinnell observed survivors in the water, and ordered rafts dropped:

> Notified plane captain to stand by with auxiliary life raft, which was dropped to survivors on second low sweep over survivors. After survivors had manned life raft made several low sweeps in order to obtain photographs of survivors. Then climbed to 1000' and circled scene of attack until relief plane arrived, at which time returned to base. Excellent performance by all crew members.[6]

AWARDS FOR VALOR

The pilot and co-pilot of the patrol bomber received the Distinguished Flying Cross for their actions leading to the destruction of *U-177*, and the other members of the plane crew, Air Medals.

PB4Y-1 Liberator *107-B-3* Plane Crew
(action on 6 February 1944)

Name	Position	Awards
Lt. (jg) Carrell Ivan Pinnell, USN	Pilot	DFC
Ens. John Michael Leonard Jr., USNR	Co-pilot	DFC(2nd)
Ens. Jean Douglas Cook, USNR	3rd Pilot	AM
Ens. Robert R. Swanson, USNR	Navigator	AM
AMM1/c Stanley Smith Shedaker, USN	Plane Capt/Photographer	AM (3rd)
AMM3/c Harry Laverne Anderson, USNR	Camera/Bow Gun	AM
ARM3/c Richard Leo McKernan, USNR	Radio	AM
AOM3/c Wayne Henry Phelps, USN	Tail Turret	AM
ARM2/c William Randolph Zudrell, USN	Crown Turret	AM

SURVIVORS RECOVERED AND INTERROGATED

On 8 February, the cruiser *Omaha* picked up fourteen survivors in the rubber raft dropped by the aircraft—two officers, two petty officers and ten seamen. The men had been adrift for fifty-four hours. All were suffering from sunburn, and immersion foot (the latter ailment caused by prolonged exposure to damp, unsanitary, and cold conditions) and several men from slight bruises and cuts, as well. Most of the prisoners had no clothing, except for short drawers or bathing trunks, indicating that they may have been sun bathing or swimming when the attack on the submarine occurred. The cruiser landed the survivors in Recife. Following a preliminary interrogation, thirteen were transferred to an interrogation center in the United States.[7]

INFORMATION GLEANED ABOUT *U-177*

The second officer, Leutnant Hans-Otto Brodt, volunteered that the submarine (a 1,200 tonner) had sunk immediately after the first depth charge attack and that the captain (Korvettenkapitän Heinz Buchholz) went down with the ship. He stated that there were no other survivors except those picked up by the *Omaha*. Of the complement of sixty-five carried on *U-177*'s final patrol, the great majority of the men had been trapped in the rapidly sinking submarine. Approximately twenty escaped the boat, but six of these, including Buchholz, were killed on deck or in the water by subsequent strafing and bombing.[8]

Of the information learned from surviving crewmen, that related to a small motorless scout helicopter (employed by *U-177* and certain other 1,200-ton submarines) was particularly interesting.

Photo 19-1

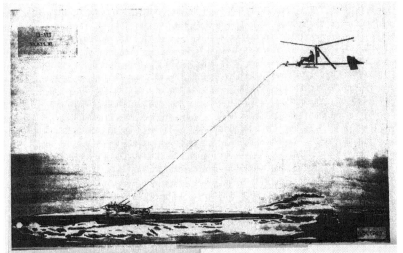

German submarine *U-177* towing a motorless-helicopter for scouting purposes.
Office of the Chief of Naval Operations, Report on the Interrogation of Survivors from *U-177* Sunk 6 February 1944

The Focke-Achgelis Fa330 Autogyro Kite—which was code named Bachstelze (Sandpiper)—was used for the purpose of observation at a considerable height. When not in use, the helicopter was disassembled and its parts stored in pressure-proof containers built into the conning tower. The fuselage was stored in the portside container, and propeller and tail assembly in the starboard container. A third container housed a winch to which was attached a 300-meter cable for towing the helicopter in the air. When the commanding officer ordered an ascent for scouting, the Bachstelze was assembled on deck.[9]

The pilot had a transceiver built into his aviator's helmet, by which he could communicate with the U-boat and dictate the altitude of his flight by giving orders for the release or retraction of the cable attached to the winch. Also, he could announce immediately the sighting of a ship or any other object he might observe, aided by binoculars if necessary. In a cold climate, the pilot wore a leather suit lined with sheepskin and sheepskin boots, and in the tropics, overalls or dark blue fatigues. For safely purposes, shoulder straps and girdle were utilized at all times.[10]

ADMIRAL INGRAM DECORATED

"All of you share this honor," said the Admiral [Jonas Ingram] to those about him as he received the [Distinguished Service] medal. He went on to state that the award was the result of the combined efforts of all the personnel of the Fleet.

—United States Naval Administration in World War II, Commander South Atlantic Force, Commander-in-Chief, Atlantic Fleet, Volume XI

In April 1943, Vice Admiral Ingram received from Secretary William F. Knox the Distinguished Service Medal for his contributions to the Allied cause. Presentation of the medal took place on 27 April, at a staff conference, with Commodore Clinton E. Braine, Fourth Fleet chief of staff, acting as the representative of the Commander-in-Chief, U. S. Atlantic Fleet, and making the bestowal.[11]

Photo 19-2

Vice Adm. Jonas H. Ingram, USN, commander Fourth Fleet.

The award made Ingram the holder of the three highest Navy decorations, having already received the Congressional Medal of Honor, for conspicuous action at Vera Cruz in 1914, and the Navy Cross for distinguished service on the staff of commander Battleship Division Nine, U. S. Atlantic Fleet, which operated with the British Grand Fleet in World War I as the 6th Battle Squadron. During his service in South America, Ingram also acquired two high Brazilian decorations; those of Grand Commander of the Southern Cross, and the Ordem do Merito Naval.[12]

TOUGHEST SUB KILL (*U-860*) BY FOURTH FLEET

Although Admiral Ingram had been rightfully feted for the work of his Fourth Fleet, its contributions to the war effort was not done. Only a month earlier, the escort carrier *Solomons* (CVE-67) had entered the area and come under the temporary operational control of Ingram. On 15 June 1944, she and her embarked aircraft encountered probably the most challenging U-boat the Fourth Fleet had dealt with to date.[13]

Photo 19-3

Escort carrier *Solomons* (CVE-67) leaving San Diego Harbor, on 31 December 1943. U.S. Naval History and Heritage Command Photograph #NH 106570

On that day, she was patrolling well to the east, and somewhat below St. Helena Island, with her embarked Avenger torpedo bombers and Wildcat fighters of Composite Squadron VC-9. Four destroyer escorts formed an anti-submarine screen around her—*Gustafson* (DE-182), *Herzog* (DE-178), *Straub* (DE-181) and *Trumpeter* (DE-180). Captain Marion Edward Crist, commanding officer of the *Solomons*, was Commander Task Group 41.6.[14]

At 0951 that morning, Ens. George E. Edwards Jr., piloting an Avenger on a regular anti-submarine patrol (along with three other torpedo bombers) reported a contact, bearing 070°T, fifty miles from the *Solomons*. There was no further communication from him. Four planes (two Avengers and two Wildcats) were launched from the carrier at 1002 to search for Edwards, and the *Straub* and *Herzog* were ordered to proceed to the position of the contact and conduct a square search. Survivors from *U-860* subsequently stated that Edwards had attacked and made four runs in the face of concentrated anti-aircraft fire. On the last run his plane was hit and crashed into the sea.[15]

Lt. Comdr. Howard M. Avery had launched from the carrier in an Avenger to conduct a normal square gambit over the reported contact and to look for Edwards and the U-boat. Shortly before sunset, at 1652, while flying at 1,500 feet, he sighted what appeared to be a wake, 10 to 12 miles distant. Two minutes later, he ascertained the wake was from a surfaced submarine about fifty miles from the position given by Edwards. As Avery approached, the U-boat instead of submerging began to maneuver, turning in circles of about 1,000 feet in diameter, to keep the aircraft on her stern. From the sub came intensive anti-aircraft fire at the plane, whose pilot circled while awaiting assistance.[16]

Ensigns Thomas J. Wadsworth, Richard E. McMahon (piloting Wildcats), and Moncrieff J. Spear (an Avenger), having found nothing of interest at the position of the contact reported by Edwards, had returned to the carrier and were preparing to land when they were vectored to the scene of the new contact. (*Straub* and *Herzog* were also ordered to proceed to the scene.) The planes arrived over *U-860* at 1743. A subsequent attack on the sub was delivered in three phases, beginning at 1746 (eight minutes after sunset) and ending at 1753.[17]

PHASE I OF THE ATTACK

Avery took charge, ordering Wadsworth and McMahon to commence strafing attacks on the starboard and port quarters respectively, while he and Spear coordinated a rocket attack. Wadsworth made his attack from the starboard quarter of the submarine, as directed (expending 400 rounds of ammunition) and pulled out at less than 100 feet over the conning tower, amid many bursts of anti-aircraft fire. McMahon, meanwhile, had commenced his strafing run in a steep dive from 3,000 feet, due to the submarine's incessant maneuvering. He peppered her deck and conning tower with 200 rounds, than pulled out to clear the target for the first rocket attack.[18]

Spear came in next, on *U-860*'s starboard beam and, on reaching 800 yards slant range, he launched eight rockets in pairs. Six of these hit a lethal area forward of the conning tower, the other two missed. After firing the last rocket, he pulled to the left and gave his gunner a chance to strafe. Almost at the same time, Avery made his attack from the port beam, and planted six projectiles in a lethal area twenty feet ahead of the conning tower.[19]

These actions constituted the first phase of the attack. All four planes had made their runs over the enemy within ten seconds. The sub was now steering a southerly course, slowing speed, trailing oil, and smoking around the conning tower—but still directing anti-aircraft fire in bursts toward the planes.[20]

Ensign Wadsworth was ordered back to the carrier, having suffered a damaged wing tank he could not jettison, but Lieutenants (jg) William F. Chamberlain and Donald E. Weigle (both flying Avengers) had meanwhile taken off from the *Solomons* and arrived almost simultaneously on the scene at 1721.[21]

PHASE II

Phase two began with McMahon making another strafing run, during which he expended the rest of his ammunition, followed by a rocket attack by Weigle. The latter fired eight more, six of which hit the area in front of the conning tower. At the conclusion of these attacks, the sub continued on course 180°T, but with speed now reduced to three knots and large quantities of greenish-yellow oil trailing her.[22]

FINAL PHASE

To commence phase three, Chamberlain came in on a depth charge run from the port quarter. He paid no heed to a burst of AA fire, and released two charges at an altitude of less than fifty feet, directly over the conning tower. The resultant violent explosion engulfed his plane, and started a fire in the bomb bay and center cockpit. He was able to maintain control just long enough to make a 180-degree turn and land in the water about 500 yards ahead of the submarine. He, as well as his gunner and radio man, could not be rescued.[23]

Avery had gone in just ahead of the depth charge run to strafe, after which he pulled up into a climbing turn to the right, enabling his gunner to get several bursts on the conning tower. Before the three remaining planes could get into position to launch another attack, *U-860* went down at 25°27'S, 05°30'W; leaving thirty to forty survivors struggling in the water.[24]

At 2300, the *Straub* reported having picked up twenty-one of these men, including the commanding officer Fregattenkapitän Paul Büchel, the second officer Otto Carls, and one deceased sailor. The prisoners were transferred to the escort carrier *Solomons* the following morning.[25]

AIR CREW LOSSES AND AWARDS FOR VALOR

The destruction of *U-860* on 15 June 1943 cost Squadron VC-9 dearly; two TBF-1c Avenger torpedo bombers and, more importantly, the six men comprising their flight crews were all lost.

TBF-1c Avenger Torpedo bomber *T-12*		
Name	**Position**	**Award/Status**
Ens. George E. Edwards Jr., USNR	Pilot	DFC (PH)/KIA
ARM2c Albert Donald Pacyna, USNR	Radioman	KIA
AMM2c Frank Kuczinski Jr., USN	Gunner	KIA
TBF-1c Avenger Torpedo bomber *T-32*		
Lt. (jg) William Francis Chamberlain, USNR	Pilot	DFC (PH)/KIA
ARM1c James Hurston Finch, USNR	Radioman	KIA
AMM2c Richard George Hennick, USNR	Gunner	KIA
TBF-1c Avenger Torpedo bomber *T-33*		
Lt. Comdr. Howard Malcolm Avery, USN	Pilot	Navy Cross
ARM2c W. J. Gorski	Radioman	
AMM1c C. D. Falwell	Gunner	
TBF-1c Avenger Torpedo bomber *T-11*		
Ens. Moncrieff J. Spear, USNR	Pilot	DFC
ARM3c Joseph Stark	Radioman	
AOM3c J. M. Chirdon	Gunner	
TBF-1d Avenger Torpedo bomber *T-1*		
Lt. (jg) Donald E. Weigle, USNR	Pilot	DFC
ARM2c J. H. Sullivan	Radioman	
AOM3c C. F. McPherson	Gunner	
FM2 Wildcat Fighter *F-17*		
Ens. Thomas J. Waldsworth, USNR	Pilot	DFC
FM2 Wildcat Fighter *F-23*		
Ens. Richard E. McMahon, USNR	Pilot	DFC[26]

VISIT BY THE FORMER HEAVYWEIGHT CHAMPION

Shortly after these losses, the Fourth Fleet got a morale boost when Comdr. Gene Tunney visited the South Atlantic area in the latter part of June. Tunney, who was the world's heavyweight boxing champion from 1926 to 1928, came to the Fourth Fleet Area to inspect the physical training program and facilities.   As the director of physical training for the entire Navy, his role was to help ensure the men of the Fleet were in shape for arduous duties they might be called upon to perform in the future.[27]

Photo 19-4

Earlier photo of then Lt. Comdr. Gene Tunney, Lt. Comdr. John Tuthill, and Joe Louis. Louis, who would rein as World Heavyweight Boxing Champion from 1937 to 1949, had just passed his army physical, in preparation for service in the U.S. Army. U.S. Naval History and Heritage Command Photograph #NH 120072

Tunney arrived at Recife just in time for a boxing "smoker." He refereed some of the bouts and made a speech to the assembled spectators, the theme being, "keep fit and, above all, learn to swim." Commander Tunney, accompanied by Lieutenant Commander McCoy, the Fleet Athletic Officer, recommended that more athletic specialists be assigned to the area to assist in the sports program.[28]

ENEMY SUBMARINE ATTACKS CONTINUE

In July 1944, the action continued to be light, yet there was enough to show that Germany's submarine campaign in the area had not ended. U-boats continued at intervals to sink or damage vessels. The *U-861* sank the Brazilian troop transport *Vital de Oliveira* on 20 July about twenty-five miles south of São Tomé lighthouse. Her sole escort, the sub-chaser *Javarí* (CS 51), had been missed by a torpedo and initially searched for the attacker, but then rescued the ship's captain and sixty-nine other survivors together with the fishing vessel *Guanabara*.[29]

Evidence of another sinking came on 24 July, when a plane of Patrol Squadron VP-203 sighted three lifeboats with survivors. The seaplane tender *Matagorda* (AVP-22) was dispatched to the scene and the next day took on board the entire crew of the Liberty ship *William Gaston*. The ship had been sunk in early morning darkness about 150 miles southeast of Florianopolis, Brazil, by two torpedoes fired by *U-861*. The eight officers, 33 crewmen and 26 armed guards abandoned ship in four lifeboats and one raft, but one boat broke up on launching. The *Matagorda* delivered the survivors to Florianopolis that same day.[30]

TURNOVER OF DESTROYERS TO BRAZILIAN NAVY

I say 'epochal' because 15 days ago two U. S. DEs [destroyer escorts] were turned over to and manned by the Brazilian Navy. These same ships steamed out of here four days later and today are in active operation with the South Atlantic Forces. Today we turn over the Reybold and the McAnn. This makes a homogeneous division of ships that will act as a Brazilian Convoy Escort to carry the big Allied convoys from a Northern point to the deep South Atlantic. It will be the first time that a unified combat escort unit will enter the great naval base . . . . under the Brazilian flag and under the command of an officer of the Brazilian Navy . . . .

The final test is the ability of you officers and men of the Brazilian Navy to carry on and operate these ships in an efficient manner. I have the utmost faith in your ability to do so. It is you who are going to set the standards for the operations of the new and modern Brazilian Navy. Make them high . . . .

My friends, speaking for and in the name of President Roosevelt, I officially turn over to the Brazilian government the Reybold and McAnn.

—Speech by Vice Adm. Jonas H. Ingram, commander Fourth Fleet, in which he referred to the turnover of two destroyers as an unparalleled ceremony in the relations between the navies of Brazil and the United States.[31]

On 1 August 1944, the Brazilian Navy received two destroyer escorts from the Fourth Fleet. The *Pennewill* (DE-175) and the *Herzog* (DE-178) became the Brazilian ships *Bertioga* and *Beberibe*. The transfer was the occasion for a presentation ceremony at Natal, attended by U.S. and Brazilian officials. Admiral Ingram made a speech presenting the ships and Rear Adm. Aria Parreiras, director of the Natal Naval Base, accepted them on behalf of his government.[32]

As the ceremony began, both ships were moored on opposite sides of a pier, with the stars and stripes still flying and an honor guard aboard. Each commanding officer read the orders decommissioning his ship, and the American flags came down. The two admirals made their speeches of presentation and reception, before the Brazilian Flag Secretary read orders to commission the ships in his country's navy. The Fourth Fleet Band then broke into the Brazilian Navy March and the new crews marched aboard the *Bertioga* and *Beberibe*.[33]

Much the same ceremony occurred two weeks later on 15 August when the destroyer escorts *McAnn* (DE-179) and *Reybold* (DE-177) became the *Bauru* and *Bracui*. As before, the principal speakers were Ingram and Parreiras.[34]

FINAL SUBMARINE KILL IN THE SOUTH ATLANTIC

The last occurrence of the destruction of a German submarine came on 29 September. At 0702 on that date, a Liberator of Squadron VB-107 piloted by Lt. John T. Burton, sighted, attacked and seriously damaged the *U-863* east-southeast of Recife. He then "homed" a second aircraft to the scene piloted by Lt. Edward A. Krug Jr. The two Liberators subsequently made three coordinated attacks, in the face of heavy anti-aircraft fire. At 0722, twenty minutes after the first contact, they destroyed the submarine (Kapitänleutnant Dietrich von der Esch); Krug's plane made the kill at position 10°45'S, 25°30'W.[35]

Life rafts were dropped to the many survivors in the water, and at 0748, both planes departed for base, having reached their prudent limit of endurance.[36]

Coastal navigation lights were turned on that night, 29 September 1944, in Brazil to increase safety of shipping. The coastline had been darkened previously to help prevent the illumination of ships in transit and thereby inadvertently aid submarines in attacking them.[37]

AWARDS FOR VALOR

The pilots of the two bombers received the Distinguished Flying Cross and their crews, Air Medals.

Plane Crews of Liberators *107-B-7* and *107-B-9*
(for action on 28 September 1944)

Name	Award
Lt. John Thomas Burton, USNR (pilot of *107-B-9*)	DFC
Lt. Edward Arthur Krug Jr., USNR (pilot of *107-B-7*)	DFC
Lt. (jg) Morton Marcus Deutsch, USNR	Air Medal
Ens. Pete William Gallagher, USNR	Air Medal
Ens. George Henry Helfenbein, USNR	Air Medal
Lt. (jg) Robert Amory Riley, USNR	Air Medal
ARM2/c Murray Irving Jorgenson, USN	Air Medal (2nd)
ARM2/c Charles William Hilgeman, USNR	Air Medal
AMM2/c Douglas Melvin Laux, USNR	Air Medal
Sea1/c Guy Benito Mangano, USNR	Air Medal
AOM2/c William Howard Mosher, USNR	Air Medal
AMM2/c Edmond Albert Nicpon, USNR	Air Medal
AMM3/c Luther Adam Palmer Jr., USN	Air Medal
ARM3/c Calvin Arthur Pollard, USN	Air Medal
AMM3/c Floyd Edward Resner, USN	Air Medal
AMM1/c Charles Walter Richards, USN	Air Medal
AOM3/c Clark Barnaby Taylor, USNR	Air Medal
ARM3/c Arnold Howell Verity, USNR	Air Medal

Waning Months of the War

The South Atlantic campaign helped win the war. The men who waged it, living and dead, are satisfied with that statement. They do not ask that any more be said.

—United States Naval Administration in World War II, Commander South Atlantic Force, Commander-in-Chief, Atlantic Fleet, Volume XI

CHANGE OF FOURTH FLEET LEADERSHIP

On 11 November 1944, Vice Adm. Jonas H. Ingram was relieved by Rear Adm. William R. Munroe as commander Fourth Fleet. Ingram became commander-in-chief Atlantic Fleet with the rank of Admiral. Munroe was similarly promoted to Vice Admiral, reflecting his new status as the commander of a numbered fleet.[1]

FLEET SHIPS ORDERED TO PACIFIC, OR TO OTHER DUTIES, OR TRANSFERRED TO BRAZILIAN NAVY

By this point, Allied forces had control of the Mediterranean Sea, and had liberated France, Belgium and part of Holland. It thus became almost a certainty that Germany, no matter how long she might postpone her ultimate defeat, could no longer send submarines to a theater as distant as the South Atlantic. As a result, on 22 November all escort vessels except four DEs were ordered detached from Fourth Fleet to return to the United States for further assignment to the Pacific.[2]

Less than three weeks later, as a result of the greatly diminished submarine threat, the JT-TJ convoy system (Rio to Trinidad, and return Trinidad to Rio) was placed on a five-day cycle to speed shipping. These convoys were suspended on 9 March 1945, and never sailed again.[3]

The last sinking of a merchant ship by a submarine in the South Atlantic occurred a day later. On 10 March, the unescorted British *Baron Jedburgh* was torpedoed and sunk by *U-532* northeast of Bahia in the area 09°S, 24°W. One gunner was lost. The master, Eric

Alexander Brown, fifty-two crew members and five gunners were rescued. Brown and thirty-two survivors landed at Cabedello, Brazil, on 22 March. The remaining twenty-five survivors were picked up on 16 March by the British merchantman *Sandown Castle* and landed at Montevideo ten days later. The German submarine, commanded by Fregattenkapitän Ottoheinrich Junker, surrendered on 13 May 1945 at Loch Eriboll, Scotland.[4]

Photo 20-1

Vice Adm. William R. Munroe, USN
U.S. National Archives Photograph #80-G-49323

Between mid-December 1944 and V-E (Victory in Europe) on 8 May 1945, the transfer of ships by the Fourth Fleet, along with aircraft squadrons continued. The First Brazilian Catalina Air Group, Rio, became operational on 12 December, with planes of the former U.S. Patrol Squadron VP-94. A week later, Admiral Munroe presented two more destroyer escorts to Brazil at Natal; *Cannon* (DE-99) and *Christopher* (DE-100), which were re-christened *Baependi* and *Benevente*. In late winter, Brazil received the last two American DEs to be transferred to its navy; *Alger* (DE-101) on 10 March and the *Marts* (DE-174) on 21 March 1945.[5]

FOURTH FLEET DOWNGRADED TO A TASK FORCE

On 15 April 1945, the U.S. Fourth Fleet was redesignated Task Force 27 of the Atlantic Fleet; Admiral Munroe retained his concurrent title, commander South Atlantic Force. That same day, the fleet oiler *Patoka* (AO-9) detached from his force, and reported to commander Service Force Atlantic. This trend continued on 20 April when the fleet tug *Seneca* (ATF-91) detached after long service in the South Atlantic Force in salvage and training.[6]

A similar process of downsizing naval aviation assets was also in progress. Patrol squadron VP-45 was withdrawn from Belém on 15 April; Bombing Squadron VPB-125 detached on 24 April; and the Igarape Assu airfield was transferred on 30 April 1945 to U.S. Army Forces South Atlantic.[7]

TRANSFER OF TASK FORCE UNITS CONTINUE

Patrol Bombing Squadrons VPB-48, VPB-125, VPB-126, VPB-211 and VPB-203 were ordered decommissioned on 19 May 1945. Ten days later, the South Atlantic was officially designated a non-combat area. On 30 May, the *Cincinnati* (CL-6) detached from the South Atlantic Force. The cruiser was followed on 11 June by the yard minesweepers *YMS-44*, *45*, *60* and *76*, which reported to CTG 29; and on 18 June by the salvage ship *Chain* (ARS-20) to commander Service Force Atlantic. Fleet Air Wing Sixteen was decommissioned on 27 June 1945.[8]

LEST WE FORGET

Traditional Navy Hymn

Eternal Father, strong to save,
Whose arm hath bound the restless wave,
Who bidd'st the mighty ocean deep
Its own appointed limits keep;
Oh, hear us when we cry to Thee,
For those in peril on the sea!

O Christ! Whose voice the waters heard
And hushed their raging at Thy word,
Who walkedst on the foaming deep,
And calm amidst its rage didst sleep;
Oh, hear us when we cry to Thee,
For those in peril on the sea!

Most Holy Spirit! Who didst brood
Upon the chaos dark and rude,
And bid its angry tumult cease,
And give, for wild confusion, peace;
Oh, hear us when we cry to Thee,
For those in peril on the sea!

O Trinity of love and power!
Our brethren shield in danger's hour;
From rock and tempest, fire and foe,
Protect them wheresoe'er they go;
Thus evermore shall rise to Thee
Glad hymns of praise from land and sea.

The original words of the "Navy Hymn" were written as a poem, titled *Eternal Father, Strong to Save*, in 1860 by William Whiting of Winchester, England, for a student who was about to sail for the United States.

Appendix A: Medal Citations for USS *Eberle* Crewmembers

LIEUTENANT FREDERICK L. EDWARDS JR.

The President of the United States of America takes pleasure in presenting the Navy Cross to Lieutenant Frederick L. Edwards, Jr., United States Naval Reserve, for extraordinary heroism and distinguished service in the line of his profession as Boarding Officer on board the Destroyer U.S.S. *EBERLE* (DD-430), when an enemy blockade runner was intercepted and destroyed on 10 March 1943, in the South Atlantic Ocean. When the *EBERLE* was ordered to put a boarding party on the hostile ship, Lieutenant Edwards courageously led his party to the runner and was the first to board her. In the face of grave danger from the rapidly spreading fires and explosion of demolition charges, he made an energetic and determined effort to salvage the ship and to obtain information of the enemy. Only after several explosions had rocked the vessel and she began to sink did he dive over the stern into the sea, from which he was later rescued. His conduct throughout was in keeping with the highest traditions of the Navy of the United States.

SEAMAN FIRST ALEXANDER JOSEPH BISHEIMER

The President of the United States of America takes pleasure in presenting the Navy Cross to Seaman First Class Alexander Joseph Bisheimer, United States Navy, for extraordinary heroism and devotion to duty while serving on board the Destroyer U.S.S. *EBERLE* (DD-430), in action against the enemy in the Atlantic Ocean, on 10 March 1943. When an enemy blockade runner was intercepted, Seaman First Class Bisheimer, as a member of a boarding party from the U.S.S. *EBERLE*, assisted in an effort to salvage her and obtain information regarding the enemy. He remained on board the Blockade Runner until several explosions rocked her and forced him to dive overboard into the water from whence he was recovered. The bravery, intrepidity and heroism displayed by Seaman First Class Bisheimer in the action described reflected great credit upon himself and upheld the highest traditions of the United States Naval Service.

SIGNALMAN THIRD WILLIAM JOSEPH PATTISON

The President of the United States of America takes pride in presenting the Navy Cross (Posthumously) to Signalman Third Class William Joseph Pattison, United States Navy, for extraordinary heroism and devotion to duty while serving on board the Destroyer U.S.S. *EBERLE* (DD-430), in action against the enemy in the Atlantic Ocean, on 10 March 1943. When a hostile blockade runner was intercepted and attacked, Signalman Third Class

Pattison, as a member of a boarding party attempting to salvage the vessel, was the second man to reach her deck. Despite grave danger from threatening flames and the powerful explosions of demolition charges, he courageously assisted in conducting a determined effort to execute salvage operations, and by his skillful use of semaphore flags kept his own ship accurately informed of the situation, remaining at his post until the runner began to sink. His conduct throughout was in keeping with the highest traditions of the Navy of the United States.

FIREMAN FIRST DENNIS JOSEPH BUCKLEY JR.

The President of the United States of America takes pride in presenting the Silver Star (Posthumously) to Fireman First Class Dennis Joseph Buckley, Jr., United States Navy, for conspicuous gallantry and intrepidity in action as a member of the boarding party from the U.S.S. *EBERLE* (DD-430), on 10 March 1943, when he endeavored to board an intercepted Blockade Runner in the face of grave danger from fire and the explosions of demolition charges. In this action he lost his life when an explosion occurred as he was preparing to climb the ladder leading to the deck of the Blockade Runner. The bravery and intrepidity displayed by Fireman First Class Buckley in the action described were in keeping with the highest traditions of the United States Naval Service.

SEAMAN SECOND WILBURN GAYLORD DAVIS

The President of the United States of America takes pride in presenting the Silver Star (Posthumously) to Seaman Second Class Wilbur Gaylord Davis, United States Navy, for conspicuous gallantry and intrepidity in action as a member of the boarding party from the U.S.S. *EBERLE* (DD-430), on 10 March 1943, when he endeavored to board an intercepted Blockade Runner in the face of grave danger from fire and the explosions of demolition charges. In this action he lost his life when an explosion occurred as he was preparing to climb the ladder leading to the deck of the Blockade Runner. The bravery and intrepidity displayed by Seaman Second Class Davis in the action described were in keeping with the highest traditions of the United States Naval Service.

WATERTENDER SECOND ALEX M. DIACHENKO

The President of the United States of America takes pride in presenting the Silver Star (Posthumously) to Watertender Second Class Alex M. Diachenko, United States Navy, for conspicuous gallantry and intrepidity in action as a member of the boarding party from the U.S.S. *EBERLE* (DD-430), on 10 March 1943, when he endeavored to board an intercepted Blockade Runner in the face of grave danger from fire and the explosions of demolition charges. In this action he lost his life when an explosion occurred as he was preparing to climb the ladder leading to the deck of the Blockade Runner. The bravery and intrepidity displayed by Watertender Second Class

Diachenko in the action described were in keeping with the highest traditions of the the United States Naval Service.

FIREMAN FIRST WILLIAM J. JONES

The President of the United States of America takes pride in presenting the Silver Star (Posthumously) to Fireman First Class William J. Jones, United States Navy, for conspicuous gallantry and intrepidity in action as a member of the boarding party from the U.S.S. *EBERLE* (DD-430), on 10 March 1943, when he endeavored to board an intercepted Blockade Runner in the face of grave danger from fire and the explosions of demolition charges. In this action he lost his life when an explosion occurred as he was preparing to climb the ladder leading to the deck of the Blockade Runner. The bravery and intrepidity displayed by Fireman First Class Jones in the action described were in keeping with the highest traditions of the United States Naval Service.

COXSWAIN JOSEPH E. H. METIVIER

The President of the United States of America takes pride in presenting the Silver Star (Posthumously) to Coxswain Joseph E. H. Metivier, United States Navy, for conspicuous gallantry and intrepidity in action as a member of the boarding party from the U.S.S. *EBERLE* (DD-430), on 10 March 1943, when he endeavored to board an intercepted Blockade Runner in the face of grave danger from fire and the explosions of demolition charges. In this action he lost his life when an explosion occurred as he was preparing to climb the ladder leading to the deck of the Blockade Runner. The bravery and intrepidity displayed by Coxswain Metivier in the action described were in keeping with the highest traditions of the United States Naval Service.

MOTOR MACHINIST'S MATE MERTON B. MYERS

The President of the United States of America takes pride in presenting the Silver Star (Posthumously) to Motor Machinist's Mate First Class Merton Bernell Myers, United States Navy, for conspicuous gallantry and intrepidity in action as a member of the boarding party from the U.S.S. *EBERLE* (DD-430), on 10 March 1943, when he endeavored to board an intercepted Blockade Runner in the face of grave danger from fire and the explosions of demolition charges. In this action he lost his life when an explosion occurred as he was preparing to climb the ladder leading to the deck of the Blockade Runner. The bravery and intrepidity displayed by Motor Machinist's Mate First Class Myers in the action described were in keeping with the highest traditions of the United States Naval Service.

CARPENTER'S FIRST ROBERT M. SHOCKLEY

The President of the United States of America takes pride in presenting the Silver Star (Posthumously) to Carpenter's Mate First Class Robert Merrill Shockley, United States Navy, for gallantry in action while boarding an enemy blockade runner on 10 March 1943 when it was intercepted by the U.S.S. *EBERLE* (DD-430). Carpenter's Mate First Class Shockley disregarded fires and explosions of demolition charges. As he started aboard, an explosion blew him into the sea.

SEAMAN SECOND CARL WELBY TINSMAN

The President of the United States of America takes pride in presenting the Silver Star (Posthumously) to Seaman Second Class Carl Welby Tinsman, United States Navy, for conspicuous gallantry and intrepidity in action as a member of the boarding party from the U.S.S. *EBERLE* (DD-430), on 10 March 1943, when he endeavored to board an intercepted Blockade Runner in the face of grave danger from fire and the explosions of demolition charges. In this action he lost his life when an explosion occurred as he was preparing to climb the ladder leading to the deck of the Blockade Runner. The bravery and intrepidity displayed by Seaman Second Class Tinsman in the action described were in keeping with the highest traditions of the United States Naval Service.

Appendix B: HMNZS *Achilles*, HMS *Ajax*, and HMS *Exeter*'s Casualties

Light Cruiser *Achilles*
GRANT, Ian, Ordinary Seaman, 1734 (NZD), killed
MILBURN, Neville, Ordinary Telegraphist, D/SSX 23288, killed
SHAW, Archibald, Able Seaman, 1030 (NZD), killed
STENNETT, Frank, Telegraphist, D/JX 148899, killed

Light Cruiser *Ajax*
BASHFORD, Cyril, Corporal, CH/X 959, killed
BURRELLS, Albert, Marine, CH/X 1688, killed
CLEMENTS, James, Marine, CH/X 654, killed
FARLEY, William, Ordinary Seaman, C/JX 151605, killed
FOLLETT, Harry, Sergeant, CH/X 688, killed
FRANCOM, Ernest, Steward, C/LX 21835, killed
LAMBARD, William, Marine, CH/X 1663, killed

Heavy Cruiser *Exeter*
AINGE, Walter, Chief Petty Officer, D/J 52100, DOW
BACK, Frederick, Engine Room Artificer 4c, D/MX 54489, killed
BETHELL, Frank, Able Seaman, D/JX 151055, killed
BETHELL, Joseph, Able Seaman, D/SSX 22452, killed
BLANDFORD, Bert, Marine, PLY/X 711, killed
BOWES, Raymond, Ordinary Seaman, D/JX 150342, killed
BOWMAN-MANIFOLD, John, Lieutenant Commander, killed
BRIGHT, Daniel, Stoker Petty Officer, D/KX 78984, killed
BURRAS, Stanley, Stoker 1c, D/KX 92228, killed
CAMPBELL, Frederick, Stoker 1c, D/KX 88775, killed
CLARKSON, Richard, Able Seaman, D/JX 151372, killed
CROKER, Alfred, Marine, PLY/X 835, killed
DAVIES, Gilbert, Able Seaman, D/SSX 22679, killed
DOVE, Gilbert, Act/Petty Officer, D/JX 134624, killed
DYER, Frederick, Shipwright 3c, D/MX 47145, killed
FRENCH, Frederick, Able Seaman, D/SSX 20765, killed
GIBSON, Stanley, Able Seaman, D/JX 139907, killed
HARRINGTON, Stanley, Marine, PLY/ 22286, killed
HARRIS, Hugh, Petty Officer Telegraphist, D/J 51924, killed
HIGGINBOTTOM, Alan, Chief Yeoman of Signals, D/J 100565, killed
HILL, Ronald, Boy Bugler, PLY/X 2238, killed
HONEY, Leslie, Leading Signalman, D/JX 138212, killed
JONES, Albert, Stoker Petty Officer, D/K 65933, killed

KAVANAGH, Michael, Telegraphist, D/SSX 16949, killed
KELLY, Albert, Stoker 1c, D/KX 82448, killed
LUMSDEN, Arthur, Telegraphist, D/JX 142445, killed
MACLEOD, William, Stoker 1c, D/KX 81482, killed
MANNING, George, Stoker 1c, D/K 59242, killed
MARSH, William, Corporal, PLY/X 1361, killed
MCDONNELL, Francis, Able Seaman, D/SSX 15579, killed
MCEVOY, James, Marine, PO/X 2091, killed
MILLS, Edward, Marine, PLY/X 1914, killed
MONKS, Christoper, Stoker 2c, D/KX 96243, killed
MORSE, Clyde, Act/Sub Lieutenant, MPK
NAYLOR, Thomas, Able Seaman, D/JX 138243, killed
O'LEARY, Patrick, Stoker 1c, D/KX 92212, killed
PARRY, David, Telegraphist, D/JX 141568, killed
PETT, Bryan, Stoker 1c, D/KX 92198, killed
PULLYBLANK, Leslie, Leading Supply Assistant, D/MX 50647, killed
RANDLE, Frank, Stoker Petty Officer, D/K 37155, killed
REMICK, Tom, Chief Yeoman of Signals, D/J 45240, killed
RICHARDS, Brynmor, Able Seaman, D/JX 141181, killed
RICHARDS, Glyndwr, Leading Seaman, D/JX 127862, killed
RICKCORD, John, Midshipman, killed
RIGLAR, Arthur, Telegraphist, D/JX 144826, killed
SMALL, Richard, Blacksmith 3c, D/MX 51352, killed
SPENCER, Harry, Able Seaman, D/SSX 16592, DOW
SQUIRE, Ernest, Boy 1c, D/JX 158659, killed
STEELE, Robert, Stoker Petty Officer, D/K 60833, killed
STUBBS, Agean, Marine, PLY/X 1370, killed
TAYLOR, Robert, Telegraphist, D/JX 146419, killed
TEAGUE, Samuel, Chief Stoker, D/K 57454, killed
THOMPSON, James, Stoker 1c, D/KX 81575, killed
TOVEY, George, Stoker Petty Officer, D/KX 80186, killed
TREGIDGO, Albert, Chief Petty Officer, D/J 89888, killed
TYLER, Donald, Paymaster Sub Lieutenant, killed
WILSON, Patrick, Stoker 1c, D/KX 86441, killed
WOODS, Humphrey, Captain, RM, killed

Appendix C: Royal Navy's Armed Merchant Cruisers

Ship	Former Name Type Vessel	Commanding Officer(s)	Notes
Alaunia (F17)	*Alaunia* passenger ship	Capt. (retired) Hugh Joseph Woodward, RN	
Alcantara (F88)	*Alcantara* passenger ship	Capt. (retired) James Geoffrey Penrose Ingham, RN; A/Capt. (retired) John Douglas Harvey, RN	Jan 40-Apr 43: South Atlantic Station
Andania	*Andania* passenger ship	Capt. Donald Keppel Bain, RN	Sunk on 16 Jun 40 by the German submarine *U-A*
Antenor (F21)	*Antenor* passenger ship	Capt. (retired) Arthur Bannatyne Arnold Baker, RN	
Arawa (F12)	*Esperance Bay*, renamed *Arawa* passenger ship	A/Capt. George Robert Deverell, RN	Nov 40-Jul 41: South Atlantic Station
Ascania (F68)	*Ascania* passenger ship	Capt. (retired) Christopher Hildyard Ringrose-Wharton, RN	
Asturias (F71)	*Asturias* passenger ship	Capt. John Robert Sutherland Haines, RN; Capt. (retired) Hubert Ardill, RN; Capt. Richard Meuric Southern, RN; Capt. (retired) John Meynell Alleyne, RN	Jul 40-Apr 43: South Atlantic Station; May-Jul 43: West Africa Command
Aurania (F28)	*Aurania* passenger ship	Capt. Harry William Cuthbert Hughes, RN	Damaged on 21 Oct 41 by *U-123*
Ausonia (F53)	*Ausonia* passenger ship	Capt. Charles Thomas Mark Pizey, RN	
Bulolo (F82)	*Bulolo* passenger ship	A/Capt. (retired) Christopher Henry Petrie, RN; Capt. (retired) Richard Lloyd Hamer, RN	Jan-Apr 40: South Atlantic Station; May 40-Nov 41: Freetown Escort Force; Dec 41-Mar 42: South Atlantic Station
California (F55)	*California* passenger ship	A/Capt. Gerald Seymour Tuck, RN; Capt. (retired) Edward	Nov 41-Mar 42: South Atlantic Station. Damaged

		Wollaston Kitson, RN	on 11 Jul 43 by a German Fw200 aircraft, scuttled the next day by HMS *Douglas*
Canton (F97)	*Canton* passenger ship	A/Capt. Charles Alfred Godfrey Nichols, RN; A/Capt. Geoffrey Neame Loriston-Clarke, RN	Aug 40-Nov 41: Freetown Escort Force; Dec 41-Aug 42: South Atlantic Station
Carinthia	*Carinthia* passenger ship	Capt. (retired) John Francis Benjamin Barrett, RN	Sunk on 6 Jun 40 by *U-46*
Carnarvon Castle (F25)	*Carnarvon Castle*	Capt. (retired) George Bridges Lewis, RN; Capt. Martin John Coucher de Meric, RN; Capt. (retired) Henry Noel Marryat Hardy, RN; Capt. (retired) Edward Wollaston Kitson, RN	Oct 39-Apr 40: South Atlantic Station; May 40-Jun 41: Freetown Escort Force; Jul 41-Apr 42: South Atlantic Station; Jun 42-Apr 43: South Atlantic Station; May-Nov 43: West Africa Command
Carthage (F99)	*Carthage* passenger ship	A/Capt. Cyril William Archie Gooding Hamley, RN; A/Cdr. John Wyndham Cookson, RN; A/Capt. (retired) William Vesey Hamilton Harris, RN	Sep-Nov 42: South Atlantic Station; Mar-Apr 43: South Atlantic Station
Cathay (F05)	*Cathay* passenger ship	A/Capt. (retired) Christopher McCabe Merewether, RN	Sep 40-Nov 41: Freetown Escort Force; Dec 41-Jan 42: South Atlantic Station. Bombed on 11 Nov 42 by German aircraft, ship sank next day
Cheshire (F18)	*Cheshire* passenger ship	Capt. (retired) Mountague Robert Bernard, RN; Capt. (retired) James Millar Begg, RN; A/Cdr. John Martin Ashley, RN; A/Capt. Humfrey Greenwood Hopper, RN; A/Capt. (retired) Robert Douglas King-Harman, RN	Nov 39-Apr 40: South Atlantic Station; May-Nov 41: Freetown Escort Force; Dec 41-Apr 43: South Atlantic Station. Damaged on 14 Oct 40 by *U-137*, and on 18 Aug 42 by *U-214*

Chitral (F57)	*Chitral* passenger ship	Capt. (retired) Alfred Geoffrey Peace, RN	
Cilicia (F54)	*Cilicia* passenger ship	Cdr. (retired) Godfrey Herbert, RN; Capt. (retired) Vincent Byrne Cardwell, RN; A/Capt. John Mortimer Scott, RN	Oct 39-Oct 40: South Atlantic Station; May 43-Feb 44: West Africa Command
Circassia (F91)	*Circassia* passenger ship	Capt. (retired) Henry Gerard Laurence Oliphant, RN	
Comorin (F49)	*Comorin* passenger ship	Capt. (retired) John Ignatius Hallett, RN; A/Capt. (retired) Christopher Henry Petrie, RN	Jan-Apr 40: South Atlantic Station; Feb 41: South Atlantic Station; Mar 41-Apr 41: Freetown Escort Force. Ship caught fire on 6 Apr 41 and was abandoned. Sunk by the destroyer HMS *Lincoln*
Corfu (F86)	*Corfu* passenger ship	Capt. Sir William Gladstone Agnew, RN; A/Cdr. (retired) Noel Charles Mansfeldt Findlay, RN; Capt. (retired) John Palmer Landon, RN; A/Cdr. (retired) Arthur Kenneth Baxendell, RAN; Capt. (retired) Charles C. Bell, RN	Jul 40-Sep 41: Freetown Escort Force; Sep 42-Apr 43: South Atlantic Station; May 43-Feb 44: West Africa Command
Derbyshire (F78)	*Derbyshire* passenger ship	Capt. (retired) Edmond Alan Berners Stanley, RN; Capt. (retired) Charles Courtenay Bell, RN	May-Nov 41: Freetown Escort Force; Dec 41-Feb 42: South Atlantic Station
Dunnottar Castle (F34)	*Dunnottar Castle* passenger ship	Capt. (retired) Henry Edmund Harvey Spencer-Cooper, RN; Capt. (retired) Charles Thomas Alexander Bunbury, RN; Capt. (retired) Henry Edmund Harvey Spencer-Cooper, RN; Capt. (retired) Charles Thomas Alexander Bunbury, RN	Oct 39-Apr 40: South Atlantic Station; May 40-Nov 41: Freetown Escort Force; Dec 41-May 42: South Atlantic Station

Dunvegan Castle	*Dunvegan Castle* passenger ship	Capt. (retired) Hubert Ardill, RN	Jan-Apr 40: South Atlantic Station; May-Aug 40: Freetown Escort Force. Sunk on 27 Aug 40 by *U-46*
Esperance Bay (F67)	*Esperance Bay* passenger ship	Capt. (retired) Geoffrey Shuttleworth Holden, RN	Dec 39-Apr 40: South Atlantic Station; Nov 40-Aug 41: Freetown Escort Force
Forfar (F30)	*Forfar* passenger ship	Capt. (retired) Hubert Henry de Burgh, RN	Sunk on 2 Dec 40 by *U-99*
Hector (F45)	*Hector* passenger ship	Capt. (retired) Robin Wynell Mayow Lloyd, RN	Bombed on 5 Apr 42 in Japanese air attack, wreckage broken up on beach
Jervis Bay (F40)	*Jervis Bay* passenger ship	Capt. (retired) Arthur Gerald Harris, RN; Cdr. (retired) James Alexander Pollard Blackburn, RN; A/Capt. Edward Stephen Fogarty Fegen, RN	Oct 39-Apr 40: South Atlantic Station. Sunk on 5 Nov 40 by the German pocket-battleship *Admiral Scheer*
Kanimbla (F23)	*Kanimbla* passenger ship	Cdr. Frank Edmund Getting, RAN	
Laconia (F42)	*Laconia* passenger ship	Capt. (retired) Gilbert George Pearse Hewett, RN	Sunk on 12 Sep 42 by *U-156*
Laurentic (F51)	*Laurentic* passenger ship	Capt. (retired) Eric Paul Vivian, RN	Sunk on 3 Nov 40 by *U-99*
Letitia (F16)	*Letitia* passenger ship	Capt. (retired) William Reynard Richardson, RN	
Maloja (F26)	*Maloja* passenger ship	A/Capt. (retired) Vernon Hammersley-Heenan, RN	Jul-Oct 40: Freetown Escort Force
Montclare (F85)	*Montclare* passenger ship	Capt. (retired) Herbert Malcolm Spreckley, RN	Oct 39: South Atlantic Station
Mooltan (F75)	*Mooltan* passenger ship	Capt. (retired) George Ernest Sutcliff, RN	Oct 39-Apr 40: South Atlantic Station; May 40: Freetown Escort Force; Jun-Jul 40: South Atlantic Station; Aug 40-Jan 41: Freetown Escort Force

Moreton Bay (F11)	*Moreton Bay* passenger ship	Cdr. Edmund Mount Haes, RN; Capt. (retired) Charles Courtenay Bell, RN	Sep 40: South Atlantic Station; Oct 40-Jun 41: Freetown Escort Force
Patroclus	*Patroclus* passenger ship	Capt. (retired) Gerald Charles Wynter, RN	May-Jun 40: South Atlantic Station. Sunk on 4 Nov 40 by *U-99*
Pretoria Castle (F61)	*Pretoria Castle*	Capt. (retired) Eric John Shelley, RN; A/Capt. (retired) Arthur Vernon Hemming, RN	Nov 39-Apr 40: South Atlantic Station; May 40: Freetown Escort Force; Jun-Jul 40: South Atlantic Station; Aug 40-Jun 41: Freetown Escort Force; Jul 41-Jun 42: South Atlantic Station
Queen of Bermuda (F73)	*Queen of Bermuda* passenger ship	Capt. (retired) Miles Brock Birkett, RN; Capt. Geoffrey Alan Brooke Hawkins, RN; Capt. Allan Thomas George Cumberland Peachey, RN; Cdr. (retired) Geoffrey Healey, RN; A/Capt. (retired) Archibald Douglas Cochrane, RN	Nov 39-Mar 42: South Atlantic Station; Jul-Aug 42: South Atlantic Station
Rajputana (F35)	*Rajputana* passenger ship	Capt. (retired) Frederick Henry Taylor, RN	Sunk on 13 Apr 41 by *U-108*
Ranchi (F15)	*Ranchi* passenger ship	Capt. (retired) Heneage Cecil Legge, RN	
Ranpura (F93)	*Ranpura* passenger ship	Capt. (retired) Clarence Walter Eyre Trelawny, RN	Mar-Apr 40: South Atlantic Station
Rawalpindi	*Rawalpindi* passenger ship	Capt. (retired) Edward Coverley Kennedy, RN	Sunk on 23 Nov 39 by the German battlecruiser *Scharnhorst*
Salopian (F94)	*Salopian* passenger ship	Capt. (retired) John Phellips Farquharson, RN	Oct 39-Jan 40: South Atlantic Station. Sunk on 13 May 41 by *U-98*
Scotstoun	*Scotstoun* passenger ship	Capt. (retired) Sydney Keith Smyth, RN	Sunk on 13 Jun 40 by *U-25*
Transylvania (F56)	*Transylvania* passenger ship	Capt. (retired) Francis Nigel Miles, RN	Sunk on 10 Aug 40 by *U-56*

Voltaire (F47)	*Voltaire* passenger ship	A/Capt. (retired) James Alexander Pollard Blackburn, RN	Apr 41: South Atlantic Station. Sunk on 4 Apr 41 by the German raider *Thor*
Wolfe (F37)	*Montcalm* passenger ship	Capt. (retired) Charles Geoffrey Coleridge Sumner, RN	
Worcestershire (F29)	*Worcestershire* passenger ship	Capt. (retired) Frederic Archibald Hunter Russel, RN	Damaged on 3 Apr 41 by *U-74*

Appendix D: Brazilian Navy in World War II

Minas Gerais-class Battleships

Ship	Builder	Commissioned	Decommissioned
Minas Gerais	Armstrong, Newcastle-on-Tyne, U.K.	6 Jan 1910	20 Sep 1953
São Paulo	Vickers, Barrow-in-Furness, U.K.	12 Jul 1910	Sold to be broken up for scrap in 1951. Sank while under tow on 6 Nov 1951

Bahia-class Light Cruisers (Armstrong Whitworth, Elswick, U.K.)

Ship	Commissioned	Decommissioned
Rio Grande do Sul (C 11)	1910	8 Jun 1948
Bahia (C 12)	1910	Lost 4 Jul 1945 in the central Atlantic, halfway between Brazil and Africa, due to explosion of depth charges on the fantail

K-class Destroyer (Thornycroft, Southampton, U.K.)

Ship	Commissioned	Decommissioned
Maranhao (CT 12)	9 Dec 1922; ex-HMS *Porpoise*, purchased in 1920	13 Sep 1946

Para-class Torpedo Boats
(Yarrow Shipbuilders Ltd., Scotstoun, Scotland)

Ship	Commissioned	Decommissioned
Piauhy (CT 3)	31 Dec 1909	28 Jul 1944
Rio Grande do Norte (CT 4)	1909	28 Jul 1944
Paraiba (CT 5)	31 Dec 1909	28 Jul 1944
Sergipe (CT 7)	1910	28 Jul 1944
Santa Catarina (CT 9)	1910	28 Jul 1944
Mato Grosso (CT 10)	1909	16 Sep 1946

Carioca-class Minelayers (Arsenal de Marinha do Rio de Janeiro)

Ship	Commissioned	End of Service
Carioca (C 1)	16 Sep 1939	1960
Cananéia (C 2)	16 Sep 1939	1960
Camocim (C 3)	7 Jun 1940	1960
Cabedelo (C 4)	7 Jun 1940	1960
Caravelas (C 5)	7 Jun 1940	1960
Camaqua (C 6)	7 Jun 1940	Capsized and sank in a storm on 21 July 1944, some thirty nautical miles east of Recife, Brazil

Humaita- and *Tupy*-class Submarines
(Cantieri Odero Terni Orlando, La Spezia, Italy)

Submarine	Commissioned	Decommissioned
Humaita (H)	20 Jul 1929	25 Nov 1950
Tupy (T 1)	10 Oct 1937	26 Aug 1959
Tymbira (T 2)	10 Oct 1937	26 Aug 1959
Tamoyo (T 3)	10 Oct 1937	26 Aug 1959

PC-461-class Patrol Craft

Brazilian Ship/ Former USN Ship	Builder's Yard	Commis- sioned	Decommis -sioned
Guaporé (G 1)/*PC-544*	Defoe Shipbuilding Co., Bay City, Michigan	24 Sep 1942	1958
Gurupi (G 2)/*PC-547*	Defoe Shipbuilding Co., Bay City, Michigan	24 Sep 1942	
Guaíba (G 3)/*PC-604*	Luders Marine Construction Co., Stamford, Connecticut	11 Jun 1943	1952
Gurupá (G 4)/*PC-605*	Luders Marine Construction Co., Stamford, Connecticut	11 Jun 1943	1952
Guajará (G 5)/*PC-607*	Luders Marine Construction Co., Stamford, Connecticut	19 Oct 1943	
Goiana (G 6)/*PC-554*	Sullivan Dry Dock and Repair Co., Brooklyn, New York	29 Oct 1943	13 Dec 1951
Grajaú (G 7)/*PC-1236*	Sullivan Dry Dock and Repair Co., Brooklyn, New York	15 Nov 1943	11 Apr 1959
Graúna (G 8)/*PC-561*	Jeffersonville Boat and Machine Co., Jeffersonville, Indiana	30 Nov 1943	19 Apr 1950

SC-497-class Submarine Chasers
(W.A. Robinson Inc., Ipswich, Massachusetts)

Brazilian Ship/ Former USN Ship	Commissioned	Decommissioned
Javari (CS 51)/ SC-763	7 Dec 1942	
Jutai (CS 52)/ SC-762	31 Dec 1942	
Juruí (CS 53)/ SC-764	31 Dec 1942	
Juruena (CS 54)/ SC-766	31 Dec 1942	
Jaguarão (CS 55)/ SC-765	16 Feb 1943	28 Jun 1950
Jaguaribe (CS 56)/ SC-767	16 Feb 1943	
Jacuí (CS 57)/ SC-1288	19 May 1943	
Jundiaí (CS 58)/ SC-1289	26 Apr 1943	

Cannon-class Destroyer Escort
(Federal Shipbuilding & Drydock Co., Newark, New Jersey)

Brazilian Ship/ Former USN Ship	Commissioned	Decommissioned/ End of Service
Bertioga (Be 1)/ *Pennewill* (DE-175)	1 Aug 1944	1964
Beberibe (Be 2)/ *Herzog* (DE-178)	1 Aug 1944	1968
Bauru (Be 3)/ *McAnn* (DE-179)	15 Aug 1944	11 Jul 1972/17 Sep 1981, preserved as museum
Bracuí (Be 4)/ *Reybold* (DE-177)	15 Aug 1944	11 Jul 1972/17 Sep 1981

(Dravo Corp., Wilmington, Delaware)

Baependi (Be 5)/ *Cannon* (DE-99)	19 Dec 1944	1973
Benevente (Be 6)/ *Christopher* (DE-100)	19 Dec 1944	1964
Babitonga (Be 7)/ *Alger* (DE-101)	10 Mar 1945	1964
Bocaina (Be 8)/ *Marts* (DE-174)	20 Mar 1945	1975

Marcílio Dias-class Destroyers (Arsenal de Marinha do Rio de Janeiro)

Ship	Commissioned	Decommissioned
Marize Barros (M 1)	29 Nov 1943	22 Aug 1972
Marcílio Dias (M 2)	29 Nov 1943	22 Aug 1972
Greenhalgh (M 3)	29 Nov 1943	1966

Henrique Dias-class ASW Trawlers (Henrique Lage, Niteroi, Brazil)

Brazilian Ship/ Former Name	Commissioned	Decommissioned
Fernandes Vieira (F 1)/*Parati*	20 Nov 1943	1 Aug 1952
Felipe Camarao (F 2)/*Papaterra*	11 Jun 1943	14 Jul 1953
Henrique Dias (F 3)/*Pargo*	9 Sep 1943	1959
Matias de Albuquerque (F 4)/*Pampano*	20 Nov 1943	7 Apr 1952
Vidal de Negreiros (F 5)/*Pelegrine*	14 Jan 1944	1959
Barreto de Menezes (F 6)/*Paru*	28 Oct 1944	4 Nov 1954

Appendix E: Organization of the U.S. Fourth Fleet

The Fourth Fleet, like other fleets, was divided into subordinate task forces, tasked with specific duties and responsibilities, and the military units comprising individual task forces were further divided into task groups and/or task units.

Fourth Fleet: Vice Adm. Jonas A. Ingram, USN
Fleet flagship: Light cruiser *Memphis* (CL-13)
Relief flagship: Coastal patrol yacht *Perseverance* (PYc-44)
Relief flagship (ordered): Yard houseboat *Big Pebble* (YHB-23)

Task Force 41 (Ocean Patrol): Rear Adm. Oliver M. Read, USN
Commander, Cruiser Division 2

Task Unit	Ship	Commanding Officer
41.1	*Omaha* (CL-4) flagship	Capt. Charles Doyle Leffler Jr., USN
41.2	*Milwaukee* (CL-5)	Capt. Charles Frederick Fielding, USN
41.3	*Cincinnati* (CL-6)	Capt. Elliott Marchant Senn, USN
41.4	*Marblehead* (CL-12)	Capt. Arthur Granville Robinson, USN
41.5	*Memphis* (CL-13)	Capt. Ralph Waldo Hungerford, USN

Task Force 42 (Escort Force): Comdr. Horace C. Robinson, USN
Commander Destroyer Squadron 9

Task Group		Commanding Officer
42.1	Destroyer Squadron 9	Comdr. H. C. Robinson, USN
	Davis (DD-395)	Comdr. William Archer Dunn
	Jouett (DD-396)	Lt. Comdr. John Calhoun Farham Jr.
	Moffett (DD-362)	Lt. Comdr. Gilbert Haven Richards Jr.
	Somers (DD-381)	Comdr. William Christopher Hughes Jr.
	Winslow (DD-359)	Lt. Comdr. Alexander Martin Kowalzyk Jr.
42.2	TF Commander	Lt. Comdr. W. H. Sanders
	Alden (DD-211)	Lt. Comdr. Wayne Herkness II
	Courage (PG-70)	Lt. J. C. Sullivan Jr., USNR
	Carnelian (PY-19)	G. B. Barry
	PC-488	Lt. (jg) J. L. Eubanks, USNR
	PC-493	Lt. (jg) J. T. Young, USNR
	PC-574	Lt. T. N. MacIntyre, USNR
	PC-575	Lt. H. M. Bashinski, USNR
42.3	TF Commander	Lt. Comdr. C. K. Post
	John D. Edwards (DD-216)	Lt. Comdr. George Hutchison, USN
	Siren (PY-13)	I. M. Shepard

	Tenacity (PG-71)	Lt. C. B. Campbell Jr., USNR
	PC-492	Lt. B. J. Dunn, USNR
	PC-494	Lt. Comdr. J. L. V. Bonney, USNR
	PC-577	Lt. (jg) E. M. Foltz, USNR
	PC-593	Lt. F. C. Heerde, USNR
42.4	*Whipple* (DD-217)	Lt. Comdr. V. J. Meola, USN
	Surprise (PG-63)	Lt. K. W. Wise, USNR
	PC-489	Lt. P. C. Nicholson Jr., USNR
	PC-495	Lt. L. R. Wallace, USNR
	PC-576	Lt. (jg) W. F. Colton, USNR
	PC-609	Lt. (jg) R. J. Wilson, USNR
	PC-610	Lt. David H. Pabst, USNR
42.5	TF Commander	Comdr. C. E. Weakley
	John D. Ford (DD-220)	Lt. Comdr. J. S. Slaughter, USN
	Saucy (PG-65)	Lt. H. G. Doyle Jr., USNR
	Spry (PG-64)	Lt. Benjamin F. Uran, USNR
	PC-490	Lt. D. Kirk Gunby, USNR
	PC-491	Lt. (jg) G. W. Clark, USNR
	PC-592	Lt. Selwyn Eddy, USNR
	PC-594	Lt. C. S. Small, USNR
	PC-595	Lt. S. F. Morris, USNR

Task Force 43: Brig. Gen. Robert L. Walsh, USN
U.S. Army Forces of the South Atlantic Theater

First Composite Squadron, Composite Force 8012, Ascension Island

Task Unit	Aircraft	Aircraft
43.1	5 B-25C Mitchell bombers	14 P-39D Airacobra fighters

Task Force 44 (Aircraft Wings): Capt. Rossmore D. Lyon, USN
Commander, Fleet Air Wing 16

Task Unit	Wing/Squadron	Commander
44.1	**Fleet Air Wing Sixteen**	Capt. Rossmore D. Lyon, USN
44.1.1	Patrol Squadron VP-74	
44.1.2	Patrol Squadron VP-94	Lt. Joseph Bonafield Tibbets, USN
44.1.3	Bombing Squadron VB-107	
44.1.4	Bombing Squadron VB-129	
44.1.5	Bombing Squadron VB-130	
44.1.6	Bombing Squadron VB-143	
44.1.7	Bombing Squadron VB-145	
44.1.8	Patrol Squadron VP-211	
44.1.9	Headquarters Squadron	
44.1.11	Utility Squadron	
44.2	**Fleet Airship Wing Four**	Capt. Walter E. Zimmerman, USN
44.2.1	Blimp Squadron 41	
44.2.2	Blimp Squadron 42	
44.2.9	Blimp Headquarters Squadron	

44.3   **Naval Air Shore Facilities**

44.3.1	NAF Amapa (LP & LTA)	44.3.9	NAF Maceió (LP & LTA)
44.3.2	NAF Belém (LP & SP)	44.3.11	NAF Bahia (Aratu) (SP)
44.3.3	NAF Igarape Assu (LTA)	44.3.12	NAF Bahia (Ipetanga) (LP & LPA)
44.3.4	NAF São Luiz (LP & LTA)	44.3.13	NAF Fernando do Noronha (LP & LTA)
44.3.5	NAF Fortaleza (LP & LTA)	44.3.14	NAF Caravellas (LTA)
44.3.6	NAF Natal (LP)	44.3.15	NAF Rio de Janeiro (Santa Cruz) (LP & LTA)
44.3.7	NAF Natal (SP)	44.3.16	NAF Montevideo (LP & SP)
44.3.8	NAF Recife (LP & LTA)	44.3.17	NAF Ascension (LP)

NAF: Naval Air Facility   LTA: Lighter than Air (Blimp)
LP: Land Plane   SP: Seaplane

44.4	**Aircraft Tenders**	**Commanding Officer**
44.4.1	*Sandpiper* (AVP-9)	Lt. Lyle Charles Bradley, USNR
44.4.2	*Barnegat* (AVP-10)	Comdr. Henry T. Dietrich Jr., USN
44.4.3	83-foot Coast Guard patrol boat *CG-83449* (used for towing targets)	

BRAZILIAN NAVAL FORCES

The Brazilian forces assigned to the Fourth Fleet were designated Task Forces 45 and 46, titled the Brazilian Naval Forces of the Center Command, and Brazilian Naval Forces of the Northeast, respectively. Per orders of President Vargas, via the Minister of Marine, the Brazilian Navy had been placed under the command of Admiral Ingram on 12 September 1942. Task Force 45 was to provide escorts for convoys from Rio de Janeiro to the south and west; escort important independent units; and provide anti-submarine security of Brazilian ports of the Center and South via patrol operations. The duties of Task Force 46 included providing convoy escort groups for Trinidad-Brazil convoys, taking over off Recife for southbound convoys, and being relieved off that port for northbound convoys. The task force was also to provide shuttle escorts between ports of the North and trade convoys, and anti-submarine security for Brazilian ports of the Northeast and North by sub-chaser patrols.

MISCELLANEOUS FORCES AND SHORE BASES

With the exception of Admiral Ingram's flagship, the cruiser *Memphis*, the ships of Task Force 47 receive scant attention in accounts of action in the South Atlantic in World War II. The Miscellaneous Force was to provide tender and supply services to the Fourth Fleet, and to vessels of Allied nations; assist the shore establishment in the performance of its mission; sweep channels clear of any enemy mines; and otherwise provide for the security of the ports as directed. The shore bases of Task Force 48 were to perform all the functions of shore activities in support of the Fleet.

Task Force 47: Miscellaneous Force

Task Group	Organization/Ships	Commanding Officer
47.1	**Fleet Flagships**	
47.1.1	*Memphis* (CL-13)	Capt. Ralph Waldo Hungerford, USN
47.1.2	*Big Pebble* (YHB-23)	
47.1.3	*Perseverance* (PYc-44)	Lt. (jg) Malcolm A. Rea, USNR
47.1.4	*Bluebird* (AM-72)	Lt. Dana Charles Wrightington, USNR
47.2	**Recife Detachment**	
47.2.1	*Melville* (AD-2)	Comdr. Rony Snyder, USN
47.2.2	*Patoka* (AO-9)	Lt. Comdr. Eugene W. Kiefer, USN
47.2.3	*Sacagawea* (YT-326)	
47.2.4	Utility towing plane 4J-13	
47.2.5	*Seneca* (ATF-91)	Lt. Herman B. Conrad, USN
47.2.6	*ATR-43*	Lt. (jg) A. C. Schoelpple, USN
47.3	**Bahia Detachment**	
47.3.2	*YR-45*	
47.4	**Natal Detachment**	
47.4.1	*YFD-38*	
47.5	**Minesweeping Group**	Lt. Comdr. Merritt Berner
	Flicker (AM-70)	Lt. E. P. Gough, USNR
	Linnet (AM-76)	Lt. Comdr. Merritt Berner, USNR
	*YMS-60**	Lt. R. C. Davidson Jr. USNR
	*YMS-76**	Lt. C. B. Tibbals, USNR
	*YMS-44***	Lt. J. E. Kuhns, USNR
	*YMS-45***	Lt. Robert B. Harrell, USNR
47.6	**Belém Detachment**	
47.6.1	*YR-35*	
	Unassigned: *YO-149*	

* To be detached   ** Upon reporting

Task Force 48: Shore Bases

Task Group	Command	Task Group	Command
48.1	U.S. Naval Operating Facility, Recife		
48.1.1	Destroyer Repair Base 12		
48.1.2	Naval Magazine, Recife		
48.1.3	Naval Dispensary, Recife		
48.2	U.S. Naval Operating Facility, Bahia		
48.2.1	Destroyer Repair Base 13	48.8	U.S. NOF, Maceió
48.3	U.S. NOB, Rio de Janeiro	48.9	U.S. NOF, Victoria
48.4	U.S. NOF, Belém	48.11	U.S. NOF, Santos
48.5	U.S. NOF, São Luiz	48.12	U.S. NOF, Florianopolis
48.6	U.S. NOF, Fortaleza	48.13	U.S. NOF, Rio Grande do Sul
48.7	U.S. NOF, Natal	48.14	U.S. NOF, Montevideo

NOB: Naval Operating Base
NOF: Naval Operating Facility

Appendix F: Medal Citations for SS *Stephen Hopkins* Crewmembers

LIEUTENANT (JG) KENNETH M. WILLETT, USNR

The President of the United States of America takes pride in presenting the Navy Cross (Posthumously) to Lieutenant Junior Grade Kenneth M. Willett, United States Naval Reserve, for extraordinary heroism and conspicuous courage as Commanding Officer of the United States Navy Armed Guard aboard the S.S. *STEPHEN HOPKINS* during action with unidentified enemy forces while en route from Capetown to Paramaribo, on 27 September 1942. In an attack launched by the enemy, and with no friendly ship in sight, Lieutenant, Junior Grade, Willett promptly manned his station at the 4-inch gun as the first shell struck, and opened fire on the most heavily armed of the two enemy raiders. Although seriously wounded in the stomach almost immediately, he kept up a sustained and rapid fire at close range, hitting his target along the water line with most of the 35 shells fired. Because of his great personal valor and gallant spirit of self-sacrifice, he was able to maintain a determined and heroic defense of his ship until forced by a magazine explosion to cease his fire. Still refusing to give up, Lieutenant, Junior Grade, Willett, obviously weakened and suffering, went down on deck and was last seen helping to cast loose the life rafts in a desperate effort to save the lives of others. The *STEPHEN HOPKINS* was shelled repeatedly from stem to stern, but before she plunged stern first, wrecked and blazing into the sea, her guns had inflicted serious damage on both enemy raiders and caused the probable destruction of one of them. His conduct throughout was in keeping with the highest traditions of the Navy of the United States. He gallantly gave his life for his country.

PAUL BUCK, MASTER OF SS *STEPHEN HOPKINS*

For distinguished service in enemy action.

Two enemy surface raiders suddenly appeared out of the mist to attack the small merchantman in which he was serving as Master. Heavy guns of one raider pounded his ship, and machine gun fire from the other sprayed her decks. He skillfully maneuvered his ship so that the heavier guns could be trained on the raider, and under his supervision his ship exchanged shot for shot with the enemy until the crew of one raider was forced to abandon its sinking ship, and the other enemy ship was forced to withdraw. His calmness under fire and his fearlessness in defending his ship were an inspiration to his crew. With boilers blown up and engines damaged, masts shot away, and ablaze from stem to stern, he reluctantly gave the order to abandon ship. The only serviceable lifeboat being overcrowded, he, unselfishly and heroically, remained on the bridge and went down with his battered ship.

His determination to fight his ship and his perseverance in engaging the enemy to the utmost until his ship was rendered helpless and sinking were in keeping with the finest traditions of the United States Merchant Marine.

RICHARD MOCZKOWSKI, CHIEF MATE OF SS *STEPHEN HOPKINS*

For extraordinary heroism beyond the call of duty.

Two enemy surface raiders suddenly appeared out of the mist to attack the small merchantman in which he was serving. Heavy guns of one raider pounded his ship, and machine gun fire from the other sprayed her decks until she was a complete wreck and afire fore and aft. The merchantman exchanged shot for shot with the enemy raiders until the crew of one raider was forced to abandon their sinking ship, and the other was forced to withdraw. The mate, shot in the chest and in the left forearm early in the action, continued at his exposed post abaft the wheelhouse rallying his men and directing orders to the bridge to enable his ship to keep her guns bearing on the enemy ships.

Weakened by rapid loss of blood from a severed artery, he collapsed to the deck, but refused to stay down, and ordered a seaman to assist him to his feet and prop him in a doorway that he might better discharge his duties. With her boilers blown up, engines destroyed, masts shot away, and ablaze from stem to stern, orders were finally given to abandon the gallant merchantman. Moczkowski was carried to the boat deck, and propped against the housing while the only usable lifeboat was lowered away. His shipmates carried the mortally wounded man to the side, but seeing the crowded boat already released and clear of the ship, the mate commanded his men to leave him rather than further jeopardize their own safety.

His fearless determination to fight his ship, and his perseverance in engaging the enemy to the utmost until his ship was rendered helpless and sinking, constitute a degree of heroism which will be an enduring inspiration to seamen of the United States Merchant Marine.

JOSEPH EARL LAYMAN, SECOND MATE OF SS *STEPHEN HOPKINS*

For distinguished service in enemy action.

Two enemy surface raiders suddenly appeared out of the morning mist to attack the small merchantman upon which he was serving. Heavy guns of one raider pounded his ship, and machine guns from the other, sprayed her decks until she was a complete wreck and afire fore and aft. His ship exchanged shot for shot with the enemy raiders until the crew of one raider was forced to abandon its sinking ship, and the other was forced to withdraw. Layman, who was in charge of the two 37 mm guns forward, put shell after shell into the larger raider and courageously maintained the fire until all his shell handlers were killed and the gun platform wrecked. With her boilers blown up, engines destroyed, masts shot away, and ablaze from stem to stern, orders were finally given to abandon ship. The only serviceable lifeboat being overcrowded, Layman, unselfishly and heroically, remained on board and went down with his battered ship.

His fearless determination to fight his ship to the end, and his self-sacrifice constitute a degree of heroism which will be an enduring inspiration to seamen of the United States Merchant Marine everywhere.

GEORGE S. CRONK,
SECOND ENGINEER OF SS *STEPHEN HOPKINS*

For meritorious service under unusual hazards.

Two enemy surface raiders attacked the merchantman upon which he was serving. Heavy guns of one raider pounded his ship, and machine gun fire from the other sprayed her decks at close quarters. Answering shot for shot, the gallant merchantman succeeded in sinking one of the raiders before she finally went under carrying many of her fighting crew with her. Engineer Cronk, sole surviving officer of the stricken ship, took command of the only lifeboat which could be launched. In heavy rain squalls and seas running high, he succeeded in rescuing six survivors who had jumped from the sinking ship.

Then, with nineteen aboard, including four badly wounded, and with no navigational instruments other than the boat compass, a westward course was set to fetch the nearest land 2,200 miles away. The small boat beat her way westward for thirty-one days. Many times heavy weather was encountered, forcing the survivors to put out a sea anchor and heave-to because of high seas. In spite of all efforts in their behalf, three of the wounded died and there were times when delirium threatened, but Cronk's firm leadership overcame all emergencies until a safe landing was made.

His courage and practical leadership, so largely contributory to the ultimate rescue of his shipmates, are in keeping with the highest traditions of the United States Merchant Marine.

FORD STILSON,
CHIEF STEWARD OF SS *STEPHEN HOPKINS*

For meritorious service under unusual hazards.

Two enemy surface raiders attacked the merchantman upon which he was serving. Heavy guns of one raider pounded his ship, and machine gun fire from the other sprayed her decks at close quarters. Answering shot for shot, the gallant merchantman succeeded in sinking one of the raiders before she finally went under carrying many of her fighting crew with her. With complete disregard for his own safety, Stilson repeatedly exposed himself to heavy enemy fire in ministering to his wounded shipmates during the engagement. Later, in a lifeboat with eighteen others, he continued to attend the seriously injured and assisted materially in maintaining morale for the thirty-one days before the lifeboat succeeded in making a landing.

His courage and outstanding devotion to duty, in keeping with the highest traditions of American seamanship, will be a lasting inspiration to seamen of the United States Merchant Marine everywhere.

CADET EDWIN JOSEPH O'HARA (POSTHUMOUSLY)

For extraordinary heroism under unusual hazards.

Two enemy surface raiders suddenly appeared out of the morning mist to attack the small merchantman upon which he was serving. Heavy guns of one raider pounded his ship, and machine guns from the other, sprayed her decks for one-half hour at close quarters. The heroic gun crew of O'Hara's ship exchanged shot for shot with the enemy, placing thirty-five shells into the waterline of one of the raiders until its crew was forced to abandon their sinking ship. The gun commander was mortally wounded early in the action, and all of the gun crew were killed or wounded when an enemy shell exploded the magazine of their gun.

At the explosion, O'Hara ran aft and single-handedly served and fired the damaged gun with five live shells remaining in the ready box, scoring direct hits near the waterline of the second raider. O'Hara was mortally wounded in this action. With boilers blown up, engines destroyed, masts shot away, and ablaze from stem to stern, the gallant merchantman finally went under carrying O'Hara and several of his fighting shipmates with her.

The magnificent courage of this young cadet constitutes a degree of heroism which will be an enduring inspiration to seamen of the United States Merchant Marine everywhere.

Appendix G: Medal Citations for USS *Borie* Crewmembers

LIEUTENANT CHARLES HARRIS HUTCHINS, USNR

The President of the United States of America takes pleasure in presenting the Navy Cross to Lieutenant Charles Harris Hutchins, United States Naval Reserve, for extraordinary heroism and distinguished service in the line of his profession as Commanding Officer of the Destroyer U.S.S. *BORIE* (DD-215), when that vessel attacked and sank an enemy submarine in the waters of the Caribbean Sea on the morning of 1 November 1943. His conduct throughout was in keeping with the highest traditions of the Navy of the United States.

LIEUTENANT MORRISON ROPES BROWN, USNR

The President of the United States of America takes pride in presenting the Navy Cross (Posthumously) to Lieutenant Morrison Ropes Brown, United States Naval Reserve, for extraordinary heroism and distinguished service in the line of his profession as Engineering Officer aboard the Destroyer U.S.S. *BORIE* (DD-215), when that vessel attacked and sank an enemy submarine in the waters of the Caribbean Sea on the morning of 1 November 1943. To keep the engines of the *BORIE* operative in order to complete her mission, despite serious damage sustained during the prolonged battle, Lieutenant Brown remained steadfastly at his post, buffeted by debris in the heavy rolling of the vessel and with water pouring into the forward engine room. As the flooding increased and the compartment became untenable, he calmly ordered his men to safety while he stayed below, standing neck-deep in water at the throttle until the *BORIE* had completely destroyed the submarine. The conduct of Lieutenant Brown throughout this action reflects great credit upon himself, and was in keeping with the highest traditions of the United States Naval Service.

MACHINIST'S MATE SECOND IRVING R. SAUM JR.

The President of the United States of America takes pleasure in presenting the Navy Cross to Machinist's Mate Second Class Irving Randolph Saum, Jr., United States Naval Reserve, for extraordinary heroism and devotion to duty while serving on board the Destroyer U.S.S. *BORIE* (DD-215), in action against the enemy when that vessel attacked and sank an enemy submarine in the waters of the Caribbean Sea on the morning of 1 November 1943. When the forward engine room was severely holed by enemy action, resulting in rapid flooding to the vessel's water line, Machinist's Mate Second Class Saum unhesitatingly volunteered to enter the damaged compartment in order to close the secondary drain suction, enabling all available pumps to be placed on the suction of the after engine room and prevent its flooding. At great risk to his own life, he courageously descended ten feet below the surface of the debris-filled water and, despite heavy rolling of the ship, succeeded in accomplishing the hazardous task. The conduct of Machinist's Mate Second Class Saum throughout this action reflects great credit upon himself, and was in keeping with the highest traditions of the United States Naval Service.

LIEUTENANT PHILIP BAUSCHE BROWN, USNR

The President of the United States of America takes pleasure in presenting the Legion of Merit to Lieutenant Philip Bausche Brown, United States Naval Reserve, for exceptionally meritorious conduct in the performance of outstanding services to the Government of the United States as Executive Officer of the U.S.S. *BORIE* from June until 15 November 1943. During his five months as Executive Officer of the U.S.S. *BORIE*, Lieutenant Brown, by constant drills and carefully supervised, foresighted training, brought his crew to a state of maximum efficiency as an effective fighting unit. With rare foresight, he trained the crew and modified the ship's life lines so that effective gunfire could be brought to bear on an enemy in an area which previously had been a blanked sector, His careful training culminated in a virtual hand-to-hand action with an enemy submarine in the early morning of 1 November. By virtue of its previous schooling and indoctrination, the entire crew functioned in the most meritorious manner, performing all duties instinctively and with a minimum of orders from the bridge. During the long drawn out action he furnished the Commanding Officer with all information and assistance required to press the action. In addition, at intervals when the ships were in close contact, he manned a sub-machine gun, and despite the enemy counterfire directed at the bridge, his accurate fire assisted in clearing exposed personnel from the deck of the submarine. Lieutenant Brown's efficient conduct and inspiring example in operational and administrative capacities aided materially in the victory of his ship over a determined, skillful enemy, and in the efficient manner in which the entire Task Force carried out its difficult missions.

Bibliography

PUBLISHED WORKS

Abbazia, Patrick. *Mr. Roosevelt's Navy*. Annapolis, Md: Naval Institute, 1975.

Bertke, Donald A., Don Kindell, Gordon Smith. *World War II Sea War: France Falls, Britain Stands Alone*. Dayton, Ohio: Bertke Publishing, 2011.

—*World War II Sea War: Germany Sends Russia to the Allies*. Dayton, Ohio: Bertke Publications, 2012.

Breitman, Richard, Norman J. W. Goda, Timothy Naftali, Robert Wolfe. *U.S. Intelligence and the Nazis*. Cambridge and New York: Cambridge University Press, 2005.

Brice, Martin. *Axis Blockade Runners of World War II*. Anapolis, Md: Naval Institute Press, 1981.

Bruhn, David D. *Battle Stars for the "Cactus Navy": America's Yachts and Fishing Vessels in World War II*. Berwyn Heights, MD: HeritageBooks, 2014.

Conn, Stetson, Byron Fairchild. *United States Army in World War II, The Western Hemisphere, The Framework of Hemisphere Defense*. Washington, D.C.: U.S. Army Center of Military History, 1989.

Department of the Army. *Medical Department, United States Army, Preventive Medicine in World War II, Vol. VI, Communicable Diseases*. Washington, DC: Department of the Army, 1963.

Duffy, James P. *Hitler's Secret Pirate Fleet: The Deadliest Ships of World War II*. Lincoln, Nebraska: University of Nebraska Press, 2005.

Hilton, Stanley E. *Hitler's Secret War in South America, 1939-1945*. Baton Rouge, Louisiana: Louisiana State University Press, 1981.

Kerr, George F. *Business in Great Waters*. London, UK: Faber & Faber, 1951.

Lott, Arnold S. *Most Dangerous Sea*. Annapolis: U.S. Naval Institute, 1959.

McGaha, Richard L. Dissertation, *The Politics of Espionage: Nazi Diplomats and Spies in Argentina, 1933-1945*. Athens, Ohio: Ohio University, 2009.

Morison, Samuel Eliot. *History of United States Naval Operation in World War II: The Battle of the Atlantic September 1939-May 1943*. Boston: Little, Brown, 1984.

—*The Two-Ocean War*. Boston: Little, Brown, 1963.

Office of the CNO. *Post Mortems on Enemy Submarines, Report on the Interrogation of Survivors from U-128 Sunk on May 17, 1943*. Washington, DC: Office of the CNO, 1943.

—*Report on the Interrogation of Survivors from U-513 Sunk on July 19, 1943*. Washington DC: Office of the CNO, 1943.

—*Report on the Interrogation of Survivors from U-591 Sunk on 30 July 1943*. Washington DC: Office of the CNO, 1943.

Penteado, Carlos José Asumpção. Thesis *The Brazilian Participation in World War II*. Fort Leavenworth, Kansas: U.S. Army Command and General Staff College, 2006.

Piekalkiewicz, Janusz. *Sea War*. London: Blandford Press, 1987.

Pope, Dudley. *The Battle of the River Plate: The Hunt for the German Pocket Battleship Graf Spee*. Ithaca, New York: McBooks, 2005.

Ragnarsson, Ragnar J. *US Navy PBY Catalina Units of the Atlantic War*. Oxford, U.K.: Osprey, 2006.

Roberts, Michael D. *Dictionary of American Naval Aviation Squadrons, Volume 2*. Washington, D.C.: Naval Historical Center, 2000.

Roosevelt, Franklin Delano. *F. D. R. His Personal Letters 1928-1945 II*. New York: Duell, Sloan and Pearce, 1950.

Stern, Robert S. *Big Gun Battles: Warship Duels of the Second World War*. Barnsley, Great Britain: Seaforth, 2015.

U.S. Government Printing Office. *Building the Navy's Bases in World War II: History of the Bureau of Yards and Docks and the Civil Engineer Corps 1940-1946 Volume II*. Washington, DC: U.S. Government Printing Office, 1947.

U.S. Government Printing Office, *Final Report on the Interrogation of Survivors from German Blockade Runner Kota Nopan Scuttled on March 10, 1943 and of Sole Survivor from German Blockade Runner Speybank Sunk on March 3, 1943*. Washington, DC: U.S. Government Printing Office, 1943.

West, Nigel. *Historical Dictionary of World War II Intelligence*. Plymouth, UK: Scarecrow Press, 2008.

Wise, James E. *Sailors' Journey into War*. Kent, Ohio: Kent State University Press, 1998.

WAR DIARIES

British Admiralty, Commandant Fifteenth Naval District, Commander South Atlantic Force, Commander Task Group 23.1, Patrol Bombing Squadron VB-107, USS *Barry*, USS *Card*, USS *Cincinnati*, USS *Goff*, USS *Humboldt*, USS *Milwaukee*, USS *Moffett*, USS *Omaha*, USS *PC-494*, USS *Santee*, USS *Saucy*, USS *Seneca*, USS *Siren*, USS *Somers*, USS *Thrush*.

WAR HISTORIES

Commander-in-Chief Atlantic Fleet, Composite Squadron VC-9, Fleet Air Wing 16, Patrol Bombing Squadron VPB-74, Patrol Bombing Squadron VPB-94, Patrol Bombing Squadron VPB-127, Patrol Bombing Squadron VPB-129, Patrol Squadron VP-74, Patrol Squadron VP-83 and Bombing Squadron VB-107, USS *Barnegat*.

Notes

ACRONYMS USED IN CHAPTER NOTES

CincLantFlt	Commander in Chief, Atlantic Fleet
CNO	Chief of Naval Operations
Com 15	Commandant Fifteenth Naval District
ComSoLantFor	Commander South Atlantic Force
CTG	Commander Task Group
CTF	Commander Task Force
DANAS	Dictionary of American Aviation Squadrons
DANFS	Directory of American Naval Fighting Ships
HMAS	His/Her Majesty's Australian Ship
HMS	His/Her Majesty's Ship (Royal Navy)
ONI	Office of Naval Intelligence
USS	United States Ship
VB	Bombing Squadron
VP	Patrol Squadron
VPB	Patrol Bombing Squadron

PREFACE NOTES
[1] CTF 23 serial 0026 of 15 May 1942.
[2] Jonas Ingram, *DANFS*.
[3] Jonas Ingram, *DANFS*; *United States Naval Administration in World War II, Commander South Atlantic Force, Commander-in-Chief, Atlantic Fleet, Vol. XI*, 1 (http://www.ibiblio.org/hyperwar/USN/Admin-Hist/146-SouthAtlantic/146-SoLant-Narrative.html: accessed 3 November 2016).
[4] Jonas Ingram, *DANFS*.
[5] Marek Pruszewicz, The day the entire German fleet surrendered, BBC World Service (http://www.bbc.com/news/magazine-30128199: accessed 29 October 2016).
[6] Marek Pruszewicz, The day the entire German fleet surrendered; Eric W. Osborne, Naval Warfare (http://encyclopedia.1914-1918-online.net/article/naval_warfare: accessed 30 October 2016).
[7] ut supra.
[8] Heather Ramsey, A Young British Officer's Account of the Awful Events at Scapa Flow (http://knowledgenuts.com/2015/09/11/a-young-british-officers-account-of-the-awful-events-at-scapa-flow/: accessed 30 October 2016).
[9] Richard Cavendish, The German battle fleet scuttled at Scapa Flow, *History Today*, Volume 59 Issue 6 June 2009
[10] CincLantFlt, Atlantic Fleet History, 13 May 1946.

[11] CincLantFlt, Atlantic Fleet History, 13 May 1946; The Battle of the Atlantic, Vol. II: U-boat Operations (National Security Agency, SRH-008) (http://ibiblio.org/hyperwar/ETO/Ultra/SRH-008/SRH008-13.html: accessed 7 November 2016), 183.

[12] CincLantFlt, Atlantic Fleet History, 13 May 1946; The Battle of the Atlantic, Vol. II: U-boat Operations, 184.

[13] CincLantFlt, Atlantic Fleet History, 13 May 1946.

[14] Ibid.

[15] Ibid.

[16] Ibid.

[17] The *Scharnhorst* is sunk in 'Battle of the North Cape' (http://ww2today.com/26th-december-1943-the-scharnhorst-is-sunk-in-battle-of-the-north-cape: accessed 28 October 2016).

[18] The *Scharnhorst* is sunk in 'Battle of the North Cape,' *World War II Today*.

[19] CincLantFlt, Atlantic Fleet History, 13 May 1946; The *Scharnhorst* is sunk in 'Battle of the North Cape,' *World War II Today*; The Battleship *Scharnhorst* (http://www.kbismarck.com/scharnhorst.html: accessed 28 October 2016).

[20] CincLantFlt, Atlantic Fleet History, 13 May 1946.

[21] Alfonso Arenas, Jonathan Ryan, Hilfskreuzer (http://www.bismarck-class.dk/hilfskreuzer/hilfskreuzer_introduction.html: accessed 24 October 2016).

[22] CincLantFlt, Atlantic Fleet History, 13 May 1946.

[23] *Spreewald*, Uboat.net.

[24] *Doggerbank*, Uboat.net; Arenas and Ryan, Hilfskreuzer.

[25] CincLantFlt, Atlantic Fleet History, 13 May 1946.

[26] Ibid.

[27] Intelligence Report 42-43, Office of the CNO, 15 May 1943; The Battle of the Atlantic, Vol. II: U-boat Operations, 183.

CHAPTER 1 NOTES

[1] CTG 23.1, Report of Interception and Destruction of the German Blockade Runner "*Kota Nopan*" (Ex-Dutch "*Kota Pinang*"), 14 March 1943.

[2] The Battle of the Atlantic Vol. II: U-boat Operations, 183-184.

[3] Ibid.

[4] Final Report on the Interrogation of Survivors from German Blockade Runner *Kota Nopan* Scuttled on March 10, 1943 and of Sole Survivor from German Blockade Runner *Speybank* Sunk on March 3, 1943 (Washington, DC: Office of the CNO, U.S. Government Printing Office, 1943); German War Decorations, Uboat.net.

[5] CTG 23.1, Report of Interception and Destruction of the German Blockade Runner "*Kota Nopan*" (Ex-Dutch "*Kota Pinang*"), 14 March 1943.

[6] CTG 23.1, Report of Interception and Destruction of the German Blockade Runner "*Kota Nopan*" (Ex-Dutch "*Kota Pinang*"), 14 March 1943; Commanding Officer, USS *Savannah* (CL-42), Report of Action – Interception and scuttling of German Blockade Runner. Believed to be the

"*Kota Tjandi*" (*Karin*) March 10, 1943, 10 March 1943; *Santee* War Diary, March 1943.

[7] ut supra.

[8] ut supra.

[9] CTG 23.1, Report of Interception and Destruction of the German Blockade Runner "*Kota Nopan*" (Ex-Dutch "*Kota Pinang*"), 14 March 1943.

[10] Final Report on the Interrogation of Survivors from German Blockade Runner *Kota Nopan* Scuttled on March 10, 1943 and of Sole Survivor from German Blockade Runner *Speybank*.

[11] Ibid.

[12] Ibid.

[13] Ibid.

[14] Ibid.

[15] Ibid.

[16] CTG 23.1, Report of Interception and Destruction of the German Blockade Runner "*Kota Nopan*" (Ex-Dutch "*Kota Pinang*"), 14 March 1943.

[17] CTG 23.1, Report of Interception and Destruction of the German Blockade Runner "*Kota Nopan*" (Ex-Dutch "*Kota Pinang*"), 14 March 1943; Commanding Officer, USS *Savannah* (CL-42), Report of Action – Interception and scuttling of German Blockade Runner. Believed to be the "*Kota Tjandi*" (*Karin*) March 10, 1943, 10 March 1943.

[18] Commanding Officer, USS *Savannah* (CL-42), Report of Action – Interception and scuttling of German Blockade Runner. Believed to be the "*Kota Tjandi*" (*Karin*) March 10, 1943, 10 March 1943; Final Report on the Interrogation of Survivors from German Blockade Runner *Kota Nopan* Scuttled on March 10, 1943 and of Sole Survivor from German Blockade Runner *Speybank* Sunk on March 3, 1943.

[19] Final Report on the Interrogation of Survivors from German Blockade Runner *Kota Nopan* Scuttled on March 10, 1943 and of Sole Survivor from German Blockade Runner *Speybank* Sunk on March 3, 1943.

[20] Ibid.

[21] Ibid.

[22] Commanding Officer, USS *Savannah* (CL-42), Report of Action – Interception and scuttling of German Blockade Runner. Believed to be the "*Kota Tjandi*" (*Karin*) March 10, 1943, 10 March 1943.

[23] Commanding Officer, USS *Savannah* (CL-42), Report of Action – Interception and scuttling of German Blockade Runner. Believed to be the "*Kota Tjandi*" (*Karin*) March 10, 1943, 10 March 1943; Final Report on the Interrogation of Survivors from German Blockade Runner *Kota Nopan* Scuttled on March 10, 1943 and of Sole Survivor from German Blockade Runner *Speybank* Sunk on March 3, 1943.

[24] Ibid.

[25] General Orders: Bureau of Naval Personnel Information Bulletin No. 319 (October 1943), No. 320 (November 1943), and No. 321 (December 1943).

CHAPTER 2 NOTES

[1] Janusz Piekalkiewicz, *Sea War* (London: Blandford Press, 1987), 20.

[2] "Destroyer Escorts in the Atlantic," Destroyer Escort Historical Museum USS *Slater* DE766
(http://www.ussslater.org/history/dehistory/history_atlanticbattle.html: accessed 29 January 2016; Thomas A. Hughes, Battle of the Atlantic World War II, *Encyclopedia Britannica* (http://www.britannica.com/event/Battle-of-the-Atlantic: 29 January 2016).

[3] Foreign Stations, Naval-History.net (http://www.naval-history.net/xDKWW2-3909-04RN.htm: accessed 29 January 2016); Graham Watson, World War 2 at Sea, Organisation of the Royal Navy 1939-1945 (http://www.naval-history.net/xGW-RNOrganisation1939-45.htm: accessed 3 September 2016).

[4] Allen M. Howard, Freetown, Sierra Leone and World War II: Assessing the Impact of the War and the Contributions Made case study (http://www.ascleiden.nl/news/freetown-sierra-leone-and-world-war-ii-assessing-impact-war-and-contributions-made: accessed 29 January 2016).

[5] Foreign Stations, Naval-History.net (http://www.naval-history.net/xDKWW2-3909-04RN.htm: accessed 29 January 2016); Naval-history.net (http://www.naval-history.net/WW2CampaignRoyalNavy.htm; Robert S. Stern, *Big Gun Battles: Warship Duels of the Second World War* (Barnsley, Great Britain: Seaforth, 2015), 5.

[6] Leo Niehorster with Donald Kindell and Mark E. Horan, "Order of Battle South Atlantic Command 3 September 1939" (http://niehorster.org/017_britain/39_navy/south-atlantic.html: accessed 5 February 2016); Allied Warship finder, Uboat.net.

[7] Piekalkiewicz, *Sea War 1939-1945*, 26.

[8] Dudley Pope, *The Battle of the River Plate: The Hunt for the German Pocket Battleship Graf Spee* (Ithaca, New York: McBooks, 2005), 15-16.

[9] Ibid.

[10] German Ship Bearing Wheat Taken by British Cruiser 42 Crew Members Held as Prisoners of War, *Milwaukee (WI) Sentinel*, 5 September 1939.

[11] Ibid.

[12] HMS *Ajax* (22), Uboat.net.

CHAPTER 3 NOTES

[1] *Graf Spee* and *Altmark* in the South Atlantic 1939 Merchant Ships Sunk, part of the Acorn Archive Hearts of Oak (http://freepages.family.rootsweb.ancestry.com/~treevecwll/spees.htm: accessed 20 March 2016).

[2] Piekalkiewicz, *Sea War 1939-1945*, 16.

[3] Piekalkiewicz, *Sea War 1939-1945*, 38; *Graf Spee* and *Altmark* in the South Atlantic 1939 Merchant Ships Sunk.

[4] *Graf Spee* and *Altmark* in the South Atlantic 1939 Merchant Ships Sunk.

[5] Piekalkiewicz, *Sea War 1939-1945*, 30, 39.

[6] *Graf Spee* and *Altmark* in the South Atlantic 1939 Merchant Ships Sunk.

[7] Piekalkiewicz, *Sea War 1939-1945*, 40; *Graf Spee* and *Altmark* in the South Atlantic 1939 Merchant Ships Sunk.

[8] *Graf Spee* and *Altmark* in the South Atlantic 1939 Merchant Ships Sunk.

[9] MV *Trevanion*, part of the Acorn Archive Hearts of Oak (http://freepages.family.rootsweb.ancestry.com/~treevecwll/trevanion.htm); *Graf Spee*, RNZN Communicators Association (http://rnzncomms.org/2013/09/27/graf-spee/: all accessed 20 March 2016).

[10] MV *Trevanion*, part of the Acorn Archive Hearts of Oak.

[11] *Graf Spee* and *Altmark* in the South Atlantic 1939 Merchant Ships Sunk.

[12] Piekalkiewicz, *Sea War 1939-1945*, 44, 46; *Graf Spee* and *Altmark* in the South Atlantic 1939 Merchant Ships Sunk.

[13] Piekalkiewicz, *Sea War 1939-1945*, 47; *Graf Spee* and *Altmark* in the South Atlantic 1939 Merchant Ships Sunk.

[14] ut supra.

[15] ut supra.

[16] Rickard, J (24 November 2007), Battle of the River Plate, 13 December 1939 (http://www.historyofwar.org/articles/battles_river_plate.html: accessed 20 March 2016).

[17] Ibid.

[18] Rickard, Battle of the River Plate; Adrian Jarvis, A Gentleman's War? The Diary of Captain Albert Horace Brown of SS *Huntsman* (http://www.cnrs-scrn.org/northern_mariner/vol11/nm_11_1_39to57.pdf: accessed 23 March 2016).

[19] Rickard, Battle of the River Plate; Correspondence with Rob Hoole, 29 March 2016.

[20] Despatch sent by Rear Adm. Henry H. Harwood, K.C.B., O.B.E. to the Lords Commissioners of the Admiralty on 30 December 1939, published in the *London Gazette*, issue 37989, 17 June 1947.

[21] Piekalkiewicz, *Sea War 1939-1945*, 49; Rickard, Battle of the River Plate.

[22] ut supra.

[23] Piekalkiewicz, *Sea War 1939-1945*, 49-50; Rickard, Battle of the River Plate; Henry H. Harwood despatch of 30 December 1939.

[24] Rickard, Battle of the River Plate; Henry H. Harwood despatch of 30 December 1939.

[25] Rickard, Battle of the River Plate.

[26] Henry H. Harwood despatch of 30 December 1939.

[27] Rickard, Battle of the River Plate; Henry H. Harwood despatch of 30 December 1939.

[28] Rickard, Battle of the River Plate; HMS *Ajax* (22), Uboat.net; The Crew of HMS *Exeter* at the Battle of the River Plate, *Exeter* Memories (http://www.exetermemories.co.uk/em/_people/crewexeter.php (accessed 24 September 2016).

[29] Casualty Lists of the Royal Navy and Dominion Navies, World War 2, Naval-History.net (http://www.naval-history.net/xDKCas1939-12DEC.htm: accessed 22 March 2016)

[30] Henry H. Harwood despatch of 30 December 1939.

[31] Ibid.

[32] Ibid.

[33] Rickard, Battle of the River Plate.

[34] Ibid.

[35] Episodes & Studies Volume 1 Achilles at the River Plate, New Zealand Electronic Text Collection (http://nzetc.victoria.ac.nz/tm/scholarly/tei-WH2-1Epi-t1-g1-t2.html: accessed 25 March 2016); Rickard, Battle of the River Plate; HMS *Ajax* (22), Uboat.net.

[36] Episodes & Studies Volume 1 Achilles at the River Plate; Piekalkiewicz, *Sea War 1939-1945*, 25, 50.

[37] Rickard, Battle of the River Plate.

[38] Piekalkiewicz, *Sea War 1939-1945*, 25; Rickard, Battle of the River Plate.

[39] Piekalkiewicz, *Sea War 1939-1945*, 50; Rickard, Battle of the River Plate.

[40] Rickard, Battle of the River Plate.

[41] Piekalkiewicz, *Sea War 1939-1945*, 50; Rickard, Battle of the River Plate.

[42] Episodes & Studies Volume 1 Achilles at the River Plate; Piekalkiewicz, *Sea War 1939-1945*, 16-25; Rickard, Battle of the River Plate; HMS *Ajax* (22), Uboat.net.

[43] The Battle of the River Plate – Fleet Auxiliary Support, Historical RFA (http://www.historicalrfa.org/archived-stories/1023-the-battle-of-the-river-plate-royal-fleet-auxiliary-support: accessed 22 March 2016).

[44] Piekalkiewicz, *Sea War 1939-1945*, 52; Rickard, Battle of the River Plate.

[45] Rickard, Battle of the River Plate.

[46] Graham Watson, World War 2 at Sea, Organisation of the Royal Navy 1939-1945 (http://www.naval-history.net/xGW-RNOrganisation1939-45.htm: accessed 3 September 2016).

CHAPTER 4 NOTES

[1] CincLantFlt, Atlantic Fleet History, 13 May 1946.

[2] Morison, *Two-Ocean War*, 13-14; The Official Chronological History of the U.S. Navy in World War II (https://www.ibiblio.org/hyperwar/USN/USN-Chron/USN-Chron-1939.html: accessed 25 March 2016).

[3] Diary entry by Henry Morgenthau Jr., cited by Joseph Perisco in *Roosevelt's Secret War*; Admiral Harold R. Stark, Eighth Chief of Naval Operations, August 1, 1939–March 26, 1942 (http://www.history.navy.mil/browse-by-topic/commemorations-toolkits/cno-and-opnav-centennial/chiefs-of-naval-operations/admiral-harold-r--stark.html: accessed 31 March 2016).

[4] Morison, *Two-Ocean War*, 14-15.

[5] Atlantic Fleet History, 13 May 1946.

[6] The Official Chronological History of the U.S. Navy in World War II.

[7] Atlantic Fleet History, 13 May 1946.

[8] Morison, *Two-Ocean War*, 15; The Official Chronological History of the U.S. Navy in World War II.

[9] Atlantic Fleet, Atlantic Fleet History, 13 May 1946.

[10] Morison, *Two-Ocean War*, 15; *DANAS*, 266.

[11] The Official Chronological History of the U.S. Navy in World War II; *Lapwing*, *DANFS*.
[12] The Official Chronological History of the U.S. Navy in World War II.
[13] *Wichita*, *DANFS*.
[14] Atlantic Fleet History, 13 May 1946.
[15] Ibid.
[16] Franklin Delano Roosevelt, *F. D. R. His Personal Letters 1928-1945 II* (New York: Duell, Sloan and Pearce, 1950), 936-937; Patrick Abbazia, *Mr. Roosevelt's Navy* (Annapolis, Md: Naval Institute, 1975), 70.
[17] Atlantic Fleet History, 13 May 1946.
[18] Ibid.
[19] C. Peter Chen, Two-Ocean Navy Act 19 Jul 1940 (http://ww2db.com/battle_spec.php?battle_id=230: accessed 21 August 2016).
[20] Democratic National Convention (July 19, 1940) Franklin D. Roosevelt Transcript (http://millercenter.org/president/fdroosevelt/speeches/speech-3318: accessed 21 August 2016).

CHAPTER 5 NOTES

[1] Geoffrey B. Mason, HMS *Ark Royal*, Service Histories of Royal Navy Warships in World War 2 (http://www.naval-history.net/xGM-Chrono-04CV-HMS_Ark_Royal.htm: accessed 26 August 2016).
[2] Ibid.
[3] Ibid.
[4] Ibid.
[5] Mason, HMS *Ark Royal*; *Empire Ability*, Uboat.net.
[6] *Empire Ability*, Uboat.net.
[7] Ibid.
[8] *Empire Ability*, Uboat.net; Ships hit from convoy SL-78, Uboat.net.
[9] *Duguay-Trouin*, World War II Database (http://ww2db.com/ship_spec.php?ship_id=835: accessed 31 March 2016).
[10] Geoffrey B. Mason, HMS *Renown*, Service Histories of Royal Navy Warships in World War 2 (http://www.naval-history.net/xGM-Chrono-02BC-Renown.htm: accessed 26 August 2016).
[11] Allen Tony, SS *Adolph Woermann* (+1939) (http://www.wrecksite.eu/wreck.aspx?134447: accessed 22 August 2016); HMS *Renown*, Service Histories of Royal Navy Warships in World War 2.
[12] *Adolph Woermann*, Sixtant War II in the South Atlantic (http://www.sixtant.net/2011/artigos.php?cat=german-blockade-runners-&sub=a-z-(24-pages--105-images)&tag=3)adolph-woermann: accessed 22 August 2016).
[13] *Arandora Star*, Uboat.net; *Greenock* (https://www.britannica.com/place/Greenock: accessed 22 August 2016).
[14] *Arandora Star*, Uboat.net; Günther Prien, Uboat.net; Jan Lettens (pseudonym) (http://www.wrecksite.eu/userView.aspx?1: accessed 22 August 2016).

[15] Donald A. Hollway, The Bull of Scapa Flow, Uboat.net.

[16] Hollway, The Bull of Scapa Flow; Salvage Operations in Scapa Flow (http://www.scapaflowwrecks.com/history/salvage.php: accessed 24 August 2016)

[17] Hollway, The Bull of Scapa Flow; The sinking of 'HMS *Royal Oak*,' Remembering Scotland at War (http://www.rememberingscotlandatwar.org.uk/accessible/exhibition/190/t he-sinking-of-hms-royal-oak: accessed 24 August 2016).

[18] Hollway, The Bull of Scapa Flow.

[19] Ibid.

[20] Correspondence with Dwight Messimer, 7 December 2016.

[21] Hollway, The Bull of Scapa Flow.

[22] Hollway, The Bull of Scapa Flow; The sinking of 'HMS *Royal Oak*,' Remembering Scotland at War; History Beneath the Waves (http://www.scapaflowwrecks.com/history/: accessed 24 August 2016).

[23] The sinking of 'HMS *Royal Oak*,' Remembering Scotland at War; *Daisy II*, Aberdeen Built Ships (http://www.aberdeenships.com/single.asp?offset=700&index=99781: accessed 24 August 2016).

[24] HMS *Royal Oak* (http://www.hmsroyaloak.co.uk/: accessed 25 August 2016).

[25] Hollway, The Bull of Scapa Flow.

[26] Stephen Sherman, Grand Cross to the Iron Cross (1939) The Highest German Decoration of WWII (http://acepilots.com/medals/grand-cross-iron.html: accessed 25 August 2016).

[27] *U-47*, Uboat.net; Top U-boat Aces, Günther Prien, Uboat.net.

[28] HMS *Renown*, Service Histories of Royal Navy Warships in World War 2; The History of Simon's Town, The Simon's Town Historical Society (http://www.simonstown.com/stdc/history/history.htm: accessed 26 August 2016).

[29] HMS *Renown*, Service Histories of Royal Navy Warships in World War 2.

[30] HMS *Renown*, Service Histories of Royal Navy Warships in World War 2; Sir Charles Edward Barrington Simeon, RN, Uboat.net.

[31] Geoffrey B. Mason, HMS, later HMAS *Shropshire*, Service Histories of Royal Navy Warships in World War 2 (http://www.naval-history.net/xGM-Chrono-06CA-HMS_Shropshire.htm: accessed 26 August 2016); Capt. J. P. Gornall, SS *Adolf Leonhardt* (http://www.wrecksite.eu/wreck.aspx?59780: accessed 26 August 2016).

CHAPTER 6 NOTES

[1] Arenas and Ryan, Hilfskreuzer.

[2] Thomas A. Hughes, Marc Milner, Battle of the Atlantic, *Encyclopedia Britannica* (https://www.britannica.com/event/Battle-of-the-Atlantic: accessed 27 August 2016).

[3] SS *Wakama* [+1940], Wrecksite
(http://www.wrecksite.eu/wreck.aspx?172656: accessed 1 April 2016); HMS
Dorsetshire (40), Uboat.net.
[4] SS *Wakama* [+1940], Wrecksite; HMS *Dorsetshire* (40), Uboat.net.
[5] Ibid.
[6] The Official Chronological History of the U.S. Navy in World War II.
[7] Arenas and Ryan, Hilfskreuzer.
[8] Arenas and Ryan, Hilfskreuzer; Piekalkiewicz, *Sea War 1939-1945*, 66.
[9] Arenas and Ryan, Hilfskreuzer.
[10] Arenas and Ryan, Hilfskreuzer; Timeline for the German Commerce
Raider Schiff 16 - HSK 2 *Atlantis*
(http://ww2timelines.com/germany/raideratlantis.htm: accessed 30 August
2016).
[11] Arenas and Ryan, Hilfskreuzer.
[12] Ibid.
[13] Arenas and Ryan, Hilfskreuzer; Piekalkiewicz, *Sea War 1939-1945*, 66.
[14] Piekalkiewicz, *Sea War 1939-1945*, 70.
[15] James P. Duffy, *Hitler's Secret Pirate Fleet: The Deadliest Ships of World War II*
(Lincoln, Nebraska: University of Nebraska Press, 2005), 9.
[16] Duffy, *Hitler's Secret Pirate Fleet*, 10-11.
[17] Ibid, 11-12.
[18] Ibid, 12-13.
[19] Donald A. Bertke, Don Kindell, Gordon Smith, *World War II Sea War:
France Falls, Britain Stands Alone* (Dayton, Ohio: Bertke Publications, 2011),
190; Duffy, *Hitler's Secret Pirate Fleet*, 13;
[20] Delville Wood, South African Naval Forces
(http://www.delvillewood.com/navy.htm: accessed 31 August 2016).
[21] Ibid.
[22] Aberdeen Built Ships
(http://www.aberdeenships.com/related.asp?index=47461&shipid=101463:
accessed 7 September 2016).
[23] Arenas and Ryan, Hilfskreuzer; Piekalkiewicz, *Sea War 1939-1945*, 78.
[24] Arenas and Ryan, Hilfskreuzer; Piekalkiewicz, *Sea War 1939-1945*, 81.
[25] Arenas and Ryan, Hilfskreuzer; Piekalkiewicz, *Sea War 1939-1945*, 81.
Different sources cite different types and numbers of guns regarding the
armament of *Thor*.
[26] *Reynolds*, Uboat.net.
[27] HMS *Cornwall* (56), Uboat.net; Arenas and Ryan, Hilfskreuzer.
[28] ut supra.
[29] ut supra.
[30] The Loss of HMAS *Sydney II*
(http://www.defence.gov.au/sydneyii/finalreport/Report/Chapter%204.pdf:
accessed 31 August 2016).
[31] The Loss of HMAS *Sydney II*; Arenas and Ryan, Hilfskreuzer.
[32] Arenas and Ryan, Hilfskreuzer.
[33] Ibid.

[34] Arenas and Ryan, Hilfskreuzer; Piekalkiewicz, *Sea War 1939-1945*, 96; HMS *Alcantara* (F 88), Uboat.net.

[35] Arenas and Ryan, Hilfskreuzer.

[36] Ibid.

[37] Ibid.

[38] Ibid.

[39] Armed Merchant Cruisers, Uboat.net.

[40] Ibid.

[41] Ibid.

[42] Ibid.

[43] Arenas and Ryan, Hilfskreuzer.

[44] Ibid.

[45] Ibid.

[46] Ibid.

[47] HMS *Carnarvon Castle* (F 25), Uboat.net.

[48] Arenas and Ryan, Hilfskreuzer.

[49] Ibid.

[50] Ibid.

[51] Ibid.

[52] Ibid.

[53] Merchant Raider Badge Hilfskreuzer Kriegsabzeichen 1941-1945, Uboat.net.

CHAPTER 7 NOTES

[1] Fact File: Merchant Navy, WW2 People's War (http://www.bbc.co.uk/history/ww2peopleswar/timeline/factfiles/nonflash/a6652091.shtml: accessed 8 September 2016).

[2] Geoffrey B. Mason, HMS *Dorsetshire* Service Histories of Royal Navy Warships in World War 2 (http://www.naval-history.net/xGM-Chrono-06CA-Dorsetshire.htm: accessed 7 September 2016); Allied Convoy Codes (http://www.naval-history.net/xDKEscorts00Index.htm: accessed 7 September 2016).

[3] Mason, HMS *Dorsetshire*.

[4] Arnold Hague, WS Convoys - 1940 Sailings (http://www.naval-history.net/xAH-WSConvoys03-1940.htm: accessed 7 September 2016); Arnold Hague, Background to the WS Convoys (http://www.naval-history.net/xAH-WSConvoys02.htm: accessed 9 September 2016).

[5] Hague, WS Convoys - 1940 Sailings; Hague, Background to the WS Convoys; *Atreus* 1911 HMS - Minelayer Base Ship (http://forums.clydemaritime.co.uk/viewtopic.php?t=25463: accessed 7 September 2016).

[6] Hague, WS Convoys - 1940 Sailings.

[7] Ibid.

[8] Ibid.

[9] Ibid.

[10] C. Peter Chen, Admiral Hipper, World War II Database (http://ww2db.com/ship_spec.php?ship_id=278: accessed 7 September 2016).

[11] Hague, WS Convoys - 1940 Sailings; Gallery No 39 – Troopships (http://www.britisharmedforces.org/pages/nat_troopships.htm: accessed 7 September 2016).

[12] Hague, WS Convoys - 1940 Sailings; HMS *Berwick* (65), Uboat.net.

[13] Hague, WS Convoys - 1940 Sailings.

[14] Hague, WS Convoys - 1940 Sailings; World War II Day-By-Day (http://worldwar2daybyday.blogspot.com/2012/08/day-1079-august-14-1942.html: accessed 7 September 2016).

[15] Hague, WS Convoys - 1940 Sailings.

[16] German Surface Raiders, Naval History and Heritage Command (https://www.history.navy.mil/research/library/online-reading-room/title-list-alphabetically/n/naval-armed-guard-service-in-world-war-ii/german-surface-raiders.html: accessed 9 September 2016); *Nordmark*, German Naval History (http://www.german-navy.de/kriegsmarine/ships/auxships/nordmark/history.html: accessed 9 September 2016).

[17] Correspondence with Dwight Messimer, 9 December 2016.

[18] Ibid.

[19] Ibid.

[20] *Nordmark*, German Naval History; USS *Conecuh* (AOR-110) (http://www.navsource.org/archives/09/19/19110.htm: accessed 10 September 2016).

[21] *Nordmark*, German Naval History.

[22] War Diary records for Axis blockade runners, liners, supply ships, and cargo vessels, Stone & Stone Second World War Books (http://books.stonebooks.com/record/1004329/: accessed 10 September 2016).

[23] Arenas and Ryan, Hilfskreuzer (http://www.bismarck-class.dk/hilfskreuzer/hilfskreuzer_introduction.html: accessed 24 October 2016).

[24] Ibid.

[25] Ibid.

[26] Ibid.

[27] German Auxiliary Cruiser *Pinguin* - *Pinguin* Voyage - Norwegian Whaling Fleet Captured (http://www.liquisearch.com/german_auxiliary_cruiser_pinguin/pinguin_voyage/norwegian_whaling_fleet_captured: accessed 10 September 2016); Norwegian Victims of *Pinguin* Capture of the Whaling Fleet, Jan. 14, 1941 (http://www.warsailors.com/raidervictims/pinguin2.html: accessed 11 September 2016).

[28] ut supra.

[29] ut supra.

[30] German Auxiliary Cruiser *Pinguin - Pinguin* Voyage - Norwegian Whaling Fleet Captured.

[31] Ibid.

[32] Ibid.

[33] Ibid.

[34] German Auxiliary Cruiser *Pinguin - Pinguin* Voyage - Norwegian Whaling Fleet Captured; War Diary records for Axis blockade runners, liners, supply ships, and cargo vessels, Stone & Stone Second World War Books.

[35] ut supra.

CHAPTER 8 NOTES

[1] General Orders: War Department, General Orders No. 177 (December 4, 1915).

[2] *United States Naval Administration in World War II, Commander South Atlantic Force, Commander-in-Chief, Atlantic Fleet, Vol. XI,* 9; Samuel Eliot Morison, *The Battle of the Atlantic September 1939-May 1943* (Boston, Mass: Little, Brown, 1984), 32-33.

[3] ut supra.

[4] *Commander South Atlantic Force, Commander-in-Chief, Atlantic Fleet, Vol. XI,* 9; Morison, *The Battle of the Atlantic September 1939-May 1943,* 84.

[5] *Commander South Atlantic Force, Commander-in-Chief, Atlantic Fleet, Vol. XI,* 10.

[6] Ibid.

[8] Ibid, 11-12.

[9] Ibid, 12.

[10] Ibid, 14.

[11] ut supra.

[12] Weekly Intelligence Report, Number 56, April 4, 1941, Naval Intelligence Division, Naval Staff, Admiralty (http://www.defence.gov.au/sydneyii/NAA/NAA.006.0150.pdf: accessed 1 March 2016).

[13] Ibid.

[14] Weekly Intelligence Report, Number 56, April 4, 1941, Naval Intelligence Division, Naval Staff, Admiralty; "Six Axis ships set on fire in South Atlantic," *Herald-Tribune,* April 1, 1941.

[15] Marc Milner, "The Three Princes: Navy, Part 38," April 17, 2010, *Legion Magazine* (https://legionmagazine.com/en/2010/04/the-three-princes-navy-part-38/#sthash.71pnwMLv.dpuf: accessed 29 February 2016).

[16] Ibid.

[17] Ibid.

[18] Ibid.

[19] "Six Axis ships set on fire in South Atlantic," *Herald-Tribune,* April 1, 1941.

[20] CincLantFlt, Atlantic Fleet History, 13 May 1946.

[21] Geoffrey B. Mason, Service Histories of Royal Navy Warships in World War II, HMS *London* (http://www.naval-history.net/xGM-Chrono-06CA-HMS_London.htm: accessed 18 September 2016).

[22] War Diary records for Naval operations in the South Atlantic (http://books.stonebooks.com/record/1000398/: accessed 28 September 2016).

[23] HMS *London* (69), Uboat.net; Donald A. Bertke, Don Kindell, Gordon Smith, *World War II Sea War: Germany Sends Russia to the Allies* (Dayton, Ohio: Bertke Publications, 2012), 43-44.

[24] *Egerland*, War II in the South Atlantic (http://www.sixtant.net/2011/artigos.php?cat=german-blockade-runners-&sub=a-z-(24-pages--105-images)&tag=9)egerland: accessed 18 September 2016).

[25] *Egerland*, War II in the South Atlantic; Bertke, Kindell, Smith, *World War II Sea War*, 43-44.

[26] HMS *London* (69), Uboat.net; Bertke, Kindell, Smith, *World War II Sea War*, 57; Arenas and Ryan, Hilfskreuzer.

[27] George F. Kerr, *Business in Great Waters* (London, UK: Faber & Faber, 1951), 59-60.

[28] Ibid.

[29] Bertke, Et Al., *World War II Sea War*, 117.

[30] Auke Visser´s German Esso Tanker's site (http://www.aukevisser.nl/german/id125.htm: accessed 18 September 2016)

[31] Lloyd Godman, Codes of Survival (http://www.lloydgodman.net/codes/Text/1939.htm: accessed 27 September 2016).

[32] Gaby Klika, What Happened to the Chinese Crew of the SS *Erlangen*?, 20 May 2014 (http://www.newlandmagazine.com.au/vision/article/794: accessed 25 September 2016).

[33] Klika, What Happened to the Chinese Crew of the SS *Erlangen*?; Lloyd Godman, Codes of Survival.

[34] ut supra.

[35] ut supra.

[36] ut supra.

[37] Klika, What Happened to the Chinese Crew of the SS *Erlangen*?

[38] Story: Subantarctic islands, *Teara* (http://www.teara.govt.nz/en/subantarctic-islands/page-1: accessed 25 September 2016); The Merchant Navy – Under the Southern Cross, New Zealand at War (http://www.nzhistory.net.nz/war/the-merchant-navy/under-the-southern-cross: accessed 27 September 2016.

[39] Klika, What Happened to the Chinese Crew of the SS *Erlangen*?; Hans Peter Jürgens, Last Rounding of the "Priwall" (http://www.caphorniers.cl/priwall/last_rounding.htm: 27 September 2016).

[40] Geoffrey B. Mason, Service Histories of Royal Navy Warships in World War II, HMS *Despatch* (http://www.naval-history.net/xGM-Chrono-06CL-Despatch.htm: accessed 18 September 2016).

[41] The Atlantic Charter, FDR Presidential Library & Museum (https://fdrlibrary.org/atlantic-charter: accessed 29 September 2016).

[42] The Atlantic Charter, FDR Presidential Library & Museum; The Atlantic Conference & Charter, 1941, Office of the Historian (https://history.state.gov/milestones/1937-1945/atlantic-conf: accessed 29 September 2016).

[43] The Atlantic Conference & Charter, 1941, Office of the Historian.

[44] Ibid.

[45] Ibid.

[46] *Somers, DANFS*; Morison, *The Battle of the Atlantic September 1939-May 1943*, 83-84; Admiralty War Diaries, 18 November 1941.

[47] Personal Interview of Chief Charles J. Martin, War Patrol – DD *SOMERS*, 29 October 1943, CNO Naval Records and Library.

[48] *Somers, DANFS*.

[49] The Last "Prize" Awards in the U.S. Navy?, Strategy Page, 10 October 2016 (https://www.strategypage.com/cic/docs/cic205b.asp#one: accessed 10 October 2016).

[50] Ibid.

[51] Ibid.

CHAPTER 9 NOTES

[1] Breitman, Richard; Goda, Norman J.W.; Naftali, Timothy; Wolfe, Robert, *U.S. Intelligence and the Nazis* (Cambridge and New York: Cambridge University Press, 2005).

[2] David P. Mowry, German Clandestine Activities in South America in World War II, Office of Archives and History National Security Agency/Central Security Service, 1989 (https://www.nsa.gov/news-features/declassified-documents/cryptologic-histories/assets/files/german_clandestine_activities.pdf: accessed 17 October 2016).

[3] Mowry, German Clandestine Activities.

[4] Mowry, German Clandestine Activities; Ronald C. Newton, *The "Nazi Menace" in Argentina, 1931-1947* (Stanford, CA: Stanford Press, 1992), 181.

[5] Richard L. McGaha, *The Politics of Espionage: Nazi Diplomats and Spies in Argentina, 1933-1945* (Ohio University, 2009), 170-174 (https://etd.ohiolink.edu/rws_etd/document/get/ohiou1256330041/inline: accessed 17 October 2016).

[6] McGaha, *The Politics of Espionage*, 174; Newton, *The "Nazi Menace"*, 53, 244.

[7] McGaha, *The Politics of Espionage*, 175.

[8] Nigel West, *Historical Dictionary of World War II Intelligence* (Plymouth, UK: Scarecrow Press, 2008), 4; Newton, *The "Nazi Menace"*, 176.

[9] Newton, *The "Nazi Menace"*, 176-178.

[10] Stanley E. Hilton, *Hitler's Secret War in South America, 1939-1945* (Baton Rouge, Louisiana: Louisiana State University Press, 1981), 29; German Espionage and Sabotage, Naval History and Heritage Command (http://www.history.navy.mil/research/library/online-reading-room/title-

list-alphabetically/g/german-espionage-and-sabotage.html: accessed 19 March 2016).

[11] Mowry, German Clandestine Activities in South America in World War II: Spying and Counterintelligence – Germany (http://histclo.com/essay/war/ww2/code/sci/sci-ger.html: accessed 17 October 2016).

[12] Battle of the Atlantic – Its Development 1939-1942 (http://www.naval-history.net/WW2CampaignsAtlanticDev.htm: accessed 18 October 2016).

[13] World War II: Spying and Counterintelligence – Germany.

[14] Christopher Klein, How South America Became a Nazi Haven (http://www.history.com/news/how-south-america-became-a-nazi-haven: accessed 18 October 2016).

[15] World War II Country Trends: Chile (http://histclo.com/essay/war/ww2/cou/reg/la/sa/ww2-chile.html: accessed 18 October 2016).

CHAPTER 10 NOTES

[1] Carlos José Asumpção Penteado, Thesis: "The Brazilian Participation in World War II" (Fort Leavenworth, Kansas: U.S. Army Command and General Staff College, 2006).

[2] *Nau Brasilis: The history, trajectory and resumption of Brazilian shipbuilding* (http://www.solariseditora.com.br/nau-brasilis-the-history-trajectory-and-resumption-of-brazilian-shipbuilding.htm: accessed 2 March 2016); Morison, *The Battle of the Atlantic September 1939-May 1943*, 378.

[3] Morison, *The Battle of the Atlantic September 1939-May 1943*, 378.

[4] Ibid, 378-379.

[5] ut supra.

[6] Army Air Forces in World War II, Vol. VII: Services Around the World, Prepared Under the Editorship of Wesley Frank Craven, Princeton University, and James Lea Cate, University of Chicago (https://www.ibiblio.org/hyperwar/AAF/VII/index.html#contents: accessed 5 March 2016), 51-52.

[7] CincLantFlt, Atlantic Fleet History, 13 May 1946.

[8] CincLantFlt, Atlantic Fleet History, 13 May 1946; Morison, *The Battle of the Atlantic September 1939-May 1943*, 379-380.

[9] Morison, *The Battle of the Atlantic September 1939-May 1943*, 379-380.

[10] Ibid.

[11] CincLantFlt, Atlantic Fleet History, 13 May 1946; *Commander South Atlantic Force, Commander-in-Chief, Atlantic Fleet, Vol. XI*, 10; Bruhn, *Battle Stars for the "Cactus Navy": America's Fishing Vessels and Yachts in World War II*, 182.

[12] Com 15 War Diary, 7 December 1941 to 1 June 1942.

[13] Bruhn, *Battle Stars for the "Cactus Navy"*, 183.

[14] *Commander South Atlantic Force, Commander-in-Chief, Atlantic Fleet, Vol. XI*, 10, 54.

[15] Bruhn, *Battle Stars for the "Cactus Navy"*, 183.

[16] Cristiano D'Adamo, Boats, Regia Marina Italiana (http://www.regiamarina.net/detail_text_with_list.asp?nid=84&lid=1&cid=9 : accessed 19 October 2016).

[17] *Commander South Atlantic Force, Commander-in-Chief, Atlantic Fleet, Vol. XI,* 10; *Milwaukee, Omaha* War Diary, May 1942; Cristiano D'Adamo, Boats, Regia Marina Italiana; *Milwaukee* War Diary, May 1942.

[18] *Commander South Atlantic Force, Commander-in-Chief, Atlantic Fleet, Vol. XI,* 10; *Moffett* War Diary, May 1942.

[19] *Thrush* War Diary, May 1942.

[20] *Thrush, DANFS.*

[21] *Thrush* War Diary, May 1942.

[22] Ibid.

[23] *Moffett, Thrush* War Diary, May 1942.

[24] *Milwaukee, Thrush* War Diary, May 1942.

[25] *Moffett* War Diary, May 1942.

[26] Ibid.

[27] Ibid.

[28] Ibid.

[29] Ibid.

[30] Ibid.

[31] Ibid.

[32] *Thrush* War Diary, May 1942.

[33] Ibid.

[34] *Commander South Atlantic Force, Commander-in-Chief, Atlantic Fleet, Vol. XI,* 10, 55, 57.

[35] Stetson Conn and Byron Fairchild, *United States Army in World War II, The Western Hemisphere, The Framework of Hemisphere Defense* (Washington, D.C.: U.S. Army Center of Military History, 1989), 323-324; Morison, *The Battle of the Atlantic September 1939-May 1943,* 276; *Commander South Atlantic Force, Commander-in-Chief, Atlantic Fleet, Vol. XI,* 62-63.

[36] CincLantFlt, Atlantic Fleet History, 13 May 1946.

[37] Conn and Fairchild, *United States Army in World War II,* 322-323.

[38] CincLantFlt, Atlantic Fleet History, 13 May 1946; Conn and Fairchild, *United States Army in World War II,* 322; *Commander South Atlantic Force, Commander-in-Chief, Atlantic Fleet, Vol. XI,* 50-51.

[39] CincLantFlt, Atlantic Fleet History, 13 May 1946; Conn and Fairchild, *United States Army in World War II,* 322-323.

[40] CincLantFlt, Atlantic Fleet History, 13 May 1946; Conn and Fairchild, *United States Army in World War II,* 324; *Commander South Atlantic Force, Commander-in-Chief, Atlantic Fleet, Vol. XI,* 68.

[41] CincLantFlt, Atlantic Fleet History, 13 May 1946; The Brazilian Navy, Uboat.net.

[42] *Commander South Atlantic Force, Commander-in-Chief, Atlantic Fleet, Vol. XI,* 68.

[43] Fourth Fleet Operation Plan No. 2-43, 4 September 1943.

[44] Ibid.

[45] *Commander South Atlantic Force, Commander-in-Chief, Atlantic Fleet, Vol. XI,* i.

CHAPTER 11 NOTES

[1] Arenas and Ryan, Hilfskreuzer.

[2] Ibid.

[3] Ibid.

[4] Intelligence Division, Office of CNO Intelligence Report Serial 77-43, of 28 October 1943, Subject: Raider "J" (Case History); Jon Guttman, The Last Raider (http://www.historynet.com/the-last-raider-july-97-world-war-ii-feature.htm: accessed 29 March 2016); The Gallant Liberty Ship SS *Stephen Hopkins* Sinks a German Raider, American Merchant Marine at War (http://www.usmm.org/hopkins.html: accessed 27 March 2016); Arenas and Ryan, Hilfskreuzer.

[5] Raider "J" (Case History); Guttman, "The Last Raider."

[6] ut supra.

[7] Raider "J" (Case History); Guttman, "The Last Raider"; Duffy, *Hitler's Secret Pirate Fleet,* 191; MV *Dalhousie* (+1942) (http://www.wrecksite.eu/wreck.aspx?137037: accessed 29 March 2016); *Stanvac Calcutta*: the Gallant Ship that Fought a German Raider (http://www.usmm.org/calcutta.html: accessed 29 March 2016).

[8] Raider "J" (Case History); German Surface Raiders, Naval History and Heritage Command (http://www.history.navy.mil/research/library/online-reading-room/title-list-alphabetically/n/naval-armed-guard-service-in-world-war-ii/german-surface-raiders.html: accessed 27 March 2016).

[9] "O'Hara, Edwin Joseph," Kings Pointers in World War II (http://kingspointww2.org/ohara-edwin-joseph/: accessed 28 March 2016); Account of Mr. Cronk, Second Assistant Engineer, SS *Stephen Hopkins,* Naval Warfare blog, 16 December 2008; Antiaircraft Action Summary, United States Fleet Information Bulletin No. 22, 217-221; "SS *Stephen Hopkins,*" Naval Warfare blog 16 December 2008 (http://navalwarfare.blogspot.com/2008/12/ss-stephen-hopkins.html: accessed 28 March 2016); German Surface Raiders, Naval History and Heritage Command; SS *Stephen Hopkins* (http://www.marad.dot.gov/about-us/maritime-administration-history-program/usdot-maritime-gallant-ship-award/ss-stephen-hopkins/: accessed 29 March 2016); The Gallant Liberty Ship SS *Stephen Hopkins* Sinks a German Raider.

[10] SS *Stephen Hopkins,* Naval Warfare blog 16 December 2008;

[11] Raider "J" (Case History); Account of Mr. Cronk; German Surface Raiders, Naval History and Heritage Command; The Gallant Liberty Ship SS *Stephen Hopkins* Sinks a German Raider; Arenas and Ryan, Hilfskreuzer.

[12] Guttman, "The Last Raider."

[13] Naval Warfare blog, 16 December 2008; German Surface Raiders, Naval History and Heritage Command.

[14] Account of Mr. Cronk.

[15] Guttman, "The Last Raider."

[16] Raider "J" (Case History); Account of Mr. Cronk; Guttman, "The Last Raider"; "American Merchant Marine Heroes and their Gallant Ships in World War II," American Merchant Marine at War (www.usmm.org: accessed 28 March 2016).

[17] Raider "J" (Case History); "American Merchant Marine Heroes and their Gallant Ships in World War II"; German Surface Raiders, Naval History and Heritage Command.

[18] Guttman, "The Last Raider."

[19] Account of Mr. Cronk.

[20] Ibid.

[21] Ibid.

[22] Account of Mr. Cronk; "O'Hara, Edwin Joseph," Kings Pointers in World War II.

[23] Raider "J" (Case History); Gallant Ships of World War II Merchant Marine (http://www.usmm.org/gallantships.html); The Gallant Ship Award (http://www.marad.dot.gov/about-us/maritime-administration-history-program/usdot-maritime-gallant-ship-award/: both accessed 30 March 2016).

[24] "O'Hara, Edwin Joseph."

CHAPTER 12 NOTES

[1] CincLantFlt, Atlantic Fleet History, 13 May 1946.

[2] *Milwaukee* War Diary, November 1942.

[3] *Somers, Milwaukee* War Diary, November 1942.

[4] *Cincinnati, Somers* War Diary, November 1942.

[5] *Cincinnati, Milwaukee, Somers* War Diary, November 1942.

[6] *Cincinnati, Somers* War Diary, November 1942.

[7] Ibid.

[8] Personal Interview of Chief Charles J. Martin, War Patrol – DD *SOMERS*, 29 October 1943, CNO Naval Records and Library.

[9] *Milwaukee* War Diary, November 1942.

CHAPTER 13 NOTES

[1] The Battle of the Atlantic, Vol. II: U-boat Operations, 181

[2] Ibid, 181-210.

[3] Ibid, 186

[4] Office of the CNO Intelligence Report 42-43 of 15 May 1943, titled Blockade Runner Summary (May 15, 1943); Allied Warship Finder, Uboat.net.

[5] The Battle of the Atlantic, Vol. II: U-boat Operations, 187.

[6] Ibid.

[7] Ibid.

[8] CincLantFlt, Atlantic Fleet History, 13 May 1946; D'Adamo, Boats, Regia Marina Italiana.

[9] Derek Waller, U-Boats - The Italian Connection, Uboat.net.

[10] D'Adamo, Boats, Regia Marina Italiana; Derek Waller, U-Boats - The Italian Connection.

[11] Derek Waller, U-Boats - The Italian Connection; Martin Brice, *Axis Blockade Runners of World War II* (Anapolis, Md: Naval Institute Press, 1981), 131-133.

[12] Blockade-Running Between Europe and the Far East by Submarines, 1942-44 [SRH-019], 1 December 1944 (https://www.history.navy.mil/research/library/online-reading-room/title-list-alphabetically/b/blockade-running-between-europe-and-the-far-east-by-submarines-1942-44.html: accessed 22 November 2016).

CHAPTER 14 NOTES

[1] German U-Boat Casualties in World War Two, Naval History and Heritage Command http://www.history.navy.mil/research/library/online-reading-room/title-list-alphabetically/u/united-states-submarine-losses/german-u-boat-casualties-in-world-war-two.html; Italian Submarine Casualties in World War Two http://www.history.navy.mil/research/library/online-reading-room/title-list-alphabetically/u/united-states-submarine-losses/italian-submarine-casualties-in-world-war-two.html: both accessed 2 April 2016).

[2] *DANAS Vol. II* Appendix 3 Submarines Sunk by Patrol Squadrons During World War II (http://www.history.navy.mil/content/dam/nhhc/research/histories/naval-aviation/dictionary-of-american-naval-aviation-squadrons-volume-2/pdfs/Appen3.pdf: accessed 4 April 2016).

[3] Uboats Sunk in South Atlantic (http://www.sixtant.net/2011/artigos.php?cat=uboats-sunk-in-south-atlantic: accessed 1 April 2016); U-boat Finder, Uboat.net.

[4] Historical Officer VB-107, A History of Patrol Squadron 83 and Bombing Squadron 107, September 15, 1941 to December 31, 1944.

[5] Ibid.

[6] Ibid.

[7] Ibid.

[8] A History of Patrol Squadron 83 and Patrol Squadron 107; Billie Goodell Inspiration to all of us, The Rampa Foundation (http://www.fundacaorampa.com.br/goodell.html: accessed 4April 2016).

[9] Ragnar J. Ragnarsson, *US Navy PBY Catalina Units of the Atlantic War* (Oxford, U.K.: Osprey, 2006), 58.

[10] A History of Patrol Squadron 83 and Patrol Squadron 107; Billie Goodell Inspiration to all of us; Report on the Interrogation of Survivors from *U-164* Sunk on January 6, 1943, O.N.I. 250 - G/ Serial No. 8, 29 March 1943 (http://www.uboatarchive.net/U-164A/U-164INT.htm: accessed 23 April 2016).

[11] A History of Patrol Squadron 83 and Patrol Squadron 107.

[12] A History of Patrol Squadron 83 and Patrol Squadron 107; Report on the Interrogation of Survivors from *U-164*.

[13] ut supra.

[14] Report on the Interrogation of Survivors from *U-164*.

[15] Ibid.
[16] Ibid.
[17] Ibid.
[18] Ibid.
[19] Correspondence with Dwight Messimer, 6 December 2016.
[20] Report on the Interrogation of Survivors from *U-164*.
[21] Ibid.
[22] Ibid.
[23] Ibid.
[24] Ibid.
[25] Ibid.
[26] Ragnarsson, *US Navy PBY Catalina Units of the Atlantic War*, 58; VP-83 Report of Anti-Submarine Action by Aircraft, #11, 134 January 1943.
[27] Carlos José Asumpção Penteado, The Brazilian Participation in World War II, A thesis presented to the Faculty of the U.S. Army Command and General Staff College in partial fulfillment of the requirements for the degree Master of Military Art and Science (Fort Leavenworth, Kansas, 2006).
[28] Ibid.
[29] VP-83 Report of Anti-Submarine Action by Aircraft, #11, 134 January 1943.
[30] Ibid.
[31] Ibid.
[32] *U-507*, Uboat.net.
[33] Ibid.
[34] Ibid.
[35] CTG 23.1 War Diary, February 1943.
[36] Ibid.
[37] CTG 23.1 War Diary, February 1943; Commander VP-74, History of Patrol Squadron Seventy-Four – Submission of, 20 June 1945.
[38] CTG 23.1 War Diary, February 1943.
[39] Ibid.
[40] Commander VP-74, History of Patrol Squadron Seventy-Four; ComSoLantFor and *Humboldt* War Diary, February 1943.
[41] *Humboldt* War Diary, February 1943.
[42] ComSoLantFor War Diary, February 1943; *Linnet*, *DANFS*.
[43] Arnold S. Lott, *Most Dangerous Sea* (Annapolis, MD: U.S. Naval Institute, 1959), 88.
[44] ComSoLantFor War Diary, February 1943; *Linnet*, *DANFS*.
[45] Commander VP-74, History of Patrol Squadron Seventy-Four.
[46] Commander VPB-74, History of Patrol Squadron Seventy-Four.
[47] Commander VPB-74, History of Patrol Squadron Seventy-Four; *Building the Navy's Bases in World War II, History of the Bureau of Yards and Docks and the Civil Engineer Corps 1940-1946, Vol. II* (Washington, D.C.: Government Printing Office, 1947), 35.
[48] Commander VPB-74, History of Patrol Squadron Seventy-Four.
[49] Ibid.

[50] Navy Gains in U-Boat War, Bureau of Naval Personnel Information Bulletin, July 1943; Tribute to a WWII US Naval Aviator and Submarine Buster, posted 14 September 2009 (http://www.usmilitariaforum.com/forums/index.php?/topic/54580-tribute-to-a-wwii-us-naval-aviator-and-submarine-buster/: accessed 21 April 2016).

[51] The *Archimede* (1939) Diesel-Electric Attack Submarine (1939) (http://www.militaryfactory.com/ships/detail.asp?ship_id=Archimede-1939: accessed 21 April 2016).

[52] Ibid.

[53] Enclosure (A) To LANTFLT ASW UNIT Serial 0398, 7 May 1943 (http://www.uboatarchive.net/Archimedie/ArchimedeAnalysis.htm: 5 April 2016); Morison, *The Battle of the Atlantic*, 390.

[54] Enclosure (A) To LANTFLT ASW UNIT Serial 0398, 7 May 1943 (http://www.uboatarchive.net/Archimedie/ArchimedeAnalysis.htm: 5 April 2016).

[55] Con la pelle appesa a un chiodo: *Archimede* (https://translate.google.com/translate?hl=en&sl=it&u=http://conlapelleap pesaaunchiodo.blogspot.com/2013/11/archimede.html&prev=search: accessed 12 June 2016).

[56] Ibid.

[57] *DANAS* Vol. II Appendix 3 Submarines Sunk by Patrol Squadrons During World War II.

[58] A History of Patrol Squadron 83 and Patrol Squadron 107; Billie Goodell Inspiration to all of us.

[59] Report of Antisubmarine Action by Aircraft, VP-74 Report No. 10, 17 May 1943; Summary of Anti-Submarine Action, May 9-17, 1943, submitted by Mills Ton Eyck Jr., Lt(jg) A-V(S) and John G. Mulook, Lieut. A-V(S).

[60] Ibid.

[61] Report of Antisubmarine Action by Aircraft, VP-74 Report No. 10, 17 May 1943.

[62] Ibid.

[63] Post Mortems on Enemy Submarines, Report on the Interrogation of Survivors from *U-128* Sunk on May 17, 1943 (Washington, Office of the CNO, 1943).

[64] Ibid.

[65] Report of Antisubmarine Action by Aircraft, VP-74 Report No. 11, 17 May 1943.

[66] Ibid.

[67] Report of Antisubmarine Action by Aircraft, VP-74 Report No. 11, 17 May 1943; Summary of Anti-Submarine Action, May 9-17, 1943, submitted by Mills Ton Eyck Jr., Lt(jg) A-V(S) and John G. Mulook, Lieut. A-V(S).

[68] Correspondence with Dwight Messimer, 6 December 2016.

[69] Commander VP-74, History of Patrol Squadron Seventy-Four; Daily Event for July 3, 2014, Maritime Quest (http://www.maritimequest.com/daily_event_archive/2014/07_july/03_mar tin_pbm_mariner_6571.htm: accessed 12 May 2016).

CHAPTER 15 NOTES

[1] U-boat Fates, U-boat Losses in May 1943, Uboat.net.

[2] Commander VPB-94, History of Patrol Bombing Squadron Ninety-Four – Forwarding of, 8 December 1944.

[3] Ibid.

[4] Ibid.

[5] Ibid.

[6] Ibid.

[7] Ibid.

[8] Ibid.

[9] Ibid.

[10] Ibid.

[11] Ibid.

[12] Ibid.

[13] General Orders: Bureau of Naval Personnel Information Bulletin No. 328 (July 1944); Commander VPB-94, History of Patrol Bombing Squadron Ninety-Four – Forwarding of, 8 December 1944.

[14] Commanding Officer, USS *Barnegat* (AVP-19), Prisoners of War from German Submarine sunk by plane no. 5 of Patrol Squadron SEVENTY-FOUR at about 1700 Zebra on 19 July 1943 - Recovery of, Treatment of, and information learned, 24 July 1943.

[15] Commander VP-74, History of Patrol Squadron Seventy-Four.

[16] Commanding Officer, USS *Barnegat* (AVP-10), Unit History – Submission of, 28 January 1946.

[17] Ibid.

[18] *Barnegat, DANFS*.

[19] Post Mortems on Enemy Submarines, Report on the Interrogation of Survivors from *U-513* Sunk on July 19, 1943 (Washington DC: Office of the CNO, 1943).

[20] Report on the Interrogation of Survivors from *U-513*; The Men - U-boat Commanders, Ebe Schnoor, Uboat.net.

[21] ut supra.

[22] Report on the Interrogation of Survivors from *U-513*; The Men - U-boat Commanders, Top U-boat Aces, Friedrich Guggenberger, Uboat.net.

[23] Report on the Interrogation of Survivors from *U-513*.

[24] Report on the Interrogation of Survivors from *U-513*; Narrative from ASW-6 report from attacking aircraft; *Barnegat, DANFS*.

[25] Report on the Interrogation of Survivors from *U-513*.

[26] Narrative from ASW-6 report from attacking aircraft.

[27] Ibid.

[28] Report on the Interrogation of Survivors from *U-513*.

[29] Commander VPB-74, History of Patrol Bombing Squadron Seventy-Four – Submission of, 20 June 1945.

[30] *Barnegat, DANFS*.

[31] Ibid.

[32] *Richard Caswell*, Uboat.net.

[33] *Barnegat*, *DANFS*.

[34] The Men - U-boat Commanders, Top U-boat Aces, Friedrich Guggenberger, Uboat.net.

[35] Ibid.

[36] Ibid.

[37] Anti-Submarine Action by Aircraft (ASW-6) Report.

[38] *Barnegat*, *DANFS*; Anti-Submarine Action by Aircraft (ASW-6) Report.

[39] Anti-Submarine Action by Aircraft (ASW-6) Report.

[40] Ibid.

[41] Ibid.

[42] Ibid.

[43] *Barnegat*, *DANFS*.

[44] Ibid.

[45] Report on the Interrogation of Survivors from *U-199* Sunk on 31 July 1943, O.N.I. 250 – G/Serial 22, 27 September 1943.

[46] Ibid.

[47] Ibid.

[48] Ibid.

[49] Report on the Interrogation of Survivors from *U-199*; Ships hit by *U-199*, Uboat.net.

[50] Ships hit by U-boats, *Changri-Lá*, Brazilian Sailing ship, *Henzada* British Steam merchant, Uboat.net.

[51] Report on the Interrogation of Survivors from *U-199*.

[52] Ibid.

[53] Ibid.

[54] Ibid.

[55] Commander VPB-74, History of Patrol Bombing Squadron Seventy-Four – Submission of, 20 June 1945.

[56] VP-94 Report of Anti-submarine Action by Aircraft, No. 5, 21 July 1943.

[57] Report on the Interrogation of Survivors From *U-662* Sunk 21 July 1943 (Washington DC: CNO).

[58] VP-94 Report of Anti-submarine Action by Aircraft, No. 5, 21 July 1943.

[59] Ibid.

[60] Ibid.

[61] VP-94 Report of Anti-submarine Action by Aircraft, No. 5, 21 July 1943; Report on the Interrogation of Survivors From *U-662*.

[62] Report on the Interrogation of Survivors From *U-662*.

[63] *Siren*, *PC-494* War Diary, August 1943; Report on the Interrogation of Survivors From *U-662*.

[64] Report on the Interrogation of Survivors From *U-662*.

[65] Ibid.

[66] Ibid.

[67] Ibid.

[68] Op-16-Z A6-2(8) Memorandum for the Director, Subject: Op-16-W Broadcasts to German U-boats, 24 September 1943.

[69] Ibid.

[70] Ibid.

[71] Ibid.

[72] Commander VPB-94, History of Patrol Bombing Squadron Ninety-Four – Forwarding of, 8 December 1944.

[73] O.N.I. 250 – G/Serial 17 Report of the Interrogation of Survivor from U-598 Sunk on 23 July 1943, 30 August 1943; VB-107 Report of Antisubmarine Action by Aircraft #2, 22 July 1943.

[74] VB-107 Report of Antisubmarine Action by Aircraft #2, 22 July 1943.

[75] Ibid.

[76] VB-107 Report of Antisubmarine Action by Aircraft #4, 22 July 1943.

[77] Ibid.

[78] Ibid.

[79] VB-107 Report of Antisubmarine Action by Aircraft #3, 22 July 1943.

[80] Ibid.

[81] VB-107 Report of Antisubmarine Action by Aircraft #2, 22 July 1943.

[82] VB-107 Report of Antisubmarine Action by Aircraft #5, 23 July 1943.

[83] VB-107 Report of Antisubmarine Action by Aircraft #6, 23 July 1943.

[84] VB-107 Report of Antisubmarine Action by Aircraft #6, 23 July 1943; A History of Patrol Squadron 83 and Bombing Squadron 107.

[85] VB-107 Report of Antisubmarine Action by Aircraft #6, 23 July 1943.

[86] A History of Patrol Squadron 83 and Bombing Squadron 107.

[87] Ibid.

[88] *Seneca* War Diary, July 1943; VB-107 Report of Antisubmarine action by Aircraft #2, 22 July 1943.

[89] *Seneca* War Diary, July 1943.

[90] A History of Patrol Squadron 83 and Bombing Squadron 107.

[91] Ibid.

CHAPTER 16 NOTES

[1] Commander VPB-129, Squadron History, 15 January 1945.

[2] Ibid.

[3] Ibid.

[4] Ibid.

[5] Commander VPB-129, Squadron History, 15 January 1945; Medical Department, United States Army, Preventive Medicine in World War II, Vol. VI, Communicable Diseases (Washington, DC: Department of the Army, 1963).

[6] Commander VPB-129, Squadron History, 15 January 1945.

[7] Ibid.

[8] Ibid.

[9] Ibid.

[10] Ibid.

[11] Ibid.

[12] Commander VPB-129, Squadron History, 15 January 1945; VB-129 Report of Anti-Submarine Action by Aircraft, No. 1, 31 August 1943.

[13] A History of Patrol Squadron 83 and Bombing Squadron 107.

[14] Ibid.

[15] Ibid.

[16] Preliminary Report Interrogation of Survivors from *U-604*, 15 September 1943; Navy Department, Office of the CNO, Report on the Interrogation of Survivors from *U-604* and *U-185* sunk 11 August 1943 and 24 August 1943.

[17] Report on the Interrogation of Survivors from *U-604* and *U-185*.

[18] Action Report Covering USS *Moffett*'s Engagement with Enemy Submarine, August 3-4, 1943.

[19] Ibid.

[20] Ibid.

[21] Ibid.

[22] Ibid.

[23] Ibid.

[24] Ibid.

[25] Ibid.

[26] Ibid.

[27] Ibid.

[28] Report on the Interrogation of Survivors from *U-604* and *U-185*.

[29] Ibid.

[30] Ibid.

[31] Ibid.

[32] Ibid.

[33] A History of Patrol Squadron 83 and Bombing Squadron 107.

[34] Commander VPB-129, Squadron History, 15 January 1945

[35] ASW-6 Report from LTJG Young's attack.

[36] Ibid.

[37] Report on the Interrogation of Survivors from *U-591*.

[38] Ibid.

[39] *Saucy* War Diary, July 1943.

[40] Report on the Interrogation of Survivors from *U-591*; The Men – U-boat Commanders, Kapitänleutnant Reimar Ziesmer, Uboat.net.

[41] Ibid.

[42] Ibid.

[43] Ibid.

[44] Ibid.

[45] Ibid.

[46] Ibid.

[47] Ibid.

[48] Historical Officer VPB-127, History of Patrol Bombing Squadron One Hundred Twenty Seven, 28 May 1945.

[49] Ibid.

[50] Ibid.

[51] Ibid.

[52] Ibid.

[53] VP-74 ASW-6 Report #14 of 27 September 1943.

[54] Ibid.

[55] Ibid.
[56] Ibid.
[57] Ibid.
[58] Ibid.
[59] Commander VPB-74, History of Patrol Bombing Squadron Seventy-Four – Submission of, 20 June 1945.
[60] *U-161*, Uboat.net.
[61] Ships hit by U-boats *St. Usk* British Steam merchant, Uboat.net.
[62] Ibid.
[63] Ibid.
[64] Ibid.
[65] Ships hit by U-boats, *Itapagé* Brazilian Motor merchant, Uboat.net.
[66] VB-107 Report of Antisubmarine Action by Aircraft No. 11, dated 5 November 1943 (http://www.uboatarchive.net/U-848A/U-848-ASW-6.htm: accessed 22 April 2016).
[67] VB-107 War Diary, November 1943; VB-107 Report of Antisubmarine Action by Aircraft No. 10.
[68] VB-107 Report of Antisubmarine Action by Aircraft No. 10.
[69] VB-107 Report of Antisubmarine Action by Aircraft No. 10 and No. 11.
[70] VB-107 Report of Antisubmarine Action by Aircraft No. 11.
[71] Ibid.
[72] Ibid.
[73] VB-107 Report of Antisubmarine Action by Aircraft No. 10.
[74] Ibid.
[75] VB-107 Report of Antisubmarine Action by Aircraft No. 13, dated 5 November 1943.
[76] Ibid.
[77] Ibid.
[78] Ibid.
[79] Ibid.
[80] VB-107, Squadron No. 6, Report of Antisubmarine Action by Aircraft No. 14, dated 15 November 1943 (http://www.uboatarchive.net/U-849A/U-849ASW-6.htm: accessed 21 April 2016).
[81] Ibid.
[82] *U-849*, Uboat.net.
[83] VB-107, Squadron No. 6, Report of Antisubmarine Action by Aircraft No. 14, dated 15 November 1943.
[84] Ibid.
[85] Ibid.
[86] VB-107, Squadron No. 6, Report of Antisubmarine Action by Aircraft No. 14, dated 15 November 1943; *DANAS* Vol. II Appendix 3 Submarines Sunk by Patrol Squadrons During World War II.
[87] VB-107, Squadron No. 6, Report of Antisubmarine Action by Aircraft No. 14, dated 15 November 1943.

CHAPTER 17 NOTES

[1] Narrative by Lt. Comdr. Hutchins of the USS *Borie*, 17 November 1943, Naval Records and Library, CNO, Personal Interviews.

[2] *Card* War Diary, October 1943.

[3] USS *Natoma* (CVE-62) Logbook Project, History of VC-9 (http://natomabaycve62.org/logbook/VC9.html: accessed 15 November 2016).

[4] USS *Card* (http://www.navsource.org/archives/03/011.htm: accessed 13 November 2016)

[5] USS *Barry*, USS *Borie*, USS *Goff*, NavSource.

[6] *Card* War Diary.

[7] Ibid.

[8] Ibid.

[9] *Card* War Diary; HF/DF The High Frequency Direction Finder, Uboat.net.

[10] *Card* War Diary; Robert A. Maher, James E. Wise, *Sailors' Journey into War* (Kent, Ohio: Kent State University Press, 1998), 137-138; *Card*, *DANFS*.

[11] *Card* War Diary; *Card*, *DANFS*.

[12] *U-584*, Uboat.net; Harvey Ardman, German Saboteurs Invade America in 1942, *World War II* magazine, February 1997 (http://www.historynet.com/world-war-ii-german-saboteurs-invade-america-in-1942.htm: both accessed 15 November 2016).

[13] Ardman, German Saboteurs Invade America in 1942, *World War II*.

[14] Ibid.

[15] Ibid.

[16] Narrative by Lt. Comdr. Hutchins of the USS *Borie*, 17 November 1943.

[17] Narrative by Lt. Comdr. Hutchins of the USS Borie, 17 November 1943; *Card*, *DANFS*.

[18] *Card*, *DANFS*; German U-Boat Casualties in World War Two, Naval History and Heritage Command (https://www.history.navy.mil/research/library/online-reading-room/title-list-alphabetically/u/united-states-submarine-losses/german-u-boat-casualties-in-world-war-two.html: accessed 14 November 2016).

[19] Narrative by Lt. Comdr. Hutchins of the USS *Borie*, 17 November 1943.

[20] Ibid.

[21] Ibid.

[22] Ibid.

[23] Ibid.

[24] Ibid.

[25] Ibid.

[26] Ibid.

[27] Ibid.

[28] Ibid.

[29] Ibid.

[30] Ibid.

[31] Ibid.

[32] Ibid.

[33] Ibid.

[34] *Goff* War Diary, November 1943.

[35] Narrative by Lt. Comdr. Hutchins of the USS *Borie*, 17 November 1943.

[36] *Card*, *Barry*, *Goff* War Diary, November 1943.

[37] *Card* War Diary.

CHAPTER 18 NOTES

[1] CTG 41.7, Action Report, Pursuit and Sinking by Gunfire of German Blockade Runner MS *Weserland*, 1-3 January 1944, 4 January 1944.

[2] *Commander South Atlantic Force, Commander-in-Chief, Atlantic Fleet, Volume XI*, 196; Commander VB-107, Report of enemy action, 13 January 1944; Admiralty War Diaries, October 1943.

[3] *Commander South Atlantic Force, Commander-in-Chief, Atlantic Fleet, Volume XI*, 196; Commander VB-107, Report of enemy action, 13 January 1944.

[4] Commander VB-107, Report of enemy action, 13 January 1944; Fleet Air Wing 16, War History 2/16/43 to 6/27/45.

[5] Commander VB-107, Report of enemy action, 13 January 1944; VB-107 War Diary, January 1944.

[6] Ibid.

[7] Ibid.

[8] *Commander South Atlantic Force, Commander-in-Chief, Atlantic Fleet, Volume XI*, 197-198.

[9] *Commander South Atlantic Force, Commander-in-Chief, Atlantic Fleet, Volume XI*, 198; Admiralty War Diaries, January 1944.

[10] *Commander South Atlantic Force, Commander-in-Chief, Atlantic Fleet, Volume XI*, 199.

[11] Ibid, 199.

[12] Ibid, 200.

[13] Ibid, 201.

[14] Ibid, 201.

[15] Ibid, 201.

[16] Ibid, 202.

[17] Ibid, 202.

[18] Ibid, 202-203.

[19] Ibid, 202-203.

[20] Ibid, 202-203.

[21] General Orders: Commander Fourth Fleet: Serial 850 (February 8, 1944).

CHAPTER 19 NOTES

[1] *Commander South Atlantic Force, Commander-in-Chief, Atlantic Fleet, Volume XI*, 205.

[2] Report of Antisubmarine Action by Aircraft, VB-107 No. 15, 5 February 1944.

[3] Ibid.

[4] Ibid.

[5] Ibid.

[6] Ibid.

[7] Commanding Officer, USS *Omaha*, Preliminary Report on German Prisoners of War from German Submarine, 11 February 1944; Report on the Interrogation of Survivors from *U-177* Sunk 6 February 1944, Office of the CNO.

[8] Commanding Officer, USS *Omaha*, Preliminary Report on German Prisoners of War.

[9] Report on the Interrogation of Survivors from *U-177*.

[10] Ibid.

[11] *Commander South Atlantic Force, Commander-in-Chief, Atlantic Fleet, Volume XI*, 214.

[12] Ibid.

[13] Ibid, 207.

[14] *Solomons* War Diary, June 1944.

[15] *Commander South Atlantic Force, Commander-in-Chief, Atlantic Fleet, Volume XI*, 207; *Solomons* War Diary, June 1944.

[16] ut supra.

[17] ut supra.

[18] *Commander South Atlantic Force, Commander-in-Chief, Atlantic Fleet, Volume XI*, 208.

[19] Ibid.

[20] Ibid, 209.

[21] *Commander South Atlantic Force, Commander-in-Chief, Atlantic Fleet, Volume XI*, 209; *Solomons* War Diary, June 1944.

[22] *Commander South Atlantic Force, Commander-in-Chief, Atlantic Fleet, Volume XI*, 209.

[23] *Commander South Atlantic Force, Commander-in-Chief, Atlantic Fleet, Volume XI*, 209; *Solomons* War Diary, June 1944.

[24] *Commander South Atlantic Force, Commander-in-Chief, Atlantic Fleet, Volume XI*, 209- 210.

[25] *Commander South Atlantic Force, Commander-in-Chief, Atlantic Fleet, Volume XI*, 210; *Straub, DANFS*; *Solomons* War Diary, June 1944.

[26] Commanding Officer, Composite Squadron Nine, History of Composite Squadron Nine – Forwarding of, 23 July 1945; Composite Squadron VC-9 Antisubmarine Action by Aircraft (ASW-6) reports completed after the attack on *U-860*.

[27] *Commander South Atlantic Force, Commander-in-Chief, Atlantic Fleet, Volume XI*, 214-215.

[28] Ibid, 215.

[29] *Commander South Atlantic Force, Commander-in-Chief, Atlantic Fleet, Volume XI*, 210; *Vital de Oliveira*, Uboat.net.

[30] *Commander South Atlantic Force, Commander-in-Chief, Atlantic Fleet, Volume XI*, 211; *William Gaston*, Uboat.net.

[31] *Commander South Atlantic Force, Commander-in-Chief, Atlantic Fleet, Volume XI*, 216-217.

[32] Ibid, 215.
[33] Ibid, 215-216.
[34] Ibid, 216.
[35] Ibid, 211.
[36] Ibid, 211
[37] Ibid, xiv.

CHAPTER 20 NOTES

[1] *Commander South Atlantic Force, Commander-in-Chief, Atlantic Fleet, Volume XI*, xiv.
[2] Ibid, xiv-xv, 212.
[3] Ibid, xiv-xv.
[4] *Baron Jedburgh*, Uboat.net; *U-532*, Uboat.net.
[5] *Commander South Atlantic Force, Commander-in-Chief, Atlantic Fleet, Volume XI*, xv.
[6] Ibid, xvi.
[7] Ibid, xvi.
[8] Ibid, xvi-xvii.

Index

About the Author

Commander David D. Bruhn, U.S. Navy (Retired) served twenty-two years on active duty and two in the Naval Reserve, as both an enlisted man and as an officer, between 1977 and 2001.

Following completion of basic training, he served as a sonar technician aboard USS *Miller* (FF 1091) and USS *Leftwich* (DD 984). He was commissioned in 1983 following graduation from California State University at Chico. His initial assignment was to USS *Excel* (MSO 439), serving as supply officer, damage control assistant, and chief engineer. He then served in USS *Thach* (FFG 43) as chief engineer and Destroyer Squadron Thirteen as material officer.

After graduation from the Naval Postgraduate School, Commander Bruhn was assigned to Secretary of the Navy and Chief of Naval Operation staffs as a budget analyst and resources planner before attending the Naval War College in 1996, following which he commanded the mine countermeasures ships USS *Gladiator* (MCM 11) and USS *Dextrous* (MCM 13) in the Persian Gulf.

Commander Bruhn's final assignment was executive assistant to a senior (SES 4) government service executive at the Ballistic Missile Defense Organization in Washington, D.C.

Following military service, he was a high school teacher and track coach for ten years, and is now a USA Track & Field official. He lives in northern California with his wife Nancy and has two sons, David and Michael.

49082819R00232

Made in the USA
San Bernardino, CA
12 May 2017